Announcements

SUNY series, Intersections: Philosophy and Critical Theory
———————
Rodolphe Gasché, editor

Announcements
On Novelty

KRISTINA MENDICINO

Paul Klee (Swiss, 1879–1940), *Zeichensammlung Südlich* (*Collection of Southern Signs*), 1924. Watercolor and ink, 12¼ x 18⅜" (framed). Mildred Lane Kemper Art Museum, Washington University in St. Louis. Gift of Joseph Pulitzer, Jr., 1962. © 2019 Artists Rights Society (ARS), New York

Published by State University of New York Press, Albany

© 2020 State University of New York Press

All rights reserved

No part of this book may be used or reproduced in any manner whatsoever without written permission. No part of this book may be stored in a retrieval system or transmitted in any form or by any means including electronic, electrostatic, magnetic tape, mechanical, photocopying, recording, or otherwise without the prior permission in writing of the publisher.

For information, contact State University of New York Press, Albany, NY
www.sunypress.edu

Library of Congress Cataloging-in-Publication Data

Names: Mendicino, Kristina, author.
Title: Announcements : on novelty / Kristina Mendicino.
Description: Albany : State University of New York Press, [2020] | Series:
    SUNY series, Intersections: philosophy and critical theory | Includes
    bibliographical references and index.
Identifiers: LCCN 2019011268 | ISBN 9781438477558 (hardcover : alk. paper) |
    ISBN 9781438477541 (pbk. : alk. paper) | ISBN 9781438477565 (ebook)
Subjects: LCSH: New and old. | Creation (Literary, artistic, etc.)
Classification: LCC B105.N4 M46 2020 | DDC 190.9/034—dc23
LC record available at https://lccn.loc.gov/2019011268

10 9 8 7 6 5 4 3 2 1

Contents

Acknowledgments — vii

Introduction: Making and Breaking the News — ix

Chapter 1 As If Zarathustra Spoke: On the Chances of Nietzsche's Good News — 1

Chapter 2 Passing the End: Baudelaire's New Findings — 35

Chapter 3 Announcing a Stellar Possibility: Blanqui's Cosmological Hypothesis — 79

Chapter 4 Atomizing the *Communist Manifesto* — 111

Afterword: On *An*novation — 153

Notes — 157

Works Cited — 225

Index — 239

Acknowledgments

The readings offered in this book owe much to the encouragement, inspiration, and support that I have received throughout the years of its genesis from my friends and colleagues in and beyond the Department of German Studies at Brown University: Susan Bernstein, Thomas Kniesche, David Farrell Krell, Edith Anna Kunz, Michael Levine, Elissa Marder, Kevin McLaughlin, Rainer Nägele, Gerhard Richter, Thomas Schestag, Jane Sokolosky, Zachary Sng, and Dominik Zechner. Without the generous and rigorous feedback that I received on my work during fellowship terms at the Pembroke Center for Teaching and Research on Women and the Cogut Institute for the Humanities, this book surely would not have taken the shape that it has now come to have. For this reason, special thanks are owed to Amanda Anderson, Marc Redfield, and Suzanne Stewart-Steinberg, although my gratitude goes to many more colleagues than I can name for their thoughtful questions and responses to my chapters in progress. Since my project grew from my teaching, I am also deeply grateful to my students for reading many of the texts addressed in this monograph with me; especially the discussions of Charles Baudelaire's "Le Voyage" that I shared with Ethel Renia were crucial to my engagement with that text. I thank the anonymous readers of my manuscript for SUNY Press for their helpful suggestions, which provoked me to sharpen my analyses and prose in many ways, and I thank Andrew Kenyon and Rodolphe Gasché at SUNY Press for their editorial guidance. I am grateful to the editors of *Modern Language Notes* for permission to reprint portions from chapter 4, "Atomizing the Communist Manifesto," which appeared under the title, "Oppositional Views and Apositional Points: Addressing the Practice of Theory in Marx," in *MLN* 133, no. 5 (2018): 1207–33. I also thank the Kemper Art Museum and Artist Rights Society for permission to reproduce Paul Klee's *Zeichensammlung Südlich* (© 2019

Artist Rights Society (ARS) New York) on the cover of this monograph, as well as Oxford University Press, for permission through PLSclear to reproduce Charles Baudelaire's "Voyaging" from *Flowers of Evil*, trans. James McGowan (Oxford: Oxford University Press, 2008). Finally, I would like to thank my closest friends and family for the conversations and support that they have given me throughout the writing process: Marta Machabeli, Joan and Joseph Mendicino, and Didier Toussaint.

Introduction

Making and Breaking the News

> There is nothing new under the sun.
>
> —Ecclesiastes
>
> Make it new.
>
> —Ezra Pound

What is "new" to speak of? What does any talk of novelty—be it prophetic or trivial, revolutionary or commercial—promise to unsettle, or unsettle with its promise? The difficulties evoked by these questions increase rather than diminish with the apparent familiarity of novel announcements, which obscures the obscurity of the "new," whatever it may mean. Even when news items are called into question or simply said to be "fake," for instance, the newness of the purported "news" is supposed to remain beyond a shadow of a doubt, nor does "faking" it seem to lessen its appeal. Whether a purported *novum* is announced or denounced, however, word of the "new" keeps escaping, from antiquity through to current affairs—and in ways that keep escaping examination of the word.

It was because the new could still be called a "new" question that Ernst Bloch would write in 1953—after Francis Bacon's *Novum Organum Scientiarum*, after the emphatically "new" art of high modernism, and after the flood of *nouveautés* on the global market of high capitalism: "[T]he Not-Yet-Conscious, Not-Yet-Become [. . .] has not even broken through as a word, let alone as a concept. [. . .] Hope [. . .] does not therefore occur in the history of the sciences, either as a psychological or as a cosmic entity, and least of all as a functionary of what has never been, of the possible New."[1] Yet even with his large-scale exposition of the dynamics of "real possibility"—which should open all possible matters to novel futures, from the conditions of the present to the latent potentials of the most distant past[2]—the prospect of "blueprint[s] for *planned or outlined* utopias" that Bloch advances presupposes that one might attain conscious clarity with regard to novel alternatives and work to "overtak[e] the natural course of events."[3] At such moments, Bloch's extensively rigorous and expansively erudite elaboration of "the New" runs the risk of understating the possibility that addressing "what has never been" may turn the thought of a radical *novum* into a known, rather than letting it be the unprecedented arrival that the "new" otherwise seems to signify in his text. In another context, Jacques Derrida pointed to this risk, which arises whenever it is a question of the status of novel inventions. "If at first we might think that invention calls all status back into question," he writes at one point in the inaugural essay of *Psyche: Inventions of the Other*, "we also see that there could be no invention without status. To invent is to produce iterability and the machine for reproduction and simulation."[4] This is why "a programmed invention," however great its potential, could hardly turn out to be "an event through which the future [*l'avenir*] comes to us."[5] Instead, any programmed or programmable future (*futur*) would foreclose the arrival of another time to come (*à venir*) and prevent the arrival of another whose otherness could not be timed or described according to temporal categories.[6]

No newscast and no technique for drafting blueprints, in other words, allows for an other or a *novum*; hence Derrida's call to reinvent invention, as well as his suggestion to call "the only possible invention [. . .] an invention [that] has to declare itself to be the invention of that which did not appear to be possible."[7] But because this declaration too would fall into self-contradiction if it were to be made, Derrida also does not deliver said declaration; suspending its assertion, he turns to another way of formulating the problem: "It is in this paradoxy that a deconstruction gets under way."[8] Whereas the constructive rhetoric of Bloch risks building a closed view of the future, Derrida's writing advocates for what may be "called deconstruction," which is said to operate "in opening, in unclosetting, in destabilizing foreclusionary structures so as to allow for the passage toward the other."[9] The fact of recognizable phenomena, institutions, and statements notwithstanding, "the new of an event" may even emerge from out of a writing that "bend[s] these rules with respect for the rules themselves in order to allow the other to come or to announce its coming in the opening of this dehiscence."[10] Derrida thus gives word of the "new" by declining it, by giving it another bent that allows for the new of the word. Only in such an oblique and wayward way might there be a chance to speak for an invention or innovation that differs from "a program of possibilities within the economy of the same."[11] Yet because this chance would also be none, if it were guaranteed, already the plurality of participles in Derrida's remarks ("opening," "uncloseting," "destabilizing") indicates that no single word for such a wager could be definitive—neither "deconstruction" nor "the other" nor the "new"—leaving the "novelty of newness" and the otherness of an other radically open issues.[12]

What does become clearer through Derrida's analysis is the way in which language lets inventive possibilities and impossibilities, statements and destabilizations, come to pass and come undone. Insubordinate to the rules and statutes that it renders speakable, language permits novel occurrences that part from an "economy of the same," in withdrawing from any transcendental structure or theoretical model that may be formulated to account for it. In one essay from his oeuvre—which interrogates language like none other—Werner Hamacher arrives upon a similar observation with regard to the language of history in Paul Valéry's *La Jeune Parque*:

> History, the self-withdrawing reference to the other in its finitude, is—and is therefore barely—still the withdrawal of history that is formulated in cognitively graspable and phenomenally representable relations to the other. It is finite history only as a parting from itself as phenomenology and morphology, from itself as the aesthetics and logic of historical relations. Only where it itself—as, for example, in Valéry's text—is relinquished to the dephenomenalizing, deaestheticizing, anamorphizing, or amorphizing withdrawal of its relation to the other; only where it is exposed to the other in its alteration and virtual unreadability, and where it is exposed to its own relation as a dwindling one, does it begin to free itself from the ontological primacy of form and from the epistemological primacy of a presenting cognition, and thus to enter the field of its finitude. The reference to the other is then no longer to be thought of as a communicative exchange in the medium of a common share in a formative principle, no longer as a securing of the self against the loss of the other and no longer as a preservation of the other in the refuge of its presentation; rather it is to be carried out as a

parting from the other as its own and appropriable, as an interruption of the circle of communication and as an imparting of that division which separates the other not only from the self but even from itself.[13]

Novelty has yet to be addressed as this radically other and othering occurrence of language, which, as Hamacher writes elsewhere, is an "eminently historical form" whose transformability precedes and exposes each formulation to transformation in turn.[14] Bloch's three-volume aesthetic, philosophical, and political project remains one of the most sustained meditations on novelty to date, but one in which "the concept of the Novum" figures as "the goal-determination of the human will" and therefore limits the very "open possibilities of the future" toward which it should be oriented.[15] By contrast, other recent investigations of the new tend to address it in terms of relatively constant structures or rules. Scholars of aesthetics and literature, such as Harold Rosenberg and Hans Robert Jauss, characterize the appeals to novelty that were made by modernist poets and artists as expressions of a consistent desire to break with tradition,[16] while scholars of cultural studies such as Boris Groys consider the production of novelties in and beyond the literary marketplace under the auspices of a more general cultural economy that demands what he calls, in Nietzschean fashion, a perpetual "revaluation of values": "One does not [. . .] break with the old by a free decision that presupposes human autonomy, gives it expression, or offers it social guarantees. One does so, rather, only by complying with the rules that determine the way our culture works."[17] Turning to various discussions of novelty in the "sciences, the social sciences, and the arts" from classical antiquity to the twentieth century, Michael North has elaborated a broad historical account of what he finds to be relatively stable "conceptual models" for the new, which he articulates in terms of "recurrence" and "recombination."[18] However, the specific language for various novel announcements tends to remain unaddressed, even when scholars such as Nicolas Dierks turn to language in order to come to terms with the new.[19] Drawing on Ludwig Wittgenstein's theory of language games, he aims to establish a basic, albeit variable grammar of novelty.[20] Yet the form of a grammar would not speak to that which escapes "communicative exchange in the medium of a common share in a formative principle;" nor would a language game, however flexible its rules may be, "free [. . .] itself from the ontological primacy of form and from the epistemological primacy of a presenting consciousness."[21] Only a philology that inclines toward "the dephenomenalizing, deaestheticizing, anamorphizing, or amorphizing withdrawal of its relation to the other" could begin to expose what the specificity of singular utterances may otherwise have to say of the new.

Even the most commonplace announcements on novelty escape the theoretical frameworks that have shaped many of its discussions to date and give anything but a straightforward indication of what is called "new" or what the "new" calls for. The often-cited verse of Ecclesiastes, "There is nothing new under the sun" (Ecc. 1.9),[22] for example, presents more than merely the denial that an unprecedented phenomenon may arrive within a divinely created cosmos, where god "has made everything suitable for its time" (Ecc. 3.11), and where solely oblivion obscures the fact that each apparent novelty "has already been, in the ages before us" (Ecc. 1.10). For if men can only say, "See, this is new," because they lack insight into "the ages before us" (Ecc. 1.10)—and these ages are "obscure" (עֹלָם, *olam*) to the same extent that they are "before" (עוֹלָם, *olam*)—what can be said is also shown through this very utterance to exceed what can be seen, what can be known, and what can be. The distinction that is drawn between word of the "new" (חָדָשׁ, *chadash*) and the unseen things of the past—in a language where the word for "word" is at once the word for "thing" (דָּבָר, *dabar*)—therefore fundamentally unsettles any assurance that speech will have corresponded to the things of which it speaks, including all that may be said of divine plans, and including this very saying on the "new."[23] The impossibility or possibility of any particular novelty cannot be judged on these terms, or any others, for that matter; rather, even the Ecclesiast's authoritative word on things undermines any supposable foundation for a decision over the issue. At the same time, however, *the* "new"—as a matter of words, if nothing else—emerges in the Ecclesiast's speech as that which is other than any known or unknown thing in the world, and perhaps the very thing that troubles any evident or speakable world order. The question as to how the new may be addressed, and what may take place in addressing it, thus opens rather than closes with the Ecclesiast's famous pronouncement.

Yet if the most categorical denial of novelty suspends any decision over its possibility, then no affirmation of novelty could be upheld either upon the same grounds. Nor does the new become a more promising prospect when the modus of speech shifts from the register of constative utterances to poetic imperatives, as in the oeuvre of Ezra Pound, whose phrase, "make it new," would become one of the most widespread clichés on novelty, beside the Ecclesiast's verse. Rather, in its iterations—at least in Pound's poetry—this seemingly simple appeal to the "new" is made over from a complex of motifs drawn from other texts, which render it more and other than the announcement of a directive that could be directly understood, let alone followed. In "Canto LIII" from the *Cantos*, where "make it new" repeats twice in a passage devoted to the reign of the ancient Chinese Emperor Tching Tang, nothing could be less certain than the force of this imperative, as the demand for novelty emerges in the midst of a sequence of verses devoted to dried up resources and prayers for replenishment, futile technological inventions and natural renewal, ancient inscriptions and modern turns of phrase. According to Pound's main source, Joseph-Anne-Marie de Moyriac de Mailla's *Histoire générale de la Chine*, Tching Tang had opened a copper mine and organized the minting of coins, which he "furnished to the poor" in order to remedy the problems of destitution and scarcity that had arisen during an extended drought.[24] But it is not to this innovation that Pound refers when he delivers his famous sentence on novelty, most likely because Tching Tang's new coinage does nothing to compensate for the lack of rain and grain. Instead, the copper turns out to quicken the depletion of resources according to de Mailla: "the granaries were depleted without the earth reproducing the harvests to replenish them."[25] "After seven years of frightful sterility," however, the Emperor utters prayers on a mountaintop, calling upon the sky to strike him and spare the people—at which point rain miraculously begins to fall, and the renewed source of water rejuvenates the land.[26] In thanks, the Emperor proceeds to engrave "the following words on the basin that he used every morning to wash his face: *Remember to renew yourself each day, and many times a day* [*Souviens-toi de te renouveller chaque jour, & plusieurs fois le jour*],"[27] aligning regular cleansing with the latest precipitation, whose regularity cannot be taken for granted, at the latest, since the recent drought. The Emperor's ineffectual political and technological innovation thus gives way to an otherwise unspecified call for renewal, which itself corresponds to no natural cycle, and no memorable model of achievement. If the reminder to renew recalls anything, then, it would be the possibility that renewal may be foreclosed or forgotten, rendering the Emperor's imperative one that does not so much urge one to follow than to give an example for the course of nature. Everyday existence becomes an urgent issue of novelty and renewal because the everyday also can *not* exist.

Taking up the motif of Tching Tang's prayer and inscription—and eliminating the divine intervention or natural event that came between—Pound writes:

> Tching prayed on the mountain and
>   wrote MAKE IT NEW
> on his bath tub
>   Day by day make it new
> cut underbrush,
> pile the logs,
> keep it growing.[28]

Memory goes lost between the lines, leaving the "new" alone as a matter of indefinite, if not absolute importance, irrespective of any outcome and without any record of the miraculous reprieve that, in de Mailla's history, had replenished the resources of the community and motivated the Emperor's inscription. Far from figuring within a historical sequence, the "new" breaks from the history that Pound will have related up to this point: no event so much as seems to answer or interrupt the Emperor's prayer, whose words are indistinguishable here from those he is said to write. The phrase, "Day by day make it new," not only appears to be the complement of both verbs for speech ("prayed," "wrote"); it also literally falls between the mountain and the basin in place of the water that had washed away Tching Tang's concerns before filling his bathtub, and thus drowns out both crisis and resolution. "Make it new" makes—transitively—nothing of all that had been said to intervene in de Mailla's account. Hence, by the time "make it new" repeats, it no longer pertains to Tching Tang in particular, but emerges instead as an impersonal and immemorial renewal of the imperative to "make it new" that thereby undercuts its novely in the language of the poem, which itself renews the call to "make it new."

It is with a view to such gestures of erasure that Paul de Man writes in his essay on "Literary History and Literary Modernity": "Modernity exists in the form of a desire to wipe out whatever came earlier, in the hope of reaching at last a point that could be called a true present, a point of origin that marks a new departure. This combined interplay of deliberate forgetting with an action that is also a new origin reaches the full power of the idea of modernity."[29] Whereas de Mailla's history suggests that the new should preserve and protect against the occurrence of natural failure, Pound's modern version of the story seems to make that failure history, by seeking to surpass or suppress ordinary and historical occurrences at all costs. But if the absolute imperative to "make it new" demands nothing but absolution from all that had been before, then its "present" could only be bereft of all determinations, including "originality." In this case, the modern pursuit of obliteration would be an acceleration of the fall into the oblivion that obscures "the ages before us," and that the Ecclesiast remembers just enough in order to conclude: "There is nothing new under the sun" (Ecc. 1.9–10). The imperative to "make it new" would be another instance of empty coinage that speeds depletion, rather than a prayer that might allow for everyday survival despite the exceptional capacity of natural occurrences to default. In other words, were this demand or desire to "make it new" to be realized at any point, there would also be no "now" and no "age;" nothing "new" and nothing at all that could remain to be said or seen, which would not at the same time have to obliterate itself, and make any explicit or implicit demand for erasure forgotten as well. Yet insofar as such demands as Pound's could only be made in being said, they would also always speak before or beyond oblivion, and they would give testimony *nolens volens* to the fact that language—immemorial—cannot be reduced or restricted to the cognition or volition of subject. For the same reason, whatever news language may give of itself could not be made according to the poetic intention to "make it new."

There is therefore no telling exactly what "it" is that occurs in Pound's poem, besides the suspension of narrative and the reduction of history to an indeterminate "it" in "Day by day make it new." But whatever "it" may have been, activities of clearing rather than cultivation are enjoined next—"cut underbrush"—which process should still, paradoxically, "keep it growing."[30] This time, "it" may refer to the "pile of logs" that arises through an accumulation of cut timber or to the cutting itself, or to something else that as yet eludes naming and knowing. Precisely because the status of "it" remains undecided, however, "its" growth becomes drawn in proximity not only to chopped wood, but also to chopped words, as the "logs" to which "it" could refer become correspondingly indeterminate: instances of lumber ("logs") or records ("logs"), or instances of a *logos* cut short. It is perhaps in this way that each element of the poem can be said to grow in being cut: severed from any single signification, from all certain identification with any single lexical item, and from etymological rooting in any one language, every one becomes at once several and therefore none in particular.[31] Novelty would arise in this context, not through an effective response to Pound's imperative, but through the haphazard piling of possibilities in language that undercuts the discernibility of their relations to one another and to themselves, and that therefore culminates in neither synthesis nor erasure. This process would entail that the new cannot be *made* and cannot *be*—not even by negation—but could nonetheless chance to open through a brush with words and the alterations to which their every compilation is exposed.

In different ways, both the Ecclesiast's and Pound's announcements on novelty indicate that its possible occurrence could not but be beyond the bounds of experience and the confines of conceptual schemata, if the "new" were to correspond to its concept and exceed the given. In light of this brief passage from Pound's poem—cut from its context, to be sure—the famous phrase of the Ecclesiast could be altered and abbreviated to read: the new *is* not, and not only because the "new" does not denote the stable attribute of a being or an event, but also because its singularity cannot be singled out as a phenomenon to be defined, in turn, according to familiar categories or in contrast to historical precedents. This claim may seem to be paradoxical, as Audrey Wasser has recently argued, writing: "if, on the one hand, the truly new work must break with its existing context, then, on the other hand, it must still be recognizable in some fashion, and be recognizable as art."[32] Yet the movement in Pound's language that may have allowed a novel event in speech does not depend upon a cogito or a paradigm of cognition; rather, it may be traced beside and despite the more recognizable logic of erasure that the poem expressly promotes and performs, and it would have to escape all certain affirmations, if it were to be at all.

When it comes to the new, this "maybe" may be its only chance, as not only the wisdom of the Ecclesiast and the poetry of Pound suggest, but also that of the prophets who give word of the new as the word of god. Turning to another watershed announcement on novelty—when Isaiah declares, in verses echoed by Pound and the Ecclesiast: "For I am about to create new heavens and a new earth; the former things shall not be remembered or come to mind" (Is. 65.17)—it turns out that even announcements which suppose a transcendent foundation for being and truth do not make it or cut it. Before all else, prophets defer as they speak the news that they go about delivering—that is, their news is not the "new" itself—such that with or without a claim to divine authority, their words promise the non-attainment of novelty for the time being. Nor do these circumstances change when the author of Revelation leaps to the result of what Isaiah once foretold and claims to see the trajectory of world history culminate in a Last Judgment and in a subsequent renewal of all things. Far from surpassing his predecessor in the end, the prophet reveals not only that his vision does not coincide with its realization, but also that the prophecy itself is to culminate in reiteration rather than renewal. Just after he reports seeing "a new heaven and a new earth," he repeats hearing the words: "See, I am making all things new," followed by the imperative: "Write this, for these words are trustworthy and true" (Rev. 21.1, 21.5). This last remark may appear to legitimate the testimony that conveys it and to render the prophecy more complete by including its inscription among the things to come. But it also decisively recasts the prophecy of renewal as a repetition and memorialization of nothing other than its own inscription. The last prophet of the New Testament thus gives no last word and no new word, but remakes the announcement, "I am making all things new," and in a way that makes the proclamation of novel ends an end in itself. In this respect, the biblical text structurally and literally resembles the inscription that repeats verbatim in Pound's poem, which ultimately calls for the repetition of the call to "make it new." These similarities indicate, moreover, that the default on novel promises to provide guarantees is independent of any decision over the secularization debate that arose when Karl Löwith and Jacob Taubes argued for the messianic implications of historical time, as understood to be "directed toward something which has not yet been but will be," or "moving towards a 'new heaven and a new earth' " that "exceeds the cycle of origin."[33] Neither a biblical authority nor a poetic author could be taken at his word, should he proclaim the new, which would have to take place in other words and otherwise than in the words of a recognizable declaration or demand, if at all. Hence, Theodor Adorno does not, like Wasser, insist that recognizability is a "must," when it comes to the arrival of a *novum*, but writes in *Aesthetic Theory*: "The category of the new has been central, though admittedly in conjunction with the question of whether anything new had ever existed."[34]

It is the main argument of this book that the paradox Adorno succinctly describes not only crucially inflects evocations of novelty, but also that the fundamental uncertainty of novel announcements is precisely what troubles the status quo, including any standards or standard words for affirming or dismissing what may be called "new." Through analyses of texts in which the question of novelty becomes emphatically pronounced, this book thus elucidates how language holds open the possibility for a *novum* that is irreducible to those gestures of judgment that would deliver authoritative sentences upon it. In so doing, it marks an attempt to expose those aspects of novelty that may emerge when the accent falls less upon what does or does not take place in positing or promising something new, than upon the difference between word of the new and the new of the word, or the *logos*—or "the logs." Even the most familiar announcements on novelty from the biblical books of prophecy through to modernist poetry indicate how the question of novelty reopens through such a shift in emphasis. However, the selection of texts that will be addressed in the following chapters does not reflect a survey of such broad historical scope, but cuts to a moment in which novelty came to mark the language of many spheres to a hitherto unprecedented extent, recurring throughout the rhetoric of commerce and politics, philosophy and history, poetry and art. As writers such as Theodor Adorno, Walter Benjamin, and Martin Heidegger have emphasized in otherwise very different contexts, it was arguably in the nineteenth century that novelty emerged as an explicitly pervasive project or problem while, at the same time, the denial of novelty kept pace with its promotion, from the series of failed revolutions in Europe between 1848 and 1871, to the theories of eternal recurrence that were articulated in the later half of the nineteenth century. Writings from this period thus offer a "novel" language that especially solicits commentary—apart from any decision as to whether its emergence may be traced largely to the logic of capitalism, as Adorno and Benjamin suggested, or whether the modern "addiction to novelty [*Neuerungssucht*]"[35] is merely the latest symptom, as Heidegger argues, of an initial decision to interpret being as the question of beings, rather than inquiring into the truth of being itself. The subsequent chapters of this book will therefore trace the unsettling senses and stakes of announcements on novelty through the texts of several of those nineteenth-century writers who registered the extreme ambivalence and coincidence of extremes that novel claims may entail: namely, Friedrich Nietzsche, Charles Baudelaire, Louis-Auguste Blanqui, and Karl Marx.

This constellation of writers is motivated in particular by Walter Benjamin's frequent references to these names in the *Arcades Project*, as he addresses novelty—largely through citation—at various critical points in his manuscripts on nineteenth-century Paris. The incisive observations that Benjamin makes over the course of this work mark a point of departure for a further elaboration of the texts that he draws upon, with an eye to what may have escaped the repetitive—and therefore contradictory—character of innovation that he exposes through quotation and commentary. In the exposés and many of the convolutes that he prepared, Benjamin underscores how appeals to the "new" propelled production and consumption in the age of high capitalism, marking the moving horizon for distinctions between the new and the old, the latest craze and the outmoded, the modern and the obsolete. Despite and because of the frequent changes in fashion, however, the character of new commodities, insofar as they are "new," seemed determined to be ever the same within the sphere of the everyday, anticipating the very imperative that Pound had sought to set apart from the logic of money and commerce: "Day by day make it new."[36]

The theories of eternal recurrence in Nietzsche's *Thus Spoke Zarathustra* and Blanqui's *Eternity by the Stars* may thus be seen, as Benjamin suggests, to reflect and respond to these large-scale developments—though not without distortion and disruption—beginning with the way in which they advertise the monotony of "novelty" that otherwise goes without saying in commercial ventures. What may have seemed new is exposed through these theories to be what Benjamin would call a modus of "historical semblance": a simulation of what has never been before that perpetuates the circulation of trade, among other things.[37] In at least this respect, Nietzsche's and Blanqui's texts break the cycle in breaking news of it, raising the question as to what occurs when repetition reaches the breaking point. And although Benjamin says little on this point in his commentaries on Nietzsche and Blanqui, he does indicate the difficulties of addressing the question by demonstrating how the historical phenomenon of historical semblance will have altered the basic structure of experience, rendering whatever would differ from recycled news a radical unknown, if anything at all. In valorizing "that perishable part of things in which their novelty consists,"[38] the promotion of "new" values turns modernity into a history not of perishable *things*—which would still preserve the value of those things, for however limited a time—but of *perishing*, which sustains itself through the indifferent repetition of production and consumption.[39] On these terms, objects of experience expire upon arrival, having always already been time-stamped, disqualified, and dispatched, as Benjamin vouches with the following example: "the post-marked stamp is [. . .] probably the first sort of voucher whose validity is inseparable from its character of newness. (The registration of value goes together here with its cancellation.)"[40] And what is the case for objects goes for subjects of experience as well, whose "fall in value" Benjamin registers through the information delivered by modern news, which does not pass on experience, but simply passes: no story "survive[s] the moment in which it was new."[41]

Yet even if certain announcements *on* novelty expose nothing but the way announcements *of* novelty tend to summon more of the same, they will have made a difference with their exorbitant claims about the sphere of empty promises and voided values. Furthermore, even should the new turn out, again and again, to be indifferent, its very lack of stable significance also renders it incommensurable with the logic of equivalence that organizes commercial exchange. Precisely when that which *is* would count for nothing in itself, that which is *not*—that which parts from all that could be said or made to be—may be the only chance that could matter. This unpredictable and unaccountable chance remains when particular novel investments and claims are shown to default in theories of eternal recurrence, because the measures and standards for such claims would have had to be known quanta, and therefore never could have been the new, let alone the decisive factors for determining whether a *novum* may yet come. What Derrida writes of deconstruction could also be said of the profoundly uncertain prospects that open through those texts that expose the semblance character of novelty: "deconstruction loses nothing from admitting that it is impossible [. . .]. For a deconstructive operation, *possibility* is rather the danger, the danger of becoming an available set of rule-governed procedures, methods, accessible approaches. The interest of deconstruction [. . .] is a certain experience of the impossible [. . .] the experience of the other as the invention of the impossible."[42] Nor did an interest in a certain experience of the impossible escape Benjamin, who discovers in his examination of nineteenth-century texts not only a certain correlation between the demand for the new and the reproduction of the same, but also the way in which the coincidence of these extremes in the oeuvres of disparate writers comes to trouble the foundational assumptions that underlie distinctions between the old and the new, possibility and impotence, making room for something akin to what Derrida calls "a space of unrest or turbulence for every status assignable to it when it suddenly arrives."[43]

"Blanqui's [*Eternity by the Stars*] presents the idea of eternal return ten years before *Zarathustra*—in a manner scarcely less moving [*pathétique*] than that of Nietzsche, and with an extraordinary hallucinatory power," writes Benjamin toward the conclusion of his exposé from 1939.[44] Yet if this remark initially speaks to the denial of novelty that Blanqui and Nietzsche both impart, in accenting the "manner" in which this "idea" is conveyed, Benjamin also indicates already here that Blanqui's particular formulation for a static state of affairs would be more and other than a matter of merely affirming or recycling it. If the "moving" pathos and passion of Blanqui's rhetoric allows him to present the governing idea of the cosmos with "hallucinatory power," then he also exposes the illusory nature of that idea and the picture of nature that would correspond to it. Thus, even if Blanqui's cosmological hypothesis of eternal return might appear to be "an unconditional surrender" to the world that this professional revolutionary had resisted all his life, Benjamin adds that it is "simultaneously the most terrible indictment [*furchtbarste Anklage*] of a society that projects this image of the cosmos—understood as an image of itself—across the heavens."[45]

And in a second, more fleeting observation of the same, Benjamin writes elsewhere in *The Arcades Project*: "Blanqui yields to bourgeois society. But it is a knee-fall of such force that the throne comes to totter [*ins Wanken kommt*],"⁴⁶ with the implication that Blanqui's announcement of eternal recurrence also sends a tremor through nature and society, and in so doing may break the ground, if not the path, for a society that would differ from the established one, as well as from any new items or news items that the present establishment could produce.

Nor is Blanqui the sole writer whose case against society would profoundly shake it. As Benjamin says, it would be taken up again by Nietzsche ten years later, and before this, the tremendous force of Blanqui's fall also echoes the tremor that should have been produced through "Le Voyage," Baudelaire's closing poem to *Les Fleurs du mal,* which, as Benjamin points out, likewise revolves around a craving for novelty that turns into a cyclical repetition of identical pursuits. For when Baudelaire writes of his poem to Charles Asselineau—"I have *made* [*fait*] a long poem dedicated to Max Du Camp, which is *to make* [*à faire*] nature, and above all, the lovers of progress, shudder [*frémir*]"⁴⁷—he sends the message that this presentation of the dead ends of novel searches should trouble nature and civilization in a new way. With respect to these writers, the premise of the Ecclesiast may still hold that "there is nothing new under the sun" (Ecc. 1.9)—that is, there is no new *thing*—but only because their texts suggest that it is in breaking with the reification of the new and in thoroughly perturbing the orders it presupposes that something unforeseen may occur. Such turbulence, whenever and wherever it may take place, allows for an other that would not be merely defined by contrast to the same, nor assigned a place within a program for the future, but would be past all reckoning and recognition. Blanqui's and Baudelaire's writings on novelty, among others, thus deliver presentations of a seemingly "deterministic cosmology"⁴⁸ that, at the same time, upset the news of the present as well as any interpretation of historical progress that would relate it to a determinate and determining past. In so doing, they open all that their language touches upon to an unheard of future, without repeating the alternatives of surpassment and repetition into which thetic, prophetic, or prescriptive declarations of novelty more overtly appear to issue, from the Bible to Pound's modernist project.

This also means, however, that the staggering movements that Benjamin registers in certain nineteenth-century writings cannot be verified according to conventional standards of facticity and effects. The throne-shaking aftershocks of Blanqui's capitulation to capital and the shudder that Baudelaire's

"Le Voyage" sent through nature could never occur, if either could be taken for a historical given or a news item, made to order within a chronological continuum. According to such a scheme of things, the revolutionary efforts of the proletariat had been crushed with the fall of the Paris Commune by the time Blanqui's book was published. Nor did the poem that Baudelaire had composed in 1859 for the second edition of *Les Fleurs du mal* incite anything like an immediate natural or social disturbance, or even the scandal that his first edition of *Les Fleurs du mal* had provoked in 1857. If something takes place in these texts on modern novelty, it is not at the level of direct effectiveness, nor is it measurable according to the form of empirical facts, nor is it deferred and reiterated as a promise for the future. As Adorno has said, in words that bear repeating: "The category of the new has been central, though admittedly in conjunction with the question of whether anything new had ever existed."[49] Yet taking the questionability of novelty seriously does not foreclose attempts to address how *nouveautés* and news—and therefore the *status quo*—may be troubled by the catastrophic view that Blanqui's and Baudelaire's announcements open, in and despite their manifest impotence. For what occurs in language, as the passages discussed above suggest, escapes whatever may be assured through imperatives or conceptual frames, including that of the possible. The troubling dimension of their language may even reside in its apparent impotence, if it is the case, as Derrida has insisted with reference to deconstruction, that "*possibility* is rather the danger."[50]

Benjamin addresses the structural indeterminacy of novel announcements perhaps most clearly when he reprises one main thrust from Blanqui's and Baudelaire's writings in his commentary on Paul Klee's "Angelus Novus" or "New Angel." In his theses *On the Concept of History*, Benjamin depicts Klee's angel as one who sees what appears to us as "a chain of given events" as a piling of "wreckage upon wreckage"[51]: "*Wo eine Kette von Begebenheiten vor uns erscheint, da sieht er eine einzige Katastrophe, die unablässig Trümmer auf Trümmer häuft und sie ihm vor die Füße schleudert.*"[52] This double vision of historical phenomena has been read as the synthesis of "the paranoid fear of the past's otherness and oblivion (in their reciprocity), and the negation of that fear by hope."[53] It has been elucidated as a reminder of the original fall that precipitated man from paradise, from which man recedes further with every step of historical progress.[54] And it has been interpreted as a prospective indication that should guide the gaze of the historical materialist: "The angel is not yet the historical materialist," writes Ian Balfour, "but its precarious position and its singular insight are necessary to the revisionary materialist Benjamin delineates. If the angel's gaze is held out, for a moment, as exemplary, then the reader is enjoined through the rhetoric of the thesis to execute an about-face."[55] But the view of this "angel" or "messenger" (ἄγγελος) may also be aligned with that of the writers whom Benjamin sees to depict the catastrophic pile up of historical novelties—including Baudelaire and Blanqui, but also Nietzsche and Marx—and who thus invert the upward thrust of Pound's verses before the fact: "Day by day make it new / cut underbrush, / pile the logs, / keep it growing."[56] As with the gaze of Benjamin's "new angel"—who is likewise impotent to resist or to reverse the movements that he observes—the alternatives their texts offer would lie in the perspectives that their language discloses, as they turn the horizon of concatenated events into a single catastrophic case, and thereby open a margin of distance from that catastrophe as well, however slight it may be. As the focused commentaries in this book should bring more sharply into view, Baudelaire, Blanqui, Marx, and Nietzsche give a slant to the news of the world with announcements on novelty that shatter the entire picture. In this respect, they can be seen as angels of an angle on the new that disturbs its logic and impetus, not via a revolutionary program, but with an abrupt shift in inclination that may also give the field of history a start or jolt and thereby unsettle, however briefly, all that was trained or chained to occupy a certain place along the horizon of historical progress. They break the news by turning it down, and in revealing it to be the *same*, they show the "new" to be *other* than it appears, while speaking for the possibility of an other that could no longer be named "new" on familiar terms. Theirs may have been interventions without an event and therefore without any addition to the total and totaling sum of progress—interventions that may have at once altered and left, in all senses of the word, everything as it was. Yet because their language remains to be read anew, such ultra-revolutionary writers may also introduce a novelty *in* innovation that remains to come.

How this introduction may take place and what it may unsettle cannot be glimpsed in general terms or exhausted by any single commentary, but may only emerge through analyses of the specific terms, overdeterminations, and indeterminations of each text. The writers of the century that itself happened to give word of the new—*le dix-neuvième siècle*, or *das neunzehnte Jahrhundert*—do not address its status in ways that have become outdated. Before all, they give anouncements that can at no time have ultimately arrived, so long as their discussions—in the etymological sense of disturbance and turbulence—remain to be discussed and analyzed further.[57] Especially when it is a question of a *novum* that would bring established or novel orders to totter, it is also a matter of a tottering language whose sense and status cannot be settled once and for all. As Nietzsche would write on *Thus Spoke Zarathustra*: "It is a 'poetic work,' or a fifth 'Evangelium' or something else for which there is yet no name [. . .]."[58] The readings offered in this book thus reflect the attempt to register the contingencies, displacements, and openings that occur in those texts it addresses without aiming to give a definitive word on them. Rather than establishing a new theory of novelty, each chapter discusses an instance of novel announcement so as to expose a different angle from which certain assumptions on novelty, history, and the present might be troubled and subject to change—beginning with the "evangelical" book that most emphatically speaks of eternal recurrence and new values: Friedrich Nietzsche's *Thus Spoke Zarathustra*.

1

As If Zarathustra Spoke

On the Chances of Nietzsche's Good News

Addressing the motif of novelty in Friedrich Nietzsche's *Thus Spoke Zarathustra: A Book for All and None* would seem destined to bomb. With few exceptions, Nietzsche hardly spoke of being moved by contemporary events. Upon the burning of the Louvre during the Paris Commune, he wrote to his friend Carl von Gersdorff, "I felt for several days annihilated and was overwhelmed by fears and doubts; the entire scholarly, scientific, philosophical, and artistic existence seemed an absurdity, if a single day could wipe out the most glorious works of art."[1] And in 1879, the "Commune" still stood at the top of his list in a note that reads: "When I wept."[2] But aside from his response to this moment of mass destruction, Nietzsche kept his distance from contemporary events, even in those passages where he directly addresses them, such as the new preface to *The Birth of Tragedy* from 1886, in which he portrays himself sitting "somewhere in an Alpine nook," writing on ancient Greece "as the thunder of the Battle of Wörth was rolling over Europe,"[3] or the lines from *The Gay Science*, where he dismisses Saint Simon's brand of French Socialism and the nationalistic politics of Germany as small matters, "petty politics," preferring instead "to live on mountains, apart, 'untimely,' in past or future centuries."[4] And in *Thus Spoke Zarathustra*, Zarathustra will speak of the utterly indigestible character of mass communications, calling the news mere noise and nausea: "They are always sick; they vomit their gall and call it a newspaper. They devour each other and cannot even digest themselves" (50).[5] Nor does the issue change significantly, when the elements or aliments of public announcements shift from fodder to fire: upon encountering a firehound—which figure has been variously read as a representative of the modern state, as well as a revolutionary who would overthrow it—Zarathustra will dismiss his "smoke and bellowing" (132), as if the language of old institutions and anti-institutional figures alike goes up in smoke and reduces to inarticulate expression.[6] From this cursory survey, Nietzsche's remarks on the news would appear to move in a vicious circle from acknowledging no news to dismissing novelty *ad nauseum*—or to turn matters of purported significance into waste or exhaust.

Then again, if the loudest news says nothing, this is not to say that the new does not persist throughout Nietzsche's book. Nietzsche's *Thus Spoke Zarathustra: A Book for All and None* could also be said to revolve around nothing, if not the *novum* its eponymous protagonist announces, the new values he would seek to create, the new tablets he would inscribe, and the new cosmology or ethics that would pivot upon the thought of eternal return.[7] Nietzsche delivers a new idiom in this book that would preoccupy philosophical approaches to the text thereafter—the "transvaluation of values," the "overman," the "will to power," and "eternal return." Above all, *Thus Spoke Zarathustra* pivots upon "the new values" around which the world will be said to revolve "inaudibly" (131). These proceed, in turn, from the "stillest thought" of eternal return, the *circulus vitiosus deus*, which, as Bernard Pautrat has argued, remains virtually unspoken in Nietzsche's *Zarathustra*, however emphatically Nietzsche would proclaim it to be the central concept of that book in *Ecce Homo*.[8] Still, there is no immediate way to tell what is new about that thought or its consequences. Although its promise would seem contingent upon withholding or circumventing its pronunciation, eternal return returns in divergent passages of Nietzsche's writing. The thought was said to come upon Nietzsche suddenly and bring him to tears, marking a turning point at least as moving as the news of the Louvre. To Heinrich Köselitz, he wrote, "my eyes were inflamed—from what? Each time, I had wept too much on my previous day's walk, not sentimental tears but tears of joy; I sang and talked nonsense, filled with a glimpse of things which put me in advance of all other men."[9] It is as if the notion of the cyclical model of time had never been thought before—although it had already been proposed by the Pythagoreans and the Stoics, to name two sects to which Nietzsche referred in a discussion of recurrence several years earlier in *On the Use and Abuse of History for Life*. Furthermore, for all the differences that have been drawn by readers of Nietzsche between ancient theories and Nietzsche's thought,[10] the closure that it offers also appears to foreclose novelty. Undergoing the singular experience of this thought, the individual who could affirm the eternal repetition of his life would have to love his fate and answer to every accident of the past by speaking as Zarathustra does: "but thus I willed it, [. . .] thus I will it; thus shall I will it" (141).[11] And whether or not one will acknowledge and espouse this ring of recurrence, there would be no getting around what it entails: "this life as you now live it and have lived it, you will have to live once more and innumerable times more; and there will be nothing new in it."[12]

In this respect, the new event that repeatedly leaves its mark upon Nietzsche's biography and published writings would arguably amount to another, modern and modified version of the wisdom of the Ecclesiast: "There is nothing new under the sun" (Ecc. 1.9). Walter Benjamin suggests as much in a discussion of Nietzsche in his *Arcades Project*, where he makes a more obscure allusion to the Ecclesiast: "In the idea of eternal recurrence, the historicism of the nineteenth century capsizes. As a result, every tradition, even the most recent, becomes the legacy of something that has already run its course in the immemorial night of the ages. Tradition henceforth assumes the character of a phantasmagoria in which primal history enters the scene in ultramodern get-up."[13] The "immemorial night of the ages" recalls the Ecclesiast's reference to the "ages before us," where the word for "before" shades into "obscure" (עוֹלָם, *olam*) and renders new visions *a priori* benighted. Thus, although Nietzsche's Zarathustra will explicitly dismiss the famous opening lines of the Ecclesiast, "All is vanity," as the childish chatter of the "old books of wisdom" (204), the crux of his thinking—if not his outspoken views—suggests that all talk of novelty would be in vain.

Perhaps the best chance of tuning into the news that Nietzsche delivers, then, would be to follow those indications of novelty in his language that neither conform to the latest news reports of epochal events, nor to Nietzsche's more pronounced words on temporal cycles. For if no such alternatives were inscribed in his texts, how else could the emphatic gestures of announcement in *Thus Spoke Zarathustra* be understood? How else could Nietzsche repeatedly declare, as he did, to have made a breakthrough with this book that would culminate in his later claims to break the history of humanity in two? Perhaps the many explicit signs that Nietzsche's writing resists the new are misleading and detract from the *novum* that is at stake in its modulations and modifications of speech, which continue through to Nietzsche's last testimonies in *Ecce Homo*, where he affirms: "I have not said one word here that I did not say five years ago through the mouth of Zarathustra."[14] Perhaps the book is a bomb—a novel and explosive intervention in language—of a piece with Nietzsche's self-proclamation in *Ecce Homo*: "I am no man, I am dynamite."

Beside Zarathustra's loud and clear evocations of novelty and the more silent yet hardly mistakable indices of eternal return, *Thus Spoke Zarathustra* introduces a manner of speaking that escapes the grasp of concepts—new and old—and that breaks down any semblance of a consistent subject of speech per se.[15] Naming a speech act, the title alone announces the announcement-character of the text as a whole, before and beside the teacher or prophet who is at least nominally related to the Persian Zoroaster. In so doing, it indicates that the news of this book may be nothing other than the delivery of an announcement of the speaking of another, whose occurrence takes precedence over whatever particular message its principal persona may otherwise convey. What comes first is an index of manner: the "thus" that ostensibly refers to a foregone instance of speech and precedes whatever Zarathustra will be said to have spoken. *Thus Spoke Zarathustra* "thus" opens with a rupture that disorients when it comes to determining sequence and reference.[16] Confronted with these unprecedented words on the front or surface of the book, the reader is at a loss: something unrecorded and irrecuperable may have already been said and done before any of the sayings that the volume contains. To begin in this way thus introduces a breach and speaks to a lack that becomes all the more emphatic, as "thus spoke Zarathustra" returns throughout the book itself at the close of nearly every speech, pointing back to its beginning, and thus ultimately to the initial words: *Thus Spoke Zarathustra*. No closure would be possible with such an opening—no catching up to where things will have started—and since this first instance of "thus spoke Zarathustra" refers to no retrievable message, properly speaking, the adverb "thus" or "also" in *Also sprach Zarathustra* might also be seen to verge on its virtual variant and near homophone, "als ob," as if to read: "as if Zarathustra spoke."

Between the erasure that Nietzsche's title appears to follow, and its repetitiveness throughout the book, *Thus Spoke Zarathustra* condenses *in nuce* the problematic status of the new that pervades Nietzsche's oeuvre, as that which could only come about by returning and that which turns out to be void upon arrival. At the same time, however, it differs from Nietzsche's characterizations of modern news and ancient cycles by emerging as a sort of virtual writing, where nothing is precisely what returns; where no term reaches its telos in a single, definitive sense; and where each therefore opens—interminably—to further iterations and alterations. Of the title, one could thus repeat what Wolfram Groddeck says in a commentary on one of Nietzsche's notes on the doctrine of eternal return: "and yet the 'thought of thoughts,' at whose inception the *figura etymologica* stands, 'we teach the teaching [*wir lehren die Lehre*],' is remarkably empty [*leer*]."[17] Here, the redoubled "Lehre" creates an echo chamber that amplifies the significance of sound over sense, so that—like "also" and "als ob"—the homonyms "doctrine" (*Lehre*) and "vacancy" (*Leere*) resonate in and as one another, and thus as simulacra of 'a' word that divides and differs from itself.

Furthermore, whatever the virtues of such splits and slippages may be, this aspect of *Thus Spoke Zarathustra* also displays the consequences of Nietzsche's more theoretical remarks on the relations between words and world, from his early lectures on rhetoric through to his last notebooks, which also bear out in the announcements that make up the title and language of his book. According to premises that he repeatedly revisits and reworks, designations would be fictive abbreviations, figures fabricated for the sake of making sense of experience—in the active sense of the word—which may be reinvented without end and must be hollow at their core for such alterations to occur. As Paul de Man writes in *Allegories of Reading*, Nietzsche develops the "fundamental observation: tropes are not understood aesthetically, as ornament, nor are they understood semantically as a figurative meaning that derives from literal, proper determination. Rather, the reverse is the case. [. . .] The figurative structure is not one linguistic mode among others but it characterizes language as such."[18] With each new experience or each "new thing [*neues Ding*]," the trope or turn of phrase that is provisionally evoked to designate it marks the point of no return, and its further circulation in doctrines, discourses, and sayings does not close, but widens the gap that cleaves from the outset between words and things. Returning to the initial word of *Also sprach Zarathustra*, one might sum up thus: it not only fabricates a reference to a missing instance of speech, but can also be broken down into its virtualization—*als o(b)*—to the point where, in the last analysis, one could zero in on the final vowel *o* as a graphic index not of a vicious circle or ring of promise, but of the uncontainable *o*pening of language that will be extended in the words that follow.

It is in this manner, among others, that all speakable concepts and terms are exposed to be porous from the beginning of Nietzsche's book. For this same reason, however, the forces and impulses that Nietzsche elsewhere claims to be operative in rhetoric would escape definitive semiotic or tropological representations.[19] As *Thus Spoke Zarathustra* opens in the absence of a speaker, language goes on—and goes on vacation—in ways that affect not only the objects but also the subjects of speech, as Gilles Deleuze would emphasize, when he construed Nietzsche's notion of an "active philology" as one in which "a word only means something insofar as the speaker *wills* something by saying it." For in this case, too, possible meanings or the lack thereof would have to exceed whatever the speaker might claim or believe himself to say, rendering every sign an ambivalent symptom: "[a]ny given concept, feeling or belief will be treated as symptoms of a will that wills something."[20] Pierre Klossowski further elucidates the way in which expression in Nietzsche's oeuvre generally takes the form of "a code of designations [. . .] on which the agent depends," dissimulating a self and a speech through a system of signs devoid of the impulsion that gave them rise. As a result, this "self" and "speech" become subject to the "fluctuations" of their recipients as well, who "continually modify the system of designations" themselves.[21] Hence, in addition to all that has been said thus far of it, the title that is inscribed as the heading of Nietzsche's book and that recurs as a code throughout could be read as an extreme instance of such speaking in flux, as the exponentiation of the abandonment of any "proper" subject of speech that Klossowski retraces through Nietzsche's posthumously published notes and letters. In a letter to the composer Heinrich Köselitz, Nietzsche suggests as much, for when he draws a parallel between the impersonal motifs found in folk music and in "that which one calls a 'proverb' [*Sprichwort*]"—literally, a "word" (*Wort*) of "speaking" (*Sprechen*)—Nietzsche adds that his "Zarathustra occurs to [him]" as an example thereof, and thereby suggests that the word he gives of Zarathustra's speaking may have likewise been a proverbial find, a citation of what may have been spoken by any number of others and meant or read otherwise every time around.[22] Since no proverbial word of speaking returns so frequently as "thus spoke Zarathustra," this title, motif, and coda speaks symptomatically to the fluctuations that would affect every speaking as such, beyond the control of any nominal or traceable instance. Through its insistent returns, it takes on an importance that verges upon outweighing the speaking it would emphasize, marginalizing its content, and decentering the main speaker of the text—not least of all because "thus spoke Zarathustra" is one utterance that Zarathustra never will have spoken himself. There is at least the risk, then, that the many announcements of Zarathustra's speaking may drown out his speeches. But in so doing, they would also expose the repeated gesture of announcement and citation as one which summons new possibilities in language by voiding, altering, or cutting off the subjective and objective significance with which each recitation may have been known and spoken before.

This possibility appears all the more plausible, to the extent that the iterations of "thus spoke Zarathustra" in Nietzsche's book also indicate novel aspects of the structure of eternal return that exceed what Zarathustra or his ancient predecessors may have said directly about the thought of it. Rather, the verbal performance both in *Thus Spoke Zarathustra* and in Nietzsche's subsequent texts renders it questionable whether eternal recurrence ever were a thought, or whether it emerges instead as a function or effect of linguistic repetition. In its formulaic character, "thus spoke Zarathustra" may be read as a variant of the formula for eternal recurrence that Nietzsche will later evoke in *Beyond Good and Evil*: "da capo." There, he describes anyone who will have affirmed it as one who has opened his eyes to the

> ideal of the most high-spirited, vital, world-affirming individual, who has learned not just to accept and bear with what was and what is, but who wants it again just as it was and is through all eternity, insatiably shouting *da capo* not just to himself but to the whole play and performance, and not just to a performance, but rather, fundamentally, to the one who needs precisely this performance.[23]

Here, the "insatiabl[e] shouting" of "da capo" would not only express the need for "the whole play and performance," but would also delay its recommencement, and thereby figures as a different repetition or figure of speech that renders its speaker all the more in want. Because, however, Nietzsche's formulation also indicates that the speaker has foremost become insatiable for the shouting of "da capo," the need of which Nietzsche speaks will have been displaced from the start, in a way that voids "not just the performance, but rather, fundamentally [. . .] the one who needs precisely this performance." Taking it from the top, the recapitulation of *Thus Spoke Zarathustra* would be a more radical version of "da capo," which is not spoken by anyone who may so much as appear to think and speak for himself or his "needs." Instead, it recurs as an anonymous utterance that affirms nothing other than the sheer facticity of another's speaking both before and after the fact; or it is an enunciation that, in initially preceding the performance it advertises, also proclaims it as foregone. Eternal recurrence thus operates in language as the decapitation that takes place with each recapitulation, as it loses all capacity to hold what it would seem to reprise, and allows all that it would recollect to escape or alter beyond recall.

Taking seriously the recurring words that open Nietzsche's book for "all and none" thus raises the question of how to read and speak of Nietzsche's *Thus Spoke Zarathustra* anew. As Werner Hamacher has written on the citational character of Nietzsche's language:

> Citation makes the intention of whatever has been cited indeterminate—and more exactly, it exposes the very in-determination through which it was citable in the first place. What loses its determination in this way, however, can never appear as a finished product of the power of imagination or formation (*Bildung*). Indeterminate it remains despite the changing determinations it may undergo, open in all futures and withdrawn from the effort of propositional discourse to establish it in a statement.[24]

Reading the text along the faultlines where its often-cited novological and enunciatory promise fails—and with it, the philosophical premises it appears to put forth, such as the "thought" of eternal return—opens new approaches to how the mediations of Zarathustra's speaking operate, and how his forecasts of new values emerge as after-effects of rhetorical structures beyond any ethics of good and evil, as well as any project of creation. And beyond these aims, selected close readings of several critical breaking points—including the broken circle described by Nietzsche's title—also provide a way to describe how *Thus Spoke Zarathustra* relates historically to the traditional and modern models of writing on novelty from which it seems so radically to depart.

The prologue gives further indications of how the exposition of Zarathustra's "proper" speaking is exposed from the outset to alteration via citations and interventions on the parts of innumerable unnamed others. Like the title, the prologue marks another critical preliminary moment, another pretext or paratext that introduces the book by dividing it and bringing it to diverge from itself—it splits in the middle with the laughter of a crowd and ends twice over—in ways that trouble any initial sense of direction. The fifth and middle section of the ten-part segment entitled "Zarathustra's Prologue" is broken or capped off as follows: "And here ended Zarathustra's first speech, which one also calls 'the Prologue'; for at this point he was interrupted by the clamor and delight of the crowd."[25] These words arrive after Zarathustra has completed three separate addresses to a crowd in a marketplace, in which he had predicted the hour of the overman; proclaimed his love for the one who overcomes himself; and, finally, presented a vision of the last man, who would know nothing of love, creation, or longing, but who would take satisfaction in minor comforts und moderate work in a uniform rhythm, sated and sedated until the end. After descending from his mountain retreat and entering the public sphere, Zarathustra's speaking aims high and hits a low, before he is said to have been cut short, and ultimately goes on to speak solely with himself. This trajectory would seem, perhaps, to be straightforward, if it were not for the unsettling fact that "Zarathustra's Prologue" continues for five more sections after the speech that is also called the "Prologue": what, then, is the status of the speeches that occur past the end? What more would Zarathustra have to announce, after he has reached the "last man" and gone above and beyond him with the "overman"? And why is the initial end of his first speech characterized as an "interruption" in the first place, if the crowd's outburst of cries and laughter follows its end and culmination? At this point, the rhetoric of the "Prologue" provokes the question of not only the significance of Zarathustra's so-called "interruption," but also the discrepancy between what "one also calls 'the Prologue' " and what is called "Zarathustra's Prologue" in Nietzsche's book.[26] In the last sections of the latter, there are, moreover, strong signals that this breach—if it was one—will have changed Zarathustra's direction in decisive ways: Zarathustra will leave the marketplace, valorizing the rupture that just took place: "the man who breaks [the people's] tables of values, the breaker, the lawbreaker [. . .] is the creator;" and he will reformulate the project of public speaking that initially brought him down, now proposing to seek "fellow creatures [. . .] who write new values on new tablets" (24). What occurs to him thus reflects what just occurred to him in the market, suggesting that his "new," creative aims were not solely created by him, but arrive in the wake of his interruption, as an ambivalent response to it. With the double and duplicitous prologue that opens the book, then, nothing less is at stake than the way in which sequence and motivation are articulated in Nietzsche's book, and, consequently, the structure of a novel event or intervention in relation to former and future times.

If the initial portions of the "prologue" are only so called because an interruption alters the trajectory of Zarathustra's discourse, then they do not introduce the text to follow so much as they present Zarathustra's first oration as a "pre-speech" that is never entirely or surely realized as the "speech" that it may have otherwise been. It casts his speaking, that is, as an abortive or unrealized possibility—once more, "as if Zarathustra spoke." And if the announcements that Zarathustra initially delivered may still make up a "speech"—the "Prologue" is merely what one "also" calls this portion of the text—the emphasis upon common parlance here indicates that the status of Zarathustra's speaking remains out of his hands, just as it had when the difference between his singular idiom and the language of the crowd led to the outcries that had punctuated, if not ended, his oration. What "one" calls Zarathustra's "first speech" thus troubles any secure demarcation of where and when Zarathustra's speeches begin or end, which is shown instead to be contingent upon other voices than his "own." The same, however, may be said as well for what Zarathustra utters in the interval that falls between the public "prologue [*Vorrede*]" and the next major part of Nietzsche's book, labeled "Zarathustra's Speeches [*Zarathustras Reden*]." This interval within what Nietzsche calls "Zarathustra's Prologue [*Zarathustras Vorrede*]" lacks any proper title and, as an interpolation between Zarathustra's "prologue" and his "logoi" or speeches, it virtually takes place in no time or in a new time that not only marks a new point of departure for Zarathustra, but also revises the events that have just taken place in town and projects them into a time to come. Hence, having retreated and slept in the woods, Zarathustra awakens to the epiphany of "a new truth [*eine[r] neue[n] Wahrheit*]" (25). This new truth entails, first of all, his recognition of a need for companions who will follow him, and whom he intends to seduce from the crowds: "let Zarathustra speak not to the people but to companions. [. . .] To lure many away from the herd, for that I have come. The people and the herd shall be angry with me: Zarathustra wants to be called a robber by the shepherds" (23).[27] If at first Zarathustra came to give his word to the people, this new account of his comings and goings redefines his purpose.

Nothing that had happened before is any longer what it was said to be, and this moment of revision or retraction not only allows Zarathustra to affirm the crowd's rejection of his word—as though it were intended all along—for it is also symptomatic of the way time is told in this text: upon each return of the "same," as much is let go as is grasped, such that each return is at once opened and cut off by a rupture that does not close. With reference to another scene in *Thus Spoke Zarathustra*, where eternal recurrence appears depicted in the image of a snake—that is, in a version of the *ourobouros*, whose head and tail should come together to form a symbolic circle for eternity—Werner Hamacher incisively observes: "The snake of eternal return of the same bites its own head off [. . .]. But its bite is always already too early and too late to grasp itself. Before the bite of the moment [. . .] it must already have bitten infinitely often, and when it does bite, what it finds between its teeth is not its authentic aboriginal self, not the substrate of time, but merely something Other, the devalued repetition of itself."[28] Long before the presentation of eternal recurrence comes to a head in that scene, Zarathustra's prologue already insinuates that the past can be recollected and redeemed solely by emptying it of its previous sense and by voiding one's initial, express intentions—in a recapitulation that entails decapitation, every time around.

From the beginning, the text proceeds by circling back and cutting into itself; consequently, Zarathustra's talk of a "new truth" and "new values" emerges not from progress, but from a mode of recurrence that leaves nothing the same. Zarathustra once spoke to all, but now claims to have spoken to none, and he may have done both at once, on the slim chance of attracting new companions before expressly realizing his purpose to do so. Zarathustra claims that he will address the people again—just as he had attempted to do at first—but he will come to speak solely to those whom he can get away with seducing: "To lure many *away* [*weg*zulocken] from the herd, for that I have come" (23). And although this difference between his first arrival and his latest plans may appear to be slight, his deviation from the initial "prologue" in his later recollections of the scene grows the further one reads. Zarathustra will eventually get carried away himself, to the point where he reclaims the laughter of the crowd that had interrupted him as his own, recalling toward the end of the third book: "When I came to men [. . .] my wise longing cried and laughed thus out of me" (196–97).[29] Similarly, when Zarathustra's "stillest hour" speaks to him in the second book, one may still hear echoes of the crowd in her summary formulation: "speak your word and break!" (146).[30] What comes back to him, in other words, is each time "something Other," and the revalued, if not "devalued," "repetition of itself."[31]

These passages also imply, however, that Zarathustra does not entirely speak on his own at the lastest since he departs from the crowd. This feature of his speaking alters the way in which the remainder of the text would need to be read, including the news that Zarathustra henceforth announces. For only upon reconceiving his discourse as one that should not address a crowd directly, but should persuade companions to break from the crowd, does Zarathsutra speak in the manner for which he has perhaps become famous: "Fellow creators, the creator seeks—those who write new values on new tablets" (24).[32] Like Zarathustra's later recollections of laughter, these seductive words may be of mixed provenance, and thus simulacra of what "Zarathustra" seems to speak for himself. Many commentators on Nietzsche's *Thus Spoke Zarathustra* acknowledge the failure of his initial public speaking, and even perform elaborate exegeses of the way in which the townspeople misconstrue his speeches,[33] but they often proceed from the new premises that Zarathustra sets forth, as though they were not affected or provoked by the primary, primal scene in the marketplace. The prospective and retrospective shifts that can be traced in Zarathustra's descriptions of his activities, however, suggest that his rhetoric of the new would similarly be contingent upon the previous failure of his words to be received. The likelihood of such contingency becomes more clearly apparent, moreover, through a closer reading of Zarathustra's prologue in the context of the ancient testimonies and modern discourses that Nietzsche touches upon in his book. Returning to the prologue along these lines indicates, in turn, that it is the crowd's modern views rather than Zarathustra's proper initiative that effects the transformation of Zarathustra from the Persian prophet whom his name recalls into a spokesman for new values that would exceed his world, as well as the world of Nietzsche's contemporaries.

In adopting the name of the first founder of a world religion according to G. W. F. Hegel's historical narrative—but also according to Nietzsche's subsequent remarks on the genesis of his book—the history of moral and theological thought would have come full circle with Nietzsche's version of Zarathustra if it were not for a certain break in the cycle. In *Ecce Homo*, Nietzsche writes, "I should have been asked what the name of Zarathustra means in my mouth, the mouth of the first immoralist: for what constitutes the tremendous historical uniqueness of that Persian is just the opposite of this. Zarathustra was the first to consider the fight of good and evil the very wheel in the machinery of things."[34] Nietzsche then proceeds to turn everything around: "The self-overcoming of morality; the self-overcoming of the moralist, into his opposite—into me—that is what the name of Zarathustra means in my mouth."[35] More specifically, however, Zarathustra's interruption by "the clamor and delight of the crowd" marks the moment where Nietzsche deviates from the ancient model that he had come to know through Friedrich Creuzer's *Symbolics and Mythology of Ancient Peoples*, and where his Zoroaster becomes the new Zarathustra. Initially *Thus Spoke Zarathustra* opens with a description of Zarathustra's initial descent from the mountain along the lines Creuzer had described in his book: Nietzsche's eponymous protagonist addresses the sun and proclaims his purpose of spreading his wisdom to the people as the sun expends its light.[36] In the similar scene that Creuzer had set, Zoroastrianism was said to be centered on "the mountain of mountains, which reaches up to the ether and towers over all lands, from which the prophets and law teachers climbed down and imparted the purer light to humanity."[37] The prophets, in turn, impart light by imparting the holy word, while the word itself was said to impart the life and love of light. Creuzer elaborates: "the eternal word [. . .] is the ground of all being, all enduring, and all blessing, and Zoroaster's law is the body of that primal word from Ormuzd, and that is itself called Zendavesta, living word. [. . .] Tightly bound together with this idea of the living word is the irresistible power of prayer."[38]

But Nietzsche's Zarathustra not only seems to share his predecessor's privileged location and rhetoric of illumination; he even adopts in his "prologue" an anaphoric form that resembles the prayers J. F. Klenker had translated from Anquetil du Perron's French edition of the manuscripts that would become disseminated in Europe as the *Zend-Avesta* toward the end of the eighteenth century.[39] In his first descent to men in the city marketplace, Zarathustra proclaims his love to the people, as if to call a beloved people into being by affecting his auditors directly: "I love those who do not know how to live, except by going under, for they are those who cross over. I love the great despisers because they are the great reverers and arrows of longing for the other shore" (15). But the "irresistible power" of the prophet meets resistance when Zarathustra professes his words of love. The circulation of words comes instead to a standstill: "There they stand [. . .]; there they laugh. They do not understand me" (16). It may thus be along the lines of effective prayer in Zoroastrainism that the public can be said to fail to understand Zarathustra, because they do not respond in kind. Their laughter, that is, is disruptive not to his utterance—for he had come to the end of a speech before the interruption is said to occur—but to its effective, affective transmission. It short-circuits the process by which his utterance could be properly called "speech" according to the premises of the Zend-Avesta that Nietzsche implicitly evokes with his title character, perhaps motivating the renaming of this "speech" as a "prologue" in the sense retraced above.[40] In this case, the criterion that decides what counts as Zarathustra's speech would be its reception, which would not depend upon the cognitive capacity of listeners to associate his words with concepts, but upon their affective capacity to affirm them. Falling short of the desired effect, the speech fails and becomes a "prologue" to a very different sort of speaking, as expressions of immediate, mutual love are replaced by efforts at seduction, and general incomprehension comes to be Zarathustra's going assumption.[41]

At both the immanent level of textual composition and the historical level of world religions, Nietzsche's prologue to *Zarathustra* thus describes the break where the discourse of Zarathustra from the ancient world ends, and the more convoluted trajectory ensues as a modern quest for "new values." The new that Zarathustra bespeaks does not emerge *sui generis*, nor can it be taken at face value when it is henceforth delivered through Nietzsche's dramatis persona. Rather, the modern crowd determines the transformation of Zoroaster to Zarathustra, as they take pride in their "education" and embrace not Zarathustra's love, but the vision Zarathustra projects for "the last man." This vision—which entails moderate amounts of labor and corresponding doses of pleasure; euthanasia to induce a happy end; and insane asylums for "whoever feels different" (18)—certainly does not represent the modern industrial world of labor as it was lived in Nietzsche's nineteenth century any more than it represents Zarathustra's or Zoroaster's values. But it does represent several of the illusions that sustained nineteenth-century Europe, and in particular the vision of socialism that Eduard von Hartmann presents in his *Philosophy of the Unconscious*, in a chapter on political economy that Nietzsche had analyzed and criticized one decade earlier in the second of his *Untimely Meditations*.[42] The new projected in Nietzsche's book thus doubles between this vision and that of Zarathustra, who takes the former as his point of departure. But precisely in so doing—and this point is crucial—Zarathustra also never entirely parts from the moment that (negatively) determines his movements, or from the new goals that his new values would do away with.

Hence, it turns out that however far Zarathustra may go from the marketplace, and however great the solitude of his retreat, he will return to the old and new tablets that remain inscribed in his history, from the moment he considers "the man who breaks [the people's] tables of values" to be "the creator" (24). Esepcially in the chapter from the third book that stands under the sign, "On the Old and New Tablets," Nietzsche returns to the rhetoric of Zarathustra's prologue, combining the language of the Old and New Testaments, along with the rhetoric of modern education and its new Zarathustrian counterpart. Insofar as the very title echoes "Zarathustra's" call for "those who will write new values on new tablets" (24), it is marked in advance as the culmination of what his project will have become. But rather than representing its fulfillment, it comes to testify to the way in which his project will have gone awry and broken into a mass of *disjecta membra*. This scene, which Nietzsche would later describe as "decisive,"[43] begins with Zarathustra sitting alone on his mountaintop amidst "broken old tablets and new tablets half covered with writing," lamenting, "Nobody tells me anything new: so I tell myself—myself" (196). Far from anything like the autobiography of a person or persona, however, the speech of this self and the law tablets that surround him splinters into a variety of textual fragments that, combined with each other, become barely legible. Zarathustra was initially said to be alone, yet he just as soon appeals in his solitude to invisible and absent auditors, bidding them to "break" not only "these old tablets of the pious," but also the "new tablet" he "found hanging even in the open market places," which once again bears the marks of modern learning that had turned him off before: "Whoever learns much will unlearn all violent desire" (205). Complicating this duplicity further, his own words from the prologue come back to him estranged when he reads and repeats the words of a tablet that recapitulates his first speech on the overman—"Man is something that must be overcome"—before pointing out: "here is a new tablet; but where are my brothers to carry it down with me to the valley and into the hearts of flesh?" (199).[44] This time around, his opening oration is inscribed as a law that is not only impersonal and anonymous, but also conveyed in the medium of the commandments that Moses had received on Mount Sinai. Only in imitation of Moses does Zarathustra now dream of delivering news that is no longer his, and as he draws the terms of the prologue together with the terminology of the Hebrew Bible, he also adds the Pauline notion of the letter inscribed in the heart: "you show that you are a letter of Christ, prepared by us, written not with ink but with the Spirit of the living God, not on tablets of stone but on tablets of human hearts" (2 Cor. 3.3).[45] All of these features show the novelty of Zarathustra's speech to reside in its polyphony. But they also suggest that any plan to deliver Zarathustra's new message would have to be tabled, even if companions would assist him in getting down to carrying it out. For if the means of conveying Zarathustra's originally recoded and recorded message are now those ancient ones performed by holy men before him, then the imperative to overcome man would be undermined *a priori* by the human, all too human character of the medium for his message, whose transmission would move along the channels of the very theological tradition from which it should break. The old language, the new lingo, and Zarathustra's novel intervention thus become inextricably entangled, turning into and out of one another, in a language whose precise parsing and phrasing function to suspend all three from the communicative efficacy that they simulate. If the Persian version of a prophet's descent from the mountain fails, making a mosaic of tablets could succeed no better in the mission of bringing Zarathustra's good news to the people.

Yet beside the tablets—which literally set Zarathustra beside himself— every "Rede" of Zarathustra could more properly be called a "Vorrede" or "prologue" of sorts, affected by the way in which no public address could or should reach a particular audience in this so-called "book for all *and* none." From the title and prologue onwards, speaking instead leads to unpredictable, deviant side effects that become recast, again and again, as the primary aim all along. And because all talk of the new is, each time, contingent upon older and other things, every speech that Zarathustra will deliver can also—without contradiction—maintain the anachronistic tone of prophet rhetoric while mixing it up with messages from the modern world. One more time, *Also sprach Zarathustra* might be said to verge on its virtual variant and near homophone "als ob," to read "as if Zarathustra spoke." The new question that emerges from these preliminary descriptions of Nietzsche's book, however, is this: if Nietzsche produced a book that responds to the latest and last vision of modern society, while drawing repeatedly upon the names, figures, and models of ancient religious texts, what could have been made possible through this new manner of speaking? And if Nietzsche nonetheless considered his book to be itself a historical intervention, what sort of event could his rhetoric come out to be?

To a certain extent, Nietzsche predicted the debates that would ensue over the indeterminate—because overdetermined—linguistic character of *Thus Spoke Zarathustra*, as well as its various religious, philosophical, or literary interpretations. Announcing the first part of his new book to his publisher Ernst Schmeitzner, Nietzsche wrote:

> *Thus Spoke Zarathustra: A Book for All and None.* It is a "poetic work," or a fifth "Evangelium" or something else for which there is yet no name: by far the most serious and *also* most joyful of my productions, and accessible to everyone. And so I believe, then, that it will create an "immediate effect" [. . .].[46]

"Accessible to everyone," like all other published works in principle, this book prescribes no way in particular for anyone to enter it, its genre and character being as anonymous as the universal and nonexistent addressee for whom this book "for all and none" was intended: it is "something else for which there is yet no name." On the one hand, Nietzsche considers calling it a "fifth Evangelium," and thus a holy text of sorts that not only comprises "good" (εὖ) "news" (ἀγγελία), but that also pertains to the traditional evangelical lineage that Nietzsche betrays throughout and perverts at every turn. On the other hand, it could be designated a "poetic work [*Dichtung*]," with no pretensions to propagating a particular religious or philosophical doctrine. Remarking more generally on the rhetorical consistency of Nietzsche's oeuvre—with passing reference to "that irrepressible *orator* Zarathustra"[47]—Paul de Man points out the scandal and stumbling block that such writing poses to readers who would seek to make a positive program out of it or reduce it to performative, literary textual strategies with no serious consequences for thought: "Nietzsche's work raises the perennial question of the distinction between philosophy and literature" and confronts readers with "the patent literariness of texts that keep making claims usually associated with philosophy rather than with literature."[48] Either way, *because* the work displays a rhetorical virtuosity that renders every utterance rent in multiple directions at once, the impact of *Zarathustra* that Nietzsche predicted to his publisher could only be utterly unpredictable. For all the speaking Zarathustra does, then, it is most likely that the *novum* it permits is not one, but remains indeterminate and is perhaps left unsaid. The very condition for the immediate effects that Nietzsche promises may even lie precisely in the unprescribed and unheard of readings that his book allows, if it is also true, as Zarathustra once spoke in the chapter "On Great Events," that the world revolves "[n]ot around the inventors of new noise, but around the inventors of new values [. . .]; it revolves *inaudibly*" (131); or if it is true, as his "stillest hour" tells Zarathustra shortly thereafter: "It is the stillest words that bring on the storm. Thoughts that come on doves' feet guide the world" (146).[49] For this often-quoted, proverbial wisdom could also characterize the messages that *Thus Spoke Zarathustra* withdraws by conveying so many crossed signals. Like the "first speech" that is also the "prologue," and like the title that is also a coda, the "stillest words" may be the very ones that are loudly proclaimed, but that still prevent the text from saying any one thing. It is equally possible, in other words, that the *novum* at stake here may be no silenced secret and no esoteric wisdom, but the accessible expressions of the text that explode each announcement, because each is laden with overdeterminations to the breaking point.

The sort of unpredictability that cuts to the core or the heart of Zarathustra's recorded diction and written tablets also characterizes the more drastic event that Nietzsche explicitly and repeatedly declared when he proclaimed himself to deliver an enunciation that would "break the history of humanity in two" in his correspondence with Franz Overbeck, August Strindberg, and Georg Brandes, and again in *Ecce Homo*.[50] For if he envisioned the immediate impact of his work as a clean break, this too is overdetermined: Nietzsche's new chronology would have had theological and political precedents, both in the calendar that begins again with the Christian Era, as Hans Blumenberg has pointed out in *The Legitimacy of the Modern Age*,[51] and in the calendar that was temporarily inaugurated with the French Revolution, as Alain Badiou emphasizes in his account of

Nietzsche's anti-philosophical and anti-theological politics.[52] Yet not only are the consequences and effects of Nietzsche's intervention no more self-evident or straightforward than a poetic fifth gospel would be; his reiterated assertions of a world-historical rupture imply that it could not have arrived once and for all, and therefore provide no definitive confirmation of its occurrence. Whereas the Christian and revolutionary chronologies eventually found institutional support for the revision and division of the calendar—for however limited a time—the scission that may have taken place upon the appearance of Nietzsche's book remains outstanding and undecided. Badiou therefore goes on to argue that Nietzsche's "archi-political event" could not take place for anyone but the one who declares it, since "this event does not succeed in distinguishing itself from its own announcement, from its own declaration."[53] Yet it may be the unsuccess and indistinction of word or event in *Thus Spoke Zarathsutra* that renders it without precedent and opens it to a history that would, for the first time, differ from any that would conform to the law of succession or map onto a timeline. Regardless of any decision over its actual or possible consequences, however, *Thus Spoke Zarathustra* figures as one instance, if not *the* instant, of Nietzsche's often announced break, which implies that all of its sayings take place in and as the interim between times. And if only in this respect, the interval marked by the entire book, like the interruption of Zarathustra's prologue, suspends to great effect the distinction between before and after, pre-speech and speech, and virtually occurs in no time.

Zeroing in on the shattering impact of Nietzsche's writing on chronology, it appears that this non-time would be the new time that the chapter on the "Old and New Tablets" perhaps most pronouncedly traces—a time of anachrony that is told in a thoroughgoing revision of old and new languages drawn largely from the Old and New Testaments of the Lutheran Bible. Furthermore, it is hardly an accident that the language of these books is evoked and altered so emphatically in a text designed to break news by breaking history. It is the Bible that perhaps, like none other, even satisfies Badiou's condition for the "possibility of [a historical] intervention"—namely, "the circulation of an already decided event," or "the presupposition, implicit or not, that there has already been an intervention"[54]—insofar as its public arrival coincided with its publication, while its circulation came to affect the very terms in which belief, thought, and language would henceforth be negotiated among its readers. Nietzsche's notes from around the time of writing the fourth and final part of *Thus Spoke Zarathustra* suggest, in any case, that the poetic appropriation of Lutheran language is what Nietzsche had thought would render *Zarathustra* an epoch-making breakthrough. In one note, he writes: "the language of Luther and the poetic form of the Bible as the foundation of a new German *Poetry*—that is *my* invention!"⁵⁵ And in another, he indicates that the significance of this poetic invention would extend to history, politics, and public life, upon the premise that "our last event is ever yet *Luther*, our sole book ever yet the *Bible*."⁵⁶ History would be made, in other words, by the particular manner of speaking or writing that is introduced by books and that thereby comes to imprint the world. Nietzsche's later remarks on his proper "invention" give the answer, moreover, to what could follow our "last event" and add to the one book that ever counted; namely, another one called *Thus Spoke Zarathustra* that seconds and others it.⁵⁷ The Lutheran Bible may never have marked the European calendar as the French Revolution had done, but it marked language in a way that exceeds any particular message it may have conveyed and that turns out, in Nietzsche's book, to be anything but dated, and inestimable for any historical invention or innovation to come.

At first there would seem to be nothing radical in Nietzsche's return to the Reformation in the wake of an age of revolutions. By the time he wrote his note, it had become relatively common for German writers to construe history with a primary emphasis upon the Reformation, which Hegel had already done, and in a way that the new generation of the Hegelian Left was left to work through. In his early text on Hegel's *Philosophy of Right*, for example, Karl Marx suggests only at first that Germany, with its Reformation, remains behind the times: "If I negate the German state of affairs in 1843, then, according to the French computation of time, I am hardly in the year 1789, and still less in the focus of the present."⁵⁸ But he overturns the position of importance that he had assigned the Revolution, when he ends his text with the prediction that Germany's temporal lag and lack of revolutionary history may ground the universal emancipation of the proletariat that the French had left behind with their social and political advancements:

> The only *practically* possible liberation of Germany is liberation that proceeds from the standpoint of *the* theory which proclaims man to be the highest being for man. [. . .] In Germany *no* kind of bondage can be broken without breaking *every* kind of bondage. The *thorough* Germany cannot make a revolution without making a *thoroughgoing* revolution. The *emancipation of the German* is the *emancipation of the human being*. The *head* of this emancipation is *philosophy,* its *heart* is the *proletariat*.⁵⁹ (MECW 3: 187)

Marx concedes, moreover, that the first "theoretical" emancipation of man took place with the Reformation: "Germany's *revolutionary* past is theoretical, it is the *Reformation*. As the revolution then began in the brain of the *monk,* so now it begins in the brain of the *philosopher*" (MECW 3: 182; cf. MEGA 1.1: 615). Likewise, Marx's contemporary and friend Heinrich Heine never ceases to think in terms of the Revolution, but he articulates contemporary events throughout his writings in a biblical language that affirms the eventfulness of Luther's translation. And like Nietzsche, Heine describes the Lutheran Bible as the event that makes modern poetry possible, while implying through his rhetoric that the same would go for the possibility of significant news.[60] (Nietzsche's unique invention, in other words, is one that he shares with Heine, whom he also acknowledges as his sole poetic predecessor in *Ecce Homo*.[61]) This working premise becomes explicit toward the end of his *History of Religion and Philosophy in Germany*, where Heine writes in a tone that is at least as prophetic as Marx's, and far more parodic than prophetic, but no less devastating for that:

> In my opinion, a methodical people like us had to begin with the Reformation, only after that could it occupy itself with philosophy, and only after completion of the latter could it go on to political revolution. I find this sequence very rational. The heads that philosophy used for speculation can be cut off afterward by the revolution for any purpose it likes. But philosophy could never have used the heads cut off by a preceding revolution. [. . .] [T]he German revolution will not turn out to be any milder or gentler because it was preceded by Kant's *Critique*, Fichte's transcendental idealism, or even nature philosophy. Because of these doctrines revolutionary forces have developed that are only waiting for the day when they can break out and fill the world with terror and with admiration.[62]

For all their differences, both Marx and Heine take the event of the Reformation as their point of departure for pronouncing a revolutionary future that they explicitly distinguish from recent events in France. Thus, this historical development remains critical, however much the revolutionary movement on German soil should differ from that of its neighbor, from the ground up or the top down.

Nietzsche's remarks on Luther follow in this line of thinking, yet in distinction to these writers, Nietzsche's history breaks off before the Revolution. Badiou comments on Nietzsche's selective political history, writing: "the Nietzschean critique of the Revolution [. . .] consists in saying that, essentially, the Revolution did not take place." He interprets this silence in terms of how, for Nietzsche, the Revolution "has not truly broken the history of the world in two, thus leaving the Christian apparatus of the old values intact."[63] But Badiou does not enter into the eventful potential that Nietzsche seems to have read in the manner of speaking that Luther introduced during the Reformation. Nor can Nietzsche's reticence on the Revolution be merely symptomatic of contemporary German perspectives on politics or the lack thereof, as it was for Marx and Heine, if he considers historical eventfulness to be first of all a question of language. Rather, if there were a writer from the previous generation whose estimation of the Reformation and the Lutheran Bible comes close that of Nietzsche—and whose writings may have also marked Nietzsche's untimely meditations on these issues—it could have been Theodor Mundt, who had introduced the Reformation as *the* event of modern history in his book on the *History of Society* (1844),[64] largely because of Luther's intervention in the German language. In order to approach the sort of evangelium or novel announcement that *Thus Spoke Zarathustra* may have been, then, one might make some headway by going back to Mundt's reflections on Luther and recapitulating Nietzsche's early notes on Mundt's book.

On the one hand, Mundt considers the newest and latest "evangelium of humanity" to be the "universal right to happiness and authentic possession,"[65] which, he argues, first flourished during the Lutheran Reformation, with its proponents' valuation of the individual and his "free self-determination [*freien Selbstbestimmung*]."[66] On the other hand, the greatest testimony to the power of Luther's intervention was, for Mundt, the language that he provided for the third estate. "Its first work," writes Mundt, "was to create a language that encompasses the entire nation, a universal, formed national language, equally comprehensible and pleasant for the high as for the low, the poor as for the rich, overcoming the previous separations of German folk life."[67] The "highest meaning" of Luther's biblical language thus turns out to be its "truly political meaning," which overturns every opposition, "in that, even as new schisms in belief seemed to call forth new separations, it tore the whole German people further along in observing itself as a unified nation and holding fast to the new language of Protestantism as the organ of this unity."[68] Along these lines, what Luther achieved with his Bible translation would have been the non-dialectical establishment of synthesis and community that sustains itself through oppositions by supplying the common terms with which any opposition or agreement would be articulated.

When Nietzsche first read and commented upon Mundt's monograph in his notebooks from 1862, he would positively value the possibility of individual interventions such as Luther's that Mundt espouses in his discussions of the Reformation:

> Indeterminacy whether the concept of a people is the higher and more encompassing one as opposed to that of man or whether the concept of man, as the original source of all peoples, is also the decisive, determining and driving force. In reality the people determine man almost exclusively; but in the great moments of revolution [*Umwälzungsmomenten*], man becomes master of the spirit of the people. For revolutionary politics this speculative concept of society is the capital content.[69]

And in *The Gay Science*, Nietzsche still evokes the dynamics that he describes here, but reverses his assessment of the direct proportion between "great moments of revolution" and the force of man. Now, it is only when a society reaches a low that an individual may give it a new turn, whose personal upswing amounts to the communal failure and fall that Nietzsche will describe under the heading, "Failure of Reformations":

> That Luther's Reformation succeeded in the North suggests that the north of Europe remained behind the south and still knew only rather homogeneous and monotonous needs. [. . .] The more general and unconditional the influence of an individual or the idea of an individual can be, the more homogeneous and the lower must the mass be that it influenced [. . .]. Conversely, we may infer that a civilization is really high when powerful and domineering natures have little influence and create only sects.[70]

It was due to general weakness and corruption, then, that Luther rose to overnight success—whereby "this night," Nietzsche emphasizes, "brought the storm that put an end to all."[71] Far from Mundt's and his own earlier appraisal, Nietzsche's depiction of the Reformation as a nocturnal coup echoes his former assessment of the Paris Commune, when "the entire scholarly, scientific, philosophical, and artistic existence seemed an absurdity, if a single day could wipe out the most glorious works of art."[72] More importantly, however, it testifies to the massive work of destruction entailed in Luther's intervention, which is indissociable, as Nietzsche and Mundt both emphasized, from the perduring influence of the Lutheran Bible upon the German language. As Zarathustra's "stillest hour" would say, great events—for better or worse—come by "storm," and it is the "stillest words" that bring them on, whether they be the words Nietzsche prints in his book, or the words of Luther's Bible translation that would transform and imprint their mark on the language in which political, theological, social, and individual debates would take place thereafter. In both events, the "stillest" words would name the "Stil" or "style" inscribed into the lexical, syntactic, and rhetorical formations that carry all that might henceforth be said.

It is in this most ambivalent light, between his earlier and later assessments of individual revolutionary interventions and writings, that Nietzsche's response to the Reformation can be seen to inflect his claim to undertake a project and even produce an event on a par with Luther's in *Thus Spoke Zarathustra*. This claim, moreover—whose chances would similarly depend upon social factors that exceed any individual initiative—reformulates Luther's devastating achievement as a model and a goal, as if Nietzsche were acting like his Zarathustra, who will likewise turn failure to success by converting the incomprehension and laughter of the crowd into the force of his speech. But this analogy between the two book-events means, too, that incalculable hazards are involved in such a tentative, whose ups and downs exceed any single revolutionary turn and any reformational trajectory. For Luther's and Nietzsche's languages can operate as Nietzsche suggests they do solely if they fail to issue into a homogeneous, standardized message, and offer instead stylized words, turns of phrase, and sentences that may be cited, adopted, and adapted to any number of ends, in any number of directions. If Nietzsche began his speculations on revolution with a theory of alternating determining forces, he comes full circle in his considerations of the Reformation as a model for his own historical breakthrough—but in a recapitulation that cuts off the "capital content" of man and society alike and leaves all speakable content to be determined anew. Such books as the Bible and *Thus Spoke Zarathustra* would communicate and innovate, that is, to the extent that they empty their contents, render the meanings of communicative means indeterminate, and break down themselves.

Thus, the historical stakes and complexities of Nietzsche's reflections on the language of his *Zarathustra* cannot be underestimated when he proclaims its place in a lineage beginning with Luther. It was along these lines that he wrote of his book to the classical philologist Erwin Rohde:

> It is my theory that with this *Zarathustra* I have brought the German language to a state of perfection. After *Luther* and Goethe, a third step had to be taken—look and see [. . .] if vigor, flexibility, and euphony have ever consorted so well in our language. [. . .] My line is superior to [Goethe's] in strength and manliness, without becoming, as Luther's did, loutish. My style is a dance, a play of symmetries—and in a leap it passes beyond them and mocks them. This enters the very vowels.[73]

If Joseph Westfall, in his recent commentary on this passage and on Nietzsche's engagement with Luther, is right to point out that the German of Nietzsche's Zarathustra is directed against what Nietzsche repeatedly calls the "degenerate" German of the newspapers, and that this effort entails a return to Luther's Bible, insofar as "the German language begins with [this] first systematization and standardization,"[74] it is not merely for Nietzsche a matter of orchestrating, in language, a transition "from word to deed," which Westfall suggests with reference to Luther's and Goethe's Faust's respective translations of the opening line of the Gospel of John, "In the beginning was the Word."[75] It is a question of outdoing his predecessors in the stylistic qualities of "vigor, flexibility, and euphony," of effecting a change that carries across every word and that thereby crosses through all words as semantic units or as recognizable elements of a certain literary tradition. Hence the many, often parodic echoes of biblical rhetoric that Nietzsche speaks and breaks with, jumbling the code, the codex, the tablets, in a way that plays to alternative possibilities beyond belief. Hence Nietzsche's privileging of impersonal manners of speaking and the simulation of proverbs and rhetorical formulae, which can spread all the more rapidly, the more they are ultimately void of any particular sense and context. Hence, too, the tablets on which Zarathustra's words return, among others, as anonymous citations—not to mention the emptying out of the Persian name "Zarathustra" that nonetheless circulates after the proper communication of the prophet has short-circuited. From the title page to the last page, it is the "thus" of *Thus Spoke Zarathustra* that comes first, and that gives it a chance to be the historical event that Nietzsche had announced. In this manner, Nietzsche was taking a "leap" with his entire book, in undermining each utterance by "pass[ing] beyond" and "mock[ing]" every symmetry or common measure that it appears to present. It can therefore hardly be an accident that he begins his description of *Thus Spoke Zarathustra* for Rohde with the words: "It is a sort of *abyss* of the future."[76] To all intents and purposes, language would be reinvented over the abyss the opens with and within each utterance, as it breaks from the foundational assumptions underlying messages and testaments—new or old—and surpasses any system of measures and symmetries, including its own. Even at the asemantic level of vowels, the elements of alphabetic writing would no longer function primarily to forge correspondences between written and vocalized signs, but to dissolve significant units into elements of a symmetrical pattern to be outdone and undone in the next step. Every announcement, every part of an announcement, and every repeated enunciation would be novel to the extent that it is thus rendered incommensurable with any other or "itself."

If meaning, communication, and vocalization are silenced in these reflections, the emphasis on vowels implies an unheard of transformation of language. And it would not be new to draw attention to this change. It is with regard to these aspects of Nietzsche's writing that Friedrich Kittler quotes the same letter to Rohde as evidence of the way in which Nietzsche's experiment in the invention of rebuses—riddling, asemantic forms of inscription—evolves out of the paradigmatic shift in language that took place with the development of new writing technologies around 1900.[77] No longer borne out by the voice of the mother, techniques of learning to read and write in isolation, Kittler argues, shifted the sense and libidinal investments in language on the part of modern writers. As a correlate to the isolation of letters on the typewriter and the disembodied transmissions of the telegram, there emerged, he argues, "an intransitive writing, which does not aim for written truths and addressed readers."[78] In emphasizing intransitivity, Kittler's assessment of medial effects on Nietzsche's style leads him to similar observations to those that follow from an analysis of Nietzsche's title, prologue, and tablets, as well as the ways in which his evangelical ambition takes after Luther's.[79] Yet what no general account of the technological conditions of Nietzsche's writing can expose is how this writing specifically alters the metaphysical, theological, and historical presuppositions that it echoes, refracts, and fragments.

After Zarathustra's preliminary descriptions of socialism and the last man, Nietzsche returns to the indeterminacy of man and society in the chapter from the first book of *Thus Spoke Zarathustra* that bears the title, "On the Thousand and One Goals," which revolves around a language of estimation and measure, if not symmetry. If there were one among myriad passages that most concisely indicates several ways in which Nietzsche's incommensurable reformation or revolution of language works—beyond Zarathustra's proper or improper speaking and beyond the Lutheran Bible—it may be this section, which begins with an overview of the many societies Zarathustra has passed through: "Many lands and many peoples saw Zarathustra: thus he discovered the good and evil of many peoples. And Zarathustra found no greater power on earth than good and evil."[80] Zarathustra goes on in the first person to recapitulate the differences from people to people, and to impart his insight into the dynamics of estimation that give rise to these distinctions, at which point the chapter comes full circle, before breaking off:

> Many lands and many peoples saw Zarathustra. No greater power did Zarathustra find on earth than the works of lovers: 'good' and 'evil' is its name.
>
> Verily, a monster is the power of this praising and censuring. Tell me, who will conquer it, O brothers? Tell me, who will throw for me a yoke over the thousand necks of this beast?
>
> A thousand goals have there been so far, for there have been a thousand peoples. Only the yoke for the thousand necks is still lacking: the one goal is lacking. Humanity still has no goal.
>
> But tell me, my brothers, if humanity still lacks a goal—is humanity itself not lacking too?—
>
> Thus spoke Zarathustra. (60)[81]

Going over these words quickly, it would seem that the estimations of good and evil not only vary from land to land, but also differ so vastly that the terms become indifferent *per se*—as Zarathustra says: "Many things I found called evil here and decked out with crimson honors there" (58). All things appear, in Zarathustra's survey of the lands he saw, divested of ultimate value or meaning, but for the investments made by the people who speak of them. Hence, Zarathustra is consistent in calling the duality of "good" and "evil" a single, greatest "power" and a single "name," so as to emphasize the confounded nature of these terms for judgment and to expose the lack of foundation for determining their distinctions. This synthesis is reflected, moreover, in the way that the plurality evoked at the opening of the chapter—"many lands and many peoples"—collapses into the evaluation provided by one speaker—namely, Zarathustra—whose assessment of the power of estimation grows to the degree that any specific sense of good and evil diminishes. The persistant polarity of values that Zarathustra discovers in observing their flux thus prepares for their formulation in terms of the poles of force that Nietzsche would elaborate further in *Beyond Good and Evil*. Yet his reduction of difference among the "many" to a "homogeneous and monotonous" formula also recalls the conditions for the "event of Luther," as Nietzsche had described them in *The Gay Science*, which allowed "the more general and unconditional influence of an individual."[82] It from such a vantage point Zarathustra might even be seen to deliver the very definition of man that otherwise appears to be lacking, when he states in the midst of "On the Thousand and One Goals": "Only man placed value in things to preserve himself—he alone created a meaning for things, a human meaning. Therefore he calls himself 'man,' which means: the esteemer" (59).[83] Hence, if humanity may still, in the end, be said to lack "a goal"—as Zarathustra had indicated in the prologue: "The time has come for man to set himself a goal" (17)—it would seem that Zarathustra will have taken the first step toward this end, and that he is the man for this task. The questions that Zarathustra delivers at the close of "On the Thousand and One Goals," in other words, would barely seem to conceal an already given answer, namely, that one goal is needed from the one who understands man to be an esteemer. Such an interpretation would align with readings such as Georg Lukács's, who traces an affinity between Nietzsche's Zarathustra and the aesthetics of fascism, and argues that a leader such as Otto von Bismark, who strikes a compromise with the populace, "was not reactionary enough for Nietzsche."[84] But by reading in this relatively straightforward manner, one would have also overlooked or overleapt the innumerable ways in which the text also speaks against any hermeneutic reduction of its utterances to a single sense and breaks its word on any "time" that may be said to "come" in advance. One would have missed, in other words, the abyssal dimensions of Nietzsche's missive that break word of novel possibilities beyond any predictable—and therefore dictatorial—or prescriptive—and therefore restrictive—trajectory.

In breaking off his speech at the end of "On the Thousand and One Goals," Zarathustra is the last man to assign an "an end to all," as Luther was said to have done, or to establish an ultimate goal for humanity, as Zarathustra once may have seemed to set out to do. For in addition to the intermittent resonances between this chapter and "Zarathustra's Prologue," dissonances emerge throughout the text, beginning with the combination of a "goal," a "yoke," and "man," which recalls the "last man" that Zarathustra had depicted in his prologue as the result of the "domesticat[ion]" of the species, if not its subjugation beneath a yoke: "One day this soil will be poor and domesticated, and no tall tree will be able to grow in it" (17). Whereas Zarathustra may have announced the positing of a goal as an alternative to the last man in his earlier speech, it is now the setting of a goal that should bring about a tame end for humanity in "On the Thousand

and One Goals." If the telos that Zarathustra now seems to seek were truly what is called for, then he would be advocating for what he once protested. But something else is happening in these passages of the text, something which corresponds neither to a proto-fascist rhetoric nor to a relapse into the situation that Zarathustra had described and decried in his prologue. Far from promising any ultimate path, the language of the passage splinters the speaking of Zarathustra "himself," as well as the message it seems to convey, so as to give rise to the suggestion that the non-being of humanity, which Zarathustra so provocatively questions in the end, is what first gives so-called human life a chance. Whereas the indeterminacy of the individual and society had inspired thoughts of revolutionary politics in Nietzsche's youth and informed his later thinking on the Reformation, a still more radical—and radically anarchic—potential is bespoken as the language of Zarathustra refracts in "On the Thousand and One Goals," in a manner of speaking on values that wants to be read literally, down "the very vowels."[85]

Already Zarathustra's definition of "man" as "the esteemer" begins to undo the subject he names, in this new version of Protagoras's famous proposition, which had defined man as the measure of all things. In Protagoras's statement, which Nietzsche would have known from Diogenes Laertes's *Lives of Eminent Philosophers*, both man and measure are equated: "the measure of all things of use is man [πάντων χρημάτων μέτρον ἐστὶν ἄνθρωπος]."[86] The same goes for the definition Nietzsche had meditated upon in his earlier, philological reflections on the derivation of "man" from the Latin "mensura," or "measure"—which carried further the traditional etymology extending from Nicolas of Cusa, who derives mind (*mens*) from the notion of measure (*mensura*) as well.[87] And in *Human, All Too Human*, Nietzsche includes an aphorism that defines "man as the measuring-one [*der Mensch als der Messende*]," writing that "primal men" defined themselves according to their invention of "measure."[88] It is in line with this tradition that Zarathustra, too, calls man "the esteemer," or more precisely, "the esteeming-one," "der Schätzende" (59, *KSA* 4: 75). In both *Human, All Too Human* and *Thus Spoke Zarathustra*, however, the slight grammatical shift from Protagoras's noun "measure [μέτρον]" to participial formulations makes all the difference, giving way to a dynamic where "man" would be a function of estimation, and where no estimate or esteemed thing would preexist the operations of this function. "Estimation" therefore cannot mean, in Nietzsche's text, that a known quality or standard would be held up as the measure for whatever should enter into this relation of evaluation. Such an assumption would already imply a hypostatization of qualities into stable quanta, whereas here, all subjects and objects are said to become what they are solely *through* estimation. Likewise, "man" cannot mean a subject with attributes, insofar as he is solely defined as the agent of esteeming, who gives rise not only to good and evil, but also to himself through the affirming and denying that takes place through him. Nietzsche's participial grammar thus entails parting with subjects, substantives, and properties—and thus, too, the subject of "man," which can appear only improperly, in quotation marks, as it does in Zarathustra's speaking here: "Therefore he calls himself 'man,' which means: the esteemer" (59). Furthermore, insofar as the participles "measuring" and "esteeming" denote ongoing activities, there would be no way for "man," by definition, to define a goal or an end for himself, beyond his participation in the process that makes him and all other things what they are in the first place.[89] The definition Zarathustra gives of "man" thus emerges as the antidote to definitions which would describe the horizons and limits of that which they define. Far from any stable notion of a human being, "man" and his "goals" become subject to alteration without end.

But Zarathustra also introduces yet another difference, in that he no longer speaks the language of measuring that Nietzsche had evoked in *Human, All Too Human*. For what is translated in the English edition as "esteemer" is a nominalized participle, "der Schätzende," which no longer resonates with "Mensch" ("man") as "Messen" ("to measure") had done in Nietzsche's formulation from before, and which thus obscures the *figura etymologica* that underlies his previous remarks. In place of Nietzsche's earlier emphasis upon the similarities between *Mensch* and *Messen*, Zarathustra creates a new association through the equation he sets forth between esteeming and creating—"to esteem is to create [*Schätzen ist Schaffen*]"—whose rhetorical force owes at least as much to the symmetry in patterns of stress, alliteration, and vocalization that binds the two words, as it does to the argument Zarathustra provides, according to which the investment of things with praise first gives them their sense, and thus creates them as the things that they are esteemed to be. Nor does his innovation of measures stop at creation, but outdoes and undoes this too, when Zarathustra praises the power of estimation as the greatest good—"esteeming itself is of all esteemed things the most estimable treasure" (59)[90]—and thereby voids the value of the particular goods of "many lands and many peoples." Thus, just as it would seem that Zarathustra goes beyond a rhetoric of measure solely in order to establish a new equilibrium between estimation and creative activity, he unsettles the productive dimension of estimation (*Schätzen*) that he seems to posit and shows creating (*Schaffen*) to be at least as hollow as it is hallowed.

With this, Zarathustra gives the "scoop"—in all senses of the word—on the abyss that underlies the "Schaffen" and "Schöpfen" of "creation,"[91] which is made explicit as he adds, shortly after his praise of praising: "without esteeming, the nut of existence [*Nuss des Daseins*] would be hollow." This sentence seems to sum in a nutshell the news and new perspective on the values of the world that Zarathustra delivers from without. Once again, as Groddeck had said about the doctrine of eternal recurrence, the "doctrine [*Lehre*]" is "remarkably empty [*leer*];"[92] and what is more, Zarathustra's speech renders the virtual condition of hollowness ("would be hollow") in terms that themselves seem to void even the shell of existence they evoke. Because Zarathustra does not express any value but valuation at this point, the simile or likeness of the "nut of existence" itself rings hollow and, deprived of substance, begins to sound less like the substantive that it at first appears to be (*Nuss*), than the suffix *-nuß* (and its more common modern variant, *-niß*), which would more usually function in German morphology to transform infinitives and participial adjectives into nouns. Whether or not it is a mere coincidence, this resonance speaks for a metamorphosis in the sense and morphology of the "Nuss des Daseins," in a book that is composed, as Nietzsche had claimed in his letter to Rohde, through to its "very vowels,"[93] and in a passage where connotations are contingent upon phonetic connections, from "schätzen" to "schaffen," and beyond. This possible reading is all the more probable, not only because the usage of *-nuß* in place of *-niß* recalls distinctive features of Luther's language, which Nietzsche professes to take as the "the foundation of a new German *Poetry*;"[94] but also because the addition of the suffix "*-nuß*" performs precisely the substantivation of actions and their resulting qualities that estimation is said to do in this chapter. Just as esteeming first produces the esteemed, which can only persist, in turn, through the perpetual process of estimation, the production of a substantive with the suffix "*-nuß*" indicates that this product is a process and exists so long as it remains in the making.[95] But if the linguistic correlate to the esteeming that Nietzsche describes is *-nuss*, then the valuation of values comes down *in nuce* to this hollow form, such that the "nut of existence" is always about to crack into the *not* of existence—or the *-ness* of nothing in particular.

These features of Zarathustra's rhetoric may suffice to cast doubt on the projects that his last questions indicate in "On the Thousand and One Goals"; however, there is yet another element in the thesaurus that Zarathustra draws upon here, which deviates from any story that could make a goal its end. With, namely, the stuttering of "schä-" and "scha-" throughout the chapter (e.g., "Schätzen ist Schaffen: hört es, ihr Schaffenden! Schätzen selber ist aller geschätzten Dinge Schatz und Kleinod" [*KSA* 4: 75]), Nietzsche also disseminates the name of the Persian woman whom Zarathustra never fully evokes, but to whom he owes his title, "On the Thousand and One Goals": Scheherazade, the storyteller of *A Thousand and One Nights*, whose name itself means "of noble appearance and/or origin."[96] The intermittent evocations of this incarnation of noble values allows for the chapter to be read against the grain—against old and new values, and against the power of value-creations *per se*. What if the aims of Zarathustra's speech were not the creation of new values, nor the creation of a yoke for "the thousand necks" of man? What if at issue were instead a way to break the creations of good and evil that bind and divide collectives? If the rhetoric of valuation appears to imply the necessity of a decisive goal in Zarathustra's speech, the names for esteeming, creating, and nobility break themselves into so many echoes and refractions of one name, and perhaps one of the "stillest words" of the text—namely, Scheherazade—whose virtual inscription in *Thus Spoke Zarathustra* speaks for the scission of all teleological decisions.

Scheherazade's discourse is one that both fails and exceeds any movement that could culminate in an ultimate end or goal. In the chambers of King Shahrayar, who had decimated the female population of his realm, taking a new wife every night and "hav[ing] her put to death the next morning,"[97] she delivers stories from the closure of a story, breaking off in the midst of each narrative sequence in a way that awakens a desire on the part of the king to spare her yet another night and listen further the next time. And after every story that Scheherazade eventually completes, she comes out with a new one that will be initiated and interrupted in turn, giving her and the king—and, by extension, the community—the time of their lives. Falling short and overshooting a thousand goals is the movement that succeeds in "sav[ing] the people."[98] Thus, to the extent that Zarathustra's speech harbors and treasures "Scheherazade"—at least in part—her subtle insistence may override his more overt announcement of the need for man to "set himself a goal" (17). Following her further traces in the text, moreover, exposes how far Zarathustra veers from goal-oriented procedures from the outset. For if he will have gained his insights by traveling and coming to know "many lands and many peoples"—that is, by moving laterally and aimlessly, and by abandoning every settlement he visits—this wandering trajectory too places him on a par with Scheherazade, who owes her stories to her traversal of "historical reports" and her acquaintance "with the sayings of men and the maxims of sages and kings."[99] And ultimately, although Zarathustra does not himself tell stories of the myriad places he had visited, he, like Scheherazade, defers the "one goal" of humanity indefinitely and speaks instead for at least one more chance by presenting the "thousand goals" of humanity to date in such a way that unsettles their status as ends. Hence, Zarathustra's speech breaks off without coming to any final decision over the existence of humanity—and without over-estimating his proper insights into values: "But tell me, my brothers, if humanity still lacks a goal—is humanity itself not lacking too?" (60).

This similarity between Zarathustra's story of humanity and the stories of Scheherazade emerges through a movement of wayward discourse that leaves all valuation processes, all humanity—and as a result, all things in creation—utterly open-ended. Rather than targets, the Persian Zarathustra, famed for "speak[ing] the truth and handl[ing] the bow and arrow well" (59), evokes the Persian Scheherazade to imply that humanity has a shot only if it lacks and fails itself, and only if the grounds for positing a comprehensive concept grasping man, society, and state alike are undermined. Furthermore, if it is masculine virtues that Zarathustra otherwise espouses throughout Nietzsche's book, at this most crucial passage, it will have been the voice of a woman that intervenes without force to allow him, among others, to go on.

Nothing new comes under the sun that Zarathustra evokes, again and again, to describe his cycles of rising to his mountaintop retreat and descending into the underworld of men. But the shards of speech from *A Thousand and One Nights* come to shed a different light, if only for a moment, on the aims of the text and the novel announcements it delivers: one can only break word of the new by breaking every promise and every given that may appear to mark an end. It is in this light that the other ruptures in Zarathustra's language might be read, too, which render each speech a virtual communication that promises nothing, but for the possibility of departing from whatever may have seemed to be said and done. It is these measures that mark Zarathustra's intervention in the German languages of Luther and Goethe, as well as the languages of creating and valuing. Ultimately, it is in this sense too that the imperative of Zarathustra's self-proclaimed "awesome mistress," the "stillest hour," would hold good: "speak your word and break!" (146). In Nietzsche's book, the scriptural monuments of the Zend-Avesta, the Lutheran Bible, *A Thousand and One Nights*—and *Thus Spoke Zarathustra*—explode into scraps, and thus liberate their language from delivering a single message or tracing a certain destiny. The decisive announcement "thus" appears to be the suspension of all decisive announcements, words, and works. And although there is no telling, this news may even allow for a way to trace a different trajectory through the overnight uprisings, downfalls, and endings that had proven so catastrophic for Nietzsche during the Paris Commune, when "the entire scholarly, scientific, philosophical, and artistic existence seemed an absurdity, if a single day could wipe out the most glorious works of art."[100] A far cry from contemporary reports, and long after Nietzsche's retreat to the mountains in 1871, the rips and tears of *Thus Spoke Zarathustra* open the language for events to speak otherwise than in terms of judgment, and perhaps mark his most valuable, value-free response to the ongoing battle of W*o*rth.

2

Passing the End

Baudelaire's New Findings

After the publication of *Thus Spoke Zarathustra*—and through to the last pages of his notebooks—Nietzsche did not stop thinking of the last man and the ends of humanity, in all senses of the word. In his notebooks from November 1887 through March 1888, for example, he reformulates the trajectories for humanity that had concerned Zarathustra throughout "On the Thousand and One Goals" in terms of cyclical and teleological models of history:

> That humanity has a collective-task to solve, that it runs as a whole towards some goal, this unclear and arbitrary notion is still very young. Perhaps one will cut loose from it again, before it becomes an *idée fixe* . . . It is no whole, this humanity: it is an insoluble manifold of rising and declining life processes—it has no youth, followed upon by maturity and finally age. Namely, the layers [*Schichten*] lie thoroughly deranged and heaped upon one another—and in several millennia there can yet be younger types of men than those whom we can point to today. *Décadence*, on the other hand, belongs to all epochs of humanity: everywhere there are excremental and decaying matters, it is the life process itself, this excising of formations of decline and fall-out.[1]

Here, Nietzsche suggests that the "layers" or "Schichten" of all that will have been give evidence for neither a progressive development toward one goal, nor does their examination reveal a sedimented pattern that could be described according to the life-cycle of youth, maturity, and old age. Hence, these layers cannot even be recollected in the name of "history," or "Geschichte," however much "Schichten" may recall this word or concept. Without a discernible arrangement or order, and therefore without definite traits that would allow for their conceptual grasp, these layers appear to accumulate in disarray. Furthermore, if the processes of increase and derangement are, as Nietzsche says, "life processes," then even the appeals that he makes to the possibility of future "younger types" could be no more than a catachrestic abuse of terms that adds to the mix-up he addresses. According to the premises Nietzsche puts forth, life would instead be without beginning or end, and therefore without a middle, too, in the sense of a necessary and natural consequence that necessitates what follows, in turn.[2] Even if all matters were to affect one another reciprocally—which Nietzsche does not say here—the *"insoluble manifold of rising and declining life processes"* would entail that no element could be isolated in order to track its changes, and no span could be singled out to keep track of time. Nietzsche thus leaves humanity utterly open-ended and incomplete—"it is no whole, this humanity"—but he goes further than he had gone in *Thus Spoke Zarathustra*, to the point where the nominal distinction of "humanity" verges upon becoming an indeterminate matter of refuse, like all other "types" or forms of life. On these terms, "history," "humanity," "age," and "progress" would be nothing to speak of, insofar as the processes that are partially comprehended by such names exceed the delimitations of designation and observation alike. When all things are open-ended in this way, in other words, there would appear to be no way to go on or to say anything more, since all things will have always been thoroughly dis-cussed by their very nature, that is: shaken, dispersed, scattered.[3]

Nonetheless, Nietzsche continues to discuss these issues, and even in these private notebooks, he utters an address to all and none, as Zarathustra had done amidst scattered "Old and New Tablets." When it comes to fictive *universalia* such as "man," he says, ideals of human progress continue to operate as the residua of the Christian notion of salvation: "the Christian ideal" remains the "sole form in which a sort of *goal* is thought today in this history of humanity."[4] Under these circumstances and within this circumscribed sphere of Christian logic and language, Nietzsche then proceeds to deliver a new imperative concerning what is "to be grasped":

To be grasped [Zu begreifen]:

that all sorts of decay and illness have enduringly worked upon collective value judgments: that in the value judgments that have become dominant, décadence has even come to preponderant status: that we not only have to fight against the consequent circumstances of all present misery from degeneration, but also that all hitherto décadence has remained behind, that is, living.[5]

Despite all "consequent circumstances"—and despite the logical consequences of his previous remarks—Nietzsche thus calls for a fight against current circumstances and consequences. In so doing, he delivers an accusation against "all present misery" that is as contradictory and insoluble as the life processes themselves, especially since his further elaboration of the problem speaks all the more strongly against the very opposition he proposes. For if all decadence remains living, then the decayed—and, as a consequence, the dead—could never have died. This means that "we"—whoever and whenever "we" are—are involved in a mêlée and mélange of life processes that could be better described as afterlife processes, which go on past the limit of decease, and therefore proceed incessantly. How could a fight be waged "against" constant conditions, which are not destroyed by their decline and destruction? What remains to be done among remains? What alternatives could become thinkable past the past and its unending end? Nietzsche gives no initial sign for a particular direction or point of departure "we" might take, but instead introduces an asymmetry between the clause that begins, "we not only have to fight," and its conclusion, "but also [. . .] *all* hitherto décadence has remained behind, that is, *living*," where "we" will have been eliminated or evacuated from his sentence.

To broach these questions anew, Nietzsche turns away from "us" to Charles Baudelaire. At this point in his notebooks, he leaves off from the urgent task that he momentarily evoked and enters into passages drawn from a lengthy prose fragment by Baudelaire that begins with the words, "the world is going to end [*le monde va finir*],"[6] which had just appeared for the first time in the posthumously published collection of Baudelaire's *Oeuvres posthumes et correspondances inédites* from 1887.[7] Through a mixture of quotation, translation, and paraphrase, it is by way of this new fragment from the dead poet that Nietzsche continues his meditations, as he entangles several threads from Baudelaire's text with his "own" writings on the afterlife processes that concern him—an entanglement that Walter Benjamin had also noticed, writing in his *Arcades Project*: "The piece that begins, 'The world is coming to an end' ('Fusées'; no. 22), contains, interwoven with the apocalyptic reverie, a frightfully bitter critique of Second Empire society. (It reminds one here and there, perhaps, of Nietzsche's notion of 'the last man.') This critique displays, in part, prophetic features."[8]

Above all, the fragment displays resonances with Nietzsche's untimely meditation. From the start, Baudelaire shifts from an announcement that "the world is going to end," to addressing the possibility that material existence may survive nevertheless, but in such a way that it would not "be worthy of the name, or of the historical dictionary."[9] As in Nietzsche's text, then, it is a matter of sheer processes, which no longer accord with categories for historical understanding, and which appear to allow for nothing new to occur. Furthermore, it is in accord with Nietzsche's depreciation of modern progress that Baudelaire goes on in his fragment to present the depreciation of all values beside wealth—beside, that is, value in the abstract—which prevails to the detriment of justice and community, and which results in a nihilistic decline that sends the world to Pluto, the god of the underworld as well as the god of wealth: "Then, anything that resembles virtue—what am I saying—anything other than ardent devotion to Pluto will be regarded as an immense ridicule. Justice—if, in this fortunate epoch, any justice can still exist—will forbid the existence of citizens who are unable to make their fortunes."[10] In this context, where the condition of existence is a devotion to wealth and death, Baudelaire thus poses the question that had emerged, albeit through somewhat different discussions, in Nietzsche's notes: "I ask any thinking man to show me what subsists of life [*Je demande à tout homme qui pense de me montrer ce qui subsiste de la vie*]."[11] And finally, after tracing the fatal developments of the world ever further, Baudelaire leaves off his prophecies by promising these pages as his legacy: "Lost in this vile world, jostled by the crowd, I am like a weary man who sees behind him, in the depths of the years, only disabuse and bitterness, and in front of him only a tempest that brings nothing new, neither instruction nor grief. [. . .] I believe I have wandered off into what people of my trade call an *hors d'oeuvre*. All things pending, I will leave these pages,—because I want to date my rage/sorrow."[12]

As Oleg Gelikman has argued, the problem of "Le Monde va finir" becomes not the end of the world, but "the failure of ending." Hence, "[i]f one is to continue to refer to this fragment as 'The End of the World,' one has to keep in mind that, simply put, there is no world to end."[13] It is in this light that André Hirt similarly observes how Baudelaire "speaks of an *other* time, which has already arrived and which does not cease to arrive."[14] And it is most likely in light of this consideration, too, that Nietzsche does not begin at the beginning when he cites Baudelaire's fragment—that is, he does not begin with the "end" of the world—when he inscribes Baudelaire's testament into his own posthumously published notes on the interminable survival of all matters. Instead, he takes up the lines in which Baudelaire enumerates a series of dead ends, when it comes to answering the question: "What does the world henceforth have to do under the sky? [*qu'est-ce que le monde a désormais à faire sous le ciel?*]."¹⁵ Nietzsche proceeds:

> The further-development of humanity [*Weiter-Entwicklung der Menschheit*], according to Baudelaire's notion. Not that we approach a wild condition again, say, according to the mode of the buffoonish disorder of South American republics, where one, arms in hand, seeks his nourishment between the ruins of our civilization. That would presuppose a certain vital energy. Mechanics will have Americanized us in such a fashion, progress will have atrophied the spiritual part in us to such an extent that all of the crazed things that the Socialists dream of remain behind positive reality. No religion, no property, not even Revolution anymore.¹⁶

The corresponding passage from this part of Baudelaire's text—which Nietzsche only partially excerpts—reads as follows:

> I do not say that the world will be reduced to the expedients and buffoonish disorder of the South American republics; or that perhaps we may even return to a state of savagery, and prowl, gun in hand [*un fusil à la main*], in search of pasture/nourishment [*pâture*], through the grass-covered ruins of our civilisation. No;—for such adventures would suppose the survival of a certain vital energy, the echo of earlier ages. New example and new victims of the inexorable moral laws, we shall perish by the thing by which we thought to live. Mechanization will have so much Americanized us, progress will have so much atrophied our spiritual part, that nothing in the sanguinary, sacrilegious or anti-natural dreams of the Utopists [*utopistes*] will be able to be compared to their positive results [*à ses résultats positifs*]. I ask any thinking man to show me what subsists of life. As for religion, I believe it useless to speak of it and to seek for its remains [*les restes*], since in such matters the only thing that can nowadays give scandal is to take the trouble to deny God. Property virtually disappeared with the abolition of the law of primogeniture; but a time will come when humanity, like an avenging ogre, will snatch their last morsel from those who believe themselves to have legitimately inherited the revolutions.¹⁷

Both passages make clear that progress of a certain kind—mechanization, for example—presents no possibility for reversing or resisting the general decline of humanity in its "development" or in its "unraveling," as Nietzsche's word "Entwicklung" may also suggest. Similarly, grass-covered ruins offer no "pasture" and no trophic value, if the "spiritual part" of man has already atrophied and his "vital energy" all but expired. Furthermore, by excising portions of the text in his version, Nietzsche presents all the more emphatically the elimination that Baudelaire announces of religion, property, and revolution—that is, the principles of the *ancien régime*, the *status quo* of bourgeois society, and the socialist programs for the future[18]—and he cuts (Baudelaire) himself out of the picture, omitting many of the sentences that originally appeared in the first person. In all of these respects, the text becomes in Nietzsche's notebooks an even more dire expression of a state of affairs—or a state of no affairs, with nothing "henceforth [. . .] to do under the sky"—in which past epochal distinctions become blended into procedures that can neither live nor die, and the possibility of personal intervention vanishes into the "insoluble manifold."

Yet just as the world appears to be going nowhere fast and nothing new remains to be seen, Nietzsche shifts his strategies of citation in the end, replacing Baudelaire's closing profession to leave a testament to his "sadness" or "rage" with a series of exclamations:

> Lost in this pitiful world, coudoyé par les foules, I am like a weary man, who, looking backwards, sees nothing but désabusement et amertume in long profound years, and before him a storm, in which there is nothing new, neither instruction nor pain. Le soir, où cet homme a volé à la destinée quelques heures de plaisir—in the evening, when this man has stolen an hour of pleasure from fate—bercé dans sa digestion, oublieux autant que possible du passé, content du présent et résigné à l'avenir, enivré de son sang-froid et de son dandysme, fier de n'être pas aussi bas, que ceux qui passent, il se dit, en contemplant la fumée de son cigare: "Que m'importe, où vont ces consciences?"
>
> —A little pure air! This absurd condition of Europe should no longer last![19]

While the interspersion of French words throughout this passage emphasizes Baudelaire's voice, the call for air recalls Zarathustra's repeated insistence upon a pure atmosphere, as when he poses the question in his speech "On the Friend": "Are you pure air [*reine Luft*] and solitude and bread and medicine for your friend?" (57).[20] Thus, Nietzsche not only rewrites and continues Baudelaire's testament past its end, but also lets Baudelaire's words culminate in an outburst. Baudelaire and Nietzsche may deny that man still has the vital energy of those who once proceeded through the wilderness, "gun in hand [*un fusil à la main*]," but Nietzsche's explosion suggests that incendiary words may nevertheless come to life, when he takes up this fragment that was collected under the heading, "Fusées," a word that Baudelaire himself had used for a collection of fragmentary meditations, which entangles—or confuses—the traditional vocabulary of spinning with that of modern explosives: "the mass of thread rolled around the spindle," the "firework formed by a cylinder of cardboard or paper filled with gunpowder," "rocket."[21] Precisely because the decadent, the decayed, and the dead cannot die—precisely because "life processes" render events, lives, and voices indistinct—it becomes possible, in other words, to rewrite and revive a past that never was certain or conclusive and thus to intervene in the "layers" or "Schichten" of life. At this unstable and volatile point in Nietzsche's notebooks, both "Nietzsche" and "Baudelaire" enter into the impersonal processes and afterlives of which Nietzsche had spoken, and in ways that alter every ego and "alter ego" at once.[22] If it may be true that there is "nothing new" to come in the foreseeable future and nothing "to be done" about worldwide decline, this language nevertheless presents a discussion—again, in the etymological sense of the word—between Nietzsche and Baudelaire that troubles and opens their oeuvres anew, as well as the conditions they address.

The possibility of a novel announcement that lies engrained in the layers of Nietzsche's notes and especially in his rendition of Baudelaire's text is one that would entail a mode of speaking that itself cannot be attributed to a single speaker or time, and that is historical in the thoroughly anachronistic, deranged, and cumulative sense that Nietzsche addresses in his notebook and other writings. Gelikman points to the similarly anachronistic and impersonal traits that run through Baudelaire's characterization of history, when he writes, "[b]ecause oversaturated by history, modernity cannot unfold progressively. The growth of competing planetary forces locks them in a spectacular battle for survival, a battle that impedes a realization of any single tendency."[23] But whereas he goes on to propose that Baudelaire's testimonial gesture implies an aim "to rebuild the sense of the world day by day" and thereby to "inhabit modernity as a Living Present,"[24] Nietzsche's remarks suggest that it is only when the date bearing Baudelaire's signature is crossed through and moved past by another—such as "Nietzsche" or "Zarathustra"—that the fragment can show vital signs. Its survival would depend upon no embattled authors or authorities, and no historical, habitual, or quotidian constructions, but upon transpersonal and impersonal processses that belong to no one and build upon nothing but the afterlives of language.

For this reason—even before Nietzsche's intervention—Baudelaire did not merely speak for himself, nor was it solely his anger or sadness in the face of current conditions that "Le Monde va finir" exposes. The manifold layers and threads that make up Baudelaire's text themselves display traces of alternate and alternating currents that cross with its presentation of the monotony of plutocracy, the failure of revolution, the degeneration of human hearts, and the endless ending of the world, and that therefore open his prose on modern "progress" in other directions. Baudelaire's description of the accelerating dynamics of plutocracy, for instance, shows itself upon closer examination to be no straightforward movement, despite the apparently unequivocal prognosis Baudelaire delivers:

> Then, the son will flee his family, not at eighteen, as at present, but at twelve, emancipated by his gluttonous precocity; he will flee, not in search of heroic adventures, not to deliver a beautiful prisoner from a tower, not to immortalise a garret with his sublime thoughts; but to found a commerce, to enrich himself, to make a competition with his infamous papa,—founder and chief shareholder of a journal that will spread enlightenment and make the one-time *Siècle* seem like a pillar of superstition.[25]

To be sure, the main point of reference seems to be Baudelaire's century and *Le Siècle*, the major newspaper that began displaying tables of financial data on the front page of the first issue of every year, beginning in 1851 and continuing past the year marked by Baudelaire's death.[26] At the same time, however, the commercial rivalry between fathers and sons—where succession will have been reduced to competition for pecuniary success—illustrates the consequences of the Revolution. For if, as Baudelaire also says, "[p]roperty virtually disappeared with the abolition of the law of primogeniture," then money will have only gained momentum as a result; or, as Louis-Auguste Blanqui had put it in 1837: "The aristocracy of birth was abolished in July 1830. It was replaced by the aristocracy of money, which is as voracious as the one that preceded it."[27] This may be why the Revolution has none but illusory or virtual heirs, or why "humanity, like an avenging ogre, will snatch their last morsel from those who believe themselves to have legitimately inherited the revolutions."[28] In any event, rather than displaying liberty, equality, and fraternity, relations among even men of the same family are shown to be taking a compulsive, unbalanced, and inimical turn that solicits a critique of both plutocratic *and* democratic histories.[29]

The latest rush for cash is not the only problem then, for there seems to be no revolutionary past to turn back to that would not bring humanity to the same point. Yet the times and messages involved in Baudelaire's remarks are still more complex than these suggestions indicate. Beside evoking the current turbulence in household and national economies, Baudelaire's narrative of alienated fathers and precocious sons simultaneously shows strong affiliations with Hesiod's verses on the most recent phase of humanity from *Works and Days*:

> But Zeus will destroy this race of speech-endowed human beings too, when at their birth the hair on their temples will be quite gray. Father will not be like-minded with sons, nor sons at all, nor guest with host, nor comrade with comrade, nor will the brother be dear, as he once was. They will dishonor their aging parents at once; they will reproach them, addressing them with grievous words—cruel men, who do not know of the gods' retribution![30]

Along these lines, the most recent race of men can be seen as the latest version of an ancient history, through the family resemblance between the modern, plutocratic era of silver and gold and Hesiod's Iron Age. Whether or not Baudelaire meant for traces of Hesiod to surface in the text, the mythological dimension that opens with Baudelaire's allusion to Pluto—recently made popular by Pierre Leroux's *De la plutocratie, ou, du gouvernement des riches* (1848)—suggests that there would be no way and no one to draw the line. Who knows? Hesiod's ancient wisdom poetry may be all that remains vital if the storm Baudelaire sees on the horizon contains "neither instruction nor grief [*ni enseignement, ni douleur*]."[31] And if this may be the case, then Baudelaire's storm may also be just the sort of retribution Hesiod had called for: an "or-age" that literally spells the reversal and demise of the "âge d'or" that industrial developments were otherwise said to promise in recent slogans from, say, Saint Simon, and that Baudelaire's real or virtual allusion to antiquity will have already rendered *iron*ic.[32] Precisely because "nothing new is contained" in it, Baudelaire's storm may gather from sources as divergent as Hesiod, Leroux, Saint Simon, and *Le Siècle* to mark a new disturbance in the ancient and modern ages and languages that Baudelaire's writing registers. Beyond the immediate limits of the text—and beyond the present lack of prospects—the many outside layers of writing that this "hors d'oeuvre" touches trouble the *status quo* and all recent forecasts, and thereby open "Baudelaire's" words to contingencies that may yet arrive when all else falls and fails.

There would be no serious contradiction if contemporary existence were to coincide with Hesiod's Iron Age, or if novel possibilities were to emerge through Baudelaire's singular way of denouncing the news and the new, because the notion of history implied in the Baudelaire's fragment is one where, as in Nietzsche's notes, life processes amount to the derangement and accumulation of times. Rather than developing this notion through reconsiderations of humanity, decadence, and material recurrence, however, Baudelaire adopts and adapts the biblical version of eternal return at the opening of "Le Monde va finir": "The world is going to end. The only reason why it could endure is that it exists. How this reason is weak, compared with all those that announce the contrary, and particularly this one: 'What does the world henceforth have to do under the sky?'"[33] Much as Baudelaire's text may be "interwoven with apocalyptic reverie,"[34] as Benjamin had noted, this announcement is less indebted to the Book of Revelation than it is to Ecclesiastes, whose most famous sentence—"There is nothing new under the sun" (Ecc. 1.9)—recurs, modified, in Baudelaire's modern fragment. And whether it is a question of what is to be done or what may be, the premise of both writers suggests that all that might yet occur will have already happened "in the ages before us" (Ecc. 1.10). Each time would therefore be crossed by innumerable others or would contain, as Baudelaire puts it, the "echo of earlier ages" that survives with or without vital force. Hence, when Baudelaire more distantly echoes this biblical book of wisdom in claiming that he is "like a weary man who sees behind him, in the depths of the years, only disabuse and bitterness,"[35] his perspective on the "depths of the years"—"années profondes"—opens out to the bottomless stretch of repetitions and coincidences into which every moment would collapse, if there were truly nothing new to be seen or done under the sun.[36] Still more radically than in the models of recurrence propounded by the Ecclesiast's Hellenistic contemporaries, however, the depths before Baudelaire and the Ecclesiast would support no illusion of a halt or hold, because the possibilities of repetition they address are not grounded in a logic of mechanical causality that might determine their sequence or sameness.[37] Instead, symptoms of the derangement and accumulation of events and deeds might fall together at any given moment, rendering each different from its predecessor and from itself at once. The kairological theology of the Ecclesiast notwithstanding, this profound and profane consequence follows from at least several of his verses, and it is what Baudelaire's language indicates in its simultaneous evocations of Hesiodic and biblical wisdom poetry, among others. Like Nietzsche's notes, Baudelaire's writing thus poses the question as to how novelty might emerge through the most extreme formulations of its foreclosure. But this time, it is not a matter of affirming eternal recurrence in order to break history in two; rather, Baudelaire's oeuvre in and beyond "Le Monde va finir" opens to the more chaotic coincidences of history, as well as the alternatives they entail for envisioning political praxis, communication, and community.

What seems certain from the bitter and disabused manner in which Baudelaire addresses the "heirs to the revolutions" in particular is that further changes for better or worse would hinge upon no simple turn of events or clear-cut decision over what is to be done. Already in the Ecclesiastical sentence, "What does the world henceforth have to do under the sky,"[38] Baudelaire shifts the accent upon that which is "to be done [*à faire*]" in a way that at the same time recalls the forward-looking rhetoric he had promoted during the Revolution of 1848. In a propagandistic contribution to *La Tribune nationale*, for example, Baudelaire reiterated a call to political action, addressing the more conservative politicians of the Second Republic in the following words:

> But what do you want, then, to conserve of this republic that does not exist but in name? *All is yet to be done [à faire].*
> Louis-Philippe ruined millions, you ruin billions!
> What are the things? What are the forms that you have changed?
> *All is to be done [Tout est à faire]*, and you are conservatives!
> Yes, you are conservatives by temperament and by principle; conservatives torn . . . from your places![39]

By insisting that all remains "to be done" because things have changed only in name, Baudelaire gave further impetus to Blanqui's words to the democratic clubs in France from 22 March 1848: "The Republic would be a lie if it did not have to be anything more than the substitution of one form of government for another. It does not suffice to change the words, it is necessary to change the things."[40] However, nearly as radically as the Ecclesiast denies the new by reversing the language of Isaiah's prophecy, "I am about to do a new thing; now it springs forth, do you not perceive it?" (Isa. 43.19),[41] Baudelaire veers from his positive announcement in 1848 to a radical doubt in "Le Monde va finir" as to whether anything is to be done at all in the current state of affairs. The new spin that Baudelaire gives his earlier turns of phrase thus reopens issues that had once seemed positively decided and that later appeared to end in positive failure. Precisely this reversibility, however, is what renders both alternatives uncertain, while Baudelaire's decision to pose the question of future action instead of positing its outright denial indicates that "Le Monde va finir" marks no simple inversion of revolutionary proclamations. Alteration would have to take place otherwise than any decision in the form of an either-or that spans all or nothing, and although Baudelaire does not say this directly in "Le Monde va finir," the fact that the recurrence of his former slogan can take place in such a complex, modified way indicates not only that echoes from the most disparate times and texts can coincide and interfere with one another, but also that no recurrence, reversal, or revolution could be decisive or ultimate.

The antecedants and circumstances for speaking and doing, as well as the consequences of every linguistic and practical gesture, become unforeseeable to the extent that seemingly straightforward temporal and causal sequences may be split, spliced, and thereby subject to revision, as when the lines of the Ecclesiast combine with Baudelaire's revolutionary rhetoric from 1848, or when fragments from Baudelaire's prose are pieced together with a citation from *Thus Spoke Zarathustra* in Nietzsche's notes from the late 1880s. Nothing may be new under the sun, and nothing may be done about it, but novel announcements may nonetheless emerge through the layers of that which has been said before in hitherto unheard of ways. While scholars such as Philippe Murray, Dolf Oehler, and Richard Burton have debated the degree to which Baudelaire adhered to revolutionary persuasions at various stages of his career,[42] the logic of what is perhaps Baudelaire's most overtly pessimistic testimony thus opens an ultra-revolutionary perspective on history that exposes every act or tendency to uncontrollable contingencies, whether it is a matter of founding a republic or watching it founder. Past failures, in other words, may also eventually come to fail themselves and, in this case, the greatest difference between Baudelaire's journalism and his journal entry regarding that which may or may not be done does not lie in the reversal of revolutionary newswriting, but in the historical and epistemological premises that he introduces in his later text to render contemporary existence itself profoundly uncertain. The historical circumstances at any given time could not but be impenetrable to even the most perceptive subject of experience, as soon as it is acknowledged that oblivion may obscure those "former ages" that underlie and undermine each apparently "new" one. Baudelaire directly addresses the uncertain scope of historical knowledge toward the end of his fragment, when he proclaims: "Those times [of degeneration] are perhaps quite close at hand. Who knows whether they are not here already: whether it is not simply the coarsening of our natures that prevents us from perceiving the atmosphere that we already breathe?"[43] But he goes perhaps furthest to unsettle the subject of experience in the earliest passages of "Le Monde va finir," where he radicalizes the Cartesian expression of doubt in such a way that removes the subjective foundation for any confirmation of existence, let alone the extant remains of other times.

Whereas Descartes would eventually find the *cogito* to be the sole certitude that remains when all existence can be called into question—"I" can already rest assured of myself in asking: "How do I know that [God] has not brought it about that there is no earth, no sky, no extended thing, no shape, no size, no place, while at the same time ensuring that all these things appear to me to exist just as they do now?"[44]—the incoherence of every present and presence in "Le Monde va finir" renders the instance of speech or reason divided, doubled, and doubtful as well.[45] At the opening, the rational operations in Baudelaire's fragment splinter into autonomous orations that subject mundane existence to debate in the absence of a clear and distinct subject: "The only reason why [the world] could endure is that it exists. How this reason is weak, compared with all those that announce the contrary, and particularly this one: 'What does the world henceforth have to do under the sky?'"[46] Differently than in Descartes's meditations, the dubiousness of existence is not the doubt of a single (first) person, but the doubt of impersonal expressions, where announcements in the conditional ("it could endure"), indicative ("it exists"), and interrogative modes ("What does the world henceforth have to do") are said to speak against and on a par with one another. Even the apparently unequivocal thesis that the world "exists" stands not as an ontological *a priori*, but as merely one statement among others without any reason to privilege it over those which contradict it. In their rhetorical execution, then, these sentences cease to carry out the operations they appear charged to perform because their coexistence places them in a dialogue that renders "reason" at odds with itself or its "selves." In taking up the most famous moments of the Ecclesiast's wisdom and Descartes's meditations, and in turning them into a world historical issue that exceeds what anyone could think through and what any subjective certainty could decide; in articulating this issue in such a way that no positive answer could be possible—including a positive assertion on the negation of the world—Baudelaire presents a predicament in which no one could know or say what exists, let alone what is to be done. But for the same reason—or for another altogether—there once again would also be no telling what may yet occur or already be taking place through the transpersonal and transtemporal afterlives of language, action, and existence that make up the atmosphere of the text.

In his apparent resignation, Baudelaire could therefore be seen to go further in preparing conditions for change than Nietzsche, when Nietzsche writes in his notes "that we [. . .] have to fight against the consequent circumstances of all present misery from degeneration."[47] Among the most novel interventions in Baudelaire's text is precisely the anachronistic and polyvocal idiom that emerges from it and that brings possibilities of history to expression, beyond what Baudelaire or anyone else may know to say. Through this multilayered writing, Baudelaire proceeds in the wake of the collapse of cylical and progressive models of history and in the midst of thoroughly deranged "life processes" and afterlife processes, whose operations are not determined by what may or may not be reasonably expected, nor by the pressures of dire or desirable circumstances. In the end, then, it is not so much that readers of "Le Monde va finir" are left with the description of an existence unworthy "of the name, or of the historical dictionary,"[48] as Baudelaire says at one point. Instead, they are confronted with a profoundly unsettled and unsettling historical diction that refuses the decisive assignation of values and names to that which may exist, and that allows the names and "echoe[s] of earlier ages" to continue to make claims as they elude conclusive interpretation and firm conceptual grasp.

In this respect, "Le Monde va finir" illustrates what Elissa Marder has called "temporal disorders" in her important and elucidating monograph on Baudelaire and Flaubert. Marder takes up Jean-François Lyotard's remarks on the ways in which responses can be fashioned to the "speed of modernity" through processes of "free association" and "rewriting," which "register" and recompose the elements of all that may come to mind from both "the furthest and nearest past, both one's own past and others' past."[49] "By suspending knowledge or judgment about what we think we know," she continues, "in the 'hiatus' of not-knowing, the past—history—reinscribes its traces on us."[50] Retracing the ways in which Baudelaire's poems "La Chevelure" and "À une passante" register the experience of modern and "(post)modern life,"[51]

Marder exposes "Baudelaire's complicated response to [. . .] collective memory loss" and his "exhausting labor to surmount the shock experience."[52] In "Le Monde va finir," Baudelaire registers "temporal disorder" as profoundly as he does in those poems and writes in a way that reflects how history might be told when any second may coincide with innumerable others, bringing temporal and subjective orders to collapse, while remaining open to that which has grown decadent, decayed, and dead.

Any number of texts from Baudelaire's oeuvre could be opened to examine further the alternative historical diction that he offers in "Le Monde va finir." But to pursue the possibilities of novel announcements that such diction permits, Baudelaire's final poem from the 1861 edition of *Les Fleurs du mal*, "Le Voyage," offers itself as one of the most far-reaching and complex texts that traces a way toward the new through the world and its ends. There too decline in the so-called modern world is at issue; the problems insist of historical change, goals, and ends; and in the end, a lethal plunge is projected from the visible horizon of the epoynomous voyagers into depths beyond experience:

> Minds burning, we know what we have to do,
> And plunge to depths of Heaven or Hell,
> To fathom the Unknown, and find the *new*![53]

> Nous voulons, tant ce feu nous brûle le cerveau,
> Plonger au fond du gouffre, Enfer ou Ciel, qu'importe?
> Au fond de l'Inconnu pour trouver du *nouveau*![54]

More often than not, this final announcement of *Les Fleurs du Mal* tends to be read as a testimony to the modern obsession with novelty that arose in high capitalism and colonialism, whose products yield the changeless and lifeless recurrence of the ever same. As Walter Benjamin wrote in his notes on Baudelaire, collected under the heading, *Central Park*: "For people as they are now, there is only one radical novelty—and always the same one: death."[55] Baudelaire's final verse also returns as the first line of Eugene W. Holland's recent monograph on the complicities and ruptures with the codes of high capitalism that become legible in and through Baudelaire's poetics: " 'Au fond de l'Inconnu pour trouver du nouveau!' To the depths of the unknown to find something new: is this the battle cry of modernism or an advertsing slogan? Could it be both? What reading procedures would distinguish absolutely between the two?"⁵⁶ But as in "Le Monde va finir," there is more to the poem and to its concluding announcement than a pessimistic final verdict on modernity, which grows apparent through attending to the voices of the dead that haunt its topoi and open each passage to other words from other times. Furthermore, retracing the rhetoric of the first-person figures in this poem shows—in a way that "La Monde va finir" only suggests—the implications of an anachronistic and polyvocal idiom for reconsidering the language of a collective, beyond the collapse of the *ancien régime*, the failed Revolution of 1848, and the plutocracy of the present.⁵⁷ And when Baudelaire himself writes of his poem to Charles Asselineau—"I have made [*fait*] a long poem dedicated to Max Du Camp, which is to make [*à faire*] nature, and above all, the lovers of progress, shudder"⁵⁸—he sends the message that "Le Voyage" was not only made to trouble nature and civilization alike, but may also be an answer to the question he would pose in his prose fragment: "what does the world henceforth have to do [*à faire*] under the sky?"⁵⁹

Le Voyage
À Maxime du Camp
I
Pour l'enfant, amoureux de cartes
    et d'estampes,
L'univers est égal à son vaste
    appétit.
Ah! que le monde est grand à la
    clarté des lampes!
Aux yeux du souvenir que le
    monde est petit!

Un matin nous partons, le
    cerveau plein de flamme,
Le coeur gros de rancune et de
    désirs amers,
Et nous allons, suivant le rythme
    de la lame,
Berçant notre infini sur le fini
    des mers:

Les uns, joyeux de fuir une
    patrie infâme;

Voyaging
For Maxime du Camp
I
The wide-eyed child in love with
    maps and plans
Finds the world equal to his
    appetite.
How grand the universe by light of
    lamps,
How petty in the memory's clear
    sight.

One day we leave, with fire
    in the brain
Heart great with rancour, bitter in
    its mood;
Outward we travel on the rolling
    main,
Lulling infinity in finitude.

Some gladly flee their homelands
    gripped in woe,

D'autres, l'horreur de leurs
    berceaux, et quelques-uns,
Astrologues noyés dans les yeux
    d'une femme,
La Circé tyrannique aux
    dangereux parfums.

Pour n'être pas changés en bêtes,
    ils s'enivrent
D'espace et de lumière et de
    cieux embrasés;
La glace qui les mord, les soleils
    qui les cuivrent,
Effacent lentement la marque
    des baisers.

Mais les vrais voyageurs sont
    ceux-là seuls qui partent
Pour partir; coeurs légers,
    semblables aux ballons,
De leur fatalité jamais ils ne
    s'écartent,
Et, sans savoir pourquoi, disent
    toujours: Allons!

Ceux-là dont les désirs ont la
    forme des nues,
Et qui rêvent, ainsi qu'un conscrit
    le canon,
De vastes voluptés, changeantes,
    inconnues,
Et dont l'esprit humain n'a
    jamais su le nom!

II
Nous imitons, horreur! la toupie
    et la boule
Dans leur valse et leurs bonds;
    même dans nos sommeils

Some, horrors of their childhood,
    others still—
Astrologers lost in a woman's eyes—
Some perfumed Circe with a tyrant's
    will.

Not to become a beast, each
    desperate one
Makes himself drunk on space and
    blazing skies;
The gnawing ice, the copper-burning
    sun
Efface the scars of kisses and of lies.

But the true voyagers set out to sea
Just for the leaving's sake; hearts lift
    aloft,
Nothing dissuades them from their
    destiny,
Something beyond their knowing
    cries, "We're off!"

These, then, whose ecstasies are wide
    as air
As conscripts dream of cannons,
    have their dreams
Of luxuries beyond what man can
    bear,
Such as the soul has neither named
    nor seen.

II
Our actions are grotesque—in leaps
    and bounds
We waltz like balls or tops; when
    day is done

La Curiosité nous tourmente et nous roule	Our curiosity rolls us around
Comme un Ange cruel qui fouette des soleils.	As if a cruel Angel lashed the sun.
Singulière fortune où le but se déplace,	Strange thing it is, to chase a shifting fake—
Et, n'étant nulle part, peut être n'importe où!	A goal that's nowhere, anywhere at all!
Où l'Homme, dont jamais l'espérance n'est lasse,	Man, whose anticipation stays awake,
Pour trouver le repos court toujours comme un fou!	To find his rest goes racing like a fool!
Notre âme est un trois-mâts cherchant son Icarie;	Our soul's three-master seeks the blessed isle:
Une voix retentit sur le pont: "Ouvre l'oeil!"	A voice on deck shouts: "Ho there, have a look!"
Une voix de la hune, ardente et folle, crie:	Some crow's-nest spy cries in romantic style
"Amour . . . gloire . . . bonheur!" Enfer! C'est un écueil!	"Love . . . glory . . . happiness!" Damn, just a rock!
Chaque îlot signalé par l'homme de vigie	Each isle is named the long-awaited sight,
Est un Eldorado promis par le Destin;	The Eldorado of our Destiny;
L'Imagination qui dresse son orgie	Fancy, that grows us orgies in the night,
Ne trouve qu'un récif aux clartés du matin.	Breaks on a reef in morning's clarity.
Ô le pauvre amoureux des pays chimériques!	Oh, the inebriate of distant lands,
Faut-il le mettre aux fers, le jeter à la mer,	This sot who sees Americas at will,
Ce matelot ivrogne, inventeur d'Amériques	Must he be chained, abandoned on the sands,

Dont le mirage rend le gouffre plus amer?

Tel le vieux vagabond, piétinant dans la boue,
Rêve, le nez en l'air, de brillants paradis;
Son oeil ensorcelé découvre une Capoue
Partout où la chandelle illumine un taudis.

III
Étonnants voyageurs! quelles nobles histoires
Nous lisons dans vos yeux profonds comme les mers!
Montrez-nous les écrins de vos riches mémoires,
Ces bijoux merveilleux, faits d'astres et d'éthers.

Nous voulons voyager sans vapeur et sans voile!
Faites, pour égayer l'ennui de nos prisons,
Passer sur nos esprits, tendus comme une toile,
Vos souvenirs avec leurs cadres d'horizons.

Dites, qu'avez-vous vu?

IV
"Nous avons vu des astres
Et des flots, nous avons vu des sables aussi;
Et, malgré bien des chocs et d'imprévus désastres,

Whose visions make the gulf more bitter still?

So the old tramp who shuffles in the filth
Dreams of a paradise and lifts his head—
In his wild eyes, Capua and her wealth
Wherever candle glow lights up a shed.

III
Fabulous voyagers! What histories

Are there behind your deep and distant stare!
Show us the treasures of your memories,
Those jewels and riches made of stars and air.

We're travellers afraid of steam and sail!
Here in our prisons every day's the same.
Oh, paint across the canvas of our souls
Your memoirs, with horizon as their frame.

Tell us, what have you seen?

IV
"We've seen the stars
And waves, and we have seen the sandy shores;
Despite disasters, all our jolts and jars,

Nous nous sommes souvent
 ennuyés, comme ici.

La gloire du soleil sur la mer
 violette,
La gloire des cités dans le
 soleil couchant,
Allumaient dans nos coeurs une
 ardeur inquiète
De plonger dans un ciel au
 reflet alléchant.

Les plus riches cités, les plus
 grands paysages,
Jamais ne contenaient l'attrait
 mystérieux
De ceux que le hasard fait
 avec les nuages.
Et toujours le désir nous
 rendait soucieux!

—La jouissance ajoute au désir
 de la force.
Désir, vieil arbre à qui le
 plaisir sert d'engrais,
Cependant que grossit et
 durcit ton écorce,
Tes branches veulent voir le
 soleil de plus près!

Grandiras-tu toujours, grand
 arbre plus vivace
Que le cyprès?—Pourtant nous
 avons, avec soin,
Cueilli quelques croquis pour
 votre album vorace
Frères qui trouvez beau tout
 ce qui vient de loin!

On sea, on land we find that we are
 bored.

The glorious sun across the violet
 sea,
Great sunlit cities dreaming as they
 lie,
Made our heart yearn with fierce
 intensity
To plunge towards those reflections
 in the sky.

Rich cities, and the grandest
 mountain spires
Somehow could never hold the
 same allure
As shifting clouds, the shape of our
 desires,
Which left us unfulfilled and
 insecure.

—Surely enjoyment quickens
 passion's spark.
Desire, old tree, that fattens on
 delight,
As you grow older, toughening
 your bark,
You want to see the sun from
 nearer height!

Do you grow always taller, grandest
 tree,
Older than the cypress?—Still, we
 have with care
Brought sketch-book pieces from
 across the sea
For our brothers who love all that's
 strange and rare!

Nous avons salué des idoles à
    trompe;
Des trônes constellés de joyaux
    lumineux;
Des palais ouvragés dont la
    féerique pompe
Serait pour vos banquiers un rêve
    ruineux;

Des costumes qui sont pour
    les yeux une ivresse;
Des femmes dont les dents
    et les ongles sont teints,
Et des jongleurs savants
    que le serpent caresse."

V
Et puis, et puis encore?

VI
"Ô cerveaux enfantins!
Pour ne pas oublier la chose
    capitale,
Nous avons vu partout, et
    sans l'avoir cherché,
Du haut jusques en bas de
    l'échelle fatale,
Le spectacle ennuyeux de
    l'immortel péché:

La femme, esclave vile,
    orgueilleuse et stupide,
Sans rire s'adorant et s'aimant
    sans dégoût;
L'homme, tyran goulu, paillard,
    dur et cupide,

Idols with trunks we've greeted in
    our time,
Great palaces enwrought with filigree

And jeweled thrones in luminous
    design,
To send your brokers dreams of
    bankruptcy;

Scant costumes that can stupefy the
    gaze
On painted women, every nail and
    tooth,
And subtle jugglers, wise in serpents'
    ways."

V
And then, and then what more?

VI
"O childish dupes!
You want the truth? We'll tell you
    without fail—
We never thought to search it out,
    but saw
From heights to depths, through
    all the mortal scale
The numbing spectacle of human
    flaw.

Woman, vile slave, proud in
    stupidity,
Tasteless and humourless in
    self-conceit;
Man, greedy tyrant, lustful, slovenly,

Esclave de l'esclave et ruisseau
    dans l'égout;

Le bourreau qui jouit, le martyr
    qui sanglote;
La fête qu'assaisonne et parfume
    le sang;
Le poison du pouvoir énervant
    le despote,
Et le peuple amoureux du
    fouet abrutissant;

Plusieurs religions semblables
    à la nôtre,
Toutes escaladant le ciel; la
    Sainteté,
Comme en un lit de plume un
    délicat se vautre,
Dans les clous et le crin cherchant
    la volupté;

L'Humanité bavarde, ivre de
    son génie,
Et, folle maintenant comme
    elle était jadis,
Criant à Dieu, dans sa furibonde
    agonie:
'Ô mon semblable, mon maître,
    je te maudis!'

Et les moins sots, hardis amants
    de la Démence,
Fuyant le grand troupeau parqué
    par le Destin,
Et se réfugiant dans l'opium
    immense!
—Tel est du globe entier l'éternel
    bulletin."

Slave of the slave, a sewer in the
    street;

The hangman jokes, the martyr sobs
    and faints,
The feast of blood is seasoned
    perfectly;
Poison of power drains a tyrant's
    strength,
Whose subjects love the whip's
    brutality.

Religions like our own in most
    details
Climb skyward on their saints, who
    it is said
Indulge their lusts with hairshirts, or
    with nails,
As dainty fops sprawl on a feather
    bed.

Drunk on her genius, Humanity,

Mad now as she has always
    been, or worse,
Cries to her God in raging agony:

'Master, my image, damn you with
    this curse!'

Not quite so foolish, bold
    demented ones
Flee from the feeding lot that holds
    the herd;
Their boundless shelter is in opium.

—From all the world, such always
    is the word."

VII

Amer savoir, celui qu'on tire
    du voyage!
Le monde, monotone et petit,
    aujourd'hui,
Hier, demain, toujours, nous
    fait voir notre image:
Une oasis d'horreur dans un
    désert d'ennui!

Faut-il partir? rester? Si tu peux
    rester, reste;
Pars, s'il le faut. L'un court, et
    l'autre se tapit
Pour tromper l'ennemi vigilant
    et funeste,
Le Temps! Il est, hélas! des
    coureurs sans répit,

Comme le Juif errant et comme
    les apôtres,
À qui rien ne suffit, ni wagon
    ni vaisseau,
Pour fuir ce rétiaire infâme;
    il en est d'autres
Qui savent le tuer sans quitter
    leur berceau.

Lorsque enfin il mettra le pied
    sur notre échine,
Nous pourrons espérer et crier:
    En avant!
De même qu'autrefois nous
    partions pour la Chine,
Les yeux fixés au large et les
    cheveux au vent,

Nous nous embarquerons sur
    la mer des Ténèbres

VII

How bitter, what we learn from
    voyaging!
The small and tedious world gives
    us to see
Now, always, the real horror of
    the thing,
Ourselves—that sad oasis in ennui!

Must one depart? or stay? Stand it
    and stay,
Leave if you must. One runs, one
    finds a space
To hide and cheat the deadly enemy
Called Time. Alas, some run a
    constant race—

The twelve apostles, or the
    Wandering Jew—
For them no ship avails, no ways
    or means
To flee that gladiator; others know
From infancy how to defeat the
    fiend.

Finally, though, his boot is on our
    chest;
Then we may hope, and call out
    "Onward ho!"
Even as once we set out for the
    East,
Our eyes fixed widely, hair blown
    to and fro,

Now sailing on the sea of shades
    we go,

Avec le coeur joyeux d'un jeune
    passager.
Entendez-vous ces voix charmantes
    et funèbres,
Qui chantent: "Par ici vous qui
    voulez manger

Le Lotus parfumé! c'est ici
    qu'on vendange
Les fruits miraculeux dont
    votre coeur a faim;
Venez vous enivrer de la
    douceur étrange
De cette après-midi qui n'a
    jamais de fin?"

À l'accent familier nous devinons
    le spectre;
Nos Pylades là-bas tendent leurs
    bras vers nous.
"Pour rafraîchir ton coeur nage
    vers ton Électre!"
Dit celle dont jadis nous baisions
    les genoux.

VIII

Ô Mort, vieux capitaine, il est
    temps! levons l'ancre!
Ce pays nous ennuie, ô Mort!
    Appareillons!
Si le ciel et la mer sont noirs
    comme de l'encre,
Nos coeurs que tu connais
    sont remplis de rayons!

Verse-nous ton poison pour qu'il
    nous réconforte!
Nous voulons, tant ce feu nous
    brûle le cerveau,

With all the plans of passengers
    well-pleased
To hear the voice, funereal and low,
That sings: "This way! Come here
    and take your ease

And eat the Lotus! Here we
    gather in
These fruits for hearts that yearn
    for strange delights;
Intoxicate yourselves on alien
Enjoyment through these days
    without a night."

We understand the phantom's
    friendly part,
That Pylades who reaches out to
    tease:
"Swim towards Electra now, to ease
    your heart!"
She cries, and long ago we kissed
    her knees.

VIII

O Death, old captain, time to make
    our trip!
This country bores us, Death! Let's
    get away!
Even if sky and sea are black as
    pitch
You know our hearts are full of
    sunny rays!

Serve us your poison, sir, to treat us
    well!
Minds burning, we know what we
    have to do,

Plonger au fond du gouffre,
    Enfer ou Ciel, qu'importe?
Au fond de l'Inconnu pour
    trouver du *nouveau*!⁶⁰
	And plunge to depths of Heaven or
	    of Hell,
	To fathom the Unknown, and find
	    the *new*!

Whereas Nietzsche's chapter "On the Thousand and One Goals" had suggested that the traversal of myriad places might open so many alternatives to each local and definitional limit for man and human history, the promise of travel seems to have defaulted in the universe of Baudelaire's "Le Voyage." Moving quickly from start to finish, these voyagers' situation seems to be nearly uniformly bleak, as their trajectory runs its course past dazzling façades and issues into a wasteland, where global reports translate into a single newscast of "immortal sin [*l'immortel péché*]." The occasional back and forth between illusion and disillusionment—when, for instance, the utopian extremes of a golden El Dorado *and* a socialist Icaria prove nowhere to be found—appears to even out in a way that parallels the "disabuse" with which "Le Monde va finir" concludes.⁶¹ Only the carefree or careless indifference of those voyagers who simply say "let's go [*allons*]" and let go of any attempt to get anywhere seem to be light-hearted enough to avoid getting down on the world, and the same goes for the "old tramp [*vieux vagabond*]," who is tripping when he discovers Capua in every shed. But such indifferent figures appear only briefly, in passing, and therefore present no sustainable alternatives as the poem takes its course. Among the ways in which the poem shows humanity to err, however, it is in the final sections that Baudelaire most pronouncedly picks up where Nietzsche would leave off in "On the Thousand and One Goals" and in his notebooks, bringing the questions of humanity, its directions, and its possibilities to a head with the "chose capitale" of "immortal sin," or the decadence and undying decay that "belong [. . .] to all epochs of humanity."⁶²

In the sixth section especially, the voyagers' evocation of "Humanité" follows a list of atrocities that they sum up thus: "Such is the eternal bulletin of the entire globe [*Tel est du globe entier l'éternel bulletin*]." And as the voyagers' horrendous enumeration of tyrants, hangmen, and martyrs, among others, emerges as the sole headline, the "bulletin" that they deliver converges with the "boule" or ball of the globe itself, whose motions we were said imitate all along, to our horror: "Nous imitons, horreur! la toupie et la boule." Human vice thus takes on the status of an "eternal" nature, and vice versa. The texture and character of this nature turns out to be the news, recalling the survey of the press that Baudelaire had provided in his journals: "Every newspaper, from first line to last, is a tissue of horrors. Wars, crimes, thefts, acts of indecency, tortures, crimes by princes, crimes by nations, crimes by individuals, an intoxication of universal atrocity."[63] Here, atrocity is so ingrained in the "tissue" of social life that the princes, nations, and individuals who execute "crimes" appear to be transient vehicles rather than agents of this transcendental—if not natural—constant: "*crimes* des princes, *crimes* des nations, *crimes* des particuliers." In "Le Voyage," Baudelaire exposes the same inversion of the more standard relation between accident and substance or action and agent, when each persona in his cross-section of "Humanité" appears as a generic type defined by a single behavior pattern, whose continuity is conveyed through present participles: "s'adorant," "s'aimant,' "énervant," "cherchant."[64] The peculiar nature and predicament of "Humanité" is thus registered in a breakdown of predication, and even in the lines of the poem that appear to specify the subject in question—such as "Woman, vile slave, proud and stupid [*La femme, esclave vile, orgueilleuse et stupide*]"—she is named as a universal species marked by the definite article ("*la* femme"), with the implication that her every attribute is an essential constant, rather than a feature that would be accidental and alterable by choice or circumstance. All occurrences that Baudelaire's voyagers appear to recount, then, are not presented as events that could also be otherwise, but as expressions of essence. The horror is vacuity: emptied of variation and even deviation, humanity seems to have run out of time and gone on autopilot in a way that eliminates history and has its correlate in the elimination of verbal tenses. Nothing happens, but barely subsists when crime and typified incarnations of violence are the global substance and subject of all that is, was, and will be.

Here, all that remains of what Nietzsche describes as "an insoluble manifold of rising and declining life processes" are the ups and downs of despotic power and suffering at every level of the social hierarchy, which Baudelaire maps onto a vertical "fatal scale [*échelle fatale*]."[65] There is no talk of a singular destiny or will to redeem, as there was in *Thus Spoke Zarathustra*, nor is a revaluation of values possible, where it never seems to have been a question of good or evil, but of an "immortal sin" more original than even the fall of man. And in this respect, Baudelaire also goes further than even Joseph de Maistre in turning human misfortune into a general, natural law, on the premise that "[o]riginal sin, which explains everything and without which nothing is explained, unfortunately repeats itself at every moment in time."[66] For if the behavior types listed in Baudelaire's poem are not merely natural, but "immortal," then they have neither beginning nor end, neither a decisive origin nor an eschatological prospect of expiation. Instead, sin would be coeval with the deity whom humanity ultimately curses toward the close of the sixth section: "Ô mon semblable, mon maître, je te maudis!" At least as radically as in Nietzsche's notes, then, what goes on in the world of Baudelaire's voyagers seems to allow for no novel change, not even in death. As Elissa Marder writes on "Le Léthé," one of the condemned poems from the first edition of *Les Fleurs du mal*: "[w]hen 'vivre est un mal' and daily life is a living hell that is indistinguishable from death, death no longer offers the promise of repose."[67] What she says of this poem holds true to the last: "The fatal scale" of "immortal sin" is not fatal because it could lead to death or because it proceeded from a fateful decision, but because it determines the everlasting fate of all human beings as such.

The sole exception to this state of affairs may be, as Eugene Holland has suggested, voyaging, which the voyagers conspicuously do not include in their litany of atrocities, despite its earlier evocation as *the* human condition: "Man, whose anticipation stays awake / To find his rest goes racing like a fool [*l'Homme, dont jamais l'espérence n'est lasse / Pour trouver le repos court toujours comme un fou!*]." "Traveling," Holland writes, "combines the temporal succession of moments with the spatial succession of spaces: following Baudelaire, it would [. . .] become one of the few remaining touchstones of modernist narrative, a kind of last-ditch, zero-degree plot structure [. . .]."[68] Travel alone can be seen as no exit from the *status quo*, however, since it is owing to Baudelaire's voyeuristic voyagers that the global panorama of sin is portrayed in the sixth section. Hence, the "voyage" comes full circle in the next section, aligning and rhyming with the "image" of humanity from which the voyagers had just appeared to depart, but retain nevertheless as the after-image that survives their experience and allows them to recognize themselves: "bitter knowing, that which one draws from the voyage! the world, monotonous and small, today, yesterday, tomorrow, always, makes us see our image: an oasis of horror [*Amer savoir, celui qu'on tire du voyage! / Le monde, monotone et petit, aujourd'hui, / Hier, demain, toujours, nous fait voir notre image: / Une oasis d'horreur*]." But even if travel is no last resort in the face of worldwide devastation, the view of the voyagers also does not exhaust the language of the poem and therefore cannot exclude the possibility that their sentence on humanity might be entangled with others, which could be teased out to allow the issue—or tissue—of the text to unravel differently, despite all appearances of a dead end.

Within Baudelaire's oeuvre alone, the universe of "Le Voyage" recalls another version of global uniformity that Baudelaire had evoked in his earlier journalistic writings, and that seems nonetheless to be a world apart from the homogeneous realm the voyagers observe. In his contribution to *Le Salut public* from 1848, Baudelaire had imagined the following universal situation, with reference to the wanderings of a very different traveler:

> The ex-king goes always from people to people, from city to city.
> Always and always, long live the Republic! Long live liberty! The men! The cries! The tears of joy!
> He runs with all of his strength to arrive in time somewhere before the Republic, to rest his head there, that is his dream. For the entire earth is no longer anything for him but a nightmare that envelops him. But hardly does he touch the gates, and the bells gleefully begin to toll and sound the Republic to his distressed ears.[69]

Here, the world becomes an enveloping "nightmare" for the deposed and itinerant king not only because it presents an expanse in which he no longer holds a position, but also because it is as monotonous as the sphere of Baudelaire's voyagers: the surround-sound of exultation and tolling bells is what gets to him wherever he goes. This public domain is, of course, also a dream. Yet however quickly the resonance of the "Republic" should fade out—and, as Baudelaire says around the same time, the Republic may have only ever existed "in name"[70]—this earlier text suggests that the "the entire earth" was recently imagined very differently than the timeless setting of "Le Voyage," whose permanence may therefore turn out to be just as temporary and illusory. In this respect, the Republic that is temporarily called to everlasting life does not merely portray the inverse image of the neverending spectacle of despotism that the voyagers view. Taken together, the dissonant echoes between these texts show any given universe in Baudelaire's writing to be provisional and capable of taking another turn. Instead of settling anything, the doubled eternal visions expose each picture to conversions and perversions as drastic as those displayed in "Le Voyage," when "[g]reat palaces enwrought with filigree / [a]nd jeweled thrones in luminous design" simultaneously appear, from a different perspective, to "send [. . .] brokers dreams of bankruptcy."[71]

It would not be difficult to find further evidence within and beyond "Le Voyage" that speaks against all-encompassing claims on the world; however, it may be no insignificant coincidence that one of the most pronounced precedents or prototypes for the static universe of "Le Voyage" can be found in an article that promotes the Revolution. Both texts show traits or traces of the historical constants to which many of Baudelaire's revolutionary contemporaries had appealed in their efforts to overturn the *status quo*. The spectrum or specter of oppressive forms that Baudelaire evokes in "Le Voyage," ranging from slavery and tyranny to cupidity, recalls the ahistorical concept of history that Karl Marx and Friedrich Engels would present at the opening of the *Communist Manifesto* in February 1848: "Freeman and slave, patrician and plebeian, lord and serf, guild-master and journeyman, in a word, oppressor and oppressed, stood in constant opposition to one another [. . .]."[72] At the same time, these words resonate with the version of history that Blanqui had delivered in his address to the provisional government in France one month later, in March 1848: "Sparta, Rome, Venice were corrupt and oppressive oligarchies. In the United States, slavery is an institution. The formula: 'Liberty, Equality, Fraternity' could become a lie as celebrated as the truth of the charter: 'All of the French are equal before the law!' The tyranny of Capital is more pitiless than that of the sabre and the censer. The revolution of February has the aim to break it."[73] And before both of these nineteenth-century revolutionaries, Maximilien Robespierre had opened his last discourse, delivered on 8 Thermidor 2, or 26 July 1794, with a similar claim: "Up to us, the revolutions that had changed the face of empires did not have as their object anything but a change of dynasty, or the passage of power from one to many. The French Revolution is the first that was founded on the theory of the rights of humanity and on the principles of justice."[74]

In all of these cases, Marx, Engels, Blanqui, and Robespierre speak of seemingly eternal and ubiquitous despotic orders. But each species of eternity functions in these rhetorical performances for the sake of promoting a revolutionary intervention, which, because it would be the first significant change to date, would mark the beginning of history as well as its end. Lyotard considers this structure to be *the* distinguishing feature of revolutionary chronology, writing: "The game that is then played between the 'pre-' and the 're-' [. . .] aims to erase the 'pre-' implied in some at least of these old judgements. For example, this is how we must take the name 'prehistory' given by Marx to any human history preceding the socialist revolution he is expecting and preparing."[75] The further consequences of this premise, moreover, entail that not even an apparently revolutionary event would have to be decisive, since history could begin at any time. After the Revolution of 1848 had seemed to succeed, the strategy that Lyotard describes is the same game—or the same play of fact and fiction—that Baudelaire would deploy in his article for the *Tribune nationale*, when he claimed that "all is yet to be done [*tout est encore à faire*]." With these words, he indicates not only that nothing has changed yet, but also that all "things [*choses*]" and "forms [*formes*]"—all matters and activities that make up the world—can and should be remade or reinvented in the present moment.⁷⁶ Furthermore, when the stasis of all things and forms assumes a more theological inflection in "Le Voyage," this shift not only does not diminish its partial resonance with revolutionary rhetoric, but also negatively mirrors the eschatological thrust of revolutionary thought that Karl Löwith traces in Marx's historical materialism, which presents "a history of fulfillment and salvation in terms of social economy" that will end the "original sin" of "exploitation."⁷⁷ The "immortal sin" of "Le Voyage" is one more layer in these strategic histories of eternity, and therefore anything but an evocation of that which necessarily lasts. Baudelaire may give no imperatives in his poem as he had done in his journalism, but this may be because the movement that "Le Voyage" should have provoked was meant to reach not only things and forms, but also their substance and base: "I have *made* [*fait*] a long poem dedicated to Max Du Camp, which is *to make* [*à faire*] nature, and above all, the lovers of progress, shudder [*frémir*]."⁷⁸

Up to a point, then, Baudelaire's lines in "Le Voyage" can be said to resonate with the rhetorical strategies of revolutionary announcements, especially in its most seemingly ahistorical moments. But unlike Marx's and Blanqui's speeches—and unlike Baudelaire's own writings from 1848—no call for change follows upon the enumeration of the atrocities that constitute the supposedly eternal essence of human nature. Instead, visionary projects founded in conscious intentions are shown to take unforeseen courses or to remain blind to their own hazard, as when "our soul" is said to be "a three-mast ship searching its Icaria [*notre âme est un trois-mâts cherchant son Icarie*]" in homage to Étienne Cabet's utopian *Voyage en Icarie*,⁷⁹ before the announcement arrives that the voyage to Icaria is bound to crash, and that utopian pursuits come down to hell: "A voice on deck rings: 'open your eye!' / An ardent and crazed voice from the foretop cries: / 'Love . . . glory . . . happiness!' Hell, it's a reef! [*Une voix retentit sur le pont: 'Ouvre l'oeil!' / Une voix de la hune, ardente et folle, crie: / 'Amour . . . gloire . . . bonheur!' Enfer! c'est un écueil!*]."⁸⁰ By contrast, the very spatiotemporal structure that characterizes the infernal world of "immortal sin" testifies to the weak survival of the decadent, decayed, and dead revolutionary rhetoric from 1848, when the shape of human life was not decided once and for all, and when its seemingly unchanging patterns were challenged precisely by pronouncing them. Thus, if past and future promises of political change may have been wrecked—if the Revolution could never be "news" again, and if there were no place for socialist utopias—the echoes of their precondition suggest that the Revolution not only never took place definitively, but also never ceased to survive as a layer of the current state of affairs. And once it is sedimented in this way, as a layer of naturalized human history, the remaining, posthumous possibilities for the Revolution could only lie in something like the tremors of nature that Baudelaire had spoken of in his letter to Asselineau, which may yet shift the "Schichten" of life processes and expose the rifts and faultlines of their current foundations.

It is along these lines that Baudelaire troubles that which Nietzsche would later call "the consequent circumstances of all present misery," and which he presents as a transcendental and stable condition in his poem.[81] Yet there are further indications that something new is taking place even as Baudelaire delivers a damning sentence on the world of sin. The asserted permanence and pervasiveness of this state is already called into question from the way in which the voyagers fail to describe it until they are prompted by their auditors, who ask to hear more after the voyagers' first round of recollections in section four come to a close. If "immortal sin" were the universal *a priori* that it appears to be, then its description would not be required. It would seem to be so far from self-evident, however, that the voyagers open their description of immortal sin in section six with the suggestion that the whole spectacle they recount could even be forgotten: "And not to forget the capital thing [. . .] [*Pour ne pas oublier la chose capitale* . . .]."[82] What speaks most against the ubiquity and changelessness of atrocity, then, is the fact that the spectacle of sin must be absent, inapparent, and forgettable on the premises where the voyagers are solicited to deliver their news. And whether its initial inconspicuousness is due to an obscure present atmosphere, as was the case in "Le Monde va finir," or whether this moment in the poem simply marks a lapse of memory (Ecc. 1.11), it opens the supposedly stable human condition to a temporary suspension. Beyond eternity and beyond the repeated atrocities that eventually occur to the speakers in Baudelaire's "Le Voyage," then, there is at least one place and time where they do not seem to extend or last: namely, the place and time of their evocation here. If the news that the voyagers break is "the eternal bulletin of the entire globe [*du globe entier l'éternel bulletin*]," the poem thus announces at the same time a breach in the eternal, ahistorical history that it relates.

The voyagers speak in an undated interval and uncharted interstice in the spatiotemporal continuum of "immortal sin," and they thereby introduce a rupture in the state of affairs, however far Baudelaire's poem may otherwise be from his political journalism, and however oblivious, illusory, or fleeting this rupture may turn out to be. Before all, however, this passage in "Le Voyage" signals that the *status quo* must have always already been broken in order for the interval to take place. As a consequence, the speakers and addressees of Baudelaire's dialogue speak as and for an alternative to both the eternal tyranny of despotism and capital, as well as the eternal Republic Baudelaire had once imagined. And because this unlocated and literally utopic passage of the poem eventually leaves off, wanders further—and thereby fails to crystallize into a social utopia of any kind—said tableau succeeds in bringing about liberation through its very failure to remain in place, leaving room for other finite interactions that may be exempt from the sphere of "immortal sin," as well as any other immortal condition. In this respect, the event of the text is more than revolutionary: because the participants in this dialogue are not called to gather by an authoritative speech act of any kind; because they are bound by no laws and are not even called a "community;" and because they need not hold together at all, the speakers and listeners of the poem present the one situation of association in which all members are left utterly free and free to leave again. Despite all talk of news in the end, it may therefore be this most inconspicuous moment that delivers the most significant novel announcement and delivers the speakers from the perennial news they impart.

This liberation is one that rests on no foundations or founding act, and that takes place nowhere, but in language. The transitory assembly of these voyagers and their auditors will have never been formally established. It takes place contingently in and through their speaking, whereby it is telling that this scene of dialogue is also the only interaction to occur in the poem. Elsewhere, each species of humanity either affects itself, like the woman who "adores herself without laughter and loves herself without disgust [*sans rire s'adorant et s'aimant sans dégoût*];" or it performs intransitive actions, as with the "martyr who sobs [*le martyr qui sanglote*];" or it is affected by force, like the despot who is enervated by "the poison of power [*le poison du pouvoir*]."[83] The encounter between the voyagers and their auditors, on the other hand, occurs as a conversation outside the worldly scenarios depicted in the voyagers' tableau and thus escapes the anthropological, ontological, and theological categories that determine it. The voyagers' appearance is accordingly one that provokes astonishment rather than recognition, and that most closely resembles the formless figure of the sea: "Astonishing voyagers! What noble histories we read in your eyes profound as the sea [*Étonnants voyageurs! quelles nobles histoires / Nous lisons dans vos yeux, profonds comme les mers!*]."⁸⁴ This understated and unstable scene of speech, as opposed to that of "Humanité" writ large, is similarly indefinite, and therefore the refutation that "Humanité" could ever have been a finished, definite whole: "it is no whole, this humanity."⁸⁵ What occurs through speaking, in short, parts from the logic, relations, and order of the world and humanity at once. Even at its most pessimistic, then, "Le Voyage" opens a dimension in language that shatters natural constants of the worst kind, and moves on to no particular or prescribable end.⁸⁶ What remains to be said and done here—among the remains of that which, according to Nietzsche, "has remained behind, that is, living"—is not to say that "all is to be done," as Baudelaire had announced in 1848. Nor does it come down to denying the possibility that "the world henceforth" has anything "to do under the sky,"⁸⁷ as Baudelaire had suggested in "Le Monde va finir." Instead, Baudelaire's poem speaks for speaking in such a way that all speakers and listeners might take leave from all stations and status, from all affairs and pursuits. Baudelaire's depiction of world history thus approaches, by an altogether different route, the maxim of which Werner Hamacher speaks, when he writes in his *95 Theses on Philology*: "It is the movement of its becoming a world: the coming to the world of this world. This coming does not allow itself to be made, to be bargained for, to be achieved through intentional acts. The nonnegotiability of this coming (of this world) is the experience that another philology has to elucidate. Its provisional maxim: act such that you can leave acting. And further: act without a maxim, even without this one."⁸⁸

The interlocutors of section six are abruptly left behind as the dialogue breaks off, but the next section of the poem traces a course and discourse that open further possibilities not only for troubling the mundane *status quo*, but also for taking leave of the voyage that has thus far revolved around the world. Shortly after the scene in section six, the speakers of Baudelaire's poem—who may be the voyagers from before, or another contingent altogether—formulate a new maxim: "Is it a must to depart? to remain? if you can remain, remain; / depart, if it is a must [*Faut-il partir? rester? Si tu peux rester, reste: / Pars, s'il le faut*]."⁸⁹ These words could, of course, suggest that staying on or going on are indifferent; that when it comes to the world, it does not matter whether you take it or leave it; and that necessity ("il faut") lies solely in defaulting one way or the other. But these lines could reduce to such a message solely if they rested upon the premises of the world that has been traveled over the first sections of "Le Voyage," which need no longer be the case. Instead, the circular logic of "Le Voyage" as a whole would appear to have ended before it becomes a question of going or staying anywhere, as the first words of section seven suggest: "bitter knowing that one draws from the voyage! the world, monotonous and small, today, yesterday, tomorrow, always, makes us see our image [*Amer savoir, celui qu'on tire du voyage! / Le monde, monotone et petit, aujourd'hui, / Hier, demain, toujours, nous fait voir notre image*]."[90] This coda not only draws a general conclusion on voyaging, but also marks the logical conclusion of the poem, which comes full circle with these verses to the insight imparted in the opening strophe: "To the eyes of memory, how the world is small [*Aux yeux du souvenir que le monde est petit!*]."[91] If it can still be a question of going or staying, then, there is no guarantee that there remains any place to go, and insofar as the poem nonetheless speaks past its end, the seventh section will have veered off into what Baudelaire had called, in "Le Monde va finir," an "hors d'oeuvre."[92] In this respect, the questions, "Is it a must to depart? to remain?" in no way follow from anything that had come before, but let "Le Voyage" proceed instead upon the sheer premise of speaking in excess of not only all ontological categories and conventional topoi, but also its proper logic and poetological closure. Henceforth, this speaking cannot be grounded or placed, which the words to come also testify, as they appear detached from any clearly defined source and from any dialogic situation. It is therefore at this point where the lines of the poem become faultlines that open perhaps most radically to the abyss of other voices and other times, and where the rhetoric of space gives way to a rhetoric of temporality: "one runs, one crouches in hiding, to cheat / deceive [*tromper*] the vigilant and deadly enemy / Time!"[93]

This turn to time is anything but a simple inversion of the spatial rhetoric from before, despite appearances to the contrary, as Baudelaire's voyagers seem to go from pursuing to being pursued, or from facing a monotonous everyday to confronting the end of their days. There may be, as Alan Rosenthal shows in "Baudelaire's Mysterious 'Enemy,'" a long history of reading "Time" as the ultimate enemy in Baudelaire's *Les Fleurs du mal*, both here and in other passages, where exhaustion increases the more time gains on one.[94] Through a reading of its most pronounced depiction in "L'Horloge," Marder ties time to the devastating memory loss that follows from the rapidly paced conditions of modern life: "[w]ithout a temporal firmament to hold the past in place, the present moment falls out of time and cannot be remembered. [. . .] Every minute tick of this clock conveys the shock experience: it is an unstoppable alarm clock that keeps us awake in order to remind us to die."[95] And insofar as the "Time" of "Le Voyage" provokes flight at the same rate that time is fleeting, all of these observations hold true. But the turn to time in these verses also entails a turn *of* time through a trope that alters its role: "nothing suffices, neither coach nor vessel, to flee this infamous gladiator [*rien ne suffit, ni wagon ni vaisseau, / Pour fuir ce rétiaire infâme*]."[96] With this, "time" not only appears as a figure of speech but escapes even its latest identification, as it may also be cast as the net—the *rete*—through which the "gladiator" (*rétiaire*) is personified as well. As such, time not only could not have one shape or direction but would "itself" be a complex net that one will have always already been caught up in, not as an ultimate catch-all, but perhaps as the nexus of words and texts in which one would be entangled at every turn.[97]

Everything, every time, stays *and* goes through this net. Hence, as the current vehicles of poetic speech set out for "the sea of Shades [*la mer des Ténèbres*]," they just as soon encounter a manifold of voices that recalls the Lotus fields of Homer's *Odyssey* and Alfred Tennyson's "Lotus-Eaters," as well as the figures of Pylades and Electra, whose traits are drawn from both the mythic tradition of ancient Greek tragic drama and the more modern tragedy of Thomas de Quincey's *Confessions of an Opium Eater*.[98] As though in response to the initial either-or—"Is it a must to depart? to remain?"—the voyagers of the seventh section opt for the only way to go, as they pass *through* time and part *for* what remains:

> We will embark upon the sea of Shadows with the joyous heart of a young passenger. Do you hear these charming and funereal voices that sing: "Come along this way, you who want to eat the perfumed Lotus! It is here that one harvests the miraculous fruits for which your heart hungers; do you come to intoxicate yourself upon the strange sweetness of this afternoon that never ends?" From the familiar accent, we divine the specter; our Pylades' below stretch their arms towards us. "To refresh your heart, swim towards your Electra!" says she whose knees we once kissed.
>
> Nous nous embarquerons sur la mer des Ténèbres
> Avec le coeur joyeux d'un jeune passager.
> Entendez-vous ces voix charmantes et funèbres,
> Qui chantent: "Par ici vous qui voulez manger
>
> Le Lotus parfumé! c'est ici qu'on vendange
> Les fruits miraculeux dont votre coeur a faim;
> Venez vous enivrer de la douceur étrange
> De cette après-midi qui n'a jamais de fin?"

> À l'accent familier nous devinons le spectre;
> Nos Pylades là-bas tendent leurs bras vers nous.
> "Pour rafraîchir ton coeur nage vers ton Électre!"
> Dit celle dont jadis nous baisions les genoux.[99]

These voices differ from both the scene of "Humanité" that had been portrayed in the previous section, as well as the dialogic exchange through which its depiction was related. This time, words from other times are addressed to the voyagers that issue into no communication and occur in no shared space or span for call and answer, but simply come to pass and break or trail off. This goes to show that these voices from the past are not eternal in the sense of constants: because they emerge from within the nexus of temporality, they are themselves timebound, arising suddenly, contingently, and fleetingly. The afterlife that the voyagers enter in embarking upon "the sea of Shadows" is therefore radically finite and transient despite the indefinite survival of all that they encounter. The contrary to finitude in this poem is not this anachronistic realm, but the chronic hell of the mundane present and the eternity of "immortal sin" that the poem survives only by departing from that world of presence. And although this latest departure may likewise seem to promise a condition of stasis—"the strange sweetness of this afternoon that never ends [*la douceur étrange de cette après-midi qui n'a jamais de fin*]"—that promise is itself evanescent, and therefore further evidence that the afterlife delivers nothing but an infinity of endings, or what Nietzsche would call a "manifold of rising and declining life processes" that shift to no end.[100] The issues of existence that were raised before in the poem thus give way to alternations and alterations of the past, present, and future, according to no determinable trajectory, but for a voyage past the ends of the world, which renders all times utterly unpredictable, if not new.

These possibilities also exceed the bounds of any experience that could be defined or affirmed by any subject of knowledge or volition. It marks a different sort of turning point, that is, than the one which both optimistic and pessimistic interpretations of the "Le Voyage" tend to underscore in the shift toward the "sea of Shadows," from Lloyd Austin's claim that Baudelaire triumphantly "makes this last voyage the symbol of the passage from life to death, and [. . .] sweeps away all that is known or imagined of the world beyond the grave,"[101] to Nicolae Babuts's suggestion that the sudden "victory of time" over the voyagers compels them to recall voices that offer "the fulfillment of the desires they have always had: the desire to be intoxicated with some impossible fruit that suggests the preoccupations with 'artificial paradises' and the need to find Electra, the ideal wife, mother, sister, and mistress."[102] As in "Le Monde va finir," addressing historical existence in its complexity entails the breakdown of the reasoning and rhetoric of the *cogito*, which will have been underway at least since the poem parts with the coherence of life—which takes shape in this context as the constancy of "immortal sin"—and most likely long before. After all, the child's love and view of the world was said to be divided from the beginning between "maps [*cartes*]" and "prints [*estampes*]"—that is, between overviews of the whole globe and close-ups of its local parts—which separate and disparate pictures appear juxtaposed in a way that renders even the earliest desires incoherent *ab initio*. Especially when it comes to the "sea of Shadows," however, even the minimal connection between Electra and the memory of a former kiss does not necessarily—and in fact could not possibly—confirm an individual sentiment of nostalgia for a beloved sister akin to Orestes's sibling in Euripides's *Orestes* or Aeschylus's *Oresteia*, or for a beloved wife like the spouse of Thomas de Quincey, who is compared to Electra in a line that Baudelaire had translated from *The Confessions of an Opium-Eater*: "L'Oreste d'opium a trouvé son Électre, qui pendant les années a essuyé sur son front les sueurs de l'angoisse et rafraîchi ses lèvres parcheminées par la fièvre."[103] Rather, breaches in logic, grammar, and lexis characterize the gestures of Pylades and the address of Electra—and, as a consequence, the subject of their solicitations—to fragmentation. Beyond so much as a semblance of coherent categories of experience, "*the* specter" soon appears to be a multitude of Pylades, stretching out "*their* arms," and thus a plethora of simulacra for one whose proper name will have become, it seems, common currency. Halfway through the strophe, this singular multitude morphs from a vision of outstretched arms to a voice, from male to female, from the plural Pylades to the one and only Electra, and from an image of upper members (outstretched arms), to a memory of lower limbs (knees). And as these metamorphoses take place—so that the upper and lower quarters of Baudelaire's quatrain likewise seem to be broken at its midriff or mid-rift—"our" status changes as well, for Electra's invitation to swim to her is not directed to the collective "we" who embarked for the sea of Shadows, but to one person alone: "To refresh *your* heart, swim towards *your* Electra! [*Pour rafraîchir* ton *coeur nage vers* ton *Électre!*]."[104] Her solicitation thus turns out to be closest call to eliciting a singular subject of desire to respond, which is incoherent *because* the current addressees and voyagers have been plural up to this point. Furthermore, when the poem reverts again to the first-person plural in the very next verse—"says she whose knees *we* once kissed [*Dit celle dont jadis nous baisions les genoux*]"—this return restores no narrative or narratorial cogency, either. For it not only adds to the confusions between the one and the many that have occurred in these lines; the language of the verse itself complicates the "we" with the "I," as the words for "former times" and "knees"—"jadis" and "genoux"—nearly spell "je dis" and phonetically compress "je" and "nous," respectively. These verses thus mark a critical point where no determinate subject could any longer be said to speak or think, but where speaking occurs between and beyond any collective or singular version of a self. Before the famous final plunge of "Le Voyage," "I" and "we" will have already undergone a *suicide*—which also in no way kills off the possibility of going on, once the semblance is abandoned that what goes on could be the individual journey of someone or some group.

"Le Voyage" is no one's odyssey through the ends of the world and the shifting layers of historical remains.[105] This is also why the memory of her "whose knees we once kissed" does not evoke the memory of a self and does not itself constitute a memory, properly speaking. Attending to this memory more closely, in fact, could at best allow one to trace it back to words on mnemomics from an earlier poem in *Les Fleurs du mal*, where it had been claimed: "I have the art of calling forth the happy times, / Seeing again my past there curled within your knees [*Je sais l'art d'évoquer les minutes heureuses, / Et revis mon passé blotti dans tes genoux*]."[106] And even there, the art and source of recollection are ultimately interdicted: "These vows, these sweet perfumes, these kisses infinite, / Will they be reborn from a gulf *we cannot sound*? [*Ces serments, ces parfums, ces baisers infinis, / Renaîtront-ils d'un gouffre* interdit à nos sondes?]."[107] It could not be otherwise if, as Kevin Newmark has shown in his meticulous reading of Baudelaire's *The Painter of Modern Life*, memory never "simply represent[s] a past that has already been present to itself," and therefore "opens" each time to that which "remains strictly unknowable."[108] In "Le Voyage," traces of former passages emerge to form a nexus of intersecting times and terms, but in it, each recollected image or mirage is shattered from the outset through its refraction into an indefinite multiplicity of subjects. The various evocative utterances sound through no one persona, but the complex net of the "infamous gladiator [*rétiaire infâme*]" that is also called "Time;" they testify to no life experience, but the "insoluble manifold of rising and declining life processes" that replace and displace history in Nietzsche's notes;[109] and they shade into each other like the immemorial conjunction of "former ages" and "later ages" that takes place at every juncture according to the Ecclesiast (Ecc. 1.11). But whereas Nietzsche and the Ecclesiast describe the structures of similar temporal complexes, it is Baudelaire who perhaps goes furthest in speaking the language of such temporality. Sounding out the abyss of memories in "Le Voyage" and elsewhere would always be "interdicted," or "interdit," because every resonance and every statement would be itself an inter-diction that is spoken between that which will have been said otherwise at multiple times.[110]

It is along the lines of such a historical idiom that the famous final announcement of novelty in *Les Fleurs du mal* might also be read against the dominant tendency to interpret it as a testimony and last testament to the monotonous modern world:

> O Death, old captain, it is time! let us lift anchor! This country bores us, o Death! Let us set sail! If the sky and sea are black as ink, our hearts, which you know, are full of rays! Pour us your poison, so that it reinforces us! So much does this fire burn the brain, we want to plunge to the bottom of the abyss, what does it matter whether it is Hell or Heaven? To the bottom of the Unknown, to find the *new*!

> Ô Mort, vieux capitaine, il est temps! levons l'ancre!
> Ce pays nous ennuie, ô Mort! Appareillons!
> Si le ciel et la mer sont noirs comme de l'encre,
> Nos cœurs que tu connais sont remplis de rayons!

> Verse-nous ton poison pour qu'il nous réconforte!
> Nous voulons, tant ce feu nous brûle le cerveau,
> Plonger au fond du gouffre, Enfer ou Ciel, qu'importe?
> Au fond de l'Inconnu pour trouver du *nouveau*![111]

Of course, these last words appear to be the profession of a first-person plural subject seeking novelty, just as they have always done. This profession is all the more pronounced, in light of the ways in which Baudelaire's lines appear to shadow the end of the voyage that Victor Hugo had dreamt up in "The Slope of Reverie [*La pente de la rêverie*]," which adumbrates encounters with living and lost friends, traverses the ruins and crowds of past and present cities, and closes with the verses:

> My spirit dived into this unknown ocean,
> Swam down, naked, alone, to the abyss,
> Pressing on from the ineffable to the invisible—
> Suddenly it came back with a great cry,
> Dazzled, stunned, gasping, staggered and astonished:
> For in the depths it had found eternity.[112]

> Mon esprit plongea donc sous ce flot inconnu,
> Au profond de l'abîme il nagea seul et nu,
> Toujours de l'ineffable allant à l'invisible . . .
> Soudain il s'en revint avec un cri terrible,
> Ébloui, haletant, stupide, épouvanté,
> Car il avait au fond trouvé l'éternité.[113]

Whether or not these echoes were ever intended,[114] the repetition and rearrangement of Hugo's vocabulary—"plonger," "inconnu," "au fond," "trouver"—in "Le Voyage" reflect the lexicon that Baudelaire would ascribe to Hugo in an essay from 1861, writing: "I do not know in what world Victor Hugo first ate the dictionary of the language that he was called upon to speak; but I see that the French lexicon, departing from his mouth, has become a world, a colored universe, melodious and moving."[115] And when Baudelaire isolates "The Slope of Reverie" in that same essay in order to trace Hugo's more recent oeuvres as "the equally regular and enormous development of the faculty that presides in this intoxicating poem,"[116] he describes it with an epithet that suggests all the more strongly that the intoxicating draught of his voyagers may be drawn from Hugo's verses. But when Baudelaire gives the trajectory of his voyagers a "new" last word by altering Hugo's "l'éternité" to "du *nouveau*," finitude replaces eternity in the end, in more than one way: "the new" literally marks an end and a limit to Hugo's word of "eternity;" it shows a universe colored by Hugo's lexicon to be subject to change; and it marks the finitude of Baudelaire's language, whose "novelty" remains contingent in part upon his departure from Hugo. And at the same time, because the sign for finitude here is "nouveau," it suggests that the many levels of finitude that the poem traverses could never culminate in an ultimate end, but instead open to new terms, including the other words from former times that Baudelaire's lines cross through.

For this same reason, however, the "nouveau" could no more be reduced to an echo of Hugo than it could be defined as a novel goal on the voyagers' horizon. Either of these alternatives would imply the fixation of personal subjects, coherent desires, and linguistic properties that the poem speaks against, from the child's love of maps and stamps, to the departure from all subjective and substantial ontologies in the sixth section; to the apparitions of Pylades and Electra that precede the address to "Death" in the end. Once again, "Le Voyage" can be seen to expose a historical—and ahistorical—scene in which epochal distinctions and discriminate voices become blended into procedures that can neither live nor die. As such, they cannot be charted according to an economy of borrowing that capitalizes upon previous poetic inventions, in order to produce a novel product whose status could be described in terms of a "before" and an "after." In Baudelaire's closing strophes, it is not a matter of merely retrieving and moving forward from a preestablished literary thesaurus, which could culminate in what Hans Robert Jauss has summarized as Baudelaire's drive toward a "new that makes the old quotable again," and that even "revives a dead past."[117] For what lives and speaks is open at all times to occasional resonances before and beyond any imaginable scenario of deliberate "quotation" on the part of an authorial instance, and therefore bound to become entangled more or less loosely with threads from other texts. This dynamic of survival is one that cites and resuscitates nothing, but one in which one can never quite be sure whether recollections are called up at all, or whether they virtually appear to surge up and submerge again by sheer chance. And in fact, within the literal seascape here—within the letters that make up all there is to see in this "black" and "ink[y]" expanse—the word "nouveau" not only may mark a departure from "The Slope of Reverie," but also emerges as a possible effect of the intoxicating diction that immediately surrounds it. For as the sequence, "*v*erse-*n*ous [*pour us*]," gives way to "*nous v*oulons [*we want*]" in the next verse, the last word, "nou-veau [*new*]," also begins to appear as yet another altered state within these permutations of "our" will. This possibility alone would suggest that "we" cannot be taken at "our" word with respect to anything in the course of these two lines, where the call for an outpouring from death spills over into a desire to be immersed in an abyss, as though the speakers wanted to be poured to death, and not the other way around. In this context, it would be no great leap to read "nou-veau" as another word for such confusion over the waters—a word that blends "us" with them, in which the words "we" (*nous*) and "water" (*eau*) swim together and suffer a black-out. Neither death nor the new would mark an absolute end, then, but the point at which "our" demands and avowals—*nos voeux*—dissolve.

This dissolution of the subject could be the subject of an infinite analysis. It may even be the case, for example, that the initial call for an intoxicating draught was an echo all along, and that the poison was prescribed when the latest voyagers first embarked upon "the sea of Shadows [*la mer des Ténèbres*]," which phrase not only recalls the sea that Edgar Allan Poe would evoke in "A Descent into the Maelstrom," "Eleanora," and *Eureka*,[118] but also the "valley of the shadow of death" from the Psalms.[119] For not only does Baudelaire's Electra promise intoxication to the seafarers who go on to demand it of death; the Psalmist also claims to be comforted upon entering the realm of shades by a chalice that has the "force to intoxicate [*force d'enivrer*]" (Ps. 23.7),[120] according to a long tradition of mistranslation that left its traces in the Bible of Le Maistre de Sacy.[121] Via parallel, parody—or paradoxical coincidence—the verses of the psalm converge with the verses of Baudelaire's poem as well, as the force to intoxicate turns into a toxin to reinforce, and the shepherd-god of the Hebrew Bible is replaced by captain Death in Baudelaire's book.[122] These disorienting shifts and turns indicate that the plunge for the new comes down to the liquidation of the subjects of the poem, under the influence of Hugo's lexicon, Poe's prose, and biblical echoes. But "Le Voyage" goes on past even these distant points on the literary spectrum.[123] Especially in the context of the Baudelaire's dedication of "Le Voyage" to Maxime du Camp, the desire to find the new and unknown resonates with the latter's *Mémoires d'un suicidé*, whose protagonist Jean-Marc is described as belonging to "the generation gnawed by irremediable ennuis, repulsed by injust downgrading, attracted towards the unknown by the desires of unruly imaginings."[124]

In all of these ways—and in more ways than could ever be retraced exhaustively—Baudelaire's voyage is bottomless. But what is certain is that the intentional or involuntary riffs off of biblical and contemporary poetic topoi undermine the assumptions that have been harbored regarding the modern voyagers' prospects or lack thereof, which rest upon the belief that there exists a group of self-identical "voyagers" pursuing new discoveries. If this were the case, then the tendencies expressed in the end would be so many expressions of the logic of modern capital, as Benjamin had suggested when he wrote in his exposé of the *Arcades Project* from 1935:

> The last poem of *Les Fleurs du mal:* "Le Voyage." "Death, old admiral, up anchor now!" The last journey of the flaneur: death. Its destination: the new. "Deep in the Unknown to find the *new*!" Newness is a quality independent of the use value of the commodity. It is the origin of the semblance that belongs inalienably to images produced by the collective unconscious. It

is the quintessence of that false consciousness whose indefatigable agent is fashion. This semblance of the new is reflected, like one mirror in another, in the semblance of the ever recurrent.[125]

As such, the voyagers would—consciously or unconsciously—be caught up in the timeless structure of oppression that Marx, Engels, Blanqui, and Baudelaire would describe as the current or recurrent state of affairs, where "oppressor and oppressed stood in constant opposition to one another [. . .]" (MECW 6: 482). The voyagers' quest for the unknown and new would be a constant that distinguishes them as yet another universal species, like *the* woman, *the* man, *the* hangman, and *the* martyr, who were described as the representative types of "Humanité" in the sixth section of the poem, and whose continuous activities stand as stable predicates of essence.[126] But such an interpretation would stand and fall with the ways in which the voyagers' discourse in the sixth section breaks from the order of constants; and it would entail blending out the traces in the seventh section that expose the "subjects" of voyaging and speaking to be a shifting plurality of largely anonymous traces. What takes place throughout the language of the poem—and out past all of its apparent limits—speaks against any straightforward reading, and for modes of speaking that will have intersected and intertwined with countless others.

In this respect, the expropriation of all proper proclamations, claims, and ends in "Le Voyage" renders this poem perhaps less a symptom of modern malaise than a novel testimony to the uninheritable legacy of the Revolution that Baudelaire had described when he wrote: "Property virtually disappeared with the abolition of the law of primogeniture [*La propriété avait disparu virtuellement avec la suppression du droit d'aînesse*]."[127] In it, every word and topos is disowned, as the announcements of "Le Voyage" are carried out through a language that deserts the spheres of property, decadence, and plutocracy that Baudelaire and Nietzsche had more explicitly deplored in other passages; instead, this language renders every well-known word or name a many-layered unknown, if not a *novum*.[128] At issue in the passages of "Le Voyage" would be a mode of posthumous survival that crosses over and overwrites previous scripts, retracing and effacing them all the way.[129] Where words and references sink or swim, an intoxication spreads that dissolves the collective subject of speech, slurs its words, and blurs the limit of life and death. And as the voyagers' desires to drink and to drown get confused; as their articulation becomes mingled with other texts—in this writing, where the only poisonous liquid to receive explicit mention is ink, or, as Joseph de Maistre puts it elsewhere, "liqueur noire"[130]—all that has and will have been becomes rewritten and open to an unheard of future.

This may have been the purport of the importations that infiltrate the announcements on novelty at the end of "Le Voyage," creating the conditions for announcements to take place through the transpersonal and transtemporal afterlives of language.[131] "Le Voyage" would then trace a trajectory that moves poetry, language, and thought beyond the collapse of the *ancien régime*, the failed Revolution of 1848, and the plutocracy of the present. But either way, the entanglements and openings in and between the divergent ages and languages that come to pass through "Le Voyage" announce a revolution in language at every moment. And it is in this way, among others, that the diction and interdictions of "Le Voyage"—with respect to all the topoi in the world, from being and time, to existence and history—are unsettled, offset, and set off anew.

3

Announcing a Stellar Possibility

Blanqui's Cosmological Hypothesis

Before and after Baudelaire's "Le Voyage," the topos of travel circulated widely in nineteenth-century literature, from René Chateaubriand's *Itinéraire de Paris à Jérusalem* from 1811 and Alphonse Lamartine's *Voyage en Orient* from 1835, to the travelogues of Maxime du Camp, Gustave Flaubert, and Gérard de Nerval, among others. However, talk of voyaging also exceeded the sphere of what tends to be called "travel literature,"[1] and extended to the political rhetoric of the nineteenth century, especially when it came to the question of navigating the landscape of global capital and breaking new paths for communication and trade. Within this register, the motif of travel is displaced as the emphasis tends to shift from distinct national and geographical regions to the expanse of the global market, where it is less a matter of particular routes than of the ungrounded and unchartable nature of the terrain. One text that speaks to the disparity between global capital and the cartographical grid was a discourse advocating the construction of a new railway line in France, which quickly derails from praising travel over land to addressing the far more obscure foundation for railway construction in transnational, financial interests. This discourse, "Sur le chemin de fer de Paris à Avignon," was held by the voyager, poet, and politician Alphonse Lamartine on 9 April 1850 before the Legislative Assembly of the Second Republic, during a debate over financial strategies to support a railway line from Paris to Avignon. This line was, according to Lamartine, supposed to prepare the way for a still farther-reaching network that would ultimately span "India and the Occident."[2] But the scope of his aims remains indefinite, not least because, as this stretch of imagination alone suggests, this poet cum statesman amplified his calls to political action through the figures of speech that characterized his poetry, most likely in accordance with his professed political belief that the cultivation of poetic imagination correlates directly with the flourishing of society.[3] The poetic dimensions of his politics provoked ambivalent responses both before and after his term as Minister of Foreign Affairs for the Provisional Government of the Second Republic that he had helped to found during the Revolution of 1848.[4] But when it comes to laying the tracks for transportation, the grounds for his turn to tropes may lie less in his rhetorical-political persuasions, than they do in the obscure nature of the sphere of capital. And whatever the poetic or political rationale for his manner of speaking may have been, Lamartine's address on infrastructural innovation quickly gives way to areas of concern that cannot be mapped upon any geopolitical territory or natural terrain, from the moment that he proposes to fund the railway by founding a shareholding company with a governmental subvention and a guarantee of interest that would last for nearly a century.[5]

Lamartine's venture thus exceeds the Chamber's domain of jurisdiction, as he enters into one that can neither be placed anywhere in particular and nor governed by any regime. Hence, Lamartine does not and perhaps cannot directly deny his opponents' objections, when they charge him with intending to render France "feudally subject [*inféodé*]" to private interests and accuse him of throwing "parcels of soil [. . .] to speculators" by means of the state.[6] Instead, he answers by pointing to another area in which national soil will have profited to the extent that it ceased to matter: the current resistance to a company of shareholders, he argues, resembles the initial resistance to the creation of credit in France from 1815–1816, which "conquered [for France] the unlimited capital of public credit" and "sufficed for the liberation of the soil, for the renaissance of industries, and for the creation of public confidence."[7] The utopic promise of finance may not be local or locatable, then, but the thrust of Lamartine's speech seems to come down to the rhetorical question: where would we be without it? And once it is seen, he suggests, that the world revolves around the invisible principles of finance, then the semblance of ceding land to private interests quickly dissipates as well. Instead, the limitless and transcendent nature of credit alters the status of industrial millionaires or "speculators," whose prospects of personal gain from a railway venture turn out to be insubstantial in comparison to the public benefits they would dispense. Proceeding upon the premise that the impersonal forces of finance are what truly count, Lamartine argues that those nominal individuals who may buy into the shareholding company would not stand to profit, but merely figure as transient incorporations of credit themselves, whose manifestations wander irrespective of geographical, political, and personal boundaries. "[L]ike all human things," he asserts, "credit personifies itself in man; it is baptized, if you will, with the name of a man":

> In Florence and in all of Italy during the Middle Ages, it was called by the name of the Medicis; in France under the former monarchy, it was called Jacques Coeur; under the Restoration, it was called Hope and Barin, in England and in Holland; in Paris, it was called, in turn, Necker, Périer, Laffitte! At the moment, it is called Rothschild.[8]

Thus, the "capital matter"—"la chose capitale"—would be neither the concrete tentatives to build infrastructure for a national public, nor the private sources of wealth they would involve, but the inventions and investors whose names "signify confidence, security in affairs, accumulation, reservoirs of capital."[9]

In Lamartine's discourse, specific train routes and potential investors turn out to be alibis that fall out of the picture, as the agents and terrain of political activity become absorbed into another, more nebulous landscape, which is literally off the charts and therefore closer to the unspecified static spaces of Baudelaire's "Le Voyage"—or to the obscurity of the "atmosphere that we already breathe" in "Le Monde va finir"[10]—than to those places that Lamartine traverses in his *Voyage en Orient*. Already in "Sur la politique rationelle," the treatise that Lamartine had published shortly before departing for his famous journey to the East, Lamartine indicates how all spaces, from capital cities to the remotest retreats, will have been submerged within the atmosphere of modern society, whose "general thought" and "political thought" are akin to a ubiquitous element like credit, as they travel through the air and echo throughout the world:

> [G]eneral thought, political thought, social thought dominates and oppresses every individual thought. We want to depose it in vain; it is around us, in us, everywhere; the air that we breathe bears it, the echo of the whole world returns it to us. In vain we take refuge in the silence of the valleys, in the pathways most lost in our forests [. . .] we contemplate with an envious regard the peacable, starred sky that attracts us and the harmonious and durable order of the celestial army; the memory of this mortal world that trembles below our feet, the concerns of the present and provisions of the future attain us up to those very heights.[11]

It is to similar atmospheric conditions that Lamartine recurs in his speech on railroads when he describes the spread of wealth, calling the principal stakeholders in his venture the "reservoirs of industry" who "are precisely to credit and money what clouds are to the rain that renders the earth fecund."[12] After Lamartine characterizes the logic or logos of finance capital as a theology of incarnation and transmigration, the sources of "credit and money" thus transform over a metaphor of cloud formation into an impersonal process, suggesting that wealth should have always trickled down for the common good. Here too, the specificity of natural and national landscapes dissolves into a second nature that covers the full expanse of the earth and renders all terrain sheerly metaphorical, in turn, by situating the base that sustains society in the "clouds."[13]

The world of capital—and by extension, the world *tout court*—thus appears to be constitutively vague, and it is into this new, nebulous landscape that Lamartine's project should break a path. It is only when Lamartine sets out to oppose a very different shadowy phenomenon that he returns to the now unsettled notion of French soil and "the reason of State [*la raison d'État*]."[14] For aside from the fertilizing effects of a massive railway enterprise, the materialization of Lamartine's proposal would also dampen the menace posed by the socialists and communists,[15] who have spread, he claims, like a "phantom" and taken up "the luminous rays of a confused metaphysics to blind populations [. . .] with pretended truths."[16] Again, the particularities of national politics emerge as functions of meteorological trends: communism would be to capital what direct sunlight is to precipitation, with the effect of blinding the populace and drying up "commerce, which sees neither a future nor security" under its influence.[17] Yet although forecasts of sun would appear to be no less natural in this context than predictions of rain, Lamartine gives no credence to the utopic vision of his contemporaries, and appeals suddenly to firm ground. Expressing his refusal to believe that some "men in our country [. . .] have made the oath of Hannibal against society," he reintroduces the notion of national terrain, if not as a concrete referent, then as a bedrock of faith: "I am convinced that above these opinions, above these regrets, these utopias, these systems, there is [. . .] not only a mass of good sense, but also a mass of granite patriotism, so to speak."[18] In this way, Lamartine takes care to discriminate between two varieties of political and economic climate change; however, because rock-solid "patriotism" figures within a metaphoric economy, it is nothing hard and fast, especially if the patriotic aim, according to Lamartine, consists in overwhelming the land with floods of wealth. If lofty socialist ambitions should be brought back down to earth through the rise of financial speculations, the means for this move will have already unearthed, liquidated, and mobilized France. And if political opponents can be cast as both blinding sunlight and as "phantom" shades, then the republic could not "separate the true from the false, the shadows from the light [*séparer le vrai du faux, les ténèbres de la lumière*],"[19] as Lamartine suggests it should. Amidst the commotion of topoi here, there is no fixed criterion to be found for the "reason of state," and no solid guarantee that the railway venture would cause all "phantoms" of dissent to "vanish," having "no value [. . .] but for the fear they inspire in certain all too timid spirits."[20] Rather, the sphere of politics, as well as the phenomena and evidence upon which political decisions could be based, turns out to be itself an insubstantial realm figured by tropes and swayed by affects such as fear or confidence, whose fluctuations and manifestations may be as inconsistent as the weather. Hence, Lamartine's attributions of social ills to the socialists is nothing that one could bank upon, and could just as easily be reversed, as Baudelaire had done in 1848 when he praised the revolutionary "dreamers who search for an ideal republic, one that is Platonic, indefinite, unknown, invisible, intangible,"[21] while crediting to Lamartine's provisional government "the ruin of public credit, destruction of all authority, overexcitation of all passions, [and] aggravated miseries."[22]

The prospect of railway voyages thus serves a pretext for the bifurcation of two alternative politico-economic routes that open on a different plane, and for this reason, whether one heads for capitalism or communism, there is no telling where one is going from the very start. What Lamartine's announcement above all exposes is the way in which the language for financial expansion or social revolution would have to speak from and toward utterly uncertain topoi, not unlike the movement that is traced in Baudelaire's "Le Voyage." To further pursue the language of revolution, its poetics, and its obscure topographies, however, the writer to turn to is not Lamartine, but his political adversary, Louis-Auguste Blanqui, who explored like none other the possibilities and contingencies of intervention upon the *terrae incognitae* of capitalism and socialism. This claim may seem surprising, in light of the tendency to underestimate Blanqui's importance for revolutionary thought, which extends from his contemporaries through to more recent scholars. Perhaps less well known in the Anglophone world, Blanqui was involved in every "major Parisian insurrection," from the 1830s through to the Paris Commune, where he exercised a strong "symbolic presence" despite his incarceration at the time.[23] Yet he is most often portrayed as a heroic militant whose repeated revolutionary efforts had failed, or as a writer whose last published text, *Eternity by the Stars*, expresses resignation to the society that imprisoned him for decades, leading scholars such as Patrick Hutton to claim, "Blanqui is more significant for the myth of his life [. . .] than for anything he actually accomplished."[24] Karl Marx and Friedrich Engels acknowledged Blanqui's genuine commitment to the proletariat, but approached his unsystematic visions for revolution with criticism, as when Friedrich Engels wrote in 1874: "Blanqui is essentially a political revolutionary, a socialist only in sentiment, because of his sympathy for the sufferings of the people, but he has neither socialist theory nor definite practical proposals for social reforms."[25] This interpretation came to underlie many subsequent Marxist readings of Blanqui, despite later qualifications by writers such as Rosa Luxemburg, who argued in her essay from 1906, "Blanquism and Social Democracy," that "Blanqui did not foresee his group forming a 'small minority' at all; on the contrary, in a period of powerful revolutionary upsurge, he was certain that, upon his call, the entire working people—if not in France, then at least in Paris—would rise up to fight the ignominious and criminal policies of the bourgeois government."[26] Only more recent returns to Blanqui on the parts of writers such as Daniel Bensaïd and Michael Löwy situate him in a lineage of socialist dissidents including "Georges Sorel, Charles Péguy, and Bernard Lazare," whose "rejection of positivism" and "critique of the ideology of 'progress'" should "contribute to the enrichment of Marxism [. . .]."[27] Further complicating these reassessments of Blanqui's significance for Marxist theory, however, was the line of interpretation that Walter Benjamin offered in the late 1930s, reading the cosmological speculations of Blanqui's *Eternity by the Stars* as "a complement of the society to which Blanqui, in his old age, was forced to concede victory."[28] It would henceforth be with an eye to Benjamin's comparison of *Eternity by the Stars* to Nietzsche's thought of eternal return that later writers such as Jacques Rancière and Peter Hallward would seek to reconcile Blanqui's notion of repetition with his commitment to revolution.[29] In the afterword to their centenary edition of *Eternity by the Stars*, however, Miguel Abensour and Valentin Pelosse consider the text to be an experiment whose turn from the immediate political scene to the cosmos constitutes the most sweeping "affirmation and elevation of materialism to the rank of an active force,"[30] while rendering nature "the theater of permanent revolution."[31]

Yet whether one emphasizes his non-systematic political declarations or the ambivalence of his cosmological system, both Blanqui's political engagements and his astronomical hypotheses cannot be understood without attending to the problem of place that insists throughout his and his contemporaries' language. The new placelessness of global capital that Lamartine and Baudelaire register in different ways allows for any number of topoi and registers to be evoked in a discussion of political movements and matters. Reading the ways in which Blanqui addresses this novel landscape would open avenues not only for tracing the relationship between his earliest and latest texts, but also for furthering those insights that Abensour and Pelosse provide into the revolutionary significance of Blanqui's language, which bears the mark "of a particular experimentation that seeks to effectuate penetrations simultaneously upon multiple fronts, in different registers."[32] Guiding the range of announcements in Blanqui's oeuvre are the questions of how to traverse the unsettled terrain of global politics, and how to pursue novel pathways for revolution through linguistic strategies that trouble the fundamental assumptions of global capital and that do not presuppose stable or static foundations for revolutionary or reactionary theories.

The confusions that emerge in Lamartine's oration with regard to the obscure domains of capitalist credit and socialist beliefs are the ones that Blanqui would emphasize in a text dated from April 1850, "Lamartine et Rothschild," which he wrote while imprisoned in Doullens.[33] Here, Blanqui does not respond directly to Lamartine's accusations that the socialists ruin commerce by spreading beliefs that destroy faith in investment ventures.[34] Blanqui had already spoken against similar arguments when he invaded the National Assembly on 4 May 1848 with a group of protesters demanding that France take up the cause of Polish refugees, as well as the cause of the unemployed in Paris. There, Blanqui proclaimed:

> The people, citoyens, know very well that one will respond to them that the prime cause of the lack of work is precisely those popular movements that agitate the public space and cast perturbations into commerce and industry [. . .], but the people know well [. . .] that this is not the primary cause, the principal cause is the deplorable situation in which they find themselves today. The lack of work, the commercial and industrial crisis, date from before the February revolution; they date further back, they have profound causes, social ones.[35]

Instead of returning to these points, Blanqui adopts a different strategy in 1850, situating Lamartine's political discourse within Lamartine's literary oeuvre through topoi drawn from his *Voyage en Orient* and his collection of poems, *Harmonies poétiques et religieuses*:

Curious spectacle! M. de Lamartine, this Captain Cook of long-run politics, this Sinbad mariner of the nineteenth century, more marvelous than his predecessor in the *Thousand and One Nights*, this voyager no less errant than Odysseus, but happier than he, having taken the Sirens on the crew of his ship and conducted the so variegated music of his convictions along the borders of all parties, M. de Lamartine, in his endless odyssey, just beached his Aeolian ship gently under the porticos of the stock market.

Spectacle curieux! M. de Lamartine, ce capitaine Cook de la politique au long cours, ce Sindbad [sic.] le Marin du XIXe siècle, plus merveilleux que son prédécesseur des *Mille et une nuits,* ce voyageur non moins errant qu'Ulysse, mais plus heureux, qui a pris les sirènes pour équipage de son navire et promené sur les rivages de tous les partis la musique si variée de ses convictions, M. de Lamartine, dans son odyssée sans fin, vient d'échouer doucement sa barque éolienne sous les portiques de la Bourse.[36]

Already in this opening passage, Blanqui's rhetoric on the alterability of Lamartine's musical modes and convictions alludes to the preface to his *Harmonies*, where Lamartine had confessed, "[t]hese Harmonies, taken separately, seem to have no relation to one another," before asserting "a principle of unity in their very diversity."[37] The reference to the *Thousand and One Nights*, on the other hand, recalls Lamartine's remarks on a recitation of the poetry of Antar, a nomadic Bedouin poet from the sixth century CE, whose work he had favorably compared to the *Thousand and One Nights* in his *Voyage en Orient*, on the grounds that Antar "is less marvelous."[38] In Blanqui's version of the story, Lamartine's speech on communist ghosts and the powers of capital is thus set under the aegis of the very sorts of inconsistencies, marvels, and mystifications from which Lamartine had claimed to be averse in his poetry, travel writing, and political discourse.[39]

The most striking element that Blanqui highlights in Lamartine's oratory, however, is Lamartine's characterization of Rothschild as both a stellar resource for political ventures, and as "a cloud that pours fecundity in the form of rain [*une nuée qui verse la fécondité sous forme de pluie*]."[40] "But that there should be at the same time fair weather and rain," Blanqui writes, "that is [. . .] new [*Mais qu'il soit en même temps le beau temps et la pluie, c'est . . . neuf*]."[41] The news thus appears to be absurd, but attempting to resolve Lamartine's metaphoric and meteorological contradiction by focusing upon either alternative would offer no better prospect either. For if Rothschild were merely a raincloud, continues Blanqui, then "[w]e would soon be drowned! It would be the deluge. [. . .] Poor recommendation for the credit-cloud, for if one never accuses an excess of credit, one sometimes complains furiously over the rain."[42] At the same time, if Rothschild were solely a solar power, he would be more like a drain than a source: "M. de Rothschild also pumps, he pumps enormously. When he is not satisfied with the revolutionaries, he retains all of the pumped vapors and does not release a drop of water, an infallible means to roast the disturbers and to calcinate them into the state of mummies."[43] But what Blanqui clearly illustrates in his recapitulation of Lamartine's speech is that the function of drawing water, at the heights of finance, is beholden to no natural laws of eventual release. The so-called "reservoir of capital" to which Lamartine had appealed thus turns out to be a private reserve and a source of privation; contrary to his claim, money-holders wield arbitrary powers that are less like those of the sun than those of the former Sun King, whom Blanqui also evokes in suggesting that, after Rothschild, comes the "deluge."[44] In carrying Lamartine's poetic logic further, Blanqui thus shows both of Lamartine's similes to lead to the opposite conclusion than the one that Lamartine reaches: the bottom line is the leveling of the world through flood or drought. Rather than according with Lamartine's harmonious poetics, the dissonances that Blanqui registers in Lamartine's announcement anticipate Baudelaire's more prosaic remarks in "Le Monde va finir," when he says: "we shall perish by the thing by which we thought to live."[45]

However, if Blanqui exaggerates the metaphoric character of Lamartine's arguments, and thus challenges Lamartine's call for the state to separate the true from the false, or the light from the dark, Blanqui does not dismiss the meteorological register that Lamartine adopts wholesale. The imagery that Lamartine draws upon would not only be as viable a figuration for the indefinite landscape of global capital as any, but was also widespread and therefore a very real element within the social fabric and the corpus of political literature. Walter Benjamin, for example, collects passages in his *Arcades Project* that register fog or "brouillard" as the atmospheric condition of the modern city, from Baudelaire's *Spleen*-cycle,[46] to Alfred de Vigny's "La maison du berger," or "House of the Shepherd," where fog rising from steam engines obstructs both vision and breath. After enjoining "us" to avoid railway tracks because "their voyage is without grace"—"évitons ces chemins—Leur voyage est sans grâces"—de Vigny adds that these roads also lead nowhere but to environs in which "the human creature neither breathes nor sees, in all of nature, / but a suffocating fog traversed by lightning [*l'humaine créature / Ne respire et ne voit, dans toute la nature / qu'un brouillard étouffant que traverse un éclair*]."[47] Across a multitude of texts and contexts, from political to poetic discourses on railway lines, landscapes appear to go up in smoke or to be covered in haze, rendering virtually any move in national, political, industrial, and financial affairs a hazardous enterprise. But whereas Lamartine nonetheless proposes a nebulous solution, designed to innovate or at least to initiate the "rebirth [of] national activity,"[48] Blanqui responds in a way that demonstrates the difficulties of navigating a space that is saturated or desiccated by capital at every point. In such an environment, new paths for social life could not be assured by taking a blind leap of faith and placing hopes in credit or any other credo. Rather, Blanqui's commentary on Lamartine's discourse suggests—*via negativa*—that novel routes could only ever arrive as the unforseeable possibilities that may emerge after breaking down the unstable platforms and projections of the *status quo*. Exposing the groundlessness of political rhetoric and relations would seem to offer the only chance for a future that would not reduce it to an element of the present, and in this way, Blanqui's critique of Lamartine's poetic politics may also be seen to converge with Marx's answer to revolutionary politics in France, which broaches social issues through critical analyses that neither collapse into circles of inversion nor recycle a repertoire of known social visions: "The social revolution of the nineteenth century cannot draw its poetry from the past, but only from the future."[49]

The alternative to Blanqui's deconstructive approach *avant la lettre* would be to repeat tentatives for conservation, progress, or novelty on the basis of unfounded presuppositions such as national soil that will have already lost their purchase. In a written corpus where capitalist society was imagined as a nebulous cosmos ordered according to natural cycles, it therefore takes no great leap to arrive upon the problem of repetition that would concern Blanqui through to his text from 1872, *Eternity by the Stars*. The recycled nature of Lamartine's proposal, however, is emphasized less in "Lamartine et Rothschild" than in "Discours de Lamartine," a second text that Blanqui devoted to Lamartine's speech. There, Blanqui traces another trajectory through the topoi that Lamartine evokes, this time turning not to Lamartine's voyages to the East, but to Michel Chevalier's westward journey to America, in order to show Lamartine's vision to be an instance of *déjà vu*:

> This discourse is not of today, nor even of yesterday. Behold, we have been hearing it for eighteen years. It is M. Michel Chevalier

who pronounced it first. He had returned from America. There, he was already a witness to the industrial effervescence of a great people who had an entire continent to clear and to plough with routes of vapor. "Make railways!" cried Michel Chevalier. "Precipitate the devouring energy of the country into this path of material activity. Open this issue for the imprisoned floods of lava that trouble the walls of society with their assaults, and that may come to make them burst. The congealed lava becomes fertile fields."

Ce discours n'est pas d'aujourd'hui, ni même d'hier. Voici dix-huit ans que nous l'entendons. C'est M. Michel Chevalier qui l'a prononcé le premier. Il revenait d'Amérique. Il y avait été témoin de l'effervescence industrielle d'un grand peuple qui a tout un continent à défricher et à sillonner de routes à vapeur. "Faites des chemins de fer!" criait Michel Chevalier. "Précipitez dans cette voie de l'activité matérielle la dévorante énergie du pays. Ouvrez cette issue aux flots emprisonnés de la lave qui ébranlent de leurs assauts les parois de la société, et qui vont peut-être la faire éclater. Les laves refroidies deviennent des champs fertiles."[50]

Lamartine replays Chevalier's message on railway constructions, then, with the sole difference that Lamartine presents his plans in analogy to benign weather phenomena, while Chevalier appeals to forces of natural disaster. Nor are the tenets that resonate through Lamartine's proposal and Chevalier's reports from his journey to America exclusive to this pair. For although Chevalier claims to have discovered in the New World the direction that the French government should take—subsidized railways "would be a productive expenditure, and the growth proceeding from the development of transactions and consumption alone would produce for the Treasury [. . .] a sum that is at least equal to the interest of the capital that the government would have consecrated, for its part, to [their] establishment"[51]—members of the National Assembly had also independently promoted the same road to success. Turning to the speeches from a session of the Chambers in 1838 that had addressed the urgency "of undertaking railway networks,"[52] Blanqui paraphrases and parodies these speeches too, chanelling the rhetoric of floods that spills over from Chevalier to Lamartine: " 'Yes!' the monarchic tribune repeated fifteen years ago, 'railways! that is, salaries for the masses, a diversion [*dérivation*] for ideas, an outlet [*déversoir*] for the imaginations, security for the powerful, the actions, the premiums, gold for the world of speculation."⁵³ The future that Lamartine envisions thus turns out to be old news gathered from various reputable or disreputable sources, whose similarities overwhelm the many differences among the persuasions that their authors may have otherwise held.

Hence, Blanqui can already comment upon the outcome of Lamartine's unrealized project: "You have the facts, these railways! They have given work to the proletariat, fortunes to speculators, and gold-fever to the entire nation. They planted the seeds of riches and of ruin too, of enthusiasm and despair."⁵⁴ The construction of railways promises to be not only fundamentally ambivalent, but also an aggravation of the very problems that Lamartine suggests that it would solve, allowing Blanqui to assign new significance to the atmospheric disturbance that Lamartine had associated with socialism: "They [the railways] have spread the miasmas of corruption over France! And these miasmas have not at all been evaporated in the open air in following the therapeutics of Lamartine. They have only condensed into black vapors [. . .]."⁵⁵ Finally, when Blanqui returns at the end of his text to the sun that had figured so prominently in Lamartine's discourse, it is evoked only to illustrate dismal prospects:

> *Nihil sub sole novi!* This is what Lamartine says and proves to us perfectly. Nothing new under the sun! One has discussed much, imagined much in political economy. One has created, praised, combatted many systems. One wanted the new. One believed the new to be necessary upon pain of death. Eh! very well, the new is already old, and it is the old that has become new again.
>
> *Nihil sub sole novi!* nous dit et nous prouve parfaitement Lamartine. Rien de nouveau sous le soleil! On a beaucoup discuté, beaucoup imaginé en économie politique. On a créé, prôné, combattu bien des systèmes. On voulait du nouveau. On croyait le nouveau nécessaire sous peine de mort. Eh! bien, le nouveau est déjà vieux, et c'est le vieux qui est redevenu du neuf.⁵⁶

The journey over railways to questions of capital, labor, and socialism; from the oldest incarnations of wealth to the biggest names of finance; and from primordial vapors to modern steam machines thus culminates in one biblical counter-word to Lamartine's political innovation, namely, the cliché from Ecclesiastes: "There is nothing new under the sun" (Ecc. 1.9). Blanqui thus delivers the news that novelty is one of the oldest desires in the book, and anything but a likely result of Lamartine's proposal.

As a revolutionary by profession, Blanqui was also after a novel society, yet it is precisely for this reason that he refuses to buy into the belief that novelty could be brought about by proposing and executing definitive blueprints for a new establishment. But what these indications of repetition do not expressly address is a possible deviation from the logic of inversion, which could not, Blanqui implies yet again, be sought in the rhetoric of novelty at all costs. In a text from October 1866, "Les sectes et la Révolution," Blanqui expressly states that there is no way to plan the future by building upon the ground plans offered by utopian socialists, or "the founders of new worlds [*les fondateurs de mondes nouveaux*],"[57] anticipating Marx and Engels's similar refusal of such measures in *The Communist Manifesto*: "[t]he theoretical conclusions of the Communists are in no way based on ideas or principles that have been invented, or discovered by this or that would-be universal reformer" (MECW 6: 498).[58] Such plans, Blanqui continues, would amount to "prison-models where their organic pursuers pretend to wall in the future,"[59] nor is Blanqui certain that any decisive movement could be immune to an equal and opposite reaction. All that is certain with regard to capitalism, Blanqui writes, is that "it is an unknown abyss, where one cannot march but with the probe in hand," and that "it is condemned by justice, by sentiment, by all the protestations of human conscience."[60] Whatever might arise after its demolition could only become apparent through "time, groping in the dark, progressive experience, [and] an unknown current."[61] Already in 1850, while imprisoned in Doullens, Blanqui had written similar remarks:

> A revolution determines in the social body an instantaneous labor of reorganization similar to the tumultuous combinations of elements of a dissolved body that tend to recompose in a new form. This labor cannot begin so long as a gasp of life still animates the old aggregation. Thus, the reconstitutive ideas of society will never be embodied so long as a cataclysm, striking the decrepit society dead, will not have liberated the captive elements whose spontaneous and rapid fermentation would need to organize the new world. All the potentials of thought, all the tensions of intelligence would not know to anticipate this creative phenomenon that bursts solely at a given moment. [. . .] Up until the instant of death and renaissance, the doctrines, the

bases of future society, remain in the state of vague aspirations, of distant and vaporous glimpses.[62]

On these terms, the emergence of a new social organization could only occur through the dissolution of known forms and the release of all known and unknown elements into a formative process, which, as such, escapes all schemes of epistemology and ontology that would render its outcome conceivable. To borrow a formulation of Werner Hamacher, revolutionary movements would be "afformative," involved in "the event of forming, itself formless, to which all forms and all performative acts remain exposed."[63] Any revolutionary plot to found a novel society, by contrast, would have to draw upon available organs for action and therefore serve as life support for the system as it currently exists. Thus, the future for Blanqui, like the past for Baudelaire, is interdicted and a question of exposing what takes place between the lines of current diction and dictates. It is for this reason that Blanqui considers "those who pretend to have [. . .] the complete plan of this unknown terrain [*terre inconnue*]" to be "out of their senses."[64] And this characterization would hold valid not only for the utopian socialists, but also for those bourgeois republicans such as Lamartine, who refused to acknowledge the constitutive unclarity of the times in proposing "to separate the true from the false, the shadows from the light [*séparer le vrai du faux, les ténèbres de la lumière*]."[65] Should work proceed—as Blanqui nonetheless insists it should—it therefore cannot be guided by a systematic theory or praxis, but by a deconstructive effort akin to the one that he performs in showing how contemporary political discourse fails to hold together and liquidates itself. The one imperative that he gives therefore calls for a clearing and declines any terms that could solidify into foundational suppositions: "Lower the obstacles, create for it [the current] an inclination, but do not harbor the pretention to create the river."[66] This proposal marks a departure from the channeling efforts of Lamartine and Chevalier, among others: Blanqui takes the atmospheric conditions that they evoke more seriously than they do, and he acknowledges what they indicate *nolens volens*, namely, that politics and society exceed the scope of theory and volition, and that no watershed intervention may be permanent or conclusive. Engels's critique of Blanqui for having "neither socialist theory nor definite practical proposals for social reforms"[67] thus goes only part of the way to elucidate the distinctive feature of Blanqui's writing, where a refusal of method *is* his method, and one that he bases upon the lack of foundations under present conditions.

Blanqui's explicit refusal to establish a "socialist theory" and to provide "definite practical proposals for social reforms" consequently entails a reconsideration of skepticism, which may seem to be the sole viable alternative to ideologies of all kinds. If capital itself "is an unknown abyss, where one cannot march but with the probe in hand,"[68] and if one proceeds only by "groping in the dark,"[69] there would be no clear criterion to decide upon the next step or to provide for the contingencies that one might encounter along the way. Thus, in a note from March 1870 on "Political Economy without Morals," Blanqui uses the same terms to describe the paths of sceptics that he had evoked in his text on revolutionary sects: "[The skeptic] makes way by groping, notices objects individually by touch, but distinguishes nothing, perceiving neither details, nor the ensemble [*Il y chemine à tâtons, constate isolément les objets par le toucher, mais ne distingue rien, n'aperçoit ni détails, ni ensemble*]."[70] Yet Blanqui also indicates where he parts ways from this skeptical procedure: in contrast to a radical isolation of objects that renders each absolved from all others—and therefore indistinct—Blanqui cites justice as "the sole true criterion in [. . .] human matters [*le seul critérium vrai dans [l]es choses humaines*]."[71] This shift from questionable epistemological criteria to the assertion of a juridical criterion may seem to defer the problem of reaching decisions more than it resolves it. But this deferral is no mere subterfuge that substitutes one indefinite term for another, nor is it an arbitrary appeal to ethics over epistemology, which would arguably do no good without any sense for what is or is not (to be done). Recalling the movements of the amorphous and metamorphosing social body that had characterized his descriptions of revolution from 1850, Blanqui renders the vagueness of justice as a necessary consequence of society's indefinite definition: "Justice is the ferment of the social body [*La justice est le ferment du corps social*]."[72] And it is precisely because Blanqui considers justice to be a vital and changing matter—"une vitalité changeante"[73]—that it not only escapes all established and imaginable laws, but also becomes an infinite task that is anything but indifferent. Not even the skeptic could survive turning a blind eye to it,[74] which also is not to say that its extent and movements could fall within the scope of a sovereign individual or legislative power, or contract into a state apparatus, as Jean-Jacques Rousseau had suggested in his formulations for the body politic in *Du contrat social*. The critical problem thus becomes one of approaching the indefinite structure of justice more precisely, but without imposing directives or directions, which would most certainly be bound to fail it.

In its ferment, the social justice for which Blanqui speaks would have to be more and other than any juridical instance within the existing political order, or within any other order that may be envisioned or supposed to come. Nor does Blanqui's evocation of an organic process indicate that justice is grounded in natural rights, which were based upon property since their first formulations, as Lamartine had indicated when he described property as an "expression of nature"—and more precisely, as a "divine principle, as a law of God [. . .], as the constitutive fiber of the nature of man"—before elaborating: "I have traveled much [. . .] I saw the places, studied, observed, and noted the state of even the soil, cities, villages, countrysides, populations, and the result for my spirit was this conviction that the state of the constitution of property in this or that country is the rigorous scale, the exact measure for the perfection or degradation of society in those countries."[75] By contrast, even the notion of a proper person becomes untenable within Blanqui's description of the social body, where "egoism" would self-destruct by "divid[ing] men in order to isolate them [. . .] and giv[ing] birth only to concurrence, war, and [. . .] destruction."[76] The isolation of the "proper" ego dissolves by itself, however, not only because its division from society culminates in destruction, but also because isolation, as Blanqui had said of the sceptic, distinguishes nothing and would therefore extinguish the self in its very act of separation.

Justice is not only beyond law and nature, however; Blanqui also distinguishes the "justice" of the "social body" from general formulae for "civic responsibility."[77] Instead of conforming to fixed schemes for agents, objects, and actions, the "ferment of the social body" demands attention because it cannot be grasped or controlled, and at the same time must be considered before comprehending anything else: "Not to take account of this," Blanqui continues, "is equivalent to closing off one's perspective, depriving oneself of the faculty of comprehending [*N'en tenir compte équivaut à se fermer la perspective, à s'ôter la faculté de comprendre*]."[78] These remarks come no closer to limiting the open-ended issue of justice, but counterpose the ferment (*ferment*) of justice to gestures of self-enclosure (*se fermer*) in a way that shows one of the gravest mistakes within this unsystematic and uninstitutionalized sphere to be precisely the assumption of a fixed and definitive view. Such isolation or self-isolation recalls once again the blindness and indifference that Blanqui associates with skepticism, whereas justice figures as that which remains to be seen, whose maintenance *as* an outstanding task is its only decisive characteristic. Furthermore, as Blanqui's usage of reflexive verbs throughout this passage suggests, the justice in question could be sought only through the efforts on the part of every single member of the social body whose borders remain open to the extent that its continuous fermentation continually decomposes and recomposes them. It is at once a collective and distributive justice that Blanqui bespeaks, then, which departs from the classical notion, "to each his own," and renders individual accountability a matter of taking into account that which cannot be grasped, owned, or known.

Rancière addresses this aspect of Blanqui's commitments in another context, when he writes, with reference to Blanqui's defense speech before the Assize Court in 1832:

> This processing goes beyond any dialogue concerning respective interests as well as any reciprocity of rights and duties. It passes through the constitution of specific subjects that take the wrong upon themselves, give it shape, invent new forms and names for it, and conduct its processing in a specific montage of proofs: "logical" arguments that are at the same time a way of reshaping the relationship between speech and its *account* as well as the perceptible configuration that demarcates the domains and powers of the logos and the *phônê*, the spaces of the visible and the invisible, and articulates these to the allocation of parties and parts. Political subjectification redefines the field of experience that gave to each their identity with their lot. It decomposes and recomposes the relationships between the ways of *doing*, of *being*, and of *saying* that define the perceptible organization of the community.[79]

But another way to formulate Blanqui's non-formulaic notion of justice may also be found in his imperative to "lower obstacles" in "Les sectes et la Révolution," or in his trial speech from 1849, where he appeals to an extra-legal justice that would favor "those thinkers who [. . .] search to discover a promised land in the moving hazes of the horizon," and who proceed in "breaking the path, along the undulations of the soil."[80] Furthermore, for all the moving pathos that a "promised land" may convey, what guides these thinkers' conduct could be no determinate destination if the horizons consist of moving haze and the land itself is undulating; rather, what distinguishes their trajectory, as Blanqui goes on to say, is its divergence from the course of those who remain immobile, as well as those "who would cast [themselves] in a single bound towards the unknown point" and thereby "precipitate [themselves] into the void."[81] Moving in a state between settlement and abyss, solid ground and flooding waters, blindness and clear sight, what is at issue for these voyagers are the operations in speech and comportment that would prepare for novel clearings to emerge. Blanqui's proclamations on justice and revolution offer no news and no judgments, but speak to the distinction that Marx would draw between bourgeois and proletarian revolutions: "There the words went beyond the content; here the content goes beyond the words."[82] For what Blanqui addresses is the ever uncontainable and incomplete task of doing justice that emerges anew with every word and every step, that unsettles the ground of every stance, and that gives revolutionary society a future through its excess over all that may be said and done. Yet if Blanqui's notion of justice thereby goes beyond any content that could be associated with the word, then it would do so in its structural resemblance to the excess of language beyond all that may be uttered or understood by a particular utterance, marking the site where the relationships of "*doing*" and "*being*" may be articulated, disarticulated, and rearticulated.[83]

One passage in which Blanqui most pronouncedly practices the sort of justice that he describes occurs in the series of convolutes that Blanqui had sent to his sister in 1872. These comprise both a work entitled *Capital and Labor*, as well as prose fragments composed between 1849 and 1874.[84] In *Capital and Labor*, Blanqui begins a chapter entitled "Capital and Labor" with an expression of the need to labor toward precision in language, toward what he calls "the just definition [*la définition juste*]":

> The default of precision in language is the worst infirmity of human intelligence. To define is to know. Thus, the just definition is the most rare of merchandise. Knowledge of things measures itself mathematically according to this justness. Where it is lacking, there are shadows. And nowhere is it so radically absent than in economy.

> Le défaut de précision dans le langage est la pire infirmité de l'intelligence humaine. Définir, c'est savoir. Aussi la définition juste est-elle la plus rare des denrées. La connaissance des choses se mesure mathématiquement à cette justesse. Où elle manque, il y a ténèbres. Or, nulle part elle n'est aussi radicalement absente que dans l'économie.[85]

Here, the question of economy is posed in terms of the value or valence of words, but in sentences that can posit nothing to the extent that they deploy a vocabulary of economy and equivalence before a "just definition" has been given for them. By speaking in this manner, Blanqui thus not only suspends the sense of value and the value of words, but also unsettles the status of those words that he will go on to impart, which may not provide "rare merchandise" for his readers in any usual sense of the word, but something else entirely. What this something else may be is not anticipated or stated explicitly here, however, but emerges solely at the end of an analysis of "capital," which is the first word Blanqui examines and shows to default on its promise to convey a definite meaning in contemporary speech. In order to clear up some confusion—in order to do justice to "capital," and eventually, to the problem of economy in linguistic exchanges—Blanqui proceeds to illustrate its obscurities through a dialogue in which "political economy" is cited to speak for "itself."

After briefly recapitulating the most common definition of capital as "accumulated labor [*travail accumulé*]," Blanqui channels the voice of political economy in the following lines:

> When a proletariat, dying of hunger, hurls invectives at this precious lord, political economy coos to him in a paternal tone: "You are capital yourself, my good friend. Do not utter such injuries. [. . .] A lawyer has his tongue for capital; a laborer, his arms; a tailor, her ten fingers [. . .]; and each, his brain [. . .]. Yes, my friend, every man is capital. I am capital, you are capital, your brother is capital, we are all capitals. Let us embrace. If the affair does not work out, who is at fault?"
>
> Quand un prolétaire, crevant la faim, invective ce cher seigneur, l'économie politique lui gazouille d'un ton paterne: "Tu es capital toi-même, mon bon ami. Ne te dis pas d'injures. [. . .] Un avocat a pour capital sa langue, un ouvrier ses bras, une couturière ses dix doigts [. . .], et chacun son cerveau. Oui, mon ami, tout homme est un capital. Je suis capital, tu es capital, ton frère est capital, nous sommes tous capitaux. Embrassons-nous. Si l'affaire ne s'arrange pas, à qui la faute?"[86]

Here, capital identifies itself with personal and professional capacities *per se*, and thus with faculties that it must lack as a fictive talking head. In this respect, the phantasmatic and parasitic character of capital is exposed even more drastically than in the dialogue by Honoré de Balzac that Blanqui seems to adapt here from "L'illustre Gaudissart." In that text, the traveling salesman Gaudissart would similarly equate "vital forces" with the means to make a living as he attempts to promote life insurance, but he is still speaking man to man, and deploying his rhetorical skills to make the most of his time:

> It is no longer a matter of economizing time, but of giving it a price, of numbering it, of representing in pecuniary form the products that you presume to obtain from it within this intellectual space, by representing the moral qualities with which you are endowed, which are [. . .] vital forces, like a waterfall, like a steam engine [. . .].

> Il ne s'agit plus là d'économiser le temps, mais de lui donner un prix, de le chiffrer, d'en représenter pécuniairement les produits que vous présumez en obtenir dans cet espace intellectuel, en représentant les qualités morales dont vous êtes doué et qui sont [. . .] des forces vives, comme une chute d'eau, comme une machine à vapeur [. . .].[87]

Shortly thereafter, Gaudissart will speak explicitly of numerically fixing "votre capital intellectuel,"[88] appealing to a logic of embodied capital that requires statistical mediation,[89] whereas in Blanqui, virtually every property of every person is said to figure immediately as a potential source of capital (or property). Inherent in everyone—except "capital" itself—the transcendent and transcendental constant of capital has more to do with theology in Blanqui's account than numeric logic, and in Blanqui's further elaboration of its Word, this substance of all qualities and accidents accordingly becomes aligned with "the Father," who is incarnated in each "Son" and perpetuated by the "Holy Spirit" that penetrates "each one of us and infuses us with God."[90] In the same spirit, Blanqui adds that this pervasive source or resource of value is not confined to the nature of man, but extends through all of creation *per se*: "It is not only each person," Blanqui continues, "it is also every thing. Fields, meadows and woods, homes, roads and bridges, merchandise, products of every nature, furnitures and quarters [are] always capital, *accumulated labor*."[91]

With each shift in register, which moves from Balzac's prose to Christological patterns, and, ultimately, to pantheism, "capital" expands as the given of all givens and gifts—from raw talent to raw material—that seems to leave no room for critique and should simply be taken for granted. But none of these aspects of capital adds up. As Blanqui points out next, woods and meadows, as well as personal qualities and human limbs, are not products of "accumulated labor," even if they can and do function as "capital." And long before this point, capital was shown to be nothing in itself, while the disparity between the dying "laborer" and the precious "lord" spoke against the *parousia* of capital and its purported source in labor before the voice of "political economy" could so much as utter a word. The gaps between nature and labor, laborer and lord that cleave open within Blanqui's rendition of the language of political economy thus expose the faults in its logic and offer an answer to the question that "political economy" had posed in the beginning: "If the affair does not work out, who is at fault?" For if capital can accumulate without labor, and laborers do without capital to the point where their work costs them their lives, then "capital and labor" are not exchangeable terms, and capital could never have operated as the exchange of equivalents. Instead, accumulation could only occur when what is gained is not traded, and when natural and personal capacities are exploited; and as Blanqui goes on to argue, it is owing to such "lacunae of exchange" that the laborer becomes placed "at the mercy of the capitalist" who can work him to death.[92] Following the immanent logic and language of political economy thus shows capital to be not "accumulated labor," but "stolen labor [*travail volé*]."[93] Such is its "just definition," its judgment, and its condemnation in this text.

At first, this instance of a "just definition" may be more definitive than Blanqui's insistence upon the open-ended character of justice had suggested; however, the procedure that he carries out is anything but conclusive, when it comes to the future of "capital." After working through the rhetorical obscurity that is employed to occlude the workings of finance, Blanqui arrives at a reading of current discourse that displaces its operative terms and discloses the holes in its self-justification, so as to open society and economy as issues that remain to be decided. Hence, Blanqui ends his essay with questions:

> Is the human race avowed to perpetual exploitation? [. . .] Will the future find its way towards mutualism, or towards integral association, that is, towards community? Here the demonstration stops and conjectures begin. The problem that is thus posed does not unite a sufficient number of givens for a mathematical

solution. All of the anxieties of our time pertain to the current impossibility of disengaging the unknown.

> Le genre humain est-il voué à l'exploitation perpétuelle? [. . .] L'avenir trouvera-t-il sa voie dans le mutuellisme, ou dans l'association intégrale, c'est-à-dire dans la communauté? Ici s'arrête la demonstration et commencent les conjectures. Le problème posé ne réunit pas encore les données suffisantes pour une solution mathématique. Toutes les angoisses de notre temps tiennent à l'impossibilité actuelle de dégager l'inconnue.[94]

With this, the correlate to Blanqui's analytic precision is therefore an imprecision that differs from the one that had subsisted before. The aporia to which Blanqui's definition of capital leads marks the point where conjectures can begin, but where none may be justified on the basis of the givens. Since, however, Blanqui's exposition will have already liberated the capacities that had been identified with capital in its popular definition, his text demonstrates one way in which revolutionary efforts could, as he had written in his text from 1850, "liberate[] the captive elements whose spontaneous and rapid fermentation would need to organize the new world."[95] Definitional "precision" here cuts open current concepts at least as much as it describes their limits, and it yields no precious "merchandise,"[96] but releases free goods from the hold that capital had claimed to have over all of human and inanimate nature. As far as further labor on "capital" may go, Blanqui also gives at least one indication as to how it may proceed justly without forming premature judgments. As Blanqui puts it in the final paragraph of his text, "dementia is the beginning of the end [*[l]a démence est le commcement de la fin*]."[97] And with this remark, he implies that minding the symptoms of capital's faulty reasoning—of its incapacity to grasp itself—exposes not only its imminent demise, but also the strength of another, inchoate current in contemporary thought, and perhaps the emergence of another economy in its midst. The task of analysis is therefore to be continued, which forms the only conclusion and imperative that Blanqui offers: "Let us continue to show it at work [*Continuons de le montrer à l'oeuvre*]."[98]

Although Blanqui had also organized and fought from the barricades during his career as a professional revolutionary;[99] and although he had composed a toast to the provisional government of the Second Republic, proclaiming "arms and organization" to be the sole "decisive element of progress;"[100] the justice he pursues in "Capital and Labor" is sought in the uncharted, unchartable, and shifting fields of language, which may alter as we speak and therefore escape definitive grasp at all times. Similarly to Baudelaire's trajectory in "Le Voyage," Blanqui's writings begin upon a *terra incognita* from the outset; they expose the unsettled terms of socioeconomic theses; and they open to unknowns in lieu of closure. As Benjamin puts it in *The Arcades Project*, most likely with reference to *Eternity by the Stars*: "With Blanqui, the cosmos has become an abyss."[101] But when Benjamin contrasts this abyss to the space that opens within Baudelaire's oeuvre, stating that the latter "is a secularized space: the abyss of knowledge and of meanings,"[102] he underemphasizes the many ways in which Blanqui likewise seeks to sound out a social and global atmosphere that is "vague, nebulous, multiform [*vague, nuageuse, multiforme*],"[103] or that is simply "an unknown abyss, where one cannot march but with the probe in hand."[104] Such metaphorical and meteorological topoi are where Blanqui and his political opponents such as Lamartine meet—along with poets such as Balzac, Baudelaire, and de Vigny—but without coming together or going on to establish a firmer foundation.

It is also in coming to terms with the Blanqui's strategies of citation, decomposition, and recomposition that elements such as novelty, repetition, and nebulosity in *Eternity by the Stars* become legible as components of his ongoing revolutionary interventions in language.[105] Rather than representing a radical turn from the issues of justice that are raised in his political writings, the discussion of comets, stars, planets, and cosmic cycles in Blanqui's cosmological hypothesis exposes the furthest consequences of current rhetoric on the nature of capital, and in pursuing this rhetoric to its utmost limits in *Eternity by the Stars*, Blanqui gestures toward that which would exceed its compass and concepts. At first, of course, at least as much appears to speak against novel possibilities in this text as in the defense speech of capital in "Capital and Labor." In *Eternity by the Stars*, more than everything imaginable returns in a seemingly unbroken and unbreakable cycle. Given the infinity of space and the limited number of chemical elements, every possible combination thereof must not only exist, but also repeat *ad infinitum*. As a result, nature as a whole would consist of "*type-combinations*, whose endless *repetitions*" simultaneously "fill up space;"[106] and among these combinations, the globe of mankind would likewise manifest "her own rightful infinity in time and space. Each of our body-doubles is the child of an earth and each earth is the body-double of the actual earth."[107] Each earth would pass through rounds of development and extinction, while life would be perpetually renewed by the collisions of astral bodies that volatize them, until gravity eventually "gathers them into nebulae sent spinning by the shock, and assigns them a regular course around new centers."[108] At the same time, each human being would not only have at all times "complete body-doubles," but would also be multiplied by the "innumerable number of variations who [. . .] always represent his person, but who borrow only scraps of his destiny." This human condition leads to the further conclusion: "We are, somewhere else, everything that we could have been down here. In addition to our whole life, to our birth and death, which we experience on a number of earths, we also live ten thousand different versions of it on other earths."[109] Hence, "every second will bring its new bifurcation, the road taken and the road that could have been taken."[110] These are the basic premises of the text that have led to its interpretation as a meditation on the world of technological reproducibility, as Eduardo Cadava has argued;[111] as a sign of ultimate resignation, as Benjamin once asserted;[112] and as the affirmation of possible worlds and infinite future bifurcations in human history, as Rancière and Hallward have suggested more recently.[113]

But Benjamin also read this apparent capitulation to capital as one that makes its throne "totter," or "wanken,"[114] indicating that the complexities of Blanqui's text solicit ongoing analysis in order to do justice to its unsettling force. One instance of instability can be found in the variable iterations of every constellation of atomic elements—from astral to human matters—which imply that "what is reproduced is exactly the process whereby what is reproduced is also altered,"[115] as Cadava observes. But as a further consequence of Blanqui's hypothesis, the innumerable variants of every body split each so-called "body-double" into a multitude of "partial infinites," where every one figures as a member in an infinite series of variants among variants that merely partially resemble one another. Thus, no subject of reproduction could ever have been one to be simply duplicated, but will have always been infinitely divisible and divided, and therefore a composite of recycled parts that no infinity of reproductions will complete: "All those systems with all their variations and all their *repetitions* make up innumerable series of partial infinites that dissolve into the great infinite like rivers dissolve into the ocean [*Tous ces systèmes, toutes ces variantes et leurs répétitions forment d'innombrables séries d'infinis partiels, qui vont s'engouffrer dans le grand infini, comme les fleuves dans l'océan*]."[116] On these terms, the one thing that could not be in the expanse of all possible worlds, then, is one fully realized person, who would have to comprise all possible variants combined, which also partially exclude one another and therefore cannot have coalesced so much as once. Thus, the supposedly unitary status of every entity is dissolved *a priori* in *Eternity by the Stars* through a more radical analysis of property and proper persons than can be found in even Blanqui's sharpest crtiqiues of egoism and capitalism. And in this respect, Blanqui shows the universe itself to be revolutionary in precisely the sense that he had indicated in his text from 1850, where the revolution was said to take place as "the tumultuous combinations of elements of a dissolved body that tends to recompose itself in a new form."[117]

This partial resonance between Blanqui's presentation of the cosmos and his earlier description of revolution indicates, moreover, that when everything returns in *Eternity by the Stars*, elements and variants of Blanqui's earlier texts return as well in ways that open their terms to alteration and redefinition. Yet because the dynamic of repeated alteration should be universal, it would have to affect not only Blanqui's earlier writings, but also the language of *Eternity by the Stars*. Nothing in his version of the cosmos works if not by operating with the concepts of infinity and infinite iterability, which repetitions in his text would therefore seem to emphasize and illustrate. When Blanqui reiterates phrases in his text, however, he annuls rather than redoubles the evidence for his arguments, in repeating nothing less than his claim on the insufficiency of language to convey the numbers and proportions of the infinite: "In the beginning, we said: 'Let every word be the enunciation of the most frightening of distances, one would speak billions and billions of centuries, talking at a rate of one word per second, in order to express in sum nothing but an insignificance, from the moment it is a matter of the infinite' [*n'exprimer en somme qu'une insignifiance, dès qu'il s'agit de l'infini*]."[118] And what goes for words also goes for worlds, allowing Blanqui to conclude, by analogy: "the thousands of *differing* variations of the earth would not be but a point in space [*ne seraient qu'un point dans l'espace*]."[119] This means, however, not only that his writing cannot but be inadequate to that which it seems to recount and account for, but also that each infinite manifold of the cosmos becomes itself an insignificant quantum, which is comparable to the extension—and, more precisely, to the non-extension—of a single point. This text on infinity risks addressing what is nothing to speak of: the further Blanqui goes to portray the immensity of cosmic spaces, the more they paradoxically seem to be without dimensions.[120]

The point of Blanqui's meditations therefore cannot be the affirmation of infinite repetition, which could neither be affirmed nor denied if all the words in the world fail to express it or so much as approximate it. Instead, the "infinite" or the indefinite serve at most as provisional and heuristic terms, bringing Blanqui's science more within the orbit of Edgar Allan Poe's cosmological "prose-poem" *Eureka* than that of Laplace's *Exposition du système des mondes*. Especially when Blanqui writes:

> If, out of concern about our *Indefinite*, Chicanery vainly attempts to force us to understand the *Infinite* and to explain it, let us refer it to the Jupiterians, who are surely endowed with a larger brain than us. [. . .] This expression is nothing but our attempt to conceive of the *Infinite*. One adds space to space, and the mind comes easily to the conclusion that it is limitless.[121]

> Que si la chicane, à cheval sur l'*Indéfini*, nous cherche des querelles d'allemand pour nous [contraindre à] comprendre et [à] lui expliquer l'*Infini*, nous la renverrons aux jupitériens, pourvus sans doute d'une plus grosse cervelle. [. . .] C'est connu et l'on ne tente que sous cette forme de concevoir l'*Infini*. On ajoute l'espace à l'espace, et la pensée arrive fort bien à cette conclusion qu'il est sans limites.[122]

His language in this passage displays a striking affinity with that of Poe's text: " 'Infinite' [. . .], like 'God,' 'spirit' [. . .], is by no means the expression of an idea—but of an effort at one. It stands for the possible attempt at an impossible conception,"[123] which Charles Baudelaire had translated as follows: "Le mot *infini*, comme les mots *Dieu*, *esprit* [. . .] est, non pas l'expression d'une idée, mais l'expression d'un effort vers une idée. Il représente une tentative possible vers une conception impossible."[124] This is not to say that Blanqui's commentary on mathematics and astronomy is merely a parody or pleasantry: "All of this, joking aside, is very serious," he insists: "It [. . .] is a matter of mathematics and positive facts."[125] But it is serious, not because mathematics and positive facts are earnest matters *per se*, but because they lead to a serious dilemma when they are thought through to their ultimate consequences and seen to result in absurdities rather than models for making sense of the world.

This situation entails devastating consequences not only for the significance of astronomical science and probability calculations, but also for the science of political economy, whose major proponents also operate repeatedly with the notion of infinity in presenting their calculations and projections. In his pamphlet from 1849, "Gratuité du crédit," for example, Frédéric Bastiat had affirmed the theoretically perpetual installation of economic inequities through recourse to two recurring cycles. The laborer who consumes his earnings regularly, writes Bastiat, remains as poor as ever, year after year: "When New Year's Eve arrives, he does not find himself any more advanced than on the first of the year, and his sole perspective is to recommence [*recommencer*] [. . .] he is always at the point of departure."[126] By contrast, the landholding capitalist who collects rent "consumes during the year the rent of the year," and "has, the next year, the following year, and during all eternity, a rent that is always equal, inexhaustible, *perpetual* [*perpétuelle*]. Capital is thus remunerated not once or twice, but an indefinite number of times!"[127] According to Blanqui's reasoning in *Eternity by the Stars*, such a scenario is *a priori* inconceivable, and after copying these passages in *Capital and Labor*, Blanqui will also argue against Bastiat's rationale, demonstrating that the supposed continuity of landed wealth springs from a rupture in equitable exchange. The gap grows, moreover, as the accumulation of means on the parts of the privileged allows them to profit from lending or renting to laborers without laboring themselves.[128] The self-perpetuating cycles of which Bastiat speaks are thereby shown to be a myth that masks by imaginary means the historical—and therefore changeable—genesis of economic disparity.[129] Blanqui responds by rhetorically emphasizing the mythic character of capital, presenting it elsewhere in *Capital and Labor* as the inversion of the Danaids' punishment in Hades, where they were eternally condemned to fill barrels full of holes: "The barrels will refill themselves [. . .]."[130] Hence, when the same terms return in *Eternity by the Stars* to illustrate the infinite wealth of nature—which is as immoral or amoral as capital—they exaggerate, among other things, the way in which the grounds for capital and rent are fictive, bottomless, and ethically abysmal to the same extent that they function as sources of plenitude: "Nature neither knows nor practices morality. [. . .] She works blindfolded, destroys, creates, transforms. [. . .] When there is nothing left in the sack, she opens the repetition box, a bottomless barrel this one, which never runs out, as opposed to the barrel of the Danaids, which could never be filled."[131] And ultimately, in presenting the infinite resources of nature as an inversion of the Danaid-myth, Blanqui also indicates yet another way in which all talk of infinity finishes in self-contradiction, for the operations of nature would have to defy all known laws of nature, as well as all comprehension, if nature is to fulfill her task. The positive mathematical and scientific premises Blanqui sets forth in *Eternity by the Stars* collapse into a mythic "vision of hell," where, as Benjamin had said, lived experience resembles the repetitive labors of Sisyphus and the Danaids.[132] But Blanqui also turns the underworld upside down through his writing and exposes the holes of hell so as to break its circles and cycles.

Beyond repeatedly demonstrating the inadequacy of language to infinite quanta in *Eternity by the Stars*, Blanqui points out other astronomical contradictions in the nature of capital by way of cosmological speculations. Returning once more to his earlier formulation of revolution as dissolution, for example, Blanqui writes that "[t]he stellar systems finish and then begin again [*recommencent*] with similar elements that they obtain thanks to new alliances and to the indefatigable mechanisms of the reproduction of identical copies drawn from various ruins," and he adds that this movement occurs as a "perpetual exchange [*échange perpétuelle*]."[133] Once again, perpetuity is at issue; this time, however, the recommencement of natural production depends upon a notion of "perpetual exchange" where nothing is retained and nothing returns to itself—where nothing is perpetuated—while conversely, the accumulation of matter amounts to nothing but ruins.[134] Thus, the notions of exchange and perpetuity, so crucial to capital, turn out to be incommensurable with it and with each other in a manner that renders vitality and productivity contingent upon the dispossession of resources. And in another exemplary passage, Blanqui even recurs to the cycles of cloud formation that had characterized Lamartine's depictions of capital, so as to bring them to burst. Comparing the succession of suns in infinite time and space to rain, Blanqui draws together the two weather phenomena that Lamartine had once confused in his attempt to illustrate the fecundity of credit: "What are those billions of suns that succeed each other throughout time & space? A deluge of sparkles. This rain fertilizes the universe [*Que sont ces milliards de soleils se succédant à travers les siècles et l'espace? Une pluie d'étincelles. Cette pluie féconde l'univers*]."[135] Here, the suns rain down to dispense and disperse their capacities, which they take from nothing and give without holding anything back. What they offer, then, is an *an*economic version of the precipitation that Lamartine had evoked in his metaphorical elevation of stellar bankers such as Rothschild. In all of these ways and more, the eternal possibilities and realities described in *Eternity by the Stars* have their correlate not in mechanical reproduction, nor even in capitalist production, but indefinitely exceed the framework of every system by breaking it down and liberating its elements. In the exaggerated form of a cosmology that borrows its language from Laplace, as well as the advocates of finance, Blanqui brings their logic to its extremes and its collapse. This is how the throne of capital, as Benjamin also puts it, begins to "totter" in and through Blanqui's text.[136] And if the revolutionary critique of society in *Eternity by the Stars* thus resembles the one that Blanqui had pursued more directly in *Capital and Labor*, the incredibility of dominant economic theory and practice becomes most apparent, perhaps, when the nature of production is transposed to the realm of natural science and stretched beyond belief—which Blanqui stresses: "So many identical populations have come to pass without having suspected each other's existence! Well, not really: this shared existence is discovered at last in the 19th century. *But who shall believe it? [Mais qui voudra y croire?]*."[137]

The cosmological system that Blanqui presents is incommensurable with those texts composed by socialist utopists such as Charles Fourier, who sought to trace analogical alignments between the social and natural orders and to work out their implications for the further developments of society.[138] Blanqui lays no new foundation for understanding the nature of society and proposes nothing new for the future at this point. In this respect, as he says in *Eternity by the Stars* and in his "Discours de Lamartine," there is still "nothing new under the suns."[139] Yet it is in *Eternity by the Stars* where Blanqui goes furthest in following the imperative that he had uttered in his text from 1866, "Les sectes et la Révolution": "Lower the obstacles, create [. . .] an inclination [for the current]."[140] For it is in this text that the most elementary principles and rigid orders for human and cosmic matters alike are liquidated and channeled elsewhere, in ways that deviate from their purposes of perpetuating the current economic and social system. And ultimately, even the elements prove to be unstable and incalculable within Blanqui's cosmological hypothesis. For when it comes to establishing these basic components of natural products, their number— which forms the common denominator for all subsequent calculations and deductions in *Eternity by the Stars*—is said to be certain only for now: "Until further notice [*jusqu'à nouvel ordre*]," Blanqui writes, "nature has at its disposal the 64 *simple* bodies named below."[141] Similarly, the supposed simplicity of these elements holds true only for the present: "They are called *simple bodies*, because hitherto [*jusqu'à présent*], they have been found to be irreducible."[142] But if it is true, as Blanqui thereby suggests, that the most elementary truths of positive science may be uncertain and provisional, from the elements through to the expanses of space and time, then anything and everything in the world remains subject to "further notice." If nothing else, the news and the promise of Blanqui consists of this "until further notice," which renders the *status quo* on a cosmic and global scale a matter that may turn out to be a temporary and transitory arrangement at any time. It is in this way that Blanqui does justice to the inconclusiveness of the world, from the heights of the stars down to the minutest particles of matter. The cosmic trajectory that Blanqui traces does not exhaust the compass of infinite space, but zeroes in on those points where the parameters for grasping anything, from the infinitely great to infinitesimally small, are nullified.

Yet true to this methodless method, Blanqui also goes further to announce at least one sign of an element "in the moving hazes of the horizon" that already exceeds the terms of the current order.[143] For he provides a glimpse of one phenomenon that gives the "nothing" of "nothing new under the sun" a new sense: namely, the comets, or those astronomical phenomena that accord in no way with the account of the cosmos that is given in the otherwise comprehensive system of Laplace. Unlike the positive descriptions of astral bodies that Blanqui sets forth and breaks down, Blanqui proceeds *via negativa* from the outset in his discussion of the comets:

> Comets are neither ether, nor gas, nor liquid, nor solid, nor in any way akin to any of the substances found in the celestial bodies, but they are made of an undefinable substance, which appears to have none of the properties of known matter [. . .]. Between the sidereal enigma that is a comet and the stellar systems that constitute the universe, there is a radical separation. They are two isolated modes of existence, two fully distinct categories of matter with no link than the disorderly action of a near-insane gravity. There is no reason to include the comets in a description of the world. They are nothing. They do nothing, and their only role is that of an enigma.
>
> Les comètes ne sont ni de l'éther, ni du gaz, ni un liquide, ni un solide, ni rien de semblable à ce qui constitue les corps célestes, mais une substance indéfinissable, ne paraissant avoir aucune des propriétés de la matière connue [. . .]. Entre cette énigme sidérale et les systèmes solaires qui sont l'univers, radicale séparation. Ce sont deux modes d'existence isolés, deux catégories de la matière totalement distinctes, et sans autre lien qu'une gravitation désordonnée, presque folle. Dans la description du monde, il n'y a nul compte à en tenir. Elles ne sont rien, ne font rien, n'ont qu'un rôle, celui d'énigme.[144]

The comets are "nothing," then, but it is precisely in not mattering—in all senses of the word—that the comets are also a *novem* that troubles the solidity and foundation of all things under the sun. For their very appearance gives evidence for the fundamental incompletion and insufficiency of all total and totalizing explanations of the cosmos to date. For this reason, their enigmatic role in the universe renders them indefinitely significant, in contrast to the "insignificance" of the infinite sums of matter and space that Blanqui would discuss before and after them.

Among their possible meanings, Blanqui elaborates one that bears political implications when he draws an analogy between the comet and the genie in a bottle from the *Thousand and One Nights*. The comet, he continues, is "like some giant from the *Thousand and One Nights*, bottled up by Solomon, and occasionally venturing little by little out of its prison, to regain human form, before being vaporized again and sucked back into the neck of the bottle."[145] At the same time, moreover, the dynamics of vaporization and compression that Blanqui evokes in this context echo his remarks on the revolution in 1835: "The sympathies of the masses, refreshed [*retrempées*] by a system of terror, reawaken [*se réveillent*] more vivid; it is a resilience [*ressort*] rendered [*rendu*] more energetic by compression and that demands only to defend itself."[146] But whether the comet is more like the legendary genie in a bottle or the suppressed revolutionary masses—or like something else entirely—this figure may be seen as an abiding threat to those who would seek and even succeed to contain it.

For all that may be said of cosmic order, then, it is under the enigmatic sign of the comets that Blanqui points beyond the failure of the system to hold together and to encompass all things in its economy of creation, destruction, exploitation, and exhaustion. The comets may even stand as evidence for the possibility of communism, distantly echoing and distorting Lamartine's words before the Legislative Assembly on 9 April 1850: "Very well! let us not fear, we men of the State; we who have the habit of envisaging with a slightly more piercing and firm regard the doctrines that traverse the horizon of humanity like comets, and who are going to lose themselves in the inaccessible regions of utopia."[147] For despite this prediction, Blanqui shows the comets to remain, until further notice, on the horizon and to hover as a testimony to the limits of the most far-reaching and penetrating theoretical and economic visions. With the comets, Blanqui's revolutionary language leaves a place for the nothing that may yet be new under the sun. It leaves off, that is, with a sign that the days of *Eternity by the Stars*—as well as the eternal returns of capital—might be, in the end, numbered.

4

Atomizing the *Communist Manifesto*

In the middle of Convolute D, "Boredom, Eternal Return," Benjamin notes: "Analogy between Engels and Blanqui: each turned to the natural sciences late in life."[1] Like Blanqui, Friedrich Engels looked to the stars after the fall of the Paris Commune, arguing in the introduction to his unfinished *Dialectic of Nature* for the revolutionary nature of Pierre-Simon Laplace's system.[2] Parting ways with the notion that "[t]he stars remained for ever fixed [. . .] in their places [. . .] by 'universal gravitation' "—and troubling the assumption that "everything was as it had been from the beginning and [. . .] would remain as it had been since the beginning"—Laplace had introduced "the discovery of the proper motion of the fixed stars, the demonstration of a resistant medium in universal space, the proof furnished by spectral analysis of the chemical identity of the matter of the universe and of the existence of such glowing nebular masses as Kant had postulated."[3] With this, Engels claims, the conception began to dawn that "nature does not just exist, but *comes into being* and *passes away*," as the cosmologists of Ancient Greece had also maintained, when they held the world to be "something that had emerged from chaos, something that had developed, that had come into being" (MECW 25: 324, 324). This theory may entail, as a consequence, that the "world is going to end,"[4] as Baudelaire once wrote, or, as Engels puts it: "the time will come when the declining warmth of the sun will no longer suffice to melt the ice thrusting itself forward from the poles; when the human race, crowding more and more about the equator, will finally no longer find even there enough heat for life" (MECW 25: 331–32). But it also follows that "the eternally repeated succession of worlds in infinite time" is "the logical complement to the coexistence of innumerable worlds in infinite space" (MECW 25: 334).

These remarks promise an upturn to every real or imaginable catastrophe, a permanent revolution where even the worst case turns out not to end badly. For the time being, however, the significance of these scientific developments for Engels lies in the evidence that they provide for the historical nature of all things. Hence, in the interval between his meditations on Laplace and his conclusion on the "eternal cycle in which matter moves," Engels challenges the supposedly fixed laws of social and economic life as well, and calls into question the eternal condition of struggle that Charles Darwin had maintained "when he showed that free competition, the struggle for existence, which the economists celebrate as the highest historical achievement, is the normal state of the *animal kingdom*" (MECW 25: 344, 331). Just as "the whole of nature, from the smallest element to the greatest, from grains of sand to suns, from Protista to man, has its existence in eternal coming into being and passing away, in ceaseless flux, in unresting motion and change," so too would "social production" be "subject to the interplay of unintended effects from uncontrolled forces" (MECW 25: 327). Even if it were to prove true that competition once operated productively in the evolution of various species, then, it could not subsist permanently as the basis for production in society or as the primary factor in the further evolution of life forms. In principle, Engels thus clears the ground for alternative social and natural arrangements by undermining the foundational assumptions of the present. According to the same reasoning, however, nothing could be less certain than Engels's conclusion that the "conscious organisation of social production, in which production and distribution are carried on in a planned way, can lift mankind above the rest of the animal world as regards the social aspect" (MECW 25: 331). Instead, the atomistic premises that Engels hazards would unsettle all positive plans to replace the *status quo* by exposing them to factors beyond all volition and control, in turn. Whatever they may also have said to the contrary, in other words, the philosophy of nature espoused by Blanqui and Engels exposes the natural and social world alike to be "an unknown abyss, where one cannot march but with the probe in hand," and where provisions for the future cannot but be blind to what could come of them.[5]

Finding a place for revolutionary intervention becomes a problem when the field of possibilities cannot be surveyed and no foundations can be assumed. This problem extends well beyond Blanqui's and Engels's oeuvres, to the major formulations of Marxist theory in the twentieth century. Under the subheading, "Practical Solution and Theoretical Problem. Why Theory?" Louis Althusser describes the practical task of distinguishing "the

Marxist dialectic from the Hegelian dialectic" according to a positional topology whose coordinates remain problematic:

> To say that it is a theoretical *problem* implies that we are not dealing merely with an imaginary difficulty, but with a really existing difficulty posed us in the form of a *problem*, that is in a form governed by imperative conditions: definition of the field of (theoretical) knowledges in which the problem is posed (situated), of the exact *location* of its posing, and of the concepts required to pose it.[6]

> Dire que c'est un *problème* théorique, implique qu'il ne s'agit pas d'une simple difficulté imaginaire, mais d'une difficulté réellement existante posée sous forme de problème, c'est-à-dire sous une forme soumise à des conditions impératives: définition du champ de connaissances (théoriques) dans lequel on pose (situe) le problème; du *lieu* exact de sa position; des concepts requis pour le poser.[7]

As far as Althusser's historical science may be from the cosmological speculations of Blanqui and Engels, his rhetoric of positions renders the thought of revolutionary theory and practice contingent upon a shifting spatial order that shapes Althusser's discussions of the historical, geographical, economic, and ideological contexts that define the horizons for theoretical work.[8] And as in Blanqui's and Engels's appeals to natural science, Althusser's recourse to topology bears political implications, situating theoretical and practical activities within a field that is, in turn, to be defined through them. Althusser's remarks also imply, however, that space does not figure as a homogeneous continuum, but may divide among multiple, differently structured problem areas, whose condition of possibility is the logic or language of *topoi*, positions, and positing. This language, in turn, cannot itself be circumscribed by the spatial orders and limits that it sets, rendering "space" an indefinite issue. Thus, Althusser's discussion of theoretical problems makes room for at least one further problem that he does not name directly: namely, the real problem of situating space in speech, which cannot be broached without addressing the broader question of the language for positions and movements. This unposed question insists each time that the "couple" or "opposition" of theory and practice is evoked to intervene "not only in all of the classical problems of theory and experience, [. . .] but also in the problems that surge up between the ensemble of scientific research, determined as a theoretical-technical ensemble, and the field of political practice, political-economical practice," as Jacques Derrida observes in the seminar he gave in 1975–76 on *Théorie et pratique*.[9] Especially if space is conceived not as a physical or natural arena, but as a function of social dynamics, the problem that comes beyond or before any "field" would be that of "the ordinary usage of language, the whole problematic [. . .] of the 'performative' and of speech acts, not to mention the practical consequences of all sorts that a theoretical language may have."[10]

Blanqui addresses this issue in his critique of the going definition of capital, and in his *reductio ad absurdum* of infinite and infinitesimal matters on a cosmic scale. Althusser speaks to the problem that language poses to the operative terms that he adopts as well, when he cautions against the assumption that theoretical language translates in any straightforward way to other areas of praxis: "the utilization of Theory is not a matter of *applying* its formulae (the formulae of the dialectic, of materialism) to a pre-existing content."[11] Theoretical transfer would instead have to transform the knowledge of its content, and thus the object of its knowledge, altering the field in which it would organize praxis. But this condition for theoretical intervention, which entails an exhaustive "analysis of the structure of the field, of the object [. . .] of the specific raw material of political practice in general,"[12] may turn out, at times, to be impractical. Thus, Althusser also acknowledges that an imprecise theory with an imprecise relation to other fields of activity may nonetheless "be endowed with a certain *practical* meaning, serving as a reference point or index [. . .] 'in the interests of popularization' [. . .] not only in pedagogy, but also in struggle."[13] Such a premature propagation of theory may even be necessary, if his assertion is true that "the moment in which a 'theory' feels the need for the Theory of its own practice [. . .] always occurs *post festum*, to help it surmount practical or 'theoretical' difficulties, resolve problems insoluble for the movement of practice immersed in its activities and therefore theoretically blind."[14] This acknowledgment is tantamount to admitting, however, that theory would always arrive too soon or too late to grasp where it stands and that each of its constative utterances would in fact be a performative issued by those who know not what they do.

In any event, the spaces of theory and practice that Althusser delineates appear to blend into one another in ways that render the description of their relation itself an insoluble problem, which is perhaps why, when Derrida addresses the "couple" or "opposition" of "theory/practice," the conjunction of the two oscillates between coordination and disjunction.[15] The difficulties of theory and/or practice redouble in an especially pronounced way, however, when it comes to the words for opposition "itself," where positing becomes indefinitely displaced through the ambivalence of those very prepositions that should indicate its direction. The German word "gegen," for example, may describe tendencies "against" and "towards"; a state of opposition (*Gegensatz*) or the stance of an object (*Gegenstand*); an area (*Gegend*) or its surroundings (*in der Gegend von*); the direction of a desire or aim (*gegen*); an interlocutor (*Gegenüber*) or an opponent (*Gegner*).[16] "Gegen" is at once *pro* and *contra* and more—which is also why it can characterize the *quid pro quo* of exchanges when this and that are traded "against" one another. But this is not to say that the divergent and even opposed tendencies denoted by "gegen"—in theory and practice—are themselves exchangeable. Instead, its many usages suggest that the demarcation of an opposition cannot but cross (its) lines—especially when it is a question of language, be it the language for a particular opposition, the language of topologies, the language of address, or, in a word: "gegen." If revolutionary interventions should address opposition and positions, language can thus be seen to come between agent and action, speaker and addressee, so as to dispose every move within a practical course or theoretical discourse to unpredictable deviations. Speaking with or against any "Gegenüber" or "Gegner" could only take place in such a way where no position or preposition could be definitively assigned a place or direction, but where every word would, as Engels had written with regard to the nature of society, be "subject to the interplay of unintended effects from uncontrolled forces" (MECW 25: 327). As the many senses of "gegen" alone indicate, the orientation and practical outcome of any address would have to be indeterminable, whether or not it is conceived as a preliminary or conclusive announcement, rendering address the blind spot of theoretical elaboration, whose every move would be a "movement of practice immersed in its activities and therefore theoretically blind."[17]

At the same time, however, the ambivalent countertendencies of positional language would also render speech and writing critical moments where the topologies of theory and practice may undergo the most radical upheaval. Over the course of his seminar, Derrida traces the thoroughgoing displacement of "theory" and "practice" in Althusser's "discourse," calling it "an act, a political gesture, a practice, and this is no longer a purely theoretical language, nor even an essentially theoretical practice."[18] The same could be said of Marx's oeuvre, which repeatedly and explicitly speaks to the opposition between theory and practice in addresses to interlocutors and opponents that fundamentally trouble the status of philosophy and action. Hence, Derrida describes Marx's oeuvre as an "event [that] is at once singular, total, and uneffaceable" in *Specters of Marx*,[19] and Étienne Balibar claims that "after Marx, philosophy is no longer as it was before."[20] But if it is true that Marx's writings introduce a *novum* in theory and practice, they also provoke the question as to where and when this intervention may have occurred, and what it may mean for articulating the "where" and "when" of any revolutionary occurrence. To broach these questions, this chapter traverses several passages in which Marx addresses theory and practice and practices theory to address, where the moves that he makes do not align with a position in any given field, but are *pre*positional in ways that revolutionize the nature of social space.

Long before the "epistemological break" that Althusser locates between Marx's early "philosophical (ideological) conscience,"[21] and his turn to historical materialism in *The German Ideology*, Marx had given thought to a different sort of rupture that takes place when philosophy breaks off from theoretical activity and turns toward worldly praxis, toward "a task of philosophy which would not be it itself" (MECW 1: 496, MEGA 4.1: 105). In the fifth of his notebooks on Epicurean philosophy, he writes in 1839:

> As in the history of philosophy there are nodal points which raise philosophy in itself to concretion, apprehend abstract principles in a totality, and thus break off the rectilinear process, so also there are moments when philosophy turns its eyes to the external world, and no longer comprehending, but, as a practical person, weaves, as it were, intrigues with the world, emerges from the transparent kingdom of Amenthes and throws itself on the breast of the worldly Siren. That is the carnival of philosophy, whether it disguises itself as a dog like the Cynic, in priestly vestments like the Alexandrian, or in fragrant spring array like the Epicurean. It is essential that philosophy should then wear character masks. (MECW 1: 491)

> Wie es in der Philosophiegeschichte Knotenpunkte giebt, die sie in sich selbst zur Konkretion erheben, die abstrakten Prinzipien in eine Totalität befassen, und so den Fortgang der graden Linie abbrechen, so giebt es auch Momente, in welchen die Philosophie die Augen in die Aussenwelt kehrt, nicht mehr begreifend, sondern als eine praktische Person gleichsam Intriguen mit der

Welt spinnt, aus dem Durchsichtigen Reiche des Amenthes heraustritt und sich ans Herz der weltlichen Sirene wirft. Das ist die Fastnachtszeit der Philosophie, kleide sie sich nun in eine Hundetracht, wie der Cyniker, in ein Priestergewand, wie der Alexandriner oder in ein duftig Frühlingskleid, wie der Epikuräer. Es ist ihr da wesentlich, Kharaktermasken anzulegen. (MEGA 4.1: 99)

Marx elucidates these remarks with reference to the Cynic, the Alexandrian, and the Epicurean, namely, to the representatives of those Hellenistic schools that had followed upon Aristotelian philosophy, which had already "stretched itself to totality" (MECW 1: 35, MEGA 1.1: 14). But his observations are also not confined to any one moment in the history of philosophy. Rather, the tendency he describes is presented in general terms, which he emphasizes when he concludes his paragraph: "The same now with the philosophy of Hegel" (MECW 1: 491; MEGA 4.1: 99). The pragmatic "turns" of philosophy to date are thus seen to display a shift from speculative theory to the spectacle of blind practice and masked performance—that is, to the opposite of those philosophical pursuits that pretend to abstract principles and conceptual grasp. Engaged philosophers are, as Marx puts it, "no longer comprehending," and therefore no longer philosophers, but actors in all senses of the word. The line between theory and practice could therefore be described as one that distinguishes insight from blindness, or that separates mundane activities from a utopic vision with no place in the world, rendering Marx's early version of an "epistemological break" a break from epistemology altogether. In taking action, it is as if philosophers threw away their eyes, their theory, their ability to see and to know—hence, Marx illustrates this process next with an allusion to Deucalion, who throws stones backwards in the wake of the flood, acting upon an oracular injunction to "depart from the temple and veil your head and loosen your girded vestments, and throw behind your back the bones of your great mother."[22] "As Deucalion, according to the legend, cast stones behind him in creating human beings," writes Marx, "so philosophy casts its regard behind it (the bones of its mother are luminous eyes) when its heart is set on creating a world [. . .]" (MECW 1: 491, MEGA 4.1: 99). Deucalion does not understand the oracle—he is "no longer comprehending"—but hazards an interpretation, in a last-ditch—or last-pitch—attempt to save life on earth, which works only by chance, as divine intervention softens the stones he had cast into human flesh.

The characterization of such a dramatic opposition between theory and practice rests, however, upon the presupposition that philosophical labor is totally independent of the world in which it takes place, which Marx interprets as a symptom for the fact that "the totality of the world in general is divided within itself," or that it is "a world torn apart"—"eine zerrissene [Welt]" (MECW 1: 491, cf. MEGA 4.1: 100). This situation cannot be the doing of theory, because theory by definition does not do anything, which is perhaps why its practitioners are said to resemble the shades of "the transparent kingdom of Amenthes" (MECW 1: 491, cf. MEGA 4.1: 99). The sheer existence of a total philosophy would instead have to follow the totaling of a world that had already given up the ghosts. And even if these revenants return to take the world by storm—"this storm which follows a great philosophy, a world philosophy"—what returns to life is not itself philosophical or living, whether it manifests itself as a ghost or as a gust (MECW 1: 491, MEGA 4.1: 100). Philosophical "activity therefore also" appears to be "torn apart and contradictory," whence "its objective universality is turned back into the subjective forms of individual consciousness in which it has its life" (MECW 1: 491, MEGA 4.1: 100). Whatever initially tore the world apart, however, remains obscure before and after the fact, rendering—and rending—the theoretical and practical spheres the effects of an event that appears to elude explanation.

Rather than seeking to mend the split between theory and practice or to offer an account for its emergence in the first place, Marx exposes the problem of philosophical practice by drawing upon a diverse array of philosophical, mythic, organic, and poetic topoi, moving from Hegel's concept of "nodal points" in the chapter on measure from the *Science of Logic*, where quantitative change gives way to a qualitative alteration when a critical mass is reached; to Ovid's verses on the great flood. Marx even goes on to revert from Deucalion to his father Prometheus in yet another dramatic reversal and mythopoetic turn—"but as Prometheus, having stolen fire from heaven, begins to build houses and to settle upon the earth, so philosophy, expanded to be the whole world, turns against the world of appearance" (MECW 1: 491, MEGA 4.1: 99)—so as to suggest that the world may stand to profit after all from a philosophy that turns a blind eye to the phenomena. In one interpretation of this passage, Hans Blumenberg hones in on this last myth, whose counterpart he finds in the relation between Epicurus and Aristotle, as well as Marx and Hegel:

> The possibility of a turnabout is like a compensation for the late arrival of one who will never have the opportunity to construct

a classic totality. When the author understands Epicurus, not as the result of the philosophy that went before him, but as the possible turning point of its "transubstantiation into flesh and blood," he grasps the Titanic opportunity that remains for a latecomer in a world that is already occupied and allocated.[23]

However, in addition to the "turnabout" that Blumenberg notes, the relations Marx depicts between any precedent and antecedent may also be read the other way around. Marx may speak of Prometheus after Deucalion, but the flood to which Deucalion responds follows his father's Promethean feats. In this respect, blind activity is the successor and descendant of more productive and inventive practices, and if Marx thereby inverts traditional chronological and genealogical orders, then his gesture suspends any neat opposition between the two mythic figures, or between practical success and more desperate measures. It therefore remains uncertain even in Marx's most positive remarks as to how the philosopher or his mythic counterpart would address the world to any effect, in a passage that pivots upon simile after simile, tracing a vertiginous sequence of tropological turns that set his articulations of time and space spinning.

What does become possible to observe more clearly through this passage, however, is what Marx is doing in relation to the most recent version of a total philosophy that he had found in the writings of Hegel. For the heterotopic and heterogeneous descriptions of theory and praxis that Marx offers here are nothing less than a non-conceptual revision of the dialectical movement of spirit that Hegel had unfolded in the chapter from the *Phenomenology of Spirit* devoted to "the world of educational formation," or "die Welt der Bildung," whose theoretical and practical language is built upon a torn structure of address on both sides of the selfsame divide.[24] Turning to this textual source for the problem—if not to its source in the real world—therefore allows for a more precise approach to Marx's point of departure, as well as the alternative trajectories he pursues. Following the dissolution of the Greek world of ethical substance into the atomized society of juridical persons in Ancient Rome, spirit is said to form "not only *One* world," but also a world that is "doubled, separated, and opposed," having been split through an "objective *reality* that has its consciousness beyond itself."[25] Thus, Hegel sums it up as "the world torn into the here and the beyond," which he renders in a single nominal phrase that displays the tear all the more violently: "die in das Diesseits und Jenseits zerrissene Welt."[26] This split entails that both sides of the schism—namely, "consciousness" and "objective *reality*"—receive their essence or reality from the other: "[E]ach singular moment, as *essence*, receives this, and thereby reality, from another, and insofar as it is real, its essence is another than its reality."[27] The individuals who subject themselves to a process of educational formation consequently strive to match up to universal essence through the "sublation of the natural self;"[28] on the other hand, universal substance exists and becomes real only through them, rendering private matters substantial concerns as well. Thus, the tendency of education toward self-effacement comes to have another side that Hegel characterizes as a real will to power—self-consciousness seeks to attain "power over [reality] through educational formation" precisely by "measuring up" to it.[29] As a result, power itself assumes the correspondingly dichotomous forms of the universal state, which "expresses to individuals their essence," and private wealth, "which gives itself up and lets individuals take the consciousness of their singularity from it."[30]

The measures that the subjects of educational formation take in the torn world therefore not only turn out to be utterly mundane. Because they are based on a principle of adequation that presupposes the non-equivalence between objective reality and consciousness—and between the singular individual and the universal essence—they also can only be utterly incoherent and render every value judgment exchangeable with its opposite: "neither the *real essence* of power and wealth, nor [. . .] the consciousness of good and bad [. . .] have truth; but rather all of these moments turn themselves from the one to the other, and each is the opposite of itself."[31] All determinate ethical and conceptual values are thereby liquidated and, ultimately, only money talks in the exchanges that take place in this "language of tornness" or "Sprache der Zerrissenheit."[32] For like wealth—whose essence consists in being "sacrificed and given up," "aufgeopfert und preisgegeben"[33]—language "expresses as essence [. . .] that which it knows to be given up," or: "was sie als Wesen ausspricht, weiß sie als das preisgegebne."[34] As Shakespeare's Timon of Athens had said long before Hegel, money is the power that makes "wrong right," or, as August Schlegel had translated, "bad good [*schlecht gut*]."[35] Hence, the "truth" is that the good and the bad may be appreciated and depreciated at random in a world where all goods essentially owe their praise (*Preis*) to their price (*Preis*), leaving their surrender (*Preisgebung*) the only veritable thing to bank upon. Conceptual knowledge of qualitative attributes does no good when wealth (οὐσία) functions as essence (οὐσία), and when this "universal procurer" or "coupler" (*Kuppler*) determines the copula in each judgment (MECW 3: 324, MEGA 1.3: 147).

The shift from theory to praxis, in this case, would be no translation from one field to another, and there would be no philosophical, political, or personal announcement that could make a difference, because a restless logic of reversibility governs language and relations alike in a universe that is torn and turned into a universal dichotomy. Everything in the world is exchanged against every other part, while each part is the "opposite" or "the counterpart" of itself—the "Gegenteil seiner selbst"—in the double sense of "gegen" for *pro* and *contra*.[36] Amends are made only much later in the *Phenomenology*, after the essence of reality comes to be situated in the singular subject of moral conscience, and after discrete subjects come to affirm one another mutually as universal in their respective singularity.[37] But the Christological solution that Hegel offers at that point only barely masks the way in which the world where he had formed his philosophical thinking remained one in which "the sort of power that belongs to the essence of the state in our times [is] a monetary power," as Hegel had also admitted in his near-contemporaneous text "On the Constitution of Germany."[38]

What Marx does in portraying the torn world is to include Hegel in the picture, and to suggest that, far from a passing or surpassed dichotomy, the world was torn in more ways than one before anyone was looking, and that it remains riven in each attempt to comprehend it theoretically. Marx takes up the Hegelian notion of a "beyond" in his evocation of the "kingdom of Amenthes;" he recapitulates Hegel's depiction of the divided state of educational formation in his rhetoric of a "torn world;" and he recurs to Hegel's characterization of reality as that which derives from an "other," when he describes the practical relation of philosophy to the world as its confrontation with "a task of philosophy which would not be it itself" (MECW 1: 496). But the history of philosophy is driven—and riven—by its relation to the world in ways that cannot be reduced to a binary, located at any one time, or brought to a dialectical resolution in philosophical thought, owing to the "one-sidedness [. . .] by which alone it is philosophy" (MECW 1: 496). In ways for which a dialectic of spirit cannot account, the rifts that cut to the core of "the world of educational formation" therefore manifest themselves in repeated returns throughout the history of philosophy, through to the present state of affairs. Without providing a causal account for these periodic disturbances, Marx nonetheless observes that they are "[t]he same now with the philosophy of Hegel," most likely with reference to the young Hegelians as well, who, as Marx and Engels would later write in *The German Ideology*, blindly sought in Hegelian fashion to bring "existing reality [to] collapse" by turning "against" the total philosophy of Hegel (MECW 5: 23, 30).

At this point in Marx's thinking, the notion of a philosophy that would engage with world affairs leads to an irreducible dilemma for which the solution becomes not Hegelian dialectics, but Romantic irony. This shift to irony takes place as Marx diverts the focus of his notes from the various philosophical characters that emerge in the wake of Aristotle's total philosophy to the ways in which similar tensions resurface between the spheres of philosophy and praxis in Ferdinand Christian Baur's study of Christ and Socrates, *Das Christliche des Platonismus, oder Socrates und Christus*. There, Marx writes:

> Socratic irony, as understood by Baur and as it must be understood with Hegel, namely as the dialectic trap through which human common sense is precipitated out of its motley ossification, not into self-complacent knowing-better, but into the truth immanent in human common sense itself, this irony is nothing but the form of philosophy in its subjective attitude to common consciousness. The fact that in Socrates it has the form of an ironical, wise man follows from the basic character of Greek philosophy and its attitude to reality. With us irony as universal immanent formula, as philosophy so to speak, was taught by Fr. v. Schlegel. But objectively, so far as content is concerned, Heraclitus, who also not only despised, but hated human common sense, is just as much an ironist, so is even Thales, who taught that everything is water though every Greek knew that no one could live on water, so is Fichte with his world-creating *ego*, despite which even Nicolai realised that he could not create any world, and so is any philosopher who asserts immanence in opposition to the empirical person. (MECW 1: 494)

> Die sokratische Ironie, wie sie Baur auffaßt und wie sie mit Hegel aufgefaßt werden muß, nämlich die dialektische Falle, wodurch der gemeine Menschenverstand nicht in wohlbehäbiges Besserwissen, sondern in die ihm selbst immanente Wahrheit aus seiner buntscheckigen Verknöcherung hineingestürzt wird, diese Ironie ist nichts als die Form der Philosophie wie sie subjektiv zum gemeinen Bewußtsein sich verhält. Daß sie in Sokrates die Form eines ironischen Menschen, Weisen hat, folgt aus dem Grundcharakter und dem Verhältnisse griechischer Philosophie zur Wirklichkeit; bei uns ist die Ironie in Fr. v. Schlegel als allgemeine

immanente Formel, gleichsam als Philosophie gelehrt worden. Aber der Objektivität, dem Inhalt nach ist ebensogut Heraklit, der auch den gemeinen Menschenverstand nicht nur verachtet, sondern haßt, ist selbst Thales, der lehrt, alles sei Wasser, während jeder Grieche wußte, daß er vom Wasser nicht leben könnte, ist Fichte mit seinem weltschöpferischen Ich, während selbst Nicolai einsah, daß er keine Welt schaffen könne, ist jeder Philosoph, der die Immanenz gegen die empirische Person geltend macht, ein Ironiker. (MEGA 4.1: 102)

The initial description of irony that Marx provides follows the Hegelian interpretation of Socratic irony that Baur offers, according to which Socrates sets out to teach the "the true, the good, and the just," by exposing the contradictions to which individual judgments lead when they do not correspond to these ideals. Given that they are "the universal [. . .] power that stands over each singular man" and that is "contained already [. . .] in the consciousness of each," recognizing these ideals amounts to recognizing oneself, and thereby allows the individual to "raise himself above all particularities of his subjective inclinations, feelings and passions."[39] Since the universal does not and cannot "enter into men from the outside," Socratic method consists in posing leading questions to those who believe themselves to be already in the know, so as to guide them to conscious insight of the "true knowing that the inner man finds in himself."[40] Marx retraces this relatively straightforward line of thinking up to a point, but breaks with his contemporary from the moment he calls irony itself the "universal immanent form" and thereby places it on a par with "the true, the good, and the just," in whose service irony was supposedly deployed. From here on, Marx's version of Socratic irony veers off in a new direction and evolves into a further commentary upon the problematic opposition between philosophy and praxis, now mediated by irony.

The ambivalence of irony allows it to unsettle each separate domain of the torn world: irony cannot be a philosophical means to an ideal or practical end, for example, if it is the "universal immanent form;" hence, irony is not even "philosophy," but only "philosophy, so to speak," as well as a movement within philosophical language that undoes its purport. At the same time, irony changes the sense of the "universal" from an ideal to a "form" that does not correspond to the Platonic forms or any formula that could be fixed. Rather, the "universal immanent form" of irony emerges as a manner of speaking and thinking that exposes the contradictory tendencies in language, which would affect or afflict ideal truths as well as individual prejudices. This is why the examples of irony that Marx introduces after referring to Baur are the principles of Heraclitus, Thales, and Fichte, whose propositions regarding the universal substance or subject of thought, being, and creation show themselves to be insupportable to the extent that the immanent and the universal could not, on principle, be limited or opposed to empirical reality as they suggest. What Marx had initially introduced as the ironic dissolution of individual presuppositions thus turns into an ironic display of the contradictions to which philosophical universals lead, which pivots upon the "against" or "gegen" that intervenes between philosophical "immanence" and "the empirical person." Without reducing all to one or developing into a total system, irony emerges in Marx's text as a critical mode for addressing, negotiating, and unsettling the oppositions of the individual and the universal. The two poles of the torn world may not be reconciled in this way, but they do lose their places, as all theoretical and practical matters are drawn into an immanent movement of irony that shifts every speakable position in language, thought, and praxis, indefinitely.[41]

Wherever it may lead, irony also works to the detriment of all structures of dominance and control, and comes to appear as restlessly ungraspable in Marx's fragmentary note as it does in Friedrich Schlegel's essay "On Incomprehensibility," to which Marx most likely alludes when he specifies the irony of which he speaks as "die Ironie in Fr. v. Schlegel." There, Schlegel's characterization of Socratic irony as "the only involuntary and yet completely deliberate dissimulation" undermines from the start the assumption that irony could merely be a consciously adopted method for the purpose of leading individuals to overcome their particular inclinations and to arrive upon truth in the end.[42] And if Schlegel nonetheless says that one can overcome oneself through irony—"through [irony] one sets oneself out and over oneself [*durch [Ironie] setzt man sich über sich selbst weg*]"[43]—this method leads "out" or "away" ("weg") from one's "self" ("selbst") in a process of "setting over" and "translating" ("übersetzen") that has no end, because it is nothing other than this wayward motion. When Schlegel proceeds to comment on this formulation through a discussion of the "irony of irony"— and thus, through a translation of irony by itself—he therefore writes: "But here, what we initially want to know this irony of irony to be understood to be, emerges *in more than one way* [*Was wir aber hier zunächst unter Ironie der Ironie verstanden wissen wollen, das entsteht* auf mehr als einem Wege]."[44] In more than one way, irony describes the infinitely divergent directions of sense that are immanent in every expression—be it universal, particular, or otherwise—and that therefore can neither be contained by the terms of logical opposition, nor sublated in an evolving dialectic, nor directed toward an ultimate purpose. Instead, irony "no longer lets itself be ruled / directed at all [*sich gar nicht mehr regieren läßt*]."[45]

This feature of irony suggests that it is ab-positional—and more precisely, a-positional—in its movements away from each position that may be suggested, and therefore from the "from" and from the "away" as well. Without location or grounds, ironic speech opens at every moment to a novel leap within (and without) that which is said, which could also be described along the lines that Werner Hamacher has traced in his commentary on Schlegel's description of "parekbasis": "Poetic parekbasis constitutes an uncontrollable, dramatic-grammatical trope whose exorbitant movement displaces the framework for every epistemological paradigm of reflective representation."[46] Thus, when universal ideals do occur in Schlegel's redefinition of irony as "the form of paradox"—which he glosses: "[p]aradoxical is everything that is simultaneously good and great"—the qualities of the "good" and the "great" cross one another out and exceed either paradigm, insofar as "greatness," *qua* quantum, cannot but refer to finite measures from which the ideal form of the "good" should be essentially distinct. And insofar this paradoxical intersection of infinite principles and finitude parallels the interference that Marx had traced between wisdom and worldly action in his notes on Epicurean philosophy, Schlegel's ironic commentary simultaneously suggests that a total philosophy and its total opposite will have always been other than either in infinite ways.

Marx's discussion of irony, however, exposes still further consequences of this structure for theory and practice. Not only does it offer a novel critique of philosophical praxis that does not reside in a conceptual framework—which would amount to assuming a philosophical position within the torn world once again. It also does not tend toward the invention of a new myth, as thinkers from Plato to Schlegel had either done or proposed, so as to illustrate the absolute and to recast reality as "the medium through which absolute light shines," which medium should break "the absolute light" "into a fabulous play of colours" that "points to something other than itself" (MECW 1: 497, MEGA 4.1: 105–06).[47] Instead, myths and concepts both enter into play in Marx's text as allusive and elusive fragments that do not coalesce, but that dissolve the more or less fictive or factual elements of philosophical systems for elucidating the world. Precisely in avoiding the seemingly opposed and paradoxically similar media of concept and myth, Marx addresses philosophy through an ironic language which does not hinge upon the duplicitous "gegen" that tears philosophy and empirical reality apart in Heraclitus, Thales, and Fichte, among others.

Most importantly, however, when Marx evokes irony explicitly, he also does not address the dilemma of philosophy and praxis by turning every term into a trope, which would reduce the problem of philosophical and practical expressions, if not to an opposition between the figural and the literal, then to a rhetorical form that could be conceptually defined and technically mastered, and thus to another general formula. Instead, through an ironic elaboration of irony in both philosophical and common parlance, Marx indicates the wayward tendencies of language that are immanent in every utterance, which distance it from any stance and which can therefore be oriented and limited by no single conceptual, mythical, or rhetorical-technical direction. As many readers of Schlegel's remarks on irony have noticed, there is no way to translate irony into definitive descriptive terms without undermining said definition, including the standard definitions that Paul de Man rehearses in order to get away from them, "such as 'meaning one thing and saying something else,' or 'praise by blame.'"[48] If it were a trope, irony would not appear to operate according to such simplistic inversions of opposites, and in *Irony on Occasion*, Kevin Newmark therefore perceptively broaches the issue by calling it fundamentally into question:

> Is irony the name for a specific kind of philosophical masked appearance in more or less playful form; or is irony rather play as sheer dissimulation, deception, and ultimately the distortion and even destruction of truth? This question, because it states the issue in terms of truth and its manifestation in a subsidiary, and in this case, veiled form, also serves to remind us that irony is a term that always marks the encounter and potential tension between literature and philosophy, or truth and tropes.[49]

In Marx's earliest formulations of the opposition between theoretical truths and practical masks, irony similarly describes both operations in a language that always—and in all ways—departs from every persona and paradigm, turning each into a parody or paradox that opens to other readings and allows for none to be conclusive. Finally, since the only definition of the "universal immanent formula" of irony that Marx provides is the proper name "Fr. v. Schlegel," he also implies that "the name" of irony is the name of another, which may itself be nothing more than a provisional marker for a movement in language that escapes any single nomination, definition, or author, and that therefore eludes every tropological or topological horizon to speak of. Whatever it may be called, however, this movement undoes divisions of all sorts by opening the very terms along which they might be drawn to the "interplay of unintended effects" in language (MECW 25: 327). The parekbasis that thereby takes place from out of every speakable position renders both radical calls for change and appeals to more rooted foundations unpredictable, and could therefore also be called the permanent revolution of all that may appear to be said or set.

Marx's earliest ways of addressing theory and practice present the fields of their operation as impossible to chart or delineate. The heterogeneous linguistic modes he evokes, drawn from Hegel, Ovid, and Schlegel, among others, literally render his articulation of the problem all over the place and present a thoroughly aporetic situation for political theory. The question of a novel intervention would therefore have to allow for the ironies of language by eluding an oppositional logic in the first place. However, Marx would soon seem to take his distance from "irony" by adopting a different approach to the apparent division between praxis and philosophy in his writings. In *The German Ideology*, for example, he and Engels part ways with the more recent philosophical critique of the young Hegelians, beginning with the exposure of their blind spot: "It has not occurred to any one of these philosophers to inquire into the connection of German philosophy with German reality, the connection of their criticism with their own material surroundings" (MECW 5: 30, MEGA 1.5: 10). They then proceed to announce: "The premises from which we begin are not arbitrary ones, not dogmas, but real premises from which abstraction can only be made in the imagination. They are the real individuals, their activity and the material conditions of their life, both those which they find already existing and those produced by their activity. These premises can thus be constated in a purely empirical way" (MECW 5: 31, MEGA 1.5: 10). Marx and Engels thus appear to assume, as Margaret Rose has argued, a mode of "speak[ing] directly" that avoids the more wayward figures of speech that had characterized Marx's early work.[50] They also arbitrate against what their philosophical predecessors and opponents may have understood to be ahistorical "ideas" and "notions," arguing instead that such ideas have a "semblance of independence" solely because they are the "reflexes and echoes of [. . .] life-process[es]" (MECW 5: 36, MEGA 1.5: 15–16). Here, Marx revises his earlier optical metaphor for those philosophical myths that recast reality as "the medium through which absolute light shines" (MECW 1: 497, MEGA 4.1: 105–06), now suggesting that ideas and notions are projected simulacra and reflexes that remain "bound" or "verknüpft" to the sources they obscure (MECW 5: 36, MEGA 1.5: 16). Yet if the problem seems once again to be a matter of breaking points and "nodal points" in the history of philosophy, this time, the paradoxical coincidence of bondage and breakage is explained by a genetic account of the emergence of language—and with it, consciousness—"from the need, the necessity, of intercourse with other men" (MECW 5: 44, MEGA 1.5: 20). Implicitly drawing on the many senses of the Greek *lógos*—which may mean relation, proportion, concept, speech, or word—Marx and Engels gloss "the language of real life" as "the material activity and the material intercourse of men." They thereby blur the distinction between social relations and verbal expressions, in accord with the ways in which the languages of "conceiving and thinking" themselves initially "appear as the direct efflux of [. . .] material behavior" (MECW 5: 36, MEGA 1.5: 15). For a time, then, they suggest that the "language of real life" must have functioned as a homogeneous continuum in which praxis and speech flowed out of and into one another, and which has since suffered a breach.

This sounds much like an origins myth and a universal ideal, however far Marx seems to have come from his earlier mode of writing, where mythic and poetic topoi were broken down and ironically taken up as elements of his critique as well as its object. Nor is Marx and Engels's idea here particularly original, but at least as old as Epicurus, who describes the origins of languages as so many particular responses to environmental factors, practical actions, and chance encounters:

> Moreover, we must suppose that human nature too was taught and constrained to do many things of every kind merely by circumstances; and that later on reasoning elaborated what had been suggested by nature and made further inventions [. . .] And so names too were not at first deliberately given to things, but men's natures according to their different nationalities had their own peculiar feelings and received their peculiar impressions, so that each in their own way emitted air formed into shape by each of these feelings and impressions, according to the differences made in the different nations by the places of their abode as well [. . .] And sometimes those who were acquainted with them brought in things hitherto unknown and introduced sounds for them, on some occasions being naturally constrained to utter them, and on others choosing them by reasoning in

accordance with the prevailing mode of formation, and thus making their meaning clear.[51]

The continuum of language and practice once bound a cohesive community in both Epicurus's account and Marx and Engels's historical narrative, then, but whereas Epicurus allows for gradual change through cultural exchanges and rational choices, Marx and Engels break with Epicurus when it comes to the language of their world. At some unspecified point—which Marx and Engels repeatedly characterize as a "blink of an eye" or "Augenblick"—the confluence of life and language was disrupted, and the craze of refraction broke ground (MECW 5: 45, MEGA 1.5: 21). This abrupt and undated shift from practical insight to theoretical blindness recalls the instantaneous shift from theoretical insight to practical blindness that Marx had addressed in his early notebooks on Epicurean philosophy. Now, however, Marx and Engels ascribe the schism that tore the world between the "consciousness of existing practice" and "the formation of 'pure' theory, theology, philosophy, morality, etc" to the division of labor (MECW 5: 45, MEGA 1.5: 21). With this narrative—which is as much an invention as it is a critical intervention—Marx and Engels therefore seem to clarify why the return of philosophers to praxis would have had to be blind since the beginning of philosophy as such. Because theory, theology, and philosophy are produced as divisions within a particular social nexus, they are not only bound to be cut off and estranged from other areas of activity, but are also situated among them, and would therefore have to be blind to reality so long as they are blind to themselves as derivative products. For this same reason, however, no theoretical insight could dispel theoretical illusions; instead, the spectrum of "apparitions" that arose through the division of labor can be brought to disappear only "by the practical overthrow of the actual social relations which gave rise to [it]" (MECW 5: 54, MEGA 1.5: 27).[52] Thus, Marx and Engels appear, theoretically, to solve the problem of the torn world that Hegel had raised and that Marx had left in suspension in his earlier texts, but they also arrive at another insoluble paradox. For by their own lights, addressing the division that they expose can effect no fundamental change, nor may it even be possible to address it without unwittingly reproducing the specters that haunt the world within which they speak. As Jan Mieszkowski has written in his precise and elucidating reading of this passage: "As 'practical consciousness,' language is existence, or more specifically, the existence of relationships. Since consciousness can never fully master language as an object but only as a relation, it cannot know language as its own product or even as a product of society. Hence 'real' linguistic consciousness, consciousness of the relations that make consciousness possible, is impossible, and language remains in crucial respects an unknown."[53]

Marx and Engels nevertheless present a provisional way to overcome the illusory divide, however, when they state that the "presentation" or "Darstellung" of reality—presumably, their presentation in *The German Ideology*—produces the conditions for "self-sufficient philosophy" to "lose its medium of existence" by explicitly situating theoretical language in the field of practice (MECW 5: 37, MEGA 1.5: 16). By addressing the status of theoretical language in this way, presentation should also alter "the material activity and the material intercourse of men," at least when it comes to the theoretical domain. Consistent with their adoption of this new method, Marx and Engels therefore repeatedly and explicitly refuse the traditional forms of philosophy in their writing, from the notion of a "schema" (MECW 5: 37, MEGA 1.5: 16), to the search for a "category" or "idea" by which the evolution of history could be described (MECW 5: 53–54, MEGA 1.5: 27). They correct divisions in current terminology by redefining what appear to be disparate notions—notions that reflect specious divisions—in terms of the relational nexus that binds them.[54] And if appeals to totality and immanence occur in Marx and Engels's declarations in a way that might appear to place their project on a par with a total philosophy, the immanence that they bring to expression should no longer operate "in opposition to the empirical person," as the immanence of Heraclitus, Thales, and Fichte had done before (MECW 1: 494; MEGA 4.1: 102). For when Marx and Engels claim that it is possible to present the whole "matter" or "cause" ("Sache") of history "in its totality" (MECW 5: 53, MEGA 1.5: 27), this totality includes the productive and communicative relations that make up the world of praxis and ideology alike.[55] Nonetheless, the question remains as to how the theoretical representation of such a totality could remain entirely distinct from what Derrida sees to be Althusser's characteristic gesture as well, when Althusser calls for a theoretical Marxism that would establish a domain of "fundamental research" upon which all other "branches, regions, [and] derived circumscriptions" would depend. For with such gestures, Althusser—and, by implication, Marx and Engels—recapitulate, once again, "the philosophical movement that is most fundamentally traditional," which "consists in subordinating the totality of regions of theoretical and practical knowledge to one fundamental and general instance."[56] Most importantly, however, the question would remain as to how a total vision of historical reality should translate to the thoroughgoing transformation of the reality that it grasps and presents, and therefore move beyond what it sees and announces.

These questions are not answered through the arguments that Marx and Engels provide in *The German Ideology*, even though they appear to reflect what Althusser describes as Marx's most critical move from "ideological philosophy" to "a new philosophy (dialectical materialism)." This new discipline, he continues, laid the foundations for the "science of history,"[57] or for "a logic of actual experience and real emergence [. . .] that would put an end to the illusions of ideological immanence" and inaugurate "the irruption of real history in ideology itself."[58] In *Reading Capital*, Althusser further develops his thinking on Marx's practice of "Darstellung," calling it the "key epistemological concept of the whole Marxist theory of value, the concept whose object is precisely to designate the mode of presence of the structure in its effects, and therefore to designate structural causality itself."[59] But as other readers more insistent upon the parodic tendencies in Marx's oeuvre have noted, his language speaks against such a strict division between his earlier texts and a mode of "Darstellung" that would proceed without irony. Already in moving from Marx's notebooks on Epicurean philosophy to *The German Ideology*, one can see that Marx returns to a language of myths in order to account for language, which Dominick LaCapra also observes as a utopic projection: "one is close to a utopia of distortion-free language and communication as well as to a vision of the total transcendence of the division of labor."[60] Nor are the other rhetorical strategies that Marx deploys in his later texts as radically different as Althusser's announcement of an "epistemological break" might imply, from the many "character masks" that Marx adopts throughout the *The Communist Manifesto* and even *Capital*,[61] to the immanent revolutions in language that occur through these texts, which resemble the movements Marx had once called "irony."[62]

Whatever it could be called, however, the sheer indetermination of language insists before any myth of its origins can be uttered, before any distinction between "scientific" and "ideological" manners of speaking can be drawn, and before any division of labor or an oeuvre can cut in. And it is this *a priori* that both allows the most radical revisions in sense to become legible in Marx and Engels's writing, and that simultaneously renders each one the vanishing point where other possibilities and counter-possibilities might be evoked, troubling any assumption of positions and any topological determinations of *pro* or *contra*. This is true even in the case of the address that most pronouncedly appears to participate in oppositions, to present the totality of world history, and to recur to positional topologies, namely, *The Communist Manifesto*. For despite all appearances to the contrary, its "universal immanent formula" is the wayward motion of language that Marx had elaborated with reference to Friedrich Schlegel in his earliest notebooks and that escapes all ontological, geopolitical, and topological forms. Nothing less than such a novel departure from the going scheme of things is implied when Marx and Engels announce: "The theoretical conclusions of the Communists are in no way based on ideas or principles that have been invented, or discovered by this or that would-be universal reformer. They merely express, in general terms, actual relations springing from an existing class struggle, from a historical movement going on under our very eyes" (MECW 6: 498, MEGA 1.6: 538). For if the communists truly express a "historical movement" or a "total-movement" (*Gesamt-Bewegung*) this could only take place if the moves of the text were displaced in all directions—if the writing were not absolute at the level of the concept or idea, but absolved from all supposedly fixed and limiting notions. Furthermore, since Marx and Engels consider social relations to be a language of "intercourse among men," the manifestation of communism through the *Manifesto* would have to be a language that mobilizes all relations, connections, and connotations as it speaks. The *Communist Manifesto* would, in other words, have to deliver not only the famous exposition of class opposition and the novel announcement of revolution that it is said to be; it would also have to undermine the oppositions it exposes. For this reason, moreover, the *Manifesto* could not derive its speech from a subject or a collective involved in current oppositions—despite the interpretations that characterize the inaugural gesture of text as the "usurp[ation]" of "an authority it does not yet possess."[63] Unsettling all instances of authorization and all seats of power, this novel announcement is rather an absolutely prepositional and apositional text whose language troubles all fields of opposition. Thus, this universally total—and totally singular—intervention offers itself as one of the most radical and far-reaching explorations of "the practical consequences of all sorts that a theoretical language may have."[64]

To begin, the language of the prologue announces itself as a speech that comes from everywhere and nowhere and that belongs to no opposition, because all current oppositional parties are what collectively conjure it into being. After the famous opening salvo, "A spectre is haunting Europe—the spectre of Communism. All the Powers of old Europe have bound together in a holy hunt [*heiligen Hetzjagd*] against this spectre: Pope and Czar, Metternich and Guizot, French Radicals and German police-spies," the more general question of position is posed in the following way:

> Where is the oppositional party that has not been decried as Communistic by its opponents in power? Where the oppositional party that has not hurled back the branding reproach of Communism, against the more advanced oppositional peoples, as well as against their reactionary opponents? (MECW 6: 481)

> Wo ist die Oppositionspartei, die nicht von ihren regierenden Gegnern als kommunistisch verschrien worden wäre, wo die Oppositionspartei, die den fortgeschritteneren Oppositionsleuten sowohl wie ihren reaktionären Gegnern den brandmarkenden Vorwurf des Kommunismus nicht zurückgeschleudert hätte? (MEGA 1.6: 525)

With these words, everything that appears to be set—including all opponents involved in current affairs—turns out to be otherwise. The word that repeats with incantatory insistence is "opposition" and variants thereof—such as "opponent," or "Gegner"—but in ways that show communism to be a recognized power beyond all reckoning and resistance. The positions of the various parties, in turn, emerge as anything but static and stable, insofar as these powers are on the move in a "holy hunt against" the ghost of communism. At the same time, however, these parties cannot really work "against" communism, if communism is immanent in their various moves against each other, and therefore virtually everywhere. These preliminary factors alone indicate, as Marx and Engels write, that "Communism is already acknowledged by all European Powers to be itself a Power" (MECW 6: 481, cf. MEGA 1.6: 525). Far from communism representing a "usurpation" of authority, all supposed or purported authorities concur to concede power to the hitherto vague and indistinct movement whose vehicle now appears to be the *Communist Manifesto*. For this reason, moreover, communism is not just "a Power," but an infinite dynamis and dynamic, since the exclusively negative definitions of communism that come from all sides suggest that all determinations are possible for it. The conditions that give rise to communism are no limiting conditions, that is, but the practical demonstration of an infinite judgment that absolves communism from all known and nameable conditions and positions.[65]

The simultaneous ubiquity, placelessness, and indeterminacy of "communism" therefore implies not only that the communists—whoever or whatever they are—cannot be assigned a location or identity within the field of politics that they would not also exceed, but that their novel power and vision—their novel theory and praxis—would also differ from those that are available within that field, not least of all because there is no point which is not or could not be set in motion by and through them. Hence, when it is said, "[i]t is high time that Communists should openly, in the face of the whole world, publish their modes of viewing, their aims, their tendencies, and counter-pose to this fairy tale of the Spectre of Communism a Manifesto of the party itself," nothing can be presupposed regarding what an aim, tendency, or mode viewing (*Anschauungsweise*) could mean—no more than one could presuppose what communism could be (MECW 6: 481, cf. MEGA 1.6: 525). The indeterminacy of communism would have to extend to an indetermination of the very philosophical categories that appear to define it, if its recognition consists in its distinction from all that is known or represented within the sociopolitical landscape. One could thus venture to say that there "is" no such thing as communism, just as there "is" no such thing as ghosts—which is not to say that they are nothing, but that their effects and existence cannot be measured according to the premises of classical ontology or contemporary politics. Hence, as Derrida remarks on the specters of communism—and of Shakespeare—"Let us call it a *hauntology*. This logic of haunting would not be merely larger and more powerful than an ontology or a thinking of Being [. . .] It would harbor within itself, but like circumscribed places or particular effects, eschatology and teleology themselves. It would *comprehend* them, but incomprehensibly."[66] The conventional definitions of space and time, among other categories, therefore could not encompass the thoroughgoing revision of recognizable topoi that the *Manifesto* performs through its presentation. Instead, the categorical impossibility of identifying or delimiting communism—as well as the aims and views associated with it—can only become apparent through the language of the *Manifesto*, which may be why the first "goal" or "Zweck" of the communists is named in the next sentence as the production and publication of this very text: "For this goal [*Zu diesem Zweck*], Communists of various nationalities have assembled in London, and sketched the following Manifesto, to be published in the English, French, German, Italian, Flemish and Danish languages" (MECW 1: 481, MEGA 1.6: 525).

But how can the goal of the *Manifesto* be the language of the *Manifesto*, if it is said to appear only in translations, and if its linguistic specificity would therefore seem to be indifferent? What is the language of the *Manifesto*, if it cannot be identified with any language in which it happens to appear? Citing Marx and Engels's later remarks on the rise of "world literature" (MECW 6: 488), Martin Puchner draws a connection between the many translations of literary works that were disseminated on the global market, and the transnational collective writing that is announced in the prologue of the *Manifesto*: "A multinational and multilingual assembly, a veritable Babel, has somehow given rise to a text, or at least to a sketch of one, that can now be published in as many languages."[67] The goal of the text, in that case, would be to enter into the circulation of translations that "defines a bourgeois world literature driven by a global market."[68] Upon arrival, the text would therefore be reduced to an element among others within the current state of affairs, where all is universally exchangeable, tradeable, translatable. Something else is happening, however, when the publication of its text and its many translations is called its goal or "Zweck." Puchner distinguishes the textual production of Marx and Engels from translations designed for global sale, when he argues that Marx and Engels "push[ed] this capitalist world literature to an extreme, becoming more international than even the most international productions of bourgeois world literature by erasing the conception of an original altogether."[69] Beyond this feature of the text, however, the implicit indifference of its variants to its main thrust also implies that the *Manifesto* is written in a mode that would affect any language in which it may appear, which could only be the case if its language is not understood to refer primarily to the lexica and grammars of particular national idioms, but to the *lógos* of relations that it at once expresses and exposes to alteration.

This is not to say, however, that the *lógos* of the *Manifesto* is universal. Solely a language that no one speaks could be the universal language of all, and in this respect, such "a real language" would seem to exist in the way that money talks: in his account of the torn world, Hegel already showed money to transcend and cross the terms of any particular veridical or ethical judgment, and Schlegel had ironically observed around the same time that "wherever there is even a little enlightenment and education, silver and gold are comprehensible and through them everything else."[70] But the notion of universal equivalence and exchange—in whatever currency—relates nothing but the "language of tornness" or "Sprache der Zerrissenheit";[71] it eliminates the specificity of all relata; and it maintains a steady and constant circulation in which nothing otherwise moves. The language of the "total-movement" that Marx and Engels claim to present would therefore also have to unsettle this fixed circuit as well. In order to be what it says, the *Manifesto* would have to differ, that is, from national languages and the wealth of nations in a way that undermines or overthrows the universal categories of ontology and subjectivity that underlie the currently established languages and means for relations, oppositions, and exchanges. In so doing, the "Gesamt-Bewegung" that it expresses would not only translate across various local idioms, but would also render the terms for exchange incommensurable and incomprehensible, from their economies of meaning and value, to the language of being and time, to the subject and substance of all conflictual history to date.

With respect to the subject of historical divisions, the *Manifesto* soon shifts from a mode of general address to what appears to be a more personal dialogue with the current bourgeois order. After a reprisal of several accusations—"We Communists have been reproached with the desire of abolishing the right of personally acquiring property as the fruit of a man's own labour, which property is alleged to be the groundwork of all personal freedom, activity and independence"—the refutation arrives as if by itself: "Hard-won, self-acquired, self-earned property! Do you mean the property of the petty artisan and of the small peasant, a form of property that preceded the bourgeois form? There is no need to abolish that; the development of industry has to a great extent already destroyed it, and is still destroying it daily" (MECW 6: 498, MEGA 1.6: 539). Such gestures have been read as the theatrical and performative dimension of the *Manifesto*, as instances of prosopopoeia that allow the *Manifesto* to "take, preemptively, the place of the proletariat, anticipating and enacting the proletariat in the manner that is, for the time being, theatrical."[72] But just as the language of commodities in *Capital* does not arise through Marx's use of "a metaphor or a prosopopoeia," but through the fact that these manufactured commodities are "structured as a prosopopoeia,"[73] the dialogue here does not unfold between personified positions in a debate. The communists' interlocutor or "Gegenüber" is not a viable opponent or "Gegner," nor is it even a fictive persona through whom the supposedly foundational rights of a citizen might be made to resound. Instead, what speaks is the language of bourgeois ideology—the phrases for "*self*-acquired, *self*-earned property"—which rhetoric would include the self not in person, but in name. It could hardly be otherwise, if the abolition of self-acquired property has already occurred without anyone's doing. What remains of personal property and proprietors are instead citations that circulate freely, which the *Manifesto* evokes not only to expose the spectral character of property, but also to unmask its unsound and unfounded status within the very media that intermittently seem to perpetuate it. The *Manifesto* can include and nullify the speech of bourgeois ideology because it is neither the proper speech or nor the property of any person. Instead, the simulated oppositions in the *Manifesto* disclose their semblance-character as well as the semblance of all characters.

If these rhetorical strategies undermine the subject of bourgeois opposition, however, the *Manifesto* deploys other strategies to undermine its substance. The eradication of opposition at its ontological roots begins, ironically, with a description of its permanent establishment. Early in the text, it is proclaimed that those involved in the dialectic of oppressor and oppressed—from Greece and Rome to the modern world—all participate in the same scheme:

> Freeman and slave, patrician and plebeian, lord and serf, guild-master and journeyman, in a word, oppressor and oppressed, stood in constant opposition to one another, carried on an uninterrupted, now hidden, now open fight, a fight that each time ended, either in a revolutionary re-constitution of society at large, or in the common ruin of the contending classes. (MECW 6: 482)

> Freier und Sklave, Patrizier und Plebejer, Baron und Leibeigner, Zunftbürger und Gesell, kurz, Unterdrücker und Unterdrückte standen in stetem Gegensatz zueinander, führten einen ununterbrochenen, bald versteckten, bald offenen Kampf, der jedesmal mit einer revolutionären Umgestaltung der ganzen Gesellschaft endete oder mit dem gemeinsamen Untergang der kämpfenden Klassen. (MEGA 1.6: 526)

What was announced as a historical synopsis—"[t]he history of all hitherto existing society is the history of class struggles"—thus turns out to describe an apparently stable, transhistorical dynamic. More specifically, however, the division between oppressor and oppressed that characterizes all history to date is summed up as a variant of the categorial forms of action and passion, which accordingly assume the form of a pair of contraries.[74] It is owing to this structure that oppositions remain in place, even as the apparent agents of opposition are subject to change: slaveholders in Ancient Greece give way to patricians in Rome; "[t]he place of manufacture was taken by the giant, Modern Industry"; "the place of the industrial middle class, by industrial millionaires, the leaders of whole industrial armies, the modern bourgeois" (MECW 6: 485, MEGA 1.6: 527). Places are traded, and although each new occupation of positions within the dynamic of oppressor and oppressed also corresponds to a geopolitical shift in the main arena of power, the basic positions remain unmoved: "The modern bourgeois society that has gone forth from the downfall of feudal society has not done away with class antagonisms. It has only set new classes, new conditions of oppression, new forms of struggle in place of the old ones" (MECW 6: 485, MEGA 1.6: 526). And what goes for space goes for time as well, since even the historical periodization that Marx and Engels supply demands to be read as a function of oppression that itself remains constant. When they write, for example, "[t]he history of all past society has moved in the mode of class oppositions, which were differently shaped in the most different epochs" (MECW 6: 504, MEGA 1.6: 544), the distinction among "epochs" could not refer to decisive changes, if "all past society" can be described in the same manner or "mode." Instead, history would appear on hold, as the word "epochs" also implies, breaking down as it does into the Ancient Greek roots for "having a hold" (ἔχω) "upon" (ἐπί) something, be it a matter of inhibiting further motion and holding off from judgment, or practicing colonial occupation. Thus, as the epochal history of positions and oppositions undergoes permutations—as oppression changes shape over various "Epochen"—the basic structure for historical temporality stays put.

Rather than presenting history, the *Manifesto* thus describes the past as the product of historical constants, and these constants can be traced, in turn, to the natural science or physics of Aristotle—that is, the physics of "total philosophy" *par excellence*. For the constellation of action, passion, position, and contrariety that are operative in the opposition of oppressor and oppressed entails precisely the same categories that were involved in the explication of ποιεῖν and πάσχειν that Aristotle unfolds in *De generatione et corruptione*, which Marx had studied while writing his doctoral dissertation on Epicurus.[75] The implicit evocation of Aristotelian philosophy in the *Manifesto* figures critically in the address that Marx and Engels set forth, however, precisely because its sense will be transformed over the course of their speech from that of a philosophy comprising timeless categories to the temporary reflection of "a world torn apart"—"eine zerrissene [Welt]"— with no principle for its foundational *Grundriß*, for its outline or faultline (MECW 1: 491, MEGA 4.1: 100). As Althusser writes of the seemingly ahistorical, "general theory of history" that Nicolo Machiavelli evokes in *The Prince*, what matters most is "the *modality* of this theory in [the] text," or "the use" that is made of it,⁷⁶ which turns out to serve Machiavelli in introducing a radically new concept of government that breaks the cycles of history to date.⁷⁷ Similarly, the foundational categories that Marx and Engels appropriate to characterize history are eventually shown to be appropriate only for a time, and lose their ground with the critical difference in history that the *Manifesto* introduces itself.⁷⁸

Whereas ποιεῖν and πάσχειν are illustrated briefly by an appeal to the active and passive forms of certain verbs in the *Categories*—"cut, burn" and "being cut, being burned" (2a 4–5)—it is in *De generatione et corruptione* that their "what [. . .] why and how [τί . . . διὰ τί καὶ πῶς]" are elaborated at length (324b 23–24). There, it is said that these movements are contingent upon contact—"for action and passion ought properly to be possible only for such things as can touch one another [οὔτε γὰρ ποιεῖν ταῦτα καὶ πάσχειν δύναται κυρίως ἃ μὴ οἷόν τε ἅψασθαι ἀλλήλων]" (322b 23–25)— which contact can occur only between those things which "have position [τοῖς ἔχουσι θέσιν]" (323a 1–2), and which thus have a "place [τόπος]" (323a 2). Furthermore, the movements of action and passion can take place solely between things that are "alike and identical in kind, but unlike and contrary in species [ἀνάγκη καὶ τὸ ποιοῦν καὶ τὸ πάσχον τῷ γένει μὲν ὅμοιον εἶναι καὶ ταὐτό, τῷ δ᾽ εἴδει ἀνόμοιον καὶ ἐναντίον]" (323b 32–34). Color, for example, cannot be affected by something of another order, such as line, "except perhaps incidentally, if it happened that the line was white or black, for unless the two things are contraries or made up of contraries, one cannot displace the other from its natural condition" (323b 27–32).⁷⁹ Beside Aristotle's examples, however, the relation that Marx and Engels trace between oppressors and oppressed over the course of history could be seen as another illustration of Aristotle's categorial scheme: there, too, it is a matter of members of a pair alike in kind, yet opposite in class, placed in position to affect one another reciprocally. The emphasis upon constancy and stance in the language of Marx and Engels can be seen as consistent, too, with the notion that action and passion pertain only to those entities that "have position." Agents and patients in history are established, in other words, within a continuum of contingent positions and related contraries.

Thought exclusively within the Aristotelian theoretical framework, what takes place over history would therefore figure as the predictable results of a stable relation, which at first stands in contradiction to the historical claims that Marx and Engels appear to offer. The impending revolutionary change that the *Manifesto* declares would not be possible if the opposition that characterizes "the history of all hitherto existing societies" were truly ontologically grounded. Society would exist instead according to the very principle that Engels would later challenge in his *Dialectic of Nature*—the principle, namely, "of the absolute immutability of nature" (MECW 25: 321). One indication of the ungrounded nature of this assumption, however, lies already in the fact that it lacks all cause. For if the structure of previous political history operated according to the Aristotelian categories of agent and patient, then it would also have to be true that the oppositional field consists in changes and exchanges that are governed by an active first cause that remains separate from the space of interaction. Aristotle illustrates this principle along the lines of food metabolism in the restoration of health: "food, while it acts, is itself somehow acted upon, for, while it acts, it is at the same time being heated or cooled or affected in some other way [τὸ δὲ σιτίον ποιοῦν καὶ αὐτὸ πάσχει τι· ἢ γὰρ θερμαίνεται ἢ ψύχεται ἢ ἄλλο τι πάσχει ἅμα ποιοῦν]" (324b 2–3). By contrast, the art of healing operates as the first cause of the restoration of health while remaining untouched by the bodies at work: "the art of the physician which, while it causes health, is not itself acted upon by that which is being healed [ἡ ἰατρική, αὐτὴ γὰρ ποιοῦσα ὑγίειαν οὐδὲν πάσχει ὑπὸ τοῦ ὑγιαζομένου]" (324a 35–324b 2). If the contraries of action and passion essentially entail "having position"—and being in a position to touch one another—the first cause is apositional with respect to the continuum that matters, and it is utterly out of touch with what it effects and affects. Thus, Aristotle concludes: "Of the things, then, which are capable of acting, those of which the form does not consist in matter are not affected, but those of which the form consists in matter are liable to be affected [Ὅσα μὲν οὖν μὴ ἐν ὕλῃ ἔχει τὴν μορφήν, ταῦτα μὲν ἀπαθῆ τῶν ποιητικῶν, ὅσα δ' ἐν ὕλῃ, παθητικά]" (324b 5–6). These arguments introduce an asymmetry between the primary agent and its patients, and they proceed from the general distinction that Aristotle draws between first causes and material, proximate causes: "Now there are two meanings of 'cause,' one being that which, as we say, results in the beginning of motion, and the other the material cause [Οὔσης δ' αἰτίας μιᾶς μὲν ὅθεν τὴν ἀρχὴν εἶναί φαμεν τῆς κινήσεως, μιᾶς δὲ τῆς ὕλης, τὴν τοιαύτην αἰτίαν λεκτέον]" (318a 1–3). For every pair of agent and patient, then, there would be a primary agency that does not map onto the topology of positions and material media (324b 12–14). And ultimately, all that takes place follows, according to Aristotle, from the supposition of a prime, unmoved mover that remains eternally active "apart from all that is sensible [κεχωρισμένη τῶν αἰσθητῶν]," as he writes in his lengthiest elaboration of this active essence in the twelfth book of the *Metaphysics* (1073a 4–5).

In the field of praxis, Marx and Engels imply that a similar structure governs the metabolic transformations of oppressor and oppressed each time the party that appears to be the primary agent of oppression turns out to undergo change through the very production process that develops under its auspices, from the replacement of the "feudal system of industry" with manufacture, to the comparison that Marx and Engels draw between bourgeois society and a "master sorcerer" or "Hexenmeister" who has "conjured up [. . .] gigantic means of production and of exchange" that exceed all control, like the forces summoned by the "sorcerer's apprentice" in Goethe's ballad of that name (MECW 6: 485, MEGA 1.6: 526; MECW 6: 489, MEGA 1.6: 531).[80] Yet their slight adaptation of Goethe's poem already indicates that there is no first cause for the dynamic of oppression and the division of oppressor and oppressed. For in the poem, the apprentice is saved when his master returns and brings the forces that his student had released back into retreat. In the *Manifesto*, however, the master-sorcerer takes the place of the apprentice and proves to be impotent himself. Marx and Engels thus imply that the role of the master was always delusional, and that the deluge of productive forces—unlike the deluge summoned in Goethe's poem—was bound to flood the entire economy and household of the bourgeois world along with its masters, rendering the critical question of Goethe's poem moot: "Should the whole house drown? [*Soll das ganze Haus ersaufen?*]."[81] No one is master of the history that Marx and Engels describe; all are overwhelmed or devoured by the process of production that consumes them. The closest thing to a cause that transcends the particular agents and patients in Marx and Engels's presentation would be the basis of production—"the means of production and of intercourse, on whose foundation the bourgeoisie built itself up"—insofar as this "foundation" or "Grundlage" figures as the underlying substance of all that is done, as the ὑποκείμενον of all social relations (MECW 6: 489, MEGA 1.6: 530). But if such a substrate may be considered a "cause" in the Aristotelian sense—in this case, the substantial cause of the productive and communicative motions that make up the language and life of society[82]—it is not a principle like the art of healing, and nothing about it indicates necessary grounds for division and oppression. All that is certain according to Marx and Engels is, rather, that this ground surges up against the divided society that it supposedly supports.

The pressing question would then seem to be: why oppression? Yet this question would be the wrong answer to the situation that Marx and Engels describe, in that it would maintain the assumption of a cause for what manifestly has none. Instead, the adoption of Aristotelian concepts and terms in Marx and Engels's text renders the absence of a first principle for oppression all the more conspicuous and exposes the historical constant of oppression to be without principle or ἀρχή. Marx and Engels's anachronistic and ontologizing exposure of the historical dynamic of class struggle thus exposes all that is and has been to be an order that lacks essential foundation, necessity, and principle cause—and that, as such, could only be the effect of a still more basic disorder. The history of all hitherto existing society is—fundamentally—anarchic.

Lived experience may be subject to the categories of agent and patient that define the historical field. But its foundation is not. The basis of production does not coincide essentially with the field of oppositions; it does not map onto the *champ* of the *Kampf*. And since any attempt to seek a first principle for the latter appears to be a lost cause, it is at the ground level that Marx and Engels also proceed further to undo the topology of opposition that lies upon it. They begin by exposing the ways in which the space of production accords with no topological coordinates, since the development of a world market extends to encompass "the whole surface of the globe" (MECW 6: 487, MEGA 1.6: 529). As a result, the production process involves the condensation of elements drawn from the "most outlying zones," or the "entlegensten Zonen," which extreme concentration has its correlate in the equally extreme dissemination of manufactured wares. Space is therefore no longer measurable by any stretch, and distance no longer makes sense when it comes to the making and marketing of goods. To the contrary, it soon turns out that space is without measure at all: "The world market has given an immense development to commerce, to navigation, to communication by land" (MECW 6: 488, MEGA 1.6: 529; MECW 6: 486, MEGA 1.6: 527). This development is immense—and more exactly, "immeasurable," "unermeßlich"—because the geographical determinations of distance and place have been eliminated by the relations involved in production. At the same time, moreover, this also means that there is no way to locate "the means of production and of intercourse" that would make up language and life (MECW 6: 489, MEGA 1.6: 530). This problem was one that Baudelaire had spoken to in "Le Voyage," and that Blanqui had addressed in calling the world of capital an "unknown abyss," each of whom adopts different strategies for coming to terms with it. In Marx and Engels's announcement, their response consists in pulling the ground out from under the philosophical tradition of substance through a "total movement" and revolution in language like none other. For if the current situation of the globe implies, for the time being, that oppression knows no limits, the haltless mobilization of space itself—a "total movement" not unlike the "Gesamt-Bewegung" of which and as which the communists are said to speak—renders any topology of fixed positions ontologically untenable, marking the first moment in the static history that Marx and Engels have recapitulated where a historical change in the relations and fields of existence could occur.

But where could anything be heading, if capital leaves nowhere to go? Worldwide change is not necessarily a viable prospect. In his essay "The Thing," for example, Martin Heidegger also thinks of the "frantic abolition of all distance" as the result of a catastrophe long in the making.[83] Unlike Marx, however, he considers its culmination to be not the "material conditions" for "exploding [the] basis" of capital and all of its oppressive mechanisms (MECW 29: 92, MEGA 2.1/2: 582), but the atomic bomb that threatens to "snuff out all life on earth."[84] "The atom bomb and its explosion," Heidgger writes, "are the mere final emission of what has long since taken place," ever since the "bearing-upon or concern" of experience was buried and forgotten in the reified language for things, or the *"realitas of res."*[85] Nothing could be less certain, then, than the more promising interpretation that Marx offers, when he writes in his notes from 1857–1858 that the multiplication of productive forces through machinery provides the "condition for [the] emancipation" of labor—and even the "emancipation from labor"[86]—by reducing "the quantity of labour necessary for the production of a certain object [. . .] to the minimum" (MECW 29: 87, MEGA 2.1/2: 578). Attending to the problematic status of these prospects, Heidegger elaborates the ways in which Marx's emphasis upon the repurposing of industrial technological and infrastructural means in communist society may nonetheless maintain a structure of domination—namely, the technological domination over objects to be made and instrumentalized—which would speak against Marx and Engels's prediction that such reforms would put an end to exploitation and antagonism (MECW 6: 503, MEGA 1.6: 543).[87] Both divergent thinkers, however, seem to concur on one point: the structure for theory and praxis will have altered explosively in the world of modern technology, calling for a different approach to being and existence than the one that had rested upon a certain tradition of interpreting Aristotelian premises up to the present.[88]

In Marx's oeuvre, this rethinking begins with his intensive engagement with the atomization of Aristotle's "total philosophy" in the Hellenistic schools of thought that arose in its wake. But also in the *Manifesto*, the global conditions that Marx and Engels describe correspond to the first "nodal point" in the history of philosophy—the symptomatic knot and cut in the history of theory and praxis—that had preoccupied Marx in his earliest notes on the shift from Aristotelian to Epicurean thought. With the "unermeßliche Entwicklung" of production and communication, the space of the world comes to resemble the infinite—the ἄπειρον—of the atomistic universe, and this space is one in which position itself is infinitely alterable, and opposition, impossible. Thus, even if the movements of the *Manifesto* cannot be reduced to a reiteration of ancient atomistic hypotheses, the earliest elaborations of space and time in atomism may be conducive to following the movement of *Manifesto*. For it is the consequences of atomistic ontology that the language of the *Manifesto* proceeds to unfold, just as it is atomistic cosmology, and not Aristotelian ontology that Engels would later praise when he announces in his *Dialectic of Nature*: "Thus we have once again returned to the mode of outlook of the great founders of Greek philosophy, the view that the whole of nature, from the smallest element to the greatest, from grains of sand to suns, from Protista to man, has its existence in eternal coming into being and passing away, in ceaseless flux, in unresting motion and change" (MECW 25: 327). But in the *Communist Manifesto*, Marx and Engels pursue the implications of this cosmology more radically than Engels would later do, hazarding a future that would escape all plans and projections.

To be sure, in certain respects, nothing could seem to be further removed from the premises of the *Communist Manifesto* than those of atomism. The *Communist Manifesto* issues a radical intervention in history, thought, and language that should exceed the thinking and practices of the present, and that therefore surpasses the more promising predictions that Marx and Engels offer here and elsewhere. For beyond the abolition of private property, exploitation, and wars among nation states, they add that communism would also alter the "forms of consciousness" or "Bewußtseinsformen" that had arisen through exploitive property relations, and with them, the sensibility, language, truth, religion, and morals that organize language and thought under oppressive conditions (MECW 6: 504, MEGA 1.6: 544). By contrast, in the atomistic universe of Lucretius and Epicurus, nothing new could come to be that is not or has not been realized through one combinatory possibility or another over the infinite expanses of space and time: "nothing new in the all is achieved besides that which has already come to be in infinite time [οὐδὲν ξένον ἐν τῷ παντὶ ἀποτελεῖται παρὰ τὸν ἤδη γεγενημένον χρόνον ἄπειρον]."[89] *Sub specie aeternitatis*, all thinkable and unthinkable possibilities are actual. Furthermore, if various orders rise and fall according to no immanent and reasonable principle, but for the chance collisions of differently shaped and weighted atoms, then their alterations can only ever be marked *post facto*, rendering every arrangement a *fait accompli*. As Lucretius says in *De rerum natura*:

> For in very truth, not by design did the first-beginnings of things place themselves each in their order with foreseeing mind, nor indeed did they make compact what movements each should start, but because many of them shifting in many ways throughout the universe are harried and buffeted by blows from limitless time, by trying movements and unions of every kind, at last they fall into such dispositions as those, whereby our world of things is created and holds together.
>
> Nam certe neque consilio primordia rerum
> ordine se quo quaeque sagaci mente locarunt
> nec quos quaeque <darent motus pepigere profecto>
> sed quia multa modis multis mutata per omne
> ex infinito vexantur percita plagis,
> omne genus motus et coetus experiundo
> tandem deveniunt in talis dispositruas,
> qualibus haec rerum consistit summa creata.[90]

Along these lines, the positions that fall into place in the making of our world are anything but stable or anchored in an unchanging topology, nor does "time" proceed in the sense of an irreversible order according to which changes might be plotted and durations of states might be measured. But the "federations" of atoms that make up any given constitution of things would not appear open to deliberate interventions, because the time of change will have always been a missed opportunity from the perspective of any sensible being.[91] Rather, Lucretius describes time as a sense that follows as a consequence of the shifting arrangement of things: "Even so time exists not by itself, but from actual things comes a feeling, what was brought to a close in time past, then what is present now, and further what is going to be hereafter [*tempus item per se non est, sed rebus ab ipsis / consequitur sensus, transactum quid sit in aevo, / tum quae res instet, quid porro deinde sequatur*]."[92] There is therefore no place or time for things to happen, but merely things that emerge from changed dispositions and thereby signal a temporal lapse. And because time would always only follow along with events—as that which Epicurus calls, according to Sextus Empiricus, σύμπτωμα συμπτωμάτων,[93] or the "coincidence of coincidences"[94]—time also could not be contemporaneous with that which takes place, but would only ever become perceptible after the fact, and sometimes not even then.

Positional shifts consequently become manifest in the future perfect, which temporal tension resonates in the unusual word Lucretius often adopts to denote positioning: namely, the future participle, "positura."[95] Yet it is not only the case, according to these premises, that every positioning becomes recognizable only belatedly; each also will have elapsed in a time that falls out of experience and escapes all parameters, because the interval of change is a time when nothing will have yet appeared to alter.[96] Each *positura* would therefore be *pre*positional in the double sense: it would denote what will have arrived as the result of an unnoticeable and therefore immemorial transition; and its observation would occur at a moment when it may no longer even hold in place, leaving all positionings to be determined.[97] Sensing any given arrangement therefore entails witnessing the future of a positioning that may also already be foregone and will have always already opened for another. Thus, atomism not only eliminates providence from the genesis of the world, but also appears to preclude providential or provisional intervention in any given state of affairs, including the kind of intervention that the *Manifesto* appears to be, if nowhere else than in the closing call for a new configuration of things by breaking old bonds: "The proletarians have nothing to lose but their chains. They have a world to win. PROLETARIAN OF ALL COUNTRIES, UNITE" (MECW 6: 519, MEGA 1.6: 557).

For this same reason, however, the infinite from which all things will have come to be and come to pass renders the coordinates for spatial directions impossible to establish, which is illustrated in Lucretius through the relations that emerge through language. Lucretius draws an analogy between the federations of atoms that make up all things and the arrangement of letters in his verses, which allows for the emergence of "sky," "sea," and "earth"—the so-called "elements" of the older Greek physiologists—and shows them to be indebted to compositions of more elementary units to which they bear no visible resemblance: "even in my verses it is of moment with what others and in what order each letter is placed. For the same letters signify sky, sea, earth, rivers, sun, [. . .] in truth, it is positionings that render discrepant things [*quin etiam refert nostris in versibus ipsis / cum quibus et quali sint ordine quaeque locata: namque eadem caelum mare terras flumina solem / significant* [. . .] *verum positura discrepitant res*]."[98] These remarks imply that, even in the absence of a topographical order, composition allows for positions to become sensible and to make sense. But more importantly, they show the imperceptible space of atomic arrangements to be thinkable and speakable solely through the language that addresses it, without being reduced or identical to that language. In other words, there is a discrepancy between the elements of language and the elements of nature, and because letters, in the final analysis, remain distinct from atoms—because letters are distinguishable—linguistic operations may not be determined by the workings of nature that they describe after all. Furthermore, even if they were to do exactly as they say, the explanations of atomism in *De rerum natura* would then be exposed to all the hazards and contingencies that are said to affect every other natural compound and element, rendering the language of atomism and its premises uncertain.

Although neither Epicurus nor Lucretius explicitly draws this consequence, then, language becomes presented in their texts as a structure that opens the elements of language and atoms alike to alternation, alteration, and division beyond all reckoning. As Thomas Schestag writes: "In this turn, the common ground of the didactic poem, the common, becomes—example. [. . .] The common's *becoming* example, however, does not simply turn the hierarchy—the priority of the common over the particular, of the whole over its parts—around; rather, in the *turn* of the common ground towards *itself*, in the attempt of its grounding and positing, the ground—the word—becomes—the condition of the condition—the letter—*driven asunder*."[99] Because Lucretius and Epicurus also consider the delivery of speech in voice or writing to be material, however, language also matters—and it may be all that matters—when it comes to changing the natural and historical makeup of relations.[100] A similar assumption may be seen to underlie the *Communist Manifesto*, even at those moments where it gives no imperatives for change, but merely claims to "express, in general terms, actual relations springing from an existing class struggle, from a historical movement [*geschichtliche Bewegung*] going on under our very eyes" (MECW 6: 498, MEGA 1.6: 538). For the "historical movement" would not be a "*historical* movement," if it were not for the construal and expression of this history that it makes manifest. Nor would it be a "historical *movement*," if it were not for the language of the *Manifesto* that sets it in motion.

At this point, for all their differences, the worlds of atomistic thought in *De rerum natura* and the global market addressed in the *Communist Manifesto* coincide not only in their voiding of stable topologies, but also in their mobilization of language to render the positionings of things discrepent with all positional or physical logic, as well as all cyclical patterns of historical or mechanical repetition.[101] Moreover, it is the possibilities of language that show this alteration to be possible at any and every time, and to be really immanent at every point. In one of the earliest testimonies on Democritean atomism, Aristotle illustrates θέσις, the Greek variant of "positura," at the level of the single letter, along the lines of the difference between Z and N (*Metaphysics* 985b 18). Here, position differs not with respect to other elements within a combination, but with respect to the rotations of a single shape, such that every single position would at once stand for every other possible position—and such that there would be no position that is not at the same time infinitely otherwise. This consequence follows from the fact that the notion of a determinate, non-relative position would have to rest upon a notion of place along the lines of Aristotle's definition of natural *topoi* in the *Physics*. Only within a limited cosmos could a distinction be drawn between above and below that is not dependent upon viewers (212a 23): " 'Above' is not anything you like, but where fire, and what is light, move. Likewise, 'below' is not anything you like, but where heavy and earth-like things move" (208b 19–22).[102] Relatively speaking, the positionings of Epicurus and Lucretius would instead be more like the mathematical objects that Aristotle distinguishes from entities that have place, insofar as they "are not in place, but still have right and left according to their position relatively to us [. . .]" (208b 22–25). Thus, Marx comments in his dissertation on the limited perspective implied in the apparent distinction of positions that Z and N illustrate: "It is evident from this quotation that Democritus considers the properties of the atom only in relation to the formation of the differences in the world of appearances, and not in relation to the atom itself" (MECW 1: 55, MEGA 1.1: 34). In relation to the atom "itself," by contrast, all positions would have their character according to their simultaneous, differential positionings, which may temporarily draw them into certain combinations with other atoms, but which can never be fixed according to a single point of view. The "positura" of each atom is therefore already its *clinamen* or inclination away from any direct and determined line of motion, which principle of deviation forms the condition of possibility for all possible worlds in atomistic thought.[103] Z is always also N, as well as И, and all others besides, including those which would render the shapes rendered here unrecognizable or dashed through entirely—. The *positura* of the atoms are polypositional, and therefore absolutely prepositional, such that no position—not even a preposition—could be adequate to their description. When Lucretius writes, "verum positura discrepitant res," this would not only mean that discrete things emerge from the positionings of atoms, but also that the *positura* themselves are discrepant and nothing but the rendition of discrepancies. What is true of atoms and letters, however, would also extend to anything that might be said or done, insofar as the analogy indicates that the differentiations of *positura* are not particular to the infinitesimally small elements of the universe, but cut across all speakable matters.

In the *Communist Manifesto*, the sentences it sets forth display precisely the sort of polydirectional, discrepant motion that characterizes the positionings of the atomistic universe, and they show the space of theory and praxis alike to break into "total-movement" (MECW 6: 498, MEGA 1.6: 538). For example, when it comes to the rise of the productive forces that generated bourgeois society, what appears to be "conjured up"—what this society "herauf beschwor"—is already said to be an uprising, and thereby displays a differential tendency in one and the same stroke: "For many a decade past," Marx and Engels continue, "the history of industry and commerce is but the history of the uprising [*Empörung*] of modern productive forces against modern conditions of production, against the property relations that are the conditions for the existence of the bourgeoisie and of its rule" (MECW 6: 489, MEGA 1.6: 531). Such is a language of social change, in which the positive developments of an up-and-coming power are themselves overwhelming and overcome, beyond and beside whatever anyone may set out to say or do—as in the poem by Goethe to which Marx and Engels allude, where the sorcerer-apprentice's assumption of power leads to the deluge that threatens to sweep the whole household into a devastating flood: "Immer neue Güsse / bringt er schnell herein, / Ach! und hundert Flüsse / Stürzen auf mich ein."[104] The coincidence of rise and uprising here springs from the simultaneous evocation of the discrepant senses conveyed by the directional prefix *empor–*, which becomes negatively charged in its substantive and socially inflected form: "Empörung." What appears to denote the tendency of things from one perspective thus becomes visible as its opposite at one and the same time, in one and the same linguistic particle that restlessly differs from itself.

The language that Marx and Engels deploy to address these alterations of positioning is not a matter of setting up opposed notions separately and arguing for a basic *coincidentia oppositorum*, which would imply the presupposition and reinforcement of the very distinctions that the *Manifesto* breaks down. Like the positioning of atoms in Epicurean thought, the language of positioning itself moves in many ways at once, so that no thesis can be asserted without coming apart *per se*. Nor is it a matter of merely drawing analogies when the language of the *Manifesto* appears to reproduce the movement of things, for the latter *are* already language, according to

Marx and Engels's (Epicurean) conception of social relations as language, in the broadest sense of the word. Thus, when Marx and Engels describe the economic empire of the bourgeois over all lands—starting with the countryside, and extending to the worldwide expansion of markets—the words that denote the conquered are themselves words for linguistic peculiarities: "[The bourgeoisie] has created enormous cities, has greatly increased the urban population as compared with the rural, and has thus torn a significant part [*bedeutenden Teil*] of the population from the idiotism [*Idiotismus*] of rural life. Just as it has made the country dependent on the towns, so it has made barbaric and semi-barbaric lands dependent on the civilised ones, nations of peasants on nations of bourgeois, the East on the West" (MECW 6: 488, MEGA 1.6: 530). The idiotism—or singular linguistic habits—of isolated peasants is eradicated as the peasants are sent to the cities, because they break from their habitation and habitual activities in a move where nothing of their former experience translates. What this failed translation means is further indicated when their significance or *Bedeutung* as a portion of their community is reduced to a fraction and quantum in the phrase, "significant part" or "bedeutenden Teil." Here, the quantitative significance or qualitative insignificance of this segment of the population corresponds to its integration into the language of equivalence that dominates commodity and labor exchange.

Similarly, Marx and Engels's reference to "barbaric and semi-barbaric lands" evokes the onomatopoetic denotation for those non-Greek speaking peoples whom the Greeks had encountered in their travels, conquests, and wars. But if barbarism characterizes all who do not belong to the bourgeoisie—who themselves seem to have no particular means of communication but wealth—then the semantic value of "barbaric" can only translate to money as well: bare (*bar*) of cash (*Bargeld*). These implications follow from the way in which the language of relations within bourgeois society was described shortly before this paragraph: "It has pitilessly torn asunder the motley feudal ties that bound man to his 'natural superiors,' and has left remaining no other nexus between man and man than naked [*nackte*] interest, than unfeeling 'bare payment' [*'bare Zahlung'*]" (MECW 6: 486–87, MEGA 1.6: 528). These remarks would thus seem to draw a simple and universal distinction between those who have means and those who are stripped of them; however, the language of Marx and Engels discloses further complexities involved in the logic of monetary coverage. For if the language of civilization is that of "cash payment" or "bare payment" (as "bare Zahlung" implies), then both are synonymous with "bare cash" ("bares

Geld," or "Bargeld"), and therefore indistinguishable from the language of those who are bare of cash, rendering the whole world an inarticulate and linguistically impoverished one despite all its wealth: a world that is utterly bar-bar-ic. Like the flood that the uprising of productive forces had conjured, the sphere of capital not only liquidates geographical, linguistic, and lived particularity in all its idiotisms, but also voids all place for anything but the cold flow of cash. There are no holds barred: "It has drowned the most holy shudders of religious fervour, of chivalrous enthusiasm, of philistine sentimentalism, in the ice-cold water of egotistical calculation" (MECW 6: 487, MEGA 1.6: 528).

In these ways, among others, the propositions of the *Manifesto*—the positions it articulates—are set upon no grounds and settle nowhere, but present a rendition of discrepencies that render all things other than they appear. Everything becomes a matter of revolutionizing language and reality within a world where the *status quo* already does not and cannot rest in place or in peace, and where relations form a flood of activity within an immense void. This expression of current history is devastating; however, it also entails as a consequence that all things are also infinitely alterable, and that alterity already characterizes reality, in innumerable ways. The totality expressed in the *Manifesto* thus remains totally open, which Marx and Engels indicate by rendering every word an atomic bomb of sorts and make explicit when they announce: "The theoretical propositions [*Sätze*] of the Communists are in no way based on ideas or principles that have been invented, or discovered by this or that would-be universal reformer" (MECW 6: 498, MEGA 1.6: 538). For with this utterance, they not only refuse to assume the role of a "would-be reformer," but also underscore the lack of "basis" for their "theoretical propositions," and therefore the absence of propositions in their text. Instead, every theoretical "Satz" would be a theoretical leap—a "theoretischer Satz" in another sense of the word—which posits and opposes nothing, but springs toward that which is not, and thereby moves past its presentation of world movements as it speaks. These sentences are therefore not unlike the more famous leap of which Marx would speak in the *Eighteenth Brumaire of Louis Bonaparte*, where the proletarian revolution is said to culminate at a point where "a situation has been created which makes all turning back impossible, and the conditions themselves cry out: Hic Rhodus, hic salta! Here is the rose, here dance!" (MECW 11: 106–07, MEGA 1.11: 101–02).[105] As groundless leaps, the revolutionary sentences announced in the *Manifesto* outstrip past positions, current situations, and determinate projects alike, because they exceed any disposition of the world that could so much as temporarily seem to take hold. Whereas all previous history was said to lie upon specious foundations for placement, action, and passion, this text takes place in and as the time of their breakdown and uprising—it takes place as the event itself, whose outcome remains outstanding.

In this respect, Marx and Engels's language of "total movement" can only issue into blindness, and may have always been, as Althusser said of revolutionary praxis, "immersed in its activities and therefore theoretically blind."[106] If the *Communist Manifesto* should nonetheless be an instance of "presentation" or "Darstellung" that exposes reality "*under* our eyes [*unter unseren Augen*]," then it does so in the sense that it shows reality to remain below the threshold of sight and foresight, ideals and ideologies (MECW 6: 498, MEGA 1.6: 538). It therefore also provides no vision for the future, but moves beyond every place and presence to deliver a theory that is out of sight. Only the unforeseeable could come of the time that the *Manifesto* utters and ushers in, as it ousts all positionings from their apparent sites and opens an interval before the time of construable events. As Hamacher has written in a text that traces a different trajectory through Marx's writings: "This opening which is the present, must, *hic et nunc*, be something other than future, more than *a* future: pluralities of futures, but also more than futures, a pluperfect-future; not only another time and other times, but what would no longer be time. The promise would be the place where this other time and this other than time occur. It is the place—the atopic place—where possibilities are indeed opened, but only those constitutively lacking the conditions of their verification and actualization."[107]

It is this opening that structures the language of the *Manifesto* and that gives it its infinitely divergent bearings. This may be why, from the outset, the *Manifesto* was cast not as a decisive announcement or as an exemplary instance of a "new genre"[108]—but rather as a sketch that "Communists of various nationalities have [. . .] *drafted / cast off* [*entworfen*]" (MECW 6: 481, MEGA 1.6: 525, my emphasis). The deluge of production and cash-flows may mobilize the entire globe, but the "total-*movement*" of the *Manifesto* overshoots it, moves the totality of movement, and gives it a run for its money, leaping off from the history that was never the be all and end all of the world, and leaving off at the point where everything in the world remains to be seen. The practical and theoretical achievement of the *Communist Manifesto* is nothing less than this novel leap and leave. It delivers a language that casts off, over and beyond its field of vision and action, and that gainsays and gains on every against. A throw-away theory and practice. Another way. Totally.

Afterword

On Annovation

"All comes to pass as if, at the core of literature and language, beyond the apparent movements that transform them, a point of instability were reserved, a potential for substantial metamorphosis that is capable of changing everything about it without changing anything at all," writes Maurice Blanchot in his essay, "Literature and the Right to Death."[1] These remarks on literature and language could also describe the many instabilities that have been retraced throughout this book. Between all and nothing—between making "all things new" and "nothing new under the sun"—the extreme possibilities and impossibilities of novel announcements are troubled, again and again, by those movements in and of language that allow all speakable things to be offered, altered, and withdrawn. Even when a text such as Marx and Engels's *Communist Manifesto* casts the language of a "total movement" into motion, there remains all the more to say of all that they speak—for this movement could only be what it is if it too goes on and goes off in unforeseen directions. Marx and Engels's novel intervention, among others, would have to remain as provisional as the orders and situations that their writing unsettles. Their premises, like those which Blanqui sets forth in *Eternity by the Stars*,[2] may be said to persist solely "until further notice."[3]

All talk of novelty—whether it be announced or denounced—proceeds in the absence of grounds and ends, and thus proceeds along divergent trajectories where each term and coordinate for orientation may turn out to be a placeholder and alibi for that which remains unset and unsaid. It may even be that the "new" gives word of another subject entirely, as in Baudelaire's "Le Voyage," where the voyagers' last wish to plunge into the depths of the waters "to find the *new*" (*pour trouver du* nouveau) liquidates the speaking subjects and their objectives in a word that allows "we" (*nous*) and the "water" (*eau*) to swim together. The question or sense of the "new" therefore remains open-ended in all directions, which the writings of Nietzsche, Baudelaire, Blanqui, and Marx show in singular ways, even and especially when their concerns cross with one another. It is precisely because the "new" remains unsettled, however, that it may continue to figure as a pivotal term in revolutionary rhetoric, poetics, and politics.

In this respect, the language of "innovation" becomes one that might best be described as "*an*novation," both in the sense of the prefix *ad-* and in the privative modus of the *a-*, in analogy to the way in which Werner Hamacher has spoken of the *afformative* dimension of formation:

> *Afformative* is not *aformative*; afformance 'is' the event of forming, itself formless, to which all forms and all performative acts remain exposed. (The Latin *ad-*, and accordingly *af-*, marks the opening of an act, and of an act of opening, as in the very appropriate example of *affor*, meaning 'addressing,' e.g., when taking leave.) But of course, in *afformative* one must also read *aformative*, as determined by *afformative*.[4]

Thought of in this way, *an*novation would offer a new opening in speech that permits a novel announcement without delivering definite or definitive news, as when Zarathustra breaks word of "esteeming" (*Schätzen*) and "creating" (*Schaffen*) in his speech "On the Thousand and One Goals," and thereby exposes his story of creation and creative goals to the unspoken name of another—namely, "Scheherazade"—whose language breaks from all goals, ends, and stories for the precarious sake of living on. But another alternative for designating the immanent alterations that language exposes, undergoes, and bears out could also simply be "announcement," a word that adds up to "*an*novation," by adjoining *ad-* to *nuntiare* ("to bear a message"), which traces back, in turn, to *novere* ("to make new"). Announcements on novelty could then be said to address and trouble the sense of annunciatory speech *per se*, as well as all that it may be brought to bear upon. In this case, their purport would not be *a* novum or *the* new, but the disturbances that their language registers each time anew. And yet, the very structure of "announcement" would therefore also imply that there could be no one word or formulation for this movement of language toward innovation and *an*novation. To approach propositions as announcements or on "announcements" would be to trace the ways in which enunciations at once initiate and suspend the possibility of a novel intervention, so as to open each to other words that remain outstanding and unpredictable. Such an approach would entail parting with the classical *logos apophantikos* that should deliver true or false statements on beings, as well as the performatives that should make their promises true, so as to attend to a dimension of speech that is neither verifiable nor functional in a way that could be stabilized or directed to an end. And if this means that *an*novative events in language would have to elude decisive confirmation as well—if it even means that, as Blanchot says, "all comes to pass [. . .] without changing anything at all"—there would also be no way to tell for sure whether everything will not have already changed in and through the very words that lie "under our eyes" (MECW 6: 498, MEGA 1.6: 538).

There is no end to *an*novation in language, both before and after the texts of the nineteenth century of revolutions and *nouveautés*, because and not despite of the fact that there may be nothing "whereof it may be said" with certitude, "See this is new" (Ecc. 1.9–10). Any word of the "new" that could be evident or predicated of anything would not be the new of the word, where even the "nothing new" could always turn out to speak for something else. In the opening sentence of Samuel Beckett's *Murphy*—"The sun shone, having no alternative, on the nothing new"[5]—"*the* nothing new" is demarcated with a definite article that sentences it to be merely one thing among others, all or any of which may be other than this "nothing," if not "new." And at the same time, even if the sun has no alternative but to shine upon "the nothing new," the sun may not touch all there is. But whether one repeats "nothing new," or pretends to issue a novel claim, there is no last word on the new that would not solicit others: "More words. And never THE word. A novel must progress toward a word. Any word that—"[6]

Notes

Introduction

1. Ernst Bloch, *The Principle of Hope*, 6.
2. See Bloch, *The Principle of Hope*, 195–286.
3. Bloch, *The Principle of Hope*, 13, 4, 12.
4. Jacques Derrida, "Psyche: Invention of the Other," 34.
5. Derrida, "Psyche: Invention of the Other," 28.
6. For an excellent discussion of the distinction between the terms "*futur*" and "*l'avenir*" in Derrida's writings, among others, such as Jean-Luc Nancy and Catherine Malabou, see Jean-Paul Martinon, *On Futurity: Malabou, Nancy and Derrida*, esp. 1–26.
7. Derrida, "Psyche: Invention of the Other," 44.
8. Derrida, "Psyche: Invention of the Other," 44.
9. Derrida, "Psyche: Invention of the Other," 44, 45.
10. Derrida, "Psyche: Invention of the Other," 44.
11. Derrida, "Psyche: Invention of the Other," 44.
12. Derrida, "Psyche: Invention of the Other," 30. Derrida also insists, moreover, that "the other is not the new," and thus cautions against a conflation of the two. Derrida, "Psyche: Invention of the Other," 46.
13. Werner Hamacher, "History, Teary: Some Remarks on *La Jeune Parque*," 85.
14. Werner Hamacher, "What Remains to Be Said," 218.
15. Bloch, *The Principle of Hope*, 202.
16. See, for example, Harold Rosenberg's *The Tradition of the New*. In this study, he argues that "the famous 'modern break' with tradition has lasted long enough to have produced its own tradition," which he proceeds to address through analyses of specific instances of modern painting and poetry and the "unique contradictions" that arise through their aspirations and claims to innovate (*Tradition of the New*, 9–10). Peter Bürger, however, contests the relevance of "the category" of the new in his characterization of the avant-garde, arguing that "the historical avant-garde movements not only intend to break with the traditional representational system

but the total abolition of the institution that is art" (*Theory of the Avant-Garde*, 63). Hans-Robert Jauss, on the other hand, sought to approach the "quarrel of the ancients and moderns" over a broader chronological stretch. In texts such as "Ursprung und Bedeutung der Fortschrittsidee in der Querelle des Anciens et des Modernes" and *Literaturgeschichte als Provokation*, he pursues in an erudite fashion the parallel development of the notion of modernity with emergence of Christianity, which undergoes further shifts with the belief in scientific progress that arose in the early modern era (*Literaturgeschichte als Provokation*, 29). He argues that the humanistic notion of an insuperable ancient ideal was further modified as altered conditions and values came to be seen in the eighteenth century to call for new presentational practices in art, whose measure was to be found not in the past, but in the history of the present (*Literaturgeschichte als Provokation*, 35).

17. Boris Groys, *On the New*, 10, 4. Groys also challenges an overestimation of commodity exchange as the driving force behind cultural innovation, emphasizing that an "economy of sacrifice, expenditure, violence, and consequence" would also need to be "taken into consideration" (*On the New*, 12–13). He also suggests that its modern valence presupposes "the social and technical means for preserving the old [. . .], for it then seems superfluous to produce tautological, derivative works that merely repeat what has long been contained in the archives" (*On the New*, 21).

18. Michael North, *Novelty: A History of the New*, 6–7.

19. North also considers the importance of language to the process of generating novelties through "recombination," which he traces back to the analogy between letters and elements in ancient atomism and follows through to the pronunciations of conceptual artists in the twentieth century. However, he does not enter into detailed analyses with regard to how a rhetoric of novelty may operate in the various texts that he addresses, most likely due to the broader scope of his project. See, for example, North, *Novelty*, 32, 198.

20. Nicolas Dierks, *Endlose Erneuerung: Moderne Kultur und Ästhetik mit Wittgenstein und Adorno*, 161. However, he also insists upon a study of the usage of the word "new" over time, in order to trace how the rules of the language game that determines "novelty" shifted when, for example, science moved away from a "static and deterministic cosmology," and emphasis began to be placed on individual expression in the oeuvres of Jean-Jacques Rousseau and the writers of the *Sturm und Drang* movement (*Endlose Erneuerung*, 192). His Wittgenstein-inspired approach should, he argues, allow for a concept of novelty that can account for historical change and that does not entail the assumption of a radical breach, insofar the rules of language games—which are only ever realized and revised in practice—"are constitutively open for further development" (*Endlose Erneuerung*, 114).

21. Werner Hamacher, "History, Teary: Some Remarks on *La Jeune Parque*," 85.

22. Biblical quotations, unless otherwise noted, are drawn from *The New Oxford Annotated Bible*.

23. For a lengthier discussion of this passage from Ecclesiastes and several of its interpretations in theological and literary texts, see Kristina Mendicino, "Newswriting, Historiography, and the Controversion of the Present (After Heine)."

24. Joseph-Anne-Marie de Moyriac de Mailla, *Histoire générale de la Chine, ou annales de cet Empire, traduites du Tong-Kien-Kang-Mou*, 174. All translations from this work are mine. North also emphasizes the way in which Pound's famous modernist slogan can be traced back to "a historical anecdote concerning Ch'eng T'ang [. . .] first king of the Shang dynasty" (North, *Novelty*, 162). For a commentary and abbreviated bibliography on Pound's sources for this canto, see Carroll F. Terrell, *A Companion to the Cantos of Ezra Pound*, 203.

25. de Mailla, *Histoire générale de la Chine*, 174.

26. de Mailla, *Histoire générale de la Chine*, 174.

27. de Mailla, *Histoire générale de la Chine*, 175.

28. Ezra Pound, *The Cantos*, 264–65. In his translations of Confucius, Pound also records a variant of this inscription in *The Great Digest*: "In letters of gold on T'ang's bathtub: AS THE SUN MAKES IT NEW / DAY BY DAY MAKE IT NEW / YET AGAIN MAKE IT NEW" (Pound, *Confucius: The Unwobbling Pivot, The Great Digest, The Analects*, 36). This quotation is followed by a reference to "the K'ang Proclamation," which reads: "Hence the man in whom speaks the voice of his forebears cuts no log that he does not make fit to be roof-tree [does nothing that he does not bring to a maximum, that he does not carry through to a finish]. *This is the second chapter of the comment containing and getting the grist of the phrase: Renew the people. / Ideogram: axe, tree, and wood-pile*" (Pound, *Confucius*, 39).

29. Paul de Man, "Literary History and Literary Modernity," in *Blindness and Insight*, 148. See also the commentary in Hugh Kenner's major study of Pound, where he writes with regard to Pound's translation of similar words in *The Great Digest*, "Calling things by their names is an endless task. The names rust. [. . .] But by 1917 Pound had forged a new language, [. . .] a block of speech and perception new to the English poetic tradition, and a use of language that responds to the pressures of perception with (Ching Ming) accuracy and adequacy" (Kenner, *The Poetry of Ezra Pound*, 130–32). For a discussion of Pound's "new" imperative within a compendium of earlier and later quotations testifying to the modern imperative to renew, see Jed Rasula's useful survey, "Make It New," 713–33.

30. Pound, *The Cantos*, 265.

31. The emphasis upon clearing and cutting may also point toward the strain of "destructive futurity" in Pound's writing, a strain that has been aligned by other readers with his growing interest in Marinetti's Futurist movement and even fascist aesthetics. For a reading of the fascist tendencies of Pound's aesthetics, see David Barnes, "Fascist Aesthetics: Ezra Pound's Cultural Negotiations in 1930s Italy," 19–35. Barnes retraces Pound's turn from an initial distaste for Futurism to a growing interest in Marinetti as a "voice of aggressive Fascism" ("Fascist Aesthetics,"

25). The counterpart to this tendency in Pound's poetics, Barnes argues, may be found in Pound's practice of "searching through reams and reams of the past for the fresh phrase," which Barnes reads as a reflection of the way in which fascist cultural politics "trod a path between futuristic modernity and imperialistic nostalgia" (Barnes, "Fascist Aesthetics," 22).

32. Audrey Wasser, *The Work of Difference: Modernism, Romanticism, and the Production of Literary Form*, 2. Wasser also acknowledges the "not" of novelty, when she writes in her chapter on Blanchot: "Mediated by representation, newness can appear only in the guise of opposition, so that any new creation is grasped in terms of what its conditions of creation are *not*. Or else it is determined as what must lie outside of conceptual thought altogether, so that it is opposed not only to its conditions, but to everything that can appear and be conceived" (*The Work of Difference*, 68). However, that which "lies outside" of conceptual thinking cannot be "opposed" to it; rather, such a relation of opposition would entail subordinating the new to the concepts of relation and contrariety, and therefore would not describe the structure of an "outside."

33. Jacob Taubes, *Occidental Eschatology*, 12. Similarly, Karl Löwith interprets the horizon of historical meaning—understood as "a transcendent purpose" for all that occurs—through a theological genealogy that is oriented toward a future eschaton. It is within such an understanding, he argues, that novelty becomes meaningful as well, since "[n]othing really new can occur in the future when it is 'the nature of all things to grow as well as to decay'" (*Meaning in History*, 7). This is not the place to enter extensively into the debate that ensued between Löwith and Hans Blumenberg over Löwith's secularization hypothesis, or the further investigations of the modern inheritance of theological rhetoric and thought. For Blumenberg's arguments against the notion that historical theories of progress are indebted to Judeo-Christian eschatology, see *The Legitimacy of the Modern Age*. For more recent analyses of these issues, see Marcel Gauchet, *The Disenchantment of the World: A Political History of Religion*, and Jean-Luc Nancy, *Dis-Enclosure*. For an excellent collection of essays that situates Nancy's work within the context of the Blumenberg-Löwith debate, see also Alexandrova et al., *Re-treating Religion: Deconstructing Christianity with Jean-Luc Nancy*.

34. Theodor Adorno, *Aesthetic Theory*, 19.

35. Heidegger, *Basic Questions of Philosophy*, 94; *Grundfragen der Philosophie*, 106. In his texts from the late 1930s, Heidegger sharply distinguishes "the history of being," or *Seinsgeschichte*, from the modern discipline of "history" or *Historie*, which registers the "news" of the past: the "deeds, works, productions, and opinions" that are recorded "as given occurrences [*Begebenheiten*] [. . .], calculated and presented in their succession and difference" (*Contributions to Philosophy*, 105; *Beiträge zur Philosophie*, 151). What Heidegger summarizes here are the results of a tendential shift from the universal history of Hegelian idealism to what Jeffrey Andrew Barash

has traced as a fact-based approach to historiography, which emerged with the "'predominance' of the natural sciences in the 1860s and 1870s" (Barash, *Martin Heidegger and the Problem of Historical Meaning*, 16). Yet as often as Heidegger casts the nineteenth century in a negative light, he also indicates that the decisive turn in the history of being that he seeks to retrieve began then, precisely at the same time that some of the most destructive consequences of metaphysics were unfolding with industrialization. In *Contributions to Philosophy*, Heidegger writes under the heading, "Hölderlin—Kierkegaard—Nietzsche": "What hidden history of the much invoked nineteenth century happened here?" (Heidegger, *Contributions*, 143; *Beiträge*, 204). And in *Basic Questions of Philosophy*, Heidegger again asserts that the names of thinkers, poets, and artists from the nineteenth century—"Schiller, Hölderlin, Kierkegaard, van Gogh, Nietzsche"—stand as "enigmatic signs, inscribed in the most hidden ground of our history." Heidegger goes on to call them "harbingers of a change of history, lying deeper and reaching further than all 'revolutions' within the compass of the activities of men, of peoples, and of their contrivances. Here something comes to pass, for which we have no measure and no space [. . .]" (Heidegger, *Basic Questions*, 182; *Grundfragen*, 216).

36. Pound, *The Cantos*, 265.

37. Benjamin, *The Arcades Project*, 918. Similarly, Adorno aligns artistic innovation in and beyond the nineteenth century with commodity production and reproduction: "*Nouveauté* is aesthetically the result of historical development, the trademark of consumer goods appropriated by art by means of which artworks distinguish themselves from the ever-same inventory in obedience to the need for the exploitation of capital, which, if it does not expand, if it does not—in its own language—offer something new, is eclipsed. The new is the aesthetic seal of expanded reproduction, with its promise of undiminished plentitude" (Adorno, *Aesthetic Theory*, 20).

38. These words appear in a quotation from Paul Valéry that Benjamin includes in Convolute S, "Painting, Jugendstil, Novelty," *The Arcades Project* [S10, 6], 560.

39. History thereby becomes the "time of hell," where "the newest remains, in every respect, the same" (Benjamin, *The Arcades Project* [S1, 5], 544).

40. Benjamin, *The Arcades Project* [S10, 3], 560.

41. These words are drawn from Benjamin's essay, "The Storyteller," but are integral to *The Arcades Project* as well, where he explicitly refers to this essay again in his convolute on "Idleness." See Walter Benjamin, "The Storyteller," 143, 148; *The Arcades Project* [m3a 5], 804. Benjamin also opens his exposé from 1939 with a reference to the two main contrasting figures he evokes in his essay on "The Storyteller" to illustrate the depreciation of experience: "The subject of this book is an illusion expressed by Schopenhauer in the following formula: to seize the essence of history, it suffices to compare Herodotus and the morning newspaper" (*The Arcades Project*, 14). His words on information also resonate, moreover, with Jean-François

Lyotard's discussion of the way in which the news forecloses the arrival of a *novum* with its announcement, because journalistic information defines each instant and thereby precludes its opening to an uncertain future: "As soon as it is transmitted and shared, it ceases to be information, it becomes an environmental given [. . .]. The length of time it occupies is, so to speak, instantaneous. Between two pieces of information, 'nothing happens,' by definition. A confusion thereby becomes possible, between what is of interest to information and the director, and what is the question of the avant-gardes, between what happens—the new—and the *Is it happening?*, the *now*" (Lyotard, *The Inhuman*, 105–06; cf. *L'inhumain*, 116–17).

42. Derrida, "Psyche: Invention of the Other," 15.

43. Derrida, "Psyche: Invention of the Other," 22.

44. Benjamin, *The Arcades Project*, 25, 26; cf. *Gesammelte Schriften*, 5: 75, 77.

45. Benjamin, *The Arcades Project* [D5a, 6], 112.

46. Benjamin, *The Arcades Project* [D5a, 2], 111, translation modified.

47. "J'ai fait un long poème dédié à Max Du Camp, qui est à faire frémir la nature, et surtout les amateurs du progrès" (Charles Baudelaire to Charles Asselineau, 20 February 1859, in *Correspondance: 1832–1860*, 1: 553, my translation).

48. I borrow this phrase from Dierks, who claims that modern discussions of novelty in the discourse of the sciences, among others, emerged through a departure from a "static and deterministic cosmology" (Dierks, *Endlose Erneuerung*, 192). This historical trajectory is disturbed by the writings of Baudelaire, Blanqui, Marx, and Nietzsche, on which see the chapters that follow, where certain static cosmological speculations turn out to be precisely what sets the world in motion.

49. Theodor Adorno, *Aesthetic Theory*, 19.

50. Derrida, "Psyche: Invention of the Other," 15.

51. Benjamin, "On the Concept of History," 392.

52. Benjamin, *Über den Begriff der Geschichte*, 20.

53. S. D. Chrostowska, "Angelus Novus, Angst of History," 57.

54. See Irving Wohlfarth, "Die Willkür der Zeichen: Zu einem sprachphilosophischen Grundmotiv Walter Benjamins," 11–12.

55. Ian Balfour, "Reversal, Quotation (Benjamin's History)," 641.

56. Pound, *The Cantos*, 265.

57. For an excellent discussion of "discussion," to which this remark is indebted, see Thomas Schestag, *para—Titus Lucretius Carus, Johann Peter Hebel, Francis Ponge*.

58. "*Also sprach Zarathustra. Ein Buch für Alle und Keinen*. Es ist eine 'Dichtung,' oder ein fünftes 'Evangelium' oder irgend etwas, für das es noch keinen Namen giebt: bei weitem das Ernsteste und *auch* Heiterste meiner Erzeugnisse, und Jedermann zugänglich. So glaube ich denn, daß es eine 'sofortige Wirkung' thun wird" (Friedrich Nietzsche to Ernst Schmeitzner, 13 February 1883, in *Sämtliche Briefe: Kritische Studienausgabe*, 6: 327, my translation.).

Chapter 1

1. Friedrich Nietzsche to Carl von Gersdorff, 21 June 1871, in *Selected Letters of Friedrich Nietzsche*, 80.
2. Friedrich Nietzsche, *Nachgelassene Fragmente 1875–1879*, in *Kritische Studienausgabe*, 8: 583. This edition will henceforth be cited as *KSA*, followed by volume and page number.
3. Friedrich Nietzsche, *The Birth of Tragedy and The Case of Wagner*, 17.
4. Friedrich Nietzsche, *The Gay Science*, 339–40.
5. All English translations are cited parenthetically by page number on the basis of Walter Kaufmann's translation of *Thus Spoke Zarathustra*. I have occasionally modified the translation to draw out certain nuances of Nietzsche's syntax or vocabulary that are critical for my reading.
6. Reading of the firehound as a figure for the revolutionary, Alain Badiou writes: "Rapidly, it becomes clear that the fire-dog is nothing but the spokesperson, the agent, or the actor of the revolutionary political event itelf, of revolt, of the collective storm" (Badiou, "Who is Nietzsche?" 7). Gary Shapiro, on the other hand, has advanced a reading of the fire hound as a representative of "state-oriented politicians, especially Rousseauian enthusiasts," which he elaborates thus: "The firehound is an ego puffed up with a desire to expand its power in the state" (Shapiro, "Nietzsche on Geophilosophy and Geoaesthetics," 486).
7. There have been many important commentaries on the new premises that Nietzsche sets forth in this book, often through readings attentive to the literary features of the text, of which I name a few here. In his monograph, *Zarathustra's Dionysian Modernism*, Robert Gooding-Williams offers a reading of the tension between Zarathustra's investment in the "possibility of creating new values" and the difficulties that any departure from tradition and inherited vocabulary necessarily entails. He interprets this tension as one that characterizes Nietzsche's work as a modernist philosophical project, in line with contemporary modernist impulses to create "novelty-engendering interruptions of received practices and traditions" (Gooding-Williams, *Zarathustra's Dionysian Modernism*, 19, 3). Peter Sloterdijk offers another description of the "overman" in relation to modern principles of evolution and the religious practice of ascetic exercise—whose equivalent he finds in the virtuosity of the tight-rope dancer and those who surpass the human in over-bearing physical and psychic regimes. See Sloterdijk, *You Must Change Your Life*.
8. See Bernard Pautrat, "Nietzsche Medused," 159–73.
9. Friedrich Nietzsche to Heinrich Köselitz, 14 August 1881, in *Selected Letters of Friedrich Nietzsche*, 177.
10. Writers such as Gilles Deleuze have offered strong interpretations of eternal return as "the being of becoming as such, the unity of multiplicity," and thus as distinct from the ancient interpretation of repetition as "a subjugation of

becoming" (*Nietzsche and Philosophy*, 29). Several other major interpretations of eternal return, which elaborate the specific difference of Nietzsche's formulation of eternal return and the seemingly similar versions of his ancient predecessors, include Martin Heidegger, *Nietzsche*, vol. 1; Pierre Klossowski, *Nietzsche and the Vicious Circle*; and Bernd Magnus, *Nietzsche's Existential Imperative*. For further arguments that what recurs in Nietzsche's thought of eternal recurrence is never the same, but the difference produced through the pulsions of returning itself, see also Gilles Deleuze's *Difference and Repetition*. In a brilliant reading of Nietzsche's notebooks, David Farrell Krell opens further important insights into the difference of the same in his chapter, "Eternal Recurrence—of the Same? Reading Notebook M III, 1," from his monograph, *Infectious Nietzsche*, 158–76. Paolo D'Iorio adopts a historicizing approach to the differences involved in Nietzsche's version of eternal recurrence in his recent study of Nietzsche's writing in the context of the contemporary scientific discourses with which Nietzsche had intensively engaged. See Paolo D'Iorio, "The Eternal Return: Genesis and Interpretation."

11. The passage reads: "Alle 'Es war' ist ein Bruchstück, ein Räthsel, ein grauser Zufall—bis der schaffende Wille dazu sagt 'aber so wollte ich es!'—Bis der schaffende Wille dazu sagt 'Aber so will ich es! So werde ich's wollen!'" (*KSA* 4: 181). Although Zarathustra has not yet delivered his announcement explicitly, which will arrive a few chapters later, these remarks can be read as an insinuation of his later articulation of eternal return, insofar as the problem that this new version of willing should solve is "that time does not run backwards [*dass die Zeit nicht zurückläuft*]" (139, *KSA* 4: 180). When the thought of eternal return occurs to Zarathustra, however, the recursion that it induces not only controverts the unidirectional passage of time, but also deviates from the form of a circle, arriving as a shock and a rupture that cannot be charted along any straightforward or curved timeline. Immediately after Zarathustra's conjugation of past, present, and future acts of willing the same "it was," Zarathustra is said to have "suddenly stopped and looked altogether like one who has received a severe shock" (141), demonstrating a sudden withdrawal not unlike the one that follows his dialogue on eternal return with a dwarf whom he bears with for part of his journey. Upon speaking with the dwarf about the way in which all things must eternally return, Zarathustra grows "afraid of his own thoughts," at which point he "suddenly" hears sounds and sees images that recall his "most distant childhood," transporting him to another scene (158–59). Likewise, in the later chapter, "The Convalescent," Zarathustra summons his thought and just as soon "fell down as one dead and long remained as one dead" (216). All of these indices suggest that return, as Zarathustra comes to sense it, if not say it, overturns itself, as well as the self who experiences it.

12. Nietzsche, *The Gay Science*, 273.

13. Walter Benjamin, *The Arcades Project*, 116.

14. Nietzsche, *Ecce Homo*, in *On the Genealogy of Morals and Ecce Homo*, 333.

15. In emphasizing this feature of the title and the book itself, my reading in this chapter may be considered a furtherance of the approach to *Thus Spoke Zarathustra* that Gary Shapiro develops in his monograph from 1989, *Nietzschean Narratives*, where he states in his introduction: "Marxists and critical theorists from Georg Lukács to Jürgen Habermas have read *Zarathustra* as an exercise in archaicizing myth to serve the interests of imperialism and irrationalism. But I want to suggest instead that it can be seen as an exemplary postmodern philosophical tale in which are inscribed an encyclopedic variety of the narrative functions of the West. It is highly textual: as written it largely effaces the *speaking* attributed to its chief agent" (Shapiro, *Nietzschean Narratives*, 35). He also proposes to read "what are usually taken to be the chief philosophical ideas of the text" as functions of Nietzsche's narrative "reinscriptions" of Western thought (Shapiro, *Nietzschean Narratives*, 35). In this respect, too, there is a strong affinity between my project here and his. However, what I will be attending to in the pages that follow are passages and textual strategies that are not necessarily defined in terms of narrative.

16. There is a tradition of reading of Nietzsche's text by beginning with the title. Martin Heidegger, for example, states in his landmark essay, "Who is Nietzsche's Zarathustra?": "if we read the title of the work, we will find a hint. [. . .] Zarathustra speaks. He is a speaker. What sort of a speaker?" But the question of Zarathustra's speaking, as Heidegger poses it, overleaps the anonymous modus or manner bespoken with the first word: "thus." Heidegger goes on, "Is he an orator or even a preacher? No. The speaker Zarathustra is an 'advocate'—a *Fürsprecher*," before quoting from the chapter of the third book, in which Zarathustra announces himself as "the advocate of life, the advocate of suffering, the advocate of the circle." Heidegger then proceeds to comment upon the overman and the circular thought of eternal return. See Heidegger, "Who is Nietzsche's Zarathustra?" 411–12. And if Heidegger will have explicitly placed a greater emphasis on "the *how*" of Zarathustra's "imparting" in his lectures on Nietzsche from the late 1930s, Heidegger nonetheless reverts again and again to the theater of personae staged in Nietzsche's book—of men, overmen, and talking animals, and above all, speakers—who disclose who they are and how they interpret all that is through their responses to the thought of eternal return. Heidegger writes, for example, "In der Gestalt des Lehrers wird die Lehre mittelbar dargestellt. Wie schon bei der ersten Mitteilung des Wiederkunftsgedankens, so noch mehr bei dieser zweiten ist das *Wie* der Mitteilung zunächst wesentlicher als das Was, weil es vor allem darauf ankommt, daß Menschen werden, die an dieser Lehre nicht zerbrechen" (Heidegger, *Nietzsche*, 1: 284). The "how" turns out to be the sign of a "who," through whom ontological problems are interpreted. The elucidating exegesis of the "who" that Heidegger offers, however, forecloses an approach to what may be, in Nietzsche's text, a manner of speaking apart from any subject of speech. Against Philippe Lacoue-Labarthe's criticisms of Heidegger's inattentiveness to "questions of form and presentation (*Darstellung*)," specifically with

regard to Nietzsche's *Thus Spoke Zarathustra*, David Farrell Krell rightly emphasizes Heidegger's concern over the literary elements of the text in *Infectious Nietzsche*, 134–35. However, the literary elements that Heidegger addresses nonetheless presuppose the persona as a subject of sense, leaving room for very different readings of the impersonal formulae that figure at least as crucially to the structure of the book as its speakers. Another excellent critique of Heidegger's hermeneutic approach, which follows different traces in Nietzsche's oeuvre than those that will be retraced in this chapter, can be found in Jacques Derrida's *Spurs / Éperons: Nietzsche's Styles*.

17. Wolfram Groddeck, "'OH HIMMEL ÜBER MIR': Zur kosmischen Wendung in Nietzsches Poetologie," 494.

18. Paul de Man, *Allegories of Reading: Figural Language in Rousseau, Nietzsche, Rilke, and Proust*, 105.

19. For example, in a note from April–June 1885, Nietzsche writes, "Das Muster einer vollständigen Fiction ist die Logik. Hier wird ein Denken erdichtet, wo ein Gedanke als Ursache eines anderen Gedankens gesetzt wird; alle Affekte, alles Fühlen und Wollen wird hinweg gedacht. Es kommt dergleichen in der Wirklichkeit nicht vor: diese ist unsäglich anders complicirt. Dadurch daß wir jene Fiction als Schema anlegen, also das thatsächliche Geschehen beim Denken gleichsam durch einen Simplifications-Apparat filtriren: bringen wir es zu einer Zeichenschrift und Mittheilbarkeit und Merkbarkeit der logischen Vorgänge. Also: das geistige Geschehen zu betrachten, wie als ob es dem Schema jener regulativen Fiction entspräche: dies ist der Grundwille. Wo es 'Gedächtniß' giebt, hat dieser Grundwille gewaltet.—In der Wirklichkeit giebt es kein logisches Denken, und kein Satz der Arithmetik und Geometrie kann aus ihr genommen sein, weil er gar nicht vorkommt. Ich stehe anders zur Unwissenheit und Ungewißheit. Nicht, daß etwas unerkannt bleibt, ist mein Kummer; ich freue mich, daß es vielmehr eine Art von Erkenntniß geben kann und bewundere die Complicirtheit dieser Ermöglichung. Das Mittel ist: die Einführung vollständiger Fictionen als Schemata, nach denen wir uns das geistige Geschehen einfacher denken als es ist. Erfahrung ist nur möglich mit Hülfe von Gedächtniß: Gedächtniß ist nur möglich vermöge einer Abkürzung eines geistigen Vorgangs zum Zeichen. Die Zeichenschrift. Erklärung: das ist der Ausdruck eines neuen Dinges vermittelst der Zeichen von schon bekannten Dingen" (*KSA* 11: 505).

20. Deleuze, *Nietzsche and Philosophy*, 74, 78.

21. Pierre Klossowski, *Nietzsche and the Vicious Circle*, 218. The depletion of intensities and impulses once they issue into linguistic expression is emphasized earlier as well, when he writes, "an *intention* is formed through the signs—minus their impulsive intensity. The intensity oscillates while thought as such is being formed, but once the declaration is produced, it is reduced to the inertia of signs" (*Nietzsche and the Vicious Circle*, 37). The "fixity of the signs of language" thus becomes the means by which "gestures and movements" are "simulate[d]" (*Nietzsche and the Vicious Circle*, 43), or, as Klossowski puts it later, the articulated "'consciousness' of the 'unconscious' consists only in a *simulation* of forces" (*Nietzsche and the Vicious Circle*, 50).

22. Friedrich Nietzsche to Heinrich Köselitz, 24 March 1883, in *Sämtliche Briefe*, 6: 350, my translation.

23. Friedrich Nietzsche, *Beyond Good and Evil*, 50–51, translation modified. The entire passage reads, in German: "Wer, gleich mir, mit einer räthselhaften Begierde sich lange darum bemüht hat, den Pessimismus in die Tiefe zu denken und aus der halb christlichen, halb deutschen Enge und Einfalt zu erlösen, mit der er sich diesem Jahrhundert zuletzt dargestellt hat, nämlich in Gestalt der Schopenhauerischen Philosophie; wer wirklich einmal mit einem asiatischen und überasiatischen Auge in die weltverneinendste aller möglichen Denkweisen hinein und hinunter geblickt hat—jenseits von Gut und Böse, und nicht mehr, wie Buddha und Schopenhauer, im Bann und Wahne der Moral—, der hat vielleicht ebendamit, ohne dass er es eigentlich wollte, sich die Augen für das umgekehrte Ideal aufgemacht: für das Ideal des übermüthigsten lebendigsten und weltbejahendsten Menschen, der sich nicht nur mit dem, was war und ist, abgefunden und vertragen gelernt hat, sondern es, so wie es war und ist, wieder haben will, in alle Ewigkeit hinaus, unersättlich da capo rufend, nicht nur zu sich, sondern zum ganzen Stücke und Schauspiele, und nicht nur zu einem Schauspiele, sondern im Grunde zu Dem, der gerade dies Schauspiel nöthig hat—und nöthig macht: weil er immer wieder sich nöthig hat—und nöthig macht——Wie? Und dies wäre nicht—circulus vitiosus deus?" (*KSA* 5: 74–75).

24. Werner Hamacher, *Premises: Essays on Philosophy and Literature from Kant to Celan*, 170–71.

25. The German passage here reads: "Und hier endet die erste Rede Zarathustra's, welche man auch 'die Vorrede' heisst: denn an dieser Stelle unterbrach ihn das Geschrei und die Lust der Menge" (*KSA* 4: 20).

26. Among Nietzsche's many commentators, Anke Bennholdt-Thomsen is one of the few who attends to this moment of the prologue as one in which the problem of communication is announced, and who draws a connection between Zarathustra's interruption and the structure of the subsequent books: "Vielmehr—das zeigte sich bereits im Rahmen der *Vorrede*—macht er die Erfahrung unvorhergesehener Widerstände, die seinen beabsichtigten Weg zu den Menschen korrigiert und ihn zu einem Weg nicht nur der öffentlichen Lehrtätigkeit, sondern auch der eigenen Erkenntnis werden läßt" (Bennholdt-Thomsen, *Nietzsches* Also sprach Zarathustra *als literarisches Phänomen*, 57). In this context, she also emphasizes the way in which the predominance of Zarathustra's speeches in the text leads to the consequence that "[d]er Erkenntnisprozeß Zarathustras keine objektive, von auktorialer Warte übersehene Darstellung [findet], sondern er wird in status nascendi und fiendi vorgeführt" (*Nietzsches* Also sprach Zarathustra, 57).

27. The German text reads: "nicht zum Volke rede Zarathustra, sondern zu Gefährten! [. . .] Viele wegzulocken von der Heerde—dazu kam ich. Zürnen soll mir Volk und Heerde: Räuber will Zarathustra den Hirten heissen" (26).

28. Werner Hamacher, *Pleroma—Reading in Hegel*, 279.

29. "Als ich zu den Menschen kam [. . .] schrie und lachte [meine weise Sehnsucht] also aus mir" (*KSA* 4: 246–47).

30. In German, it reads: "Sprich dein Wort und zerbrich!" (*KSA* 4: 188), where the consonance and rhyme between the imperative forms of "speak" ("s*prich*") and "break to pieces" ("zer*brich*") forge a connection between speaking and breaking, while breaking down each word into the literal elements that sound the same and that also cannot but affect the status of the subject of speech, the "I" or the "ich" that returns in both "spr*ich*" and "zerbr*ich*." Subsequent readers such as Martin Heidegger would adopt and adapt this and similar passages in pursuing the question of world-historical thoughts, said to structure *a priori* whatever else might be experienced and recounted as history. "This history is the poetic and thinking struggle for the word of being as a whole," Heidegger writes in his lectures from the late 1930s on Nietzsche, before returning to these premises again in his postwar lecture course from 1951–1952, *What Is Called Thinking* or *What Does Thinking Call For?* (*Was heißt Denken?*). There, he will recur to the words that "the stillest hour" exchanges with Zarathustra: "It is the stillest words that bring on the storm. Thoughts that come on doves' feet guide the world" (146), in order to draw the conclusion that thinking differs not only from "the usual representation of objects and formation of opinions [*das gewöhnliche Vorstellen und Meinen*]," but also from the outcries against these things in Nietzsche's writings, "when they make themselves into the court of judgment of thinking [*wenn es sich zum Gerichtshof des Denkens machen will*]" (Heidegger, *Was heißt Denken?* 77–78, my translation). Instead, Heidegger suggests that Nietzsche's decisive thought would be represented in the posthumous papers, and even then, what the reader has to seek would be that which the "language of the thinker [*die Sprache des Denkers*]" says in silence: namely, what Heidegger calls the "unthought in his thought [*das Ungedachte in seinem Gedachten*]," which emerges as the source from which further thinking draws its possibility (*Was heißt Denken?* 82, my translation). Throughout this chapter, I circle around this proposal of a silencing of language in order to offer, obliquely, an alternative interpretation of the imperative of Zarathustra's "stillest hour."

31. Werner Hamacher, *Pleroma—Reading in Hegel*, 279.

32. "Die Mitschaffenden sucht der Schaffende, Die, welche neue Werthe auf neue Tafeln schreiben" (*KSA* 4: 26).

33. Gooding-Williams, in his insightful and detailed reading of the prologue, which encompasses no less than one third of his book, argues that "the difference between Zarathustra's and the townspeople's interpretations of Zarathustra's first speech is the difference between (1) viewing that speech as an attempt to perform a perlocutionary act (as an attempt to produce an effect *by* saying something) and (2) viewing it as an effort to constate a fact;" rather than responding to Zarathustra, the members of the crowd construe his talk of the overman as an announcement of the tightrope walker, whose performance they await (Gooding-Williams, *Nietzsche's Dionysian Modernism*, 69). However, this interpretation of the scene presupposes that, already here, "Zarathustra's poetic intention is to induce in his auditors a vision inspiring them to become new-values creators," which desire only dawns on

Zarathustra later (*Nietzsche's Dionysian Modernism*, 70). Likewise, Stanley Rosen glosses the scene in which Zarathustra delivers his first speech thus: "In order to produce a new order, Nietzsche must overthrow the old one," but problems arise for his initial projection of an overcoming of man when "[t]he decadent accordingly believe themselves to be the new race of mankind for whom Zarathustra calls, just as the townsfolk believe that the rope-dancer is the superman" (Rosen, *The Mask of Enlightenment: Nietzsche's Zarathustra*, 47–48).

34. Nietzsche, *Ecce Homo*, in *On the Genealogy of Morals and Ecce Homo*, 327–328. Cf. *KSA* 6: 367.

35. Nietzsche, *Ecce homo*, 328; cf. *KSA* 6: 367.

36. To the sun, Zarathustra says: "Behold, I am weary of my wisdom, like a bee that has gathered too much honey; I need hands outstretched to receive it. I would give away and distribute, until the wise among men find joy once again in their folly, and the poor in their riches. For that I must descend to the depths, as you do in the evening when you go behind the sea and still bring light to the underworld, you overrich star" (10). The analogy to honey and the conversion of wisdom to folly that he bespeaks do not figure in Creuzer's text, but these differences do not detract from the basic similarity in question. Françoise Dastur discusses the importance of Creuzer's work for Nietzsche's development of *Thus Spoke Zarathustra* in her article, "Who Is Nietzsche's Zarathustra? A Note on the Iranian-Persian Background," 39–54. She also points the reader to the second volume of Curt Paul Janz's biography of Nietzsche, in which he mentions Creuzer among the sources Nietzsche drew upon in composing his book. Instead of focusing upon the connections between Nietzsche and Creuzer in the language of Zarathustra's prologue, however, Dastur stresses the significance of Nietzsche's protagonist for the questioning of morals performed throughout his book.

37. Friedrich Creuzer, *Symbolik und Mythologie der alten Völker*, 1: 693, my translation.

38. The German text reads: "Also das ewige Wort [. . .] ist Grund alles Daseyns, alles Bleibens und alles Segens, und Zoroasters Gesetz ist der Leib jenes Urwortes von Ormuzd, und jenes heisst selbst Zendavesta, lebendiges Wort. [. . .] Mit dieser Idee von dem lebendigen Worte hängt aber die von der unwiderstehlichen Macht des Gebetes eng zusammen" (710).

39. For example, the first of the prayers that Klenker collects and translates—after introductory remarks, in which the prayers are said to be delivered upon sunrise ("beim Sonnenaufgang," Klenker, *Zend-Avesta*, 76)—opens: "Ich bete und rufe an 'Ormuzd,' den Grossen, glänzend und schimmernd in Lichtherrlichkeit—allvollkommen—allvortrefflich—allrein—allmächtig—allweise—deß Körper rein ist über alles—heilig über alles—deß Gedanke Reingutes ist—Quell aller Freuden—der mir giebt was ich habe; stark und wirksam und allernährend und über alles unaussprechlich in Herrlichkeit verschlungen! Ich bete und rufe an Bahmen, Ardibehescht, Schahriver, Sapandomad, Khordad, Amerdad, Goschorun, den Schützer der Heerden,

das Feuer Ormuzd's, den lebendigstwirksamsten der Amshaspands. Ich bete und rufe an Vendidad, der Zoroaster gegeben—heilig—rein—und groß ist" (Klenker, *Zend-Avesta*, 81). Both Klenker's and du Perron's translations are the sources to which Creuzer directly refers at the start of his chapter on Zoroastrian religion (Creuzer, *Symbolik und Mythologie*, 1: 654–55). Whether or not Nietzsche read these sources, he would have known the anaphoric style of Christ's Sermon on the Mount in the Gospel of Matthew—and that of the Hebrew prophets, whose rhetoric and imagery Creuzer considers to be testimonies to the legacy of Zoroastrianism, arguing, for example, that Ezekiel's visions contain "äusserst viel Persisches aus der Lehre der Magier" (Creuzer, *Symbolik und Mythologie*, 1: 652).

40. Interestingly, the fact that the failure of Zarathustra's speech arises from a lack of reciprocal love aligns this moment with the Pauline redefinition of sin in terms of privation, "*the lack of love*," while the good, as love, would not take the form of prohibition, but expenditure, as Abed Azzam shows in his excellent study, *Nietzsche Versus Paul*. The motives for Zarathustra's expenditure, however, differ from Pauline *agape*. If love may seem to offer a positive alternative to the prohibitions of Jewish law, Paul goes on to describe the manifestation of this love not as a noble act, but in terms of suffering and sacrifice: "the good should appear in historical reality in the same manner in which the Jewish law (as well as sin) appears in this reality" (Azzam, *Nietzsche Versus Paul*, 65). This feature of his formulation renders the Pauline transvaluation of (Jewish) values a reflection and perpetuation of the reactive "slave-morality" that Nietzsche reads in both Judaism and Christianity: "Yet, for Paul, as for Nietzsche, this reformation does not imply a cut with the concept of the suffering good of slave-morality" (Azzam, *Nietzsche Versus Paul*, 65).

41. It might be objected that the anachronism of Nietzsche's *Zarathustra* begins long before he addresses a mass that has become modern and proven unable to take up the light that he would bring to them, much as the world is said to fail to receive the luminous word of god in the prologue to the Gospel of John. After all, it is also the case that this Persian prophet, "who lived six thousand years before Christ" according to Creuzer, comes across a saintly hermit in the woods and pronounces "that God *is dead*!" (12), before arriving in the marketplace of the prologue. Furthermore, Zarathustra will later refer to "the Hebrew Jesus" (73), who happens to be the only other persona with a proper name beside himself in the entire book. However, the express function of Zarathustra's word for the people does not alter until this encounter with the crowd, whose outburst of laughter repeats with compulsion, erupting again and again in Zarathustra's language. Up to that point, Zarathustra was as unaware of modern conditions for public speech as the saintly hermit was of the death of god. Zarathustra may know better than the saint, when it comes to God's posthumous status, but the saint knows better than Zarathustra, when it comes to the possibility of delivering a missive to the public. Prescient of Zarathustra's upcoming role as a robber—and recalling a biblical topos for the second coming of Christ (cf. 1 Thess. 5.2)—he exclaims: "Give them nothing!

[. . .] They are suspicious of hermits and do not believe that we come with gifts. [. . .] They probably ask themselves, Where is the thief going?" (11). These terms return only after Zarathustra reformulates his purpose thus: "To lure many away from the herd, for that I have come. The people and the herd shall be angry with me: Zarathustra wants to be called a robber by the shepherds" (23). The reciprocal naivety between Zarathustra and the saint is perhaps what allows them to separate, "laughing as two boys laugh" (12). But Zarathustra becomes up to date only in the decisive instant where his speaking is disrupted and with it, the possibility of prophetic rhetoric as such.

42. In his article, "Foucault, Nietzsche, Enlightenment: Some Historical Considerations," Louis Miller suggests that Nietzsche models his last man on Eduard Hartmann's depiction of modern social evolution in his *Philosophie des Unbewussten*, writing, "Nietzsche's public reckoning with Hartmann in the second *Untimely Meditation* makes evident that it was first von Hartmann who conjured up for Nietzsche the specter of the last man" (Miller, "Foucault, Nietzsche, Enlightenment," 347). Statements that speak for this claim can be found in the passage where Nietzsche writes: "Zwar nennt Hartmann das Lebensalter, welchem die Menschheit sich jetzt nähert, das 'Mannesalter': das ist aber, nach seiner Schilderung, der beglückte Zustand, wo es nur noch 'gediegene Mittelmässigkeit' giebt und die Kunst das ist, was 'dem Berliner Börsenmanne etwa Abends die Posse' ist, wo 'die Genies kein Bedürfniss der Zeit mehr sind, weil es hiesse, die Perlen vor die Säue werfen oder auch weil die Zeit über das Stadium, welchem Genies gebührten, zu einem wichtigeren fortgeschritten ist,' zu jenem Stadium der socialen Entwickelung nämlich, in welchem jeder Arbeiter 'bei einer Arbeitszeit, die ihm für seine intellectuelle Ausbildung genügende Musse lässt, ein comfortables Dasein führe.' Schalk aller Schalke, du sprichst das Sehnen der jetzigen Menschheit aus: du weisst aber gleichfalls, was für ein Gespenst am Ende dieses Mannesalters der Menschheit, als Resultat jener intellectuellen Ausbildung zur gediegenen Mittelmässigkeit, stehen wird—der Ekel" (*KSA* 1: 314–15). A few lines later, Nietzsche contrasts this vision for humanity with a prophetic call for an alternative type of human, whom he represents as a bridge over the stream of becoming ("Es wird die Zeit sein, in welcher [. . .] man überhaupt nicht mehr die Massen betrachtet, sondern wieder die Einzelnen, die eine Art von Brücke über den wüsten Strom des Werdens bilden" [*KSA* 1: 317]). Thus, this passage anticipates Nietzsche's (trans-)figuration of man in *Zarathustra* as "a bridge and not an end," whereby "what can be loved in man is that he is an overture and a going under" (15). Furthermore, it is worth noting that, although Nietzsche does not mention industrial capital in this passage from his *Untimely Meditations*, nor in the passage on the last man in *Zarathustra*, the chapter he quotes from Hartmann's book, "Das Unbewusste in der Geschichte," formulates modern comfort in precisely such terms. After criticizing the way in which an increase in the "wealth of nations [*Nationalreichthum*]" at first "essentially comes to profit solely the owners of capital [*wesentlich nur den Capitalbesitzern zu*

Gute [kommt]," Hartmann suggests that the poor working conditions of the current labor force make up a passing phase, and that, once capital, the division of labor, and industrial production have fulfilled their tasks in producing a global market and superior production, they will have prepared and made possible the "fourth and *last* phase [. . .] of free association [*vierte und* letzte *Phase [. . .] der freien Association*]," in which moderate labor hours will "leave sufficient leisure [to] lead a comfortable [. . .] existence worthy of man [*genügende Müsse lässt, ein comfortables [. . .] menschenwürdiges Dasein [zu] führe[n]*]" (Eduard von Hartmann, *Philosophie des Unbewussten*, 1: 341–42, my translation and emphasis).

43. See Nietzsche, *Ecce Homo*, 302.

44. The passage reads: "Siehe, hier ist eine neue Tafel: aber wo sind meine Brüder, die sie mit mir zu Thale und in fleischerne Herzen tragen?—Also heischt es meine grosse Liebe zu den Fernsten: schone deinen Nächsten nicht! Der Mensch ist Etwas, das überwunden werden muss" (*KSA* 4: 249).

45. The biblical rhetoric of Nietzsche's Zarathustra has been noted and interpreted by many scholars. In his article, "Friedrich Nietzsche und die Bibel unter besonderer Berücksichtigung von *Also sprach Zarathustra*," Jörg Salaquarda provides a detailed inventory of the references that Nietzsche evokes. Karl Löwith perceptively remarks on how Zarathustra's aphoristic and parable-rife rhetoric splits between the form of the ancient "philosophic didactic poem," and a sheer mode of announcement that Nietzsche adopts in imitation of "the language of the Gospels" in order "to proclaim an anti-Christian message," whose "philosophic content is more veiled than apparent in the parables of Zarathustra" (Löwith, *Nietzsche's Philosophy of the Eternal Recurrence of the Same*, 18). Daniel Weidner reads Zarathustra as a prophet, according to the definition of the prophet as "jemand, der Einfluss ist: der Einfluss unterliegt und Einfluss hat, der wirkungsbewusst ist, auch wenn diese Wirkung paradox sein kann" (Weidner, "'Und ihr—ihr machtet schon ein Leier-Lied daraus': Nietzsche als Prophet," 364). In this context, he also argues that the ambivalence of the prophet's effectiveness and message lessens the difference between Biblical prophecy and Nietzsche's words, for which "es [. . .] keine Wahrheit hinter dem Diskurs [gibt]" ("'Und ihr—ihr machtet schon ein Leier-Lied daraus,'" 373). In this particular passage, however, Nietzsche not only echoes Paul; for in speaking of "hearts of *flesh*," he also reintroduces the very element that Paul had eliminated when he wrote in his Epistle to the Romans: "For a person is not a Jew who is one outwardly, nor is true circumcision something external *and fleshly*. Rather, a person is a Jew who is one inwardly, and real circumcision is a matter of *the heart*" (Rom. 2.28–29). This decision may have been motivated in part by the contemporary theologian Hermann Lüdemann's *Die Anthropologie des Apostels Paulus*, where the exact phrase that Nietzsche uses, "fleischerne[s] Herz," appears to illustrate the way in which, for Paul, "the heart, despite its spirituality, also stands in graspable relation to the σάρξ [flesh]," for at times "the apostle expressly recurs to the fleshly heart" (2. Cor. 3.3). See Hermann Lüdemann, *Die Anthropologie des*

Apostels Paulus, 19. Since Nietzsche borrowed this book in 1880 from his friend, the Protestant theologian Franz Overbeck (see *KSA* 15: 113), it is possible that he is echoing it in his new emphasis on the fleshly dimensions of even Pauline spirit.

46. "*Also sprach Zarathustra. Ein Buch für Alle und Keinen.* Es ist eine 'Dichtung,' oder ein fünftes 'Evangelium' oder irgend etwas, für das es noch keinen Namen giebt : bei weitem das Ernsteste und *auch* Heiterste meiner Erzeugnisse, und Jedermann zugänglich. So glaube ich denn, daß es eine 'sofortige Wirkung' thun wird" (Friedrich Nietzsche to Ernst Schmeitzner, 13 February 1883, in *Sämtliche Briefe: Kritische Studienausgabe*, 6: 327, my translation).

47. de Man, *Allegories of Reading*, 131.

48. de Man, *Allegoires of Reading*, 119.

49. "Nicht um die Erfinder von neuem Lärme: um die Erfinder von neuen Werthen dreht sich die Welt; *unhörbar* dreht sie sich" (*KSA* 4: 169).

50. To Overbeck, Nietzsche writes in early March of 1884, "I don't exactly know how I have come to this—but it is possible that for the first time a thought has come to me that will break the history of humanity in two. This Zarathustra is only the prologue, the preamble, the vestibule—I had to encourage myself, since only discouragement came to me from all sides: to encourage myself to bear this thought! for I am still far from being able to utter it and represent it. IF IT IS TRUE or rather if it is BELIEVED TO BE TRUE—then all things would be modified and would return, and all values hitherto will be devalued" (qtd. in Klossowski, *Nietzsche and the Vicious Circle*, 100). The passage in *Ecce Homo* is formulated somewhat differently, with reference instead to Zarathustra's exposition of Christian morality: "I have not said even one word that I had not already said five years ago through the mouth of Zarathustra. The *discovery* of Christian morality is an event that has no equivalent or like [*das nicht seines Gleichen hat*], a real catastrophe. Whosoever brings it to light [*wer über sie aufklärt*] is a *force majeure*, a fate,—he breaks the history of humanity in two pieces. One lives *before* him, one lives *after* him . . ." (*KSA* 6: 373, my translation). This passage especially makes clear that Nietzsche's rhetoric of breaking history in two—which would be inscribed in terms of living "before" and "after" the one who broke it—is itself modeled after the chronological rupture that Christianity had introduced.

51. He writes: "The question of a significant, decisive date that cuts the ages of time had its paradigm in the incision with which world history had fallen into two different parts with respect to salvation. [. . .] The fact that history finally appeared divisible once again, that a new epoch conferred itself the claim to absolve itself from the past and make a new beginning, had the foundational trait of a mythic repetition, for all of the rational features under which this claim stood. One more time and in vain, the French Revolution should attempt this, and in Nietzsche it is already the sign of impending madness, when he expects in his letter to Paul Deussen from 14 September 1888 that his revaluation of values 'cleaves the history of humanity in two halves,' or speaks one month later to Overbeck that he even

'shoots the history of humanity asunder in two halves' " (*Die Legitimität der Neuzeit*, 435–36, my translation). These sentences do not appear in the English translation of the second edition by Robert M. Wallace.

52. Quoting several lines from Nietzsche's late letter to August Strindberg, in which Nietzsche does not attribute the decisive event to his *Zarathustra*, but projects it into the near future of the current year—"I am preparing an event which, in all likelihood, will break history in two halves, to the point that one will need a new calendar, with 1888 as Year One," Badiou writes, "Here Nietzsche proposes an imitation of the French revolution" (Alain Badiou, "Who is Nietzsche?" 4).

53. Badiou, "Who is Nietzsche?" 6.

54. Badiou, *Being and Event*, 210. Cf. Badiou's discussion of the revolutionary dimensions of Nietzsche's thought and his critique of Heidegger's interpretation of Nietzsche, again with reference to Nietzsche's claim to break history in two, in *Nietzsche: L'antiphilosophie*. In Pierre Klossowski's *Nietzsche and the Vicious Circle*, Nietzsche's pronunciation of historical rupture figures crucially for his discussion of the simulacra that Nietzsche's political vision consists of, once it is founded on the basis of the experience of eternal return and the pulsions of force that propel it.

55. The German reads: "Die Sprache Luthers und die poetische Form der Bibel als die Grundlage einer neuen deutschen Poesie—das ist meine Erfindung!" (*KSA* 11: 60).

56. "Unser letztes Ereigniß ist immer noch *Luther*, unser einziges Buch immer noch die *Bibel*" (*KSA* 11: 56).

57. In Luther's German the word for "second" is the same as the word for "other": "ander."

58. Karl Marx, "Contribution to the Critique of Hegel's Philosophy of Law," in *Collected Works*, 3: 176. All subsequent references to the English edition of Marx's and Engels's works (MECW) will be cited parenthetically in the following by volume and page number. The German passage reads: "Wenn ich die deutschen Zustände von 1843 verneine, stehe ich, nach französischer Zeitrechnung, kaum im Jahre 1789, noch weniger im Brennpunkt der Gegenwart" (Karl Marx, "Zur Kritik der Hegelschen Rechtsphilosophie," in MEGA 1.1: 608). All subsequent references to the German edition of Marx's and Engels's works will be noted parenthetically by division and volume, followed by page number, according to the *Gesamtausgabe* (MEGA).

59. The German passage reads: "Die einzig *praktisch* mögliche Befreiung Deutschlands ist die Befreiung auf dem Standpunkt *der* Theorie, welche den Menschen für das höchste Wesen des Menschen erklärt. [. . .] In Deutschland kann *keine* Art der Knechtschaft gebrochen werden, ohne *jede* Art der Knechtschaft zu brechen. Das *gründliche* Deutschland kann nicht revolutionieren, ohne *von Grund aus* zu revolutionieren. Die *Emanzipation des Deutschen* ist die *Emanzipation des Menschen*. Der Kopf dieser Emanzipation ist die *Philosophie*, ihr Herz das *Proletariat*" (MEGA 1.1: 620–21).

60. On this, see Mendicino, "Newswriting, Historiography, and the Controversion of the Present (After Heine)."

61. There, Nietzsche writes of Heine: "how he has the German language in hand! People will one day say that *Heine and I* are by far the first artists of the German language [*Und wie er das Deutsche handhabt! Man wird einmal sagen, dass Heine und ich bei weitem die ersten Artisten der deutschen Sprache gewesen sind*]" (*KSA* 6: 286, my translation).

62. Heine, *History of Religion and Philosophy in Germany*, 242. He goes on to explain how these forces might work, writing: "Kantians will appear who have no more use for piety even in the world of appearances, who with sword and axe will mercilessly rummage around in the soil of our European culture in order to eradicate the last roots of the past. Armed Fichteans will enter on the scene who, in their fanaticism of will, can be restrained neither by fear nor by self-interest, for they live in the spirit and defy matter like the first Christians, who likewise could be subdued neither by bodily torture nor by bodily delights" (*History of Religion and Philosophy in Germany*, 242).

63. Badiou, "Who is Nietzsche?" 5.

64. Theodor Mundt, *Die Geschichte der Gesellschaft in ihren neueren Entwickelungen und Problemen*, 184. All translations from this text are mine.

65. Mundt, *Die Geschichte der Gesellschaft*, 1.

66. Mundt also calls the valuation of the individual that emerged with the Reformation, along with the Protestant work ethic, the "reformational elements of today's society" in the closing pages of his book. See Mundt, *Die Geschichte der Gesellschaft*, 434.

67. "[S]ein [des dritten Standes] erstes Werk war dies gewesen, sich eine neue, die ganze Nation umfassende Sprache zu erschaffen, eine allgemeine, gebildete Nationalsprache, dem Hohen wie dem Niedern, dem Armen wie dem Reichen gleich verständlich und angenehm, überwindend die bisherigen Trennungen des deutschen Volkslebens [. . .]" (Mundt, *Die Geschichte der Gesellschaft*, 78).

68. "Hierin liegt die höchste Bedeutung, welche die protestantische Bibel erlangt hat, ausgesprochen, ihre wahrhaft politische Bedeutung, indem sie, wie auch immer die neuen Glaubensspaltungen neue Trennungen hervorzurufen schienen, doch das ganze deutsche Volk mit fortriß, sich im innersten Wesen als eine einheitliche Nation zu betrachten, und als das Organ dieser Einheit zuerst die neue Sprache des Protestantismus festzuhalten" (Mundt, *Die Geschichte der Gesellschaft*, 164–65).

69. "Ungewißheit, ob der Volksbegriff der höhere u. umfassendere gegen den des Menschen oder ob der Menschenbegriff, als die ursprüngliche Quelle alles Volksthums, auch die entscheidende bedingende u. treibende Kraft ist. In der Wirklichkeit bedingt das Volk den Menschen fast ausschließlich; aber in den großen Umwälzungsmomenten wird der Mensch Meister des traditionellen Volksgeistes. Für die revolutionäre Politik ist dieser speculative Begriff der Gesellschaft der

Hauptinhalt" (Nietzsche, *Nachgelassene Aufzeichnungen Herbst 1858–Herbst 1862*, 1.2: 409, my translation).

70. Friedrich Nietzsche, *The Gay Science*, 195. The German text reads: "Dass Luther's *Reformation* im Norden gelang, ist ein Zeichen dafür, dass der Norden gegen den Süden Europa's zurückgeblieben war und noch ziemlich einartige und einfarbige Bedürfnisse kannte [. . .]. Je allgemeiner und unbedingter ein Einzelner oder der Gedanke eines Einzelnen wirken kann, um so gleichartiger und um so niedriger muss die Masse sein, auf die da gewirkt wird; während Gegenbestrebungen innere Gegenbedürfnisse verrathen, welche auch sich befriedigen und durchsetzen wollen. Umgekehrt darf man immer auf eine wirkliche Höhe der Cultur schliessen, wenn mächtige und herrschsüchtige Naturen es nur zu einer geringen und sectirerischen Wirkung bringen: diess gilt auch für die einzelnen Künste und die Gebiete der Erkenntniss" (*KSA* 3: 493–94).

71. Nietzsche, *The Gay Science*, 194, translation modified. The German text reads: "Zur Zeit der grossen Kirchen-Verderbniss war in Deutschland die Kirche am wenigsten verdorben: deshalb entstand hier die Reformation, als das Zeichen, dass schon die Anfänge der Verderbniss unerträglich empfunden wurden. Verhältnissmässig war nämlich kein Volk jemals christlicher, als die Deutschen zur Zeit Luther's: ihre christliche Cultur war eben bereit, zu einer hundertfältigen Pracht der Blüthe auszuschlagen,—es fehlte nur noch Eine Nacht; aber diese brachte den Sturm, der Allem ein Ende machte" (*KSA* 3: 492–93).

72. Friedrich Nietzsche to Carl von Gersdorff, 21 June 1871, in *Selected Letters of Friedrich Nietzsche*, 80.

73. Nietzsche to Erwin Rohde, 22 February 1884, in *Selected Letters of Friedrich Nietzsche*, 219–21. The German text reads: "ich bilde mir ein, mit diesem Z<arathustra> die deutsche Sprache zu ihrer Vollendung gebracht zu haben. Es war, nach *Luther* und Goethe, noch ein dritter Schritt zu thun—; sieh zu, alter Herzens-Kamerad, ob Kraft, Geschmeidigkeit und Wohllaut je schon in unsrer Sprache so beieinander gewesen sind. Lies Goethen nach einer Seite meines Buchs—und Du wirst fühlen, daß jenes 'Undulatorische,' das Goethen als Zeichner anhaftete, auch dem Sprachbildner nicht fremd blieb. Ich habe die strengere, männlichere Linie vor ihm voraus, ohne doch, mit *Luther*, unter die Rüpel zu gerathen. Mein Stil ist ein Tanz; ein Spiel der Symmetrien aller Art und ein Überspringen und Verspotten dieser Symmetrien. Das geht bis in die Wahl der Vokale.—" (*Sämtliche Briefe*, 6: 479).

74. Westfall, "Zarathustra's Germanity: Luther, Goethe, Nietzsche," 49.

75. Westfall, "Zarathustra's Germanity," 52.

76. Nietzsche to Erwin Rohde, 22 February 1884, in *Selected Letters of Friedrich Nietzsche*, 219–20. "Es ist eine Art Abgrund der Zukunft" (*Sämtliche Briefe*, 6: 479). Furthermore, given the echo of "Rhodus" that one may also hear in Rohde's name—as well as Nietzsche's emphasis upon stylistic leaping, or "Überspringen"—the letter may also reflect a subtle, perhaps sub-intentional attempt to call upon Rohde to take the leap into Nietzsche's writing, as if to say: "Hic Rhodus, hic salta."

77. Friedrich Kittler, *Aufschreibesysteme 1800 · 1900*, 229.
78. Kittler, *Aufschreibesysteme*, 221.
79. For an excellent study of the complexities of "afterness" in and beyond Nietzsche, see Gerhard Richter, *Afterness: Figures of Following in Modern Thought and Aesthetics*, especially 26–38.
80. "Viele Länder sah Zarathustra und viele Völker: so entdeckte er vieler Völker Gutes und Böses. Keine grössere Macht fand Zarathustra auf Erden, als gut und böse" (*KSA* 4: 74).
81. "Viele Länder sah Zarathustra und viele Völker: keine grössere Macht fand Zarathustra auf Erden, als die Werke der Liebenden: 'gut' und 'böse' ist ihr Name. Wahrlich, ein Ungethüm ist die Macht dieses Lobens und Tadelns. Sagt, wer bezwingt es mir, ihr Brüder? Sagt, wer wirft diesem Thier die Fessel über die tausend Nacken? Tausende Ziele gab es bisher, denn tausend Völker gab es. Nur die Fessel der tausenden Nacken fehlt noch, es fehlt das Eine Ziel. Noch hat die Menschheit kein Ziel. Aber sagt mir doch, meine Brüder: wenn der Menschheit das Ziel noch fehlt, fehlt da nicht auch—sie selber noch?—Also sprach Zarathustra" (*KSA* 4: 76).
82. Nietzsche, *The Gay Science*, 195.
83. "Werthe legte erst der Mensch in die Dinge, sich zu erhalten,—er schuf erst den Dingen Sinn, einen Menschen-Sinn! Darum nennt er sich 'Mensch,' das ist: der Schätzende" (*KSA* 4: 75).
84. See Georg Lukács, "Nietzsche als Vorläufer der faschistischen Ästhetik," in *Probleme der Ästhetik*, 310, 318.
85. An anarchic tendency in Zarathustra's rhetoric is suggested already in the way the abstract power of estimation that he discovers does not belong, properly speaking, to him, but appears in the form of a many-headed, personified "monster" of "praising and censuring" that no longer bears the traits of man or peoples. Uniting various estimations in a collective singular that is at odds with itself, this monster of power resembles instead Zarathustra's earlier depiction of the modern state as the incarnation of a Babelian "confusion of tongues of good and evil" that devours its subjects (49). And for all Nietzsche's ambivalence toward the work of the anarchist Mikhail Bakunin (see *KSA* 7: 580), whom he most likely learned of through his relationship to Wagner (see *KSA* 15: 30), it was precisely passages such as these on the state that most likely prompted his publisher Schmeitzner to question his political commitments, to which he replied, in a letter from 2 April 1883, "what, moreover, concerns 'the state': I know what I know. One can count me among the 'anarchists,' if one intends ill for me: but it is certain that I foresee European anarchies and earthquakes with an immense compass. All movements lead thereto—including your anti-Jewish one" (Nietzsche to Schmeitzner, 2 April 1883, *Sämtliche Briefe*, 6: 355–56, my translation).
86. Diogenes Laertes, *Lives of Eminent Philosophers: Books 6–10*, 462–63, translation modified.
87. Azadeh Ataeian provides a brief description of these etymological trajectories in *Vom Standpunkt des Erkennens: Nietzsches Philosophie des Perspektivismus*, 28.

88. Nietzsche writes: "Der Mensch als der Messende.—Vielleicht hat alle Moralität der Menschheit in der ungeheuren inneren Aufregung ihren Ursprung, welche die Urmenschen ergriff, als sie das Maass und das Messen, die Wage und das Wägen entdeckten (das Wort 'Mensch' bedeutet ja den Messenden, er hat sich nach seiner grössten Entdeckung benennen wollen!). Mit diesen Vorstellungen stiegen sie in Bereiche hinauf, die ganz unmessbar und unwägbar sind, aber es ursprünglich nicht zu sein schienen" (*KSA* 2: 554).

89. The structure of a perpetual activity that realizes itself in its very performance, and that thus will have reached its end only so long as it goes on, is teleological, insofar as it corresponds to what Aristotle describes as *entelecheia* in the *Metaphysics*. There, Aristotle privileges those actions in which the performance is the same as its fulfillment—such as seeing and having seen—over those motions where the completion of an act differs from its performance, as in the case of building a house and having built a house. It is the latter kind of teleological action that Zarathustra shifts toward at the end of his speech, when talk of estimation gives way to the projection of a goal—that is, a substantive ("Ziel") that man should have ("haben"), rather than a process that man would, by definition, continuously do.

90. "Schätzen selber ist aller geschätzten Dinge Schatz und Kleinod" (*KSA* 4: 75).

91. In this context, it is significant that "schaffen" also resonates with the etymologically and semantically related "schöpfen," which means both to "create" and to "draw" or "scoop" water. The English "scoop" derives too from this Germanic word.

92. Groddeck, "OH HIMMEL ÜBER MIR," 494.

93. For Luther's usage of this suffix, which alternates with the more common *-niß*, see Bach, *Handbuch der Luthersprache*, and more recently, Charles V. J. Russ, "Nominalization in Martin Luther's Word Formation," especially 247.

94. It was precisely this ambivalence of the suffix upon which Heine's revolutionary announcement had pivoted at the close of "Various Conceptions of History," when his neologism—"Erschaffniß" ("creation")—displaces the notion of a "Schöpfer" ("creator"). There too creation becomes suspended between an operation and a product of its process, and thereby comes to exist to the same extent that it remains unfinished and in the making. For "Erschaffniß" may, like other verbal nouns such as "Zeugnis" ("testimony"), maintain the active force of the infinitive in order to denote what creates, or it may, like "Gleichnis" ("simile") and "Geheimnis" ("secret"), be construed from the past participle, "erschaffen" ("created"), to denote that which is created. On Heine's usage of this word, see Mendicino, "Newswriting, Historiography," 101.

95. Susanne Enderwitz, "Shahrazâd is One of Us: Practical Narrative, Theoretical Discussion, and Feminist Discourse," 188.

96. *The Arabian Nights*, 11.
97. *The Arabian Nights*, 11.
98. *The Arabian Nights*, 11.

99. Friedrich Nietzsche to Carl von Gersdorff, 21 June 1871, in *Selected Letters of Friedrich Nietzsche*, 80.

Chapter 2

1. "Daß die Menschheit eine Gesammt-Aufgabe zu lösen habe, daß sie als Ganzes irgend einem Ziel entgegenlaufe, diese sehr unklare und willkürliche Vorstellung ist noch sehr jung. Vielleicht wird man sie wieder los, bevor sie eine 'fixe Idee' wird . . . Sie ist kein Ganzes, diese Menschheit: sie ist eine unlösbare Vielheit von aufsteigenden und niedersteigenden Lebensprozessen—sie hat nicht eine Jugend und darauf eine Reife und endlich ein Alter. Nämlich die Schichten liegen durcheinander und übereinander—und in einigen Jahrtausenden kann es immer noch jüngere Typen Mensch geben, als wir sie heute nachweisen können. Die décadence andererseits gehört zu allen Epochen der Menschheit: überall giebt es Auswurf- und Verfall-Stoffe, es ist ein Lebensprozeß selbst, das Ausscheiden der Niedergangs- und Abfalls-Gebilde" (*KSA* 13: 87). All translations from the notebooks are mine.

2. See Aristotle, *Poetics* 1450b 23–32: "A beginning is that which does not itself follow necessarily from something else, but after which a further event or process naturally occurs. An end, by contrast, is that which itself naturally occurs, whether necessarily or usually, after a preceding event, but need not be followed by anything else. A middle is that which both follows a preceding event and has further consequences [ἀρχὴ δέ ἐστιν ὃ αὐτὸ μὲν μὴ ἐξ ἀνάγκης μετ' ἄλλο ἐστίν, μετ' ἐκεῖνο δ' ἕτερον πέφυκεν εἶναι ἢ γίνεσθαι· τελευτὴ δὲ τοὐναντίον ὃ αὐτὸ μὲν μετ' ἄλλο πέφυκεν εἶναι ἢ ἐξ ἀνάγκης ἢ ὡς ἐπὶ τὸ πολύ, μετὰ δὲ τοῦτο ἄλλο οὐδέν· μέσον δὲ ὃ καὶ αὐτὸ μετ' ἄλλο καὶ μετ' ἐκεῖνο ἕτερον]" (*Poetics*, in *Aristotle: Poetics, Longinus: On the Sublime, and Demetrius: On Style*).

3. See the *Oxford English Dictionary*, s.v. "discuss."

4. *KSA* 13: 88, 89.

5. "Daß alle Art Verfall und Erkrankung fortwährend an den Gesammt-Werthurtheilen mitgearbeitet hat: daß in den herrschend gewordenen Werthurtheilen décadence sogar zum Übergewicht gekommen ist: daß wir nicht nur gegen die Folgezustände alles gegenwärtigen Elends von Entartung zu kämpfen haben, sondern *alle* bisherige Décadence rückständig d.h. *lebendig* geblieben ist" (*KSA* 13: 89).

6. The initial words, as Oleg Gelikman notes, are derived from a manuscript that Stéphane Mallarmé had sent to Baudelaire and that would appear in 1875 as the prose poem, "Le Phénomène futur" (Gelikman, "The Crisis of the Messianic Claim: Scholem, Benjamin, Baudelaire," 177).

7. Charles Baudelaire, *Oeuvres posthumes et correspondances inédites*, 87–94. Many of Nietzsche's notes in this notebook from November 1887–March 1888, in fact, are excerpted in French directly from this collection of Baudelaire's posthumous writings. See, for example, *KSA* 13: 75–86, 90–92. See also Baudelaire, *Oeuvres*

complètes, 1: 665–67. "Le Monde va finir" and all subsequent quotations from Baudelaire's poems and prose will be cited by volume and page number according to the *Oeuvres complètes* (*OC*). Nietzsche's sustained engagement with Baudelaire's poems and prose, from his readings of *Les Fleurs du mal* in 1885, through to his discovery of the *Oeuvres posthumes* in 1887, has been emphasized by readers such as Karl Pestalozzi and Jacques Le Rider as evidence for an ambivalent affinity toward this poet, whom Nietzsche would also align with Wagnerism in France. See Karl Pestalozzi, "Nietzsches Baudelaire-Rezeption," and Jacques Le Rider, "Nietzsche et Baudelaire." Whereas Pestalozzi traces an evolution from Nietzsche's more negative assessment to a positive reception of Baudelaire, however, Le Rider argues that "[c]ette ambivalence est à vrai dire analogue à celle qui marque les sentiments de Nietzsche envers Wagner et—peut-être aussi—de Nietzsche envers lui-même: *Haß-liebe*, amour-haine envers Wagner, envers Baudelaire, envers soi-même" ("Nietzsche et Baudelaire," 98). The emphasis of both writers, however, is upon Nietzsche's stance toward Baudelairean pessimism and decadence in general, rather than a close examination of what is at stake in the prose fragment, "Le Monde va finir," and the pages in Nietzsche's notebook where it is partially cited, translated, and paraphrased (*KSA* 13: 90–92). Le Rider sums the relation between the two passages only briefly, writing, "La démystification baudelairienne du mythe moderniste du Progrès des civilisations, la vision opposée d'une humanité en pleine décadence morale, régressant vers l'animalité, relues par Nietzsche, préfigurent de manière frappante la conscience 'postmoderne,' si l'on interprète le mépris baudelairien de l'idée de progrès comme un sentiment de 'fin de l'histoire'" ("Nietzsche et Baudelaire," 91).

8. Walter Benjamin, *The Arcades Project*, [J 47a, 3], 315. In German, the passage reads: "Das Stück 'Le monde va finir' (Fusées XXII) enthält, mit der apokalyptischen Träumerei verwoben, eine von furchtbarer Bitterkeit erfüllte Kritik der Gesellschaft des zweiten Kaiserreichs. (Sie klingt vielleicht hin und wieder an Nietzsches Vorstellung vom 'letzten Menschen' an.) Diese Kritik hat zum Teil prophetische Züge" (Benjamin, *Gesammelte Schriften*, 5: 396–97).

9. Charles Baudelaire, *My Heart Laid Bare and Other Prose-Writings*, 171, translation modified. Baudelaire, *OC* 1: 665.

10. Charles Baudelaire, *My Heart Laid Bare*, 173, translation modified. "Alors, ce qui ressemblera à la vertu,—que dis-je,—tout ce qui ne sera pas l'ardeur vers Plutus sera réputé un immense ridicule. La justice, si, à cette époque fortunée, il peut encore exister une justice, fera interdire les citoyens qui ne sauront pas faire fortune" (*OC* 1: 666–67).

11. Charles Baudelaire, *My Heart Laid Bare*, 171, translation modified. Baudelaire, *OC* 1: 666.

12. Charles Baudelaire, *My Heart Laid Bare*, 174, translation modified. "Perdu dans ce vilain monde, coudoyé par les foules, je suis comme un homme lassé dont l'œil ne voit en arrière, dans les années profondes, que désabusement et amertume, et devant lui qu'un orage où rien de neuf n'est contenu, ni enseignement,

ni douleur. [. . .] Je crois que j'ai dérivé dans ce que les gens du métier appellent un hors-d'œuvre. Cependant, je laisserai ces pages,—parce que je veux dater ma colère. [tristesse]" (*OC* 1: 667). In his monograph devoted to this text, André Hirt not only insists that the undated text dates its readers, but also that it arrives in a "siècle qui, du point de vue sérieux, du travail et de ce qu'il faut entendre par la pensée, n'en a manifestement plus rien à faire, réalité qui est devenue pour nous plus évidente encore" (André Hirt, *Baudelaire: Le monde va finir*, 15, 17).

    13. Gelikman, "The Crisis of the Messianic Claim," 180, 181.

    14. Hirt, *Baudelaire*, 20.

    15. Baudelaire, *My Heart Laid Bare*, 171, translation modified. Baudelaire, *OC* 1: 665.

    16. "Die Weiter-Entwicklung der Menschheit nach Baudelaires Vorstellung. Nicht daß wir dem wilden Zustande uns wieder näherten, etwa nach Art des désordre bouffon südamerikanischer Republiken, wo man, das Gewehr in der Hand, seine Nahrung sucht, zwischen den Trümmern unserer Civilisation. Das würde noch eine gewisse vitale Energie voraussetzen. Die Mechanik wird uns derart amerikanisirt, der Fortschritt wird die spiritualistische Partie dermaaßen in uns atrophiirt haben, daß Alles Verrückte, was geträumt worden ist von Socialisten, hinter der positiven Wirklichkeit zurück bleibt. Keine Religion, kein Eigenthum; selbst keine Revolution mehr" (*KSA* 13: 91–92).

    17. Baudelaire, *My Heart Laid Bare*, 171–72, translation modified. The passage in French reads: "Je ne dis pas que le monde sera réduit aux expédients et au désordre bouffon des républiques du Sud-Amérique,—que peut-être même nous retournerons à l'état sauvage, et que nous irons, à travers les ruines herbues de notre civilisation, chercher notre pâture, un fusil à la main. Non;—car ce sort et ces aventures supposeraient encore une certaine énergie vitale, écho des premiers âges. Nouvel exemple et nouvelles victimes des inexorables lois morales, nous périrons par où nous avons cru vivre. La mécanique nous aura tellement américanisés, le progrès aura si bien atrophié en nous toute partie spirituelle, que rien parmi les rêveries sanguinaires, sacrilèges, ou anti-naturelles des utopistes ne pourra être comparé à ses résultats positifs. Je demande à tout homme qui pense de me montrer ce qui subsiste de la vie. De la religion, je crois inutile d'en parler et d'en chercher les restes, puisque se donner encore la peine de nier Dieu est le seul scandale en pareilles matières. La propriété avait disparu virtuellement avec la suppression du droit d'aînesse; mais le temps viendra où l'humanité, comme un ogre vengeur, arrachera leur dernier morceau à ceux qui croiront avoir hérité légitimement des révolutions" (*OC* 1: 665–66).

    18. In this respect, he seems to anticipate Gelikman's reading of Baudelaire's text as one that "inscribes modernity in a register that is neither apocalyptic nor temporal" (Gelikman, "The Crisis of the Messianic Claim," 181).

    19. Nietzsche breaks off just before the lines in which Baudelaire characterizes his text as a legacy. The passage in Nietzsche's notebooks reads: "Was mich betrifft,

der ich bisweilen das Lächerliche eines Propheten in mir fühle, ich weiß, daß ich niemals la charité d'un médecin darin finden werde. Verloren in dieser erbärmlichen Welt, coudoyé par les foules, bin ich wie ein müder Mensch, der rückwärts blickend nichts sieht, als désabusement et amertume in langen tiefen Jahren und vor sich einen Sturm, in dem es Nichts Neues giebt, weder Lehre, noch Schmerz. Le soir, où cet homme a volé à la destinée quelques heures de plaisir—den Abend, an dem dieser Mensch eine Stunde Vergnügen dem Schicksale abgestohlen hat—, bercé dans sa digestion, oublieux autant que possible du passé, content du présent et résigné à l'avenir, enivré de son sang-froid et de son dandysme, fier de n'être pas aussi bas, que ceux qui passent, il se dit, en contemplant la fumée de son cigare: 'Que m'importe, où vont ces consciences?'—Ein wenig reine Luft! Dieser absurde Zustand Europa's soll nicht mehr länger dauern!" (*KSA* 13: 91–92).

20. Cf. Nietzsche, *KSA* 4: 72.

21. In the *Dictionnaire Littré*, the first definition of the word reads, "La masse de fil enroulé sur le fuseau," and after a list of usages relevant to architecture and seafaring appears the definition, "Pièce d'artifice formée d'un cylindre de carton ou de papier rempli de poudre à canon, ainsi dite par assimilation de forme avec un fuseau. Jeter, lancer des fusées," *Dictionnaire Littré*, s.v. "fusée," https://www.littre.org/definition/fus%C3%A9e. Accessed 10 March 2017. However, the inclusion of the fragment among those that Baudelaire had collected under this name is a decision of his editor. Helpfully summarizing the commentary of the editors of the Pléiade-edition of Baudelaire's oeuvre, Gelikman writes: "Even in calling it 'La Fin du monde,' we do no more than follow the decision of the editors. We don't know what Baudelaire would have called it, or how he would have used it. It may be the beginning of the novel he was planning, or a prose poem. It also could have been destined for *Fusées*, the collection of aphorisms and reflections where it is now placed" ("The Crisis of the Messianic Claim," 178). Nevertheless, the way in which Nietzsche weaves Baudelaire's words into his text suggests that Baudelaire's posthumous testimony functions along the lines that Dolf Oehler traces in his reading of Baudelaire's prose poems, namely, as an attempt to work against all current odds (and ends), in order to "jeter des éclairs et d'allumer des fusées, non pas pour faire flamber la réalité elle-même, mais pour dire les faits et frapper l'imagination du publique" (Oehler, *Le spleen contre l'oubli: Juin 1848: Baudelaire, Flaubert, Heine, Herzen*, 317–18). Oehler also makes the further argument that "[l]e nouveau qu'il [Baudelaire] a recherché, c'est d'abord ce regard neuf sur tout ce qui passe pour connu, car c'est là la condition première pour surmonter et dépasser l'ancien. Le prix à payer pour sa technique de recherché de la vérité en redisant à neuf les lieux communs de l'époque, c'est le malentendu" (*Le spleen contre l'oubli*, 325).

22. This particular passage is therefore one in which it is not a matter of Nietzsche finding in Baudelaire the "double of his proper personality," as Stéphane Michaud has suggested, than it is of exploding such distinctions. See Stéphane

Michaud, "Nietzsche et Baudelaire," 138. The phrase "alter ego" appears in Le Rider, "Nietzsche et Baudelaire," 98.

23. Gelikman, "The Crisis of the Messianic Claim," 184.

24. Gelikman, "The Crisis of the Messianic Claim," 185.

25. Baudelaire, *My Heart Laid Bare*, 172. "Alors, le fils fuira la famille, non pas à dix-huit ans, mais à douze, émancipé par sa précocité gloutonne ; il la fuira, non pas pour chercher des aventures héroïques, non pas pour délivrer une beauté prisonnière dans une tour, non pas pour immortaliser un galetas par de sublimes pensées, mais pour fonder un commerce, pour s'enrichir, et pour faire concurrence à son infâme papa,—fondateur et actionnaire d'un journal qui répandra les lumières et qui ferait considérer *Le Siècle* d'alors comme un suppôt de la superstition" (*OC* 1: 666).

26. See *Le Siècle* Nr. 5514 (1 January 1851), 1, and *Le Siècle* Nr. 11606 (1 January 1867), 1. The tables that are printed on the front pages of these and the intervening first issues of each year are not to be found before 1851. For evidence of this contrast, see *Le Siècle* Nr. 5255 (1 January 1850), 1.

27. Louis-Auguste Blanqui, "Formulaire de réception à la 'Société des Saisons' (1837)," in *Oeuvres complètes*, 128–30, 128. Baudelaire's subsequent description of the way in which "a time will come when humanity, like an avenging ogre, will snatch their last morsel from those who regard themselves as the legitimate heirs of the revolutions" also resonates with the rhetoric of voracity with which Blanqui characterizes the latest aristocracy (*My Heart Laid Bare*, 172; *OC* 1: 666).

28. Baudelaire, *My Heart Laid Bare*, 172, translation modified. The passage in French reads: "La propriété avait disparu virtuellement avec la suppression du droit d'aînesse; mais le temps viendra où l'humanité, comme un ogre vengeur, arrachera leur dernier morceau à ceux qui croiront avoir hérité légitimement des révolutions" (*OC* 1: 665–66).

29. Baudelaire, *My Heart Laid Bare*, p. 172. "La propriété avait disparu virtuellement avec la suppression du droit d'aînesse" (*OC* 1: 666).

30. Ζεὺς δ' ὀλέσει καὶ τοῦτο γένος μερόπων ἀνθρώπων, /εὖτ' ἂν γεινόμενοι πολιοκρόταφοι τελέθωσιν. /οὐδὲ πατὴρ παίδεσσιν ὁμοίιος οὐδέ τι παῖδες, /οὐδὲ ξεῖνος ξεινοδόκῳ καὶ ἑταῖρος ἑταίρῳ, /οὐδὲ κασίγνητος φίλος ἔσσεται, ὡς τὸ πάρος περ. / αἶψα δὲ γηράσκοντας ἀτιμήσουσι τοκῆας· / μέμψονται δ' ἄρα τοὺς χαλεποῖς βάζοντες ἔπεσσιν, / σχέτλιοι, οὐδὲ θεῶν ὄπιν εἰδότες· Hesiod, *Works and Days*, lines 180–87, in *Theogony, Works and Days, Testimonia*, 102–03.

31. Baudelaire, *My Heart Laid Bare*, 173; *OC* 1: 667.

32. The likelihood that Baudelaire's vision of an "orage" before or "devant" himself may be read as a phonetic inversion of the "âge d'or" is also reinforced by the way in which this collocation echoes the most famous slogan of the Saint Simonians, who had spread the word that "the age of gold, which a blind tradition has until now placed in the past, is before us [*l'âge d'or, qu'une aveugle tradition*

a placé jusqu'ici dans le passé, est devant nous]" (Enfantin and Bazard, *Le doctrine de Saint-Simon*, in *Œuvres de Saint-Simon & d'Enfantin*, 42: 303, my translation).

33. Baudelaire, *My Heart Laid Bare*, 171, translation modified. "Le monde va finir. La seule raison pour laquelle il pourrait durer, c'est qu'il existe. Que cette raison est faible, comparée à toutes celles qui annoncent le contraire, particulièrement à celle-ci : que'est-ce que le monde a désormais à faire sous le ciel ?" (*OC* 1: 665).

34. Walter Benjamin, *The Arcades Project*, [J 47a, 3], 315. Cf. Benjamin, *Gesammelte Schriften*, 5: 396–97.

35. Baudelaire, *My Heart Laid Bare*, 173; *OC* 1: 667.

36. As discussed above, the Ecclesiast's word for "in ages before us," lə·'ō·lā·mîm, derives from the verbal root ʿalam, which means "to conceal, to hide, to be secret," from which the nominalized form came to signify times "long past." Hence, as Anton Schoors writes in his commentary, the phrase indicates "an unfathomable fullness of time," and "the remotest time in the past." See Anton Schoors, *Ecclesiastes*, 86. See also *A Hebrew and English Lexicon of the Old Testament*, s.v. עוֹלָם and עָלַם.

37. For arguments tracing Ecclesiastes to the third century BCE—that is, to the era of the Stoics and Epicurean atomists—see Schoors, *Ecclesiastes*, 3–9, where both the textual evidence and a bibliography relevant to the dating of the biblical book are described. In contrast to the Epicurean school, however, the foundational assumption of the Ecclesiast is that there is "an appointed time for every matter" (Ecc. 3.17) assigned by a transcendent deity. With or without the notion of divine causality, however, his assertions on recurrence may be read to refer not to the repetition of the very same events—as one would have to conclude if space and time were infinite, and only a limited, albeit innumerable number of atomic combinations were possible—but to "*type[s]* of event[s] and deed[s]," as Michael V. Fox argues in *A Time to Tear Down and a Time to Build Up: A Rereading of Ecclesiastes*, 200.

38. Baudelaire, *My Heart Laid Bare*, 171, translation modified; *OC* 1: 665.

39. "Mais que voulez-vous donc conserver de cette république qui n'existe encore que de nom ? Tout est encore à faire. Louis-Philippe a gâché des millions, vous gâchez des milliards ! Quelles sont les choses ? quelles sont les formes que vous avez changées? Tout est à faire, et vous, vous êtes conservateurs ! Oui, vous êtes conservateurs par tempérament et par principe; conservateurs acharnés . . . de vos places!" (Baudelaire, *La Tribune nationale* 31 May 1848, in *OC* 2: 1047, my translation).

40. Blanqui, "Aux clubs démocratiques de Paris (22 mars 1848)," in *Oeuvres complètes*, 171.

41. On this relationship between the Ecclesiast's pronunciations and Isaiah, see Thomas Krüger, "Dekonstruktion und Rekonstruktion prophetischer Eschatologie im Qohelet-Buch," 112–13.

42. This would not be the place to enter into the much-debated political commitments of Baudelaire at various points in his career, which range from Philippe Murray's suggestion that Baudelaire never authentically subscribed to the Revolution,

which Richard Burton retraces and challenges in his monograph, *Baudelaire and the Second Republic: Writing and Revolution*, 46–50; to Dolf Oehler's arguments that even Baudelaire's explicit addresses to the bourgeoisie in, for example, the *Salon of 1846*, are covert appeals to a future "anti-bourgeois, if not proletarian public" (Oehler, *Pariser Bilder I: 1830–1848: Antibourgeoise Ästhetik bei Baudelaire, Daumier und Heine*, 15, my translation). Burton takes the most inclusive view: "Baudelaire was not a dandy-who-became-a-radical-who-became-a-reactionary: at every stage of his career he was simultaneously dandy, radical, *and* reactionary, with now one now another 'tendency' apparently in the ascendant, but always divided, always in conflict" (*Baudelaire and the Second Republic*, 52).

43. Baudelaire, *My Heart Laid Bare*, 173. "Ces temps sont peut-être bien proches ; qui sait même s'ils ne sont pas venus, et si l'épaississement de notre nature n'est pas le seul obstacle qui nous empêche d'apprécier le milieu dans lequel nous respirons" (*OC* 1: 667). These lines are themselves yet another instance of historical coincidence and revision, recalling Baudelaire's view of modernity in the *Salon of 1846*, where he had cast the obscurity of the present atmosphere in a more optimistic light: "Parisian life is fecund in poetic and marvelous subjects. The marvelous envelops and drenches us like the atmosphere, but we do not see it." The French text reads: "La vie parisienne est féconde en sujets poétiques et merveilleux. Le merveilleux nous enveloppe et nous abreuve comme l'atmosphère, mais nous ne le voyons pas" (Baudelaire, *Salon de 1846*, in *OC* 2: 496, my translation). Both passages also could be read to testify to the way in which, as Gelikman writes, "[t]he event of absolute modernity may have occurred already, which means that both the utopian interpretation of history and the dream of its apocalyptic interruption are kept alive only by our blindness to this event" (Gelikman, "The Crisis of the Messianic Claim," 184).

44. René Descartes, *Meditations on First Philosophy: With Selections from the Objections and Replies*, 17–18. "Or qui me peut avoir assuré que ce Dieu n'ai point fait qu'il n'y ait aucune terre, aucun ciel, aucun corps étendu, aucune figure, aucune grandeur, aucun lieu, et que néanmoins j'aie les sentiments de toutes ces choses, et que tout cela ne me semble point exister autrement que je le vois?" (Descartes, *Oeuvres philosophiques: Tome II (1638–1642)*, 409).

45. Hirt similarly points to the ways in which the text "emprunte les apparences de la philosophie," and notes that "[i]l y est question du principe de raison," but he does not analyze the specific rhetorical structures that dissolve the unity of reason. See Hirt, *Le monde va finir*, 21. For arguments that complicate the more traditional narrative of Cartesian philosophy as *the* foundation of subjectivity in the modern era, see Alain de Libera, *La double révolution*.

46. Baudelaire, *My Heart Laid Bare*, 171, translation modified; cf. *OC* 1: 665. Baudelaire's evocation of "raison" at first appears to be used in the sense of "rationale." But the way in which it gives way to hypostasized, conflicting reason*s* "qui annoncent le contraire [*that announce the contrary*]" may have been inspired

by Joseph de Maistre's etymological meditations on how oration comes "from OS and RATIO, mouth and reason, which is to say spoken reason" (de Maistre, *St. Petersburg Dialogues: Or, Conversations on the Temporal Government of Providence*, 50). After all, Baudelaire had not only read de Maistre's St. Petersburg dialogues, but also soon refers to them in his *Journaux intimes*, when he writes: "De Maistre et Edgar Poe m'ont appris à raisonner [*De Maistre and Edgar Poe have taught me to reason*]" (*OC* 1: 669).

47. Nietzsche, *KSA* 13: 89.

48. Baudelaire, *My Heart Laid Bare and Other Prose-Writings*, 171, translation modified; *OC* 1: 665.

49. Jean-François Lyotard, "Rewriting Modernity," quoted in Elissa Marder, *Dead Time: Temporal Disorders in the Wake of Modernity (Baudelaire and Flaubert)*, 12. See Lyotard, *The Inhuman*, 24–35.

50. Marder, *Dead Time*, 12.

51. Marder, *Dead Time*, 13.

52. Marder, *Dead Time*, 66, 87.

53. Baudelaire, *The Flowers of Evil*, 293. All subsequent translations from *Les Fleurs du mal* will, unless otherwise noted, be parenthetically cited by page number on the basis of McGowan's English version.

54. Baudelaire, *OC* 1: 134.

55. Walter Benjamin, "Central Park," in *Selected Writings: 1938–1940*, 171. "Es gibt für die Menschen wie sie heute sind nur eine radikale Neuigkeit—und das ist immer die gleiche: der Tod" (Benjamin, *Zentralpark*, in *Gesammelte Schriften*, 1.2: 668). Dolf Oehler similarly reads the association Baudelaire draws between novelty and death as an allegory for the trajectory of "bourgeois society"—"Curiosité, the buyer's eternal greed for the new [*Neugier*], is the principle of its deadly dynamic [. . .]. 'Au Lecteur,' like 'Le Voyage,' the introductory and closing poems of *Flowers of Evil*, will flesh out what is already set up in the "Dédicace": that this dynamic can have its end only in death, of the individual or of bourgeois society in sum" (Oehler, *Pariser Bilder I*, 69, my translation). It was on the basis of a wide reading public's familiarity with Baudelaire's final lines that the art historian Harold Rosenberg could recycle them at the beginning of his study of novelty and modernism in art, poetry, and politics, writing in *The Tradition of the New*: "The famous 'modern break with tradition' has lasted long enough to have produced its own tradition. Exactly one hundred years have passed since Baudelaire invited fugitives from the too-small world of memory to come aboard for his voyage in search of the new" (Rosenberg, *The Tradition of the New*, 9). See also Hans Robert Jauss, who reads Baudelaire's poem along the lines of the quarrel between the ancients and moderns in "Tradition, Innovation, and Aesthetic Experience," 375–88. Adopting a similar approach that navigates the interplay between ancient and modern topoi in Baudelaire, Maria Moog-Grünewald argues that a positive reassessment of *curiositas*, which Thomas Aquinas counts among the daughters of melancholic *acedia*—the medieval precursor

to modern ennui—makes up the "Besonderheit und das Neue des baudelaireschen Melancholieverständnisses" (Moog-Grünewald, "Ennui—Curiosité—Nouveau," 132). She then turns to the final two strophes of "Le Voyage," asserting that they take up "nicht allein isotopisch Thema und Struktur der gesamten Gedichtsammlung," but also formulate "die Quintessenz des baudelaireschen Oeuvre und zugleich das *punctum saliens* der Dichtung der Moderne" (Moog-Grünewald, "Ennui—Curiosité—Nouveau," 138).

56. Eugene W. Holland, *Baudelaire and Schizoanalysis: The Sociopoetics of Modernism*, 1.

57. While readers such as Richard Burton have emphasized Baudelaire's return to the first-person plural in the first and last poems of *Les Fleurs du mal*, the much more nebulous, shifting "nous" of "Le Voyage" dissolves the collective that seems to be established in Baudelaire's prefatory address "Au Lecteur." Kathryn Oliver Mills points out in her reading: "'Le Voyage' resonates with a chorus of voices [. . .] the direct and inclusive first-person plural fragments into multiple identities. If the surface of 'Le Voyage' leads us to believe that we know who is talking, and where we stand as listeners/readers, a closer reading shows this to be far from the case" (Mills, *Formal Revolution in the Work of Baudelaire and Flaubert*, 17). In his very different analysis of the poem, F. W. Leakey also draws attention to the differences among the first-person plural subjects that speak throughout, including, for example, the shift in the second section, where the "we" does not mark a return to "the original mode of address," but "refers, rather, to Humanity in general" (*Baudelaire and Nature*, 297).

58. "J'ai fait un long poème dédié à Max Du Camp, qui est à faire frémir la nature, et surtout les amateurs du progrès" (Charles Baudelaire to Charles Asselineau, 20 February 1859, in *Correspondance: 1832–1860*, 1: 553, my translation).

59. Baudelaire, *My Heart Laid Bare*, 171; *OC* 1: 665.

60. Baudelaire, *OC* 1: 129–32; McGowan, *Flowers of Evil*, 283–93. I have offered McGowan's verse translation for readers of English to gain a sense of the poem as a whole; however, in the following pages, I will offer my own prose translations of the lines that I analyze, in order to render more precisely the lexical and syntactic features of the French text that are crucial to my readings.

61. Baudelaire, *OC* 1: 667.

62. Nietzsche, *KSA* 13: 87.

63. Baudelaire, *My Heart Laid Bare*, 202; "Tout journal, de la première ligne à la dernière, n'est qu'un tissu d'horreurs. Guerres, crimes, vols, impudicités, tortures, crimes des princes, crimes des nations, crimes des particuliers, une ivresse d'atrocité universelle" (Baudelaire, *OC* 1: 705–06). As Richard Burton has put it, the travellers respond to their auditors' request for a news and world report with "a catalogue of horrors which [. . .] Baudelaire juxtaposes one against the other like so many newspaper headlines [. . .] inviting us to make just such a link with journalism and journalistic techniques" (Burton, *Baudelaire in 1859: A Study in the Sources of Poetic Creativity*, 80).

64. Burton also notices the usage of participles here (*Baudelaire in 1859*, 80).
65. Nietzsche, *KSA* 13: 87.
66. de Maistre, *St. Petersburg Dialogues*, 33.
67. Marder, *Dead Time*, 62.
68. Holland, *Baudelaire and Schizoanalysis*, 8–9.
69. "Le ex-roi va toujours de peuple en peuple, de ville en ville. Toujours et toujours, vive la République! vive la Liberté! des hommes! des cries! des pleurs de joie! Il court de toutes ses forces pour arriver à temps quelque part avant la République, pour y reposer sa tête, c'est là son rêve. Car la terre entière n'est plus pour lui qu'un cauchemar qui l'enveloppe. Mais à peine touche-t-il aux barrières, que les cloches se mettent gaiement en branle, et sonnent la République à ses oreilles éperdues" (Baudelaire, *OC* 2: 1035, my translation).
70. See above, n. 39.
71. Baudelaire, *The Flowers of Evil*, 287; cf. *OC* 1: 132: "Nous avons salué des idoles à trompe; / Des trônes constellés de joyaux lumineux; / Des palais ouvragés dont la féerique pompe / Serait pour vos banquiers un rêve ruineux."
72. Karl Marx and Friedrich Engels, *The Communist Manifesto*, in MECW 6: 482.
73. "Sparte, Rome, Venise étaient des oligarchies corrompues et oppressives. Aux États-Unis, l'esclavage est une institution. La formule: 'Liberté, Égalité, Fraternité' pourrait devenir un mensonge aussi célèbre que celui de la Charte-vérité: 'Tous les Français sont égaux devant la loi!' La tyrannie du Capital est plus impitoyable que celle du sabre et de l'encensoir. La révolution de Février a pour but de la briser" (Blanqui, *Oeuvres complètes*, 174, my translation).
74. Maximilien Robespierre, "Dernier discours," in *Oeuvres de Maximilien Robespierre*, 3: 689–736, 689, my translation.
75. Lyotard, *The Inhuman*, 26.
76. Baudelaire, *La Tribune nationale* 31 May 1848, in *OC* 2: 1047, my translation.
77. Karl Löwith, *Meaning in History*, 45, 43.
78. "J'ai fait un long poème dédié à Max Du Camp, qui est à faire frémir la nature, et surtout les amateurs du progrès" (Charles Baudelaire to Charles Asselineau, 20 February 1859, in *Correspondance: 1832–1860*, 1: 553, my translation).
79. This text, however, presents an oppressively rigid formula for communal life in its own right. For a brief and helpful discussion of the restrictive aspects of socialism as presented in the *Voyage en Icarie*, see Leslie J. Roberts, "Etienne Cabet and his *Voyage en Icarie*, 1840," 77–94.
80. Baudelaire, *The Flowers of Evil*, 285; *OC* 1: 130.
81. Nietzsche, *KSA* 13: 89.
82. Baudelaire, *The Flowers of Evil*, 289; *OC* 1: 132.
83. Baudelaire, *OC* 1: 132, my translation.

84. Baudelaire, *OC* 1: 131, my translation.

85. Nietzsche, *KSA* 13: 87.

86. Charles Baudelaire to Charles Asselineau, 20 February 1859, in *Correspondance: 1832–1860*, 1: 553, my translation.

87. Baudelaire, *My Heart Laid Bare*, 171, translation modified; Baudelaire, *OC* 1: 665.

88. Werner Hamacher, *95 Theses on Philology*, in *Minima Philologica*, 98.

89. Baudelaire, *OC* 1: 133, my translation.

90. Baudelaire, *OC* 1: 133, my translation.

91. Baudelaire, *OC* 1: 129, my translation.

92. Baudelaire, *OC* 1: 667.

93. Baudelaire, *OC* 1: 133, my translation.

94. Alan S. Rosenthal, "Baudelaire's Mysterious 'Enemy,'" 286–94. In this piece, he helpfully reminds readers of the various affirmations of this view and its limits on the parts of Antoine Adam, Jacques Crépet, and Georges Blin, among others.

95. Marder, *Dead Time*, 64. In his reading of "Le Voyage" within the broader context of a critical analysis of Ludwig Binswanger's essay on "The Problem of the Development of the Self in Art," Paul de Man reads time as a confining pressure, writing, "since the confinement is due not only to a lack of space, but is primarily caused by the excessive presence of time, these movements of horizontal expansion can never free the artist from his initial predicament" (de Man, *Blindness and Insight: Essays in the Rhetoric of Contemporary Criticism*, 45–46). For an excellent recent collection of analyses devoted to the complex and differentiated modes of temporality in Baudelaire's oeuvre, see *Time for Baudelaire (Poetry, Theory, History)*, ed. E. S. Burt, Elissa Marder, and Kevin Newmark.

96. Baudelaire, *OC* 1: 133, my translation.

97. Françoise Meltzer gestures toward such an approach to temporality in Baudelaire's poetry when she writes: "[T]he poems of Baudelaire record [. . .] a double vision: one of the world as it was, and one as it is. This double vision has been noted but usually laid on the altar of Baudelaire's drug use. I argue that it is a vision in which the past has not yet caught up with the present, and in which the future seems threatening. Baudelaire records his encounter with modernity as an unintelligible morass of contradictions that he cannot resolve. [. . .] I mean 'record' as in graphesis: the putting in writing what surrounds the poet [. . .]. Baudelaire is so much of an honest video and acoustic artist (to force an anachronism), that he registers (at times without knowing it) the dual vision that is so often his" (Meltzer, *Seeing Double: Baudelaire's Modernity*, 5–6).

98. For a helpful survey of the range of classical and contemporary sources from which Baudelaire's allusions to myth were most likely drawn, see Nicolae Babuts, "Baudelaire's 'Le Voyage': The Dimension of Myth," 348–59.

99. Baudelaire, *OC* 1: 133–34.

100. Nietzsche, *KSA* 13: 87.

101. J. L. Austin, *Poetic Principles and Practice: Occasional Papers on Baudelaire, Mallarmé, and Valéry*, 16. He goes on to argue that the final departure of the voyagers testifies to the way in which "[t]he vast appetite of the child" from the opening strophe of the poem "remains unimpaired: what he loses in his voyage through life is his illusions, not his desires. [. . .] Above all, the poet knows that to express even despair in a great poem is to have overcome despair" (*Poetic Principles*, 17). F. W. Leakey agrees, writing: "the Travellers show themselves to be essentially unchanged from the child, the 'young passengers,' of the earlier sections of the poem; their earlier condemnation of human curiosity and restlessness and self-delusion, is in effect undermined by their own unregenerate eagerness to revert to these same attitudes [. . .]" (*Baudelaire and Nature*, 309).

102. Babuts, "Baudelaire's 'Le Voyage,'" 351.

103. Baudelaire, *OC* 1: 463. See also Babuts, "Baudelaire's 'Le Voyage,'" 352, to which these remarks on Baudelaire's references are indebted. The longer passage in de Quincey's English version of the text reads: "for thou, beloved M., dear companion of my later years, thou wast my Electra! and neither in nobility of mind nor in long-suffering affection, wouldst permit that a Grecian sister should excel an English wife. For thou thoughtst not much to stoop to humble offices of kindness, and to servile ministrations of tenderest affection;—to wipe away for years the unwholesome dews upon the forehead, or to refresh the lips when parched and baked with fever; nor, even when thy own peaceful slumbers had by long sympathy become infected with the spectacle of my dread contest with phantoms and shadowy enemies that oftentimes bade me 'sleep no more!'—not even then, didst thou utter a complaint or any murmur, nor withdraw thy angelic smiles, nor shrink from thy service of love more than Electra did of old" (*Confessions of an English Opium Eater, and Other Writings*, 41). What Babuts does not discuss in his informative account of the topoi that wander from de Quincey's English text to Baudelaire's "Le Voyage" is the way in which de Quincey presents his Electra-like wife as a silent companion during his "contest with phantoms," while in the poem, Electra is herself a phantom and a speaker, who promises rather than gives refreshment to the voyagers' parched hearts.

104. Baudelaire, *OC* 1: 134, my translation and emphasis.

105. From the reference to Circe in the first section, to the evocation of Homer's and Tennyson's "Lotus Eaters" in the seventh, the poem has frequently been read as a modern adaptation of Odyssean motifs, on which see Babuts, as well as Pierre Brunel, *Baudelaire antique et moderne*, 27–42.

106. Baudelaire, *The Flowers of Evil*, 75; *OC* 1: 37. This parallel has often been registered. Claude Pichois refers to it in the commentary to his edition of Baudelaire's oeuvre (*OC* 1: 1102), and it appears in Babuts's study of the role of myth in "Le Voyage." However, Babuts seeks to draw conclusions on the basis of the parallel that suggest a more familiar structure and subject of desire than "Le

Voyage" otherwise indicates, when he writes: "Nor should one be surprised that the image of nestling on the knees of the beloved in 'Le Balcon' resembles embracing Electra's knees in 'Le Voyage': both suggest a strong sexual worship tempered by the need for maternal and sisterly compassion" ("Baudelaire's 'Le Voyage,'" 352).

107. Baudelaire, *Flowers of Evil*, 75; *OC* 1: 37.

108. Kevin Newmark, "Off the Charts: Walter Benjamin's Depiction of Baudelaire," 78. Shortly thereafter, he adds, again with reference to Baudelaire's descriptions of the mnemonic techniques of the "painter of modern life," that the scene of memory-inscription becomes one in which "the subject [. . .] forgets itself in the very act of writing" (Newmark, "Off the Charts," 83). For another excellent discussion of Baudelaire's presentations of memory in *The Painter of Modern Life*, as well as "Le Cygne," see Hans-Jost Frey, *Studies in Poetic Discourse: Mallarmé, Baudelaire, Rimbaud, Hölderlin*. Especially relevant to the commentary on "Le Voyage" that is developed in this chapter is Frey's observation that "[t]he act of remembering can never become a remembered object, in which the memory could quiet itself. It can only appear or sound out in enumeration as a never-ending distancing from the remembered or the listed. Positively speaking, this means that each single memory becomes an allegory of that memory to the extent that each is a part of the enumeration" (Frey, *Studies in Poetic Discourse*, 96).

109. Nietzsche, *KSA* 13: 87.

110. As Debrati Sanyal has written with regard to a somewhat different constellation of texts, "Baudelaire's distinctive representations of time [. . .] open up a differentiated vision of history—not just as shattering or traumatic violence, nor as unchanging recurrent catastrophe, but as a field of testimony and engagement [. . .]" (Sanyal, "Reading Baudelaire in the Age of Terror," 108). Equally important and germane to this reading of "Le Voyage" is her remark: "The temporality of melancholy, repetition, and diffraction of 'The Swan,' the singular event that elides representation but generates poetic discourse in its aftermath: these are emblems of Baudelaire's response to the terror of imperial urban modernity but they can also be read as meditations on how to conceptualize historical time and event in the wake of crisis more generally. Historical time is envisioned not as linear progress, but rather as a palimpsest that defies the notion of a singular origin or causal nexus [. . .]. An event is conceptualized not as available for visual representation nor as illegible trauma but as a complex process whose effects demand ongoing decipherment, and in alternative, multidirectional narratives of historical time" (Sanyal, "Reading Baudelaire in the Age of Terror," 115).

111. Baudelaire, *OC* 1: 134, my translation.

112. Hugo, "The Slope of Reverie," in *Selected Poems of Victor Hugo: A Bilingual Edition*, 45, translation modified. For a close reading of this poem, with brief reference to the "care and admiration" with which Baudelaire had read it, see Victor Brombert, "The Rhetoric of Contemplation: Hugo's 'La pente de la rêverie,'" 59.

113. Victor Hugo, "La pente de la rêverie," in *Oeuvres poétiques*, 1: 772.

114. The upshot and pitfalls of intertextual study in Baudelaire have, of course, become a well-established topic among his commentators, such Jonathan Culler, whose exemplary reading of "Correspondances," between Baudelaire, Lamartine, Hugo, and many others, too—ends with a cautionary note: "A criticism focused on intertextual relations discovers echoes whose significative status is uncertain, but finds that a way of discussing such echoes is to claim for them a critical, ironic force which can work in both directions, infecting what is repeated [. . .]" (Culler, "Intertextuality and Interpretation: Baudelaire's 'Correspondances,'" 135).

115. "J'ignore dans quel monde Victor Hugo a mangé préalablement le dictionnaire de la langue qu'il était appelé à parler; mais je vois que le lexique français, en sortant de sa bouche, est devenu un monde, un univers coloré, mélodieux et mouvant," Baudelaire, *OC* 2: 133, my translation.

116. The phrase reads: "le développement aussi régulier qu'énorme de la faculté qui préside à la génération de ce poème enivrant" (Baudelaire, *OC* 2: 137, my translation). "The Slope of Reverie" is also the only title of a poem, besides Hugo's *La Légende des siècles*, that Baudelaire names in his essay.

117. Hans Robert Jauss, "Tradition, Innovation, and Aesthetic Experience," 375, 383. As Paul de Man writes in another context, "Jauss and his disciples" sought to trace Baudelaire's legacy as the inauguration of a shift from mimetic to allegorical and nonrepresentational poetic language. In so doing, however, they formulated "a pattern of continuity" for "that which is, by definition, the negation of all continuity" (de Man, "Lyric and Modernity," in *Blindness and Insight*, 185–86).

118. In *Eureka*, the *Mare Tenebrarum* is significantly described as the site for the chance discovery of a message in a bottle, not unlike the messages that happen to surface in the seventh section of "Le Voyage." "And now," writes Poe toward the start of *Eureka*, "before proceeding to our subject proper, let me beg the reader's attention to an extract or two from a somewhat remarkable letter, which appears to have been found corked in a bottle and floating on the *Mare Tenebrarum*—an ocean well described by the Nubian geographer, Ptolemy Hephaestion, but little frequented in modern days unless by the Transcendentalists and some other divers for crotchets" (Poe, *Eureka*, in *Poetry and Tales*, 1263. Cf. Charles Baudelaire, *Eureka*, 9). Ironically, in the preface to his translation of this text, Baudelaire remarks: "Quand je lis *Eureka*, je ne puis m'empêcher de considérer cet ouvrage comme immensément supérieur aux *Vestiges de la Création* et comme révélant un bien autre génie; et de même que j'admire le poëme (en exceptant toutefois cette malheureuse tentative de gouaillerie humouristique incluse dans ce que l'auteur nous donne comme une lettre trouvée dans une bouteille flottant sur le *Mare tenebrarum*), de même aussi j'y vois avec chagrin le panthéisme dominant, lequel, d'ailleurs, n'était pas nécessaire à son dessein principal" (Baudelaire, *Eureka*, vi–vii). According to Jacob Bryant's *A New System; or, An Analysis of Ancient Mythology*, the source that Poe most likely drew upon for his reference to the "Nubian geographer," the *Mare*

Tenebrarum referred to the Atlantic Ocean, on which see Kent Ljungquist, "Poe's Nubian Geographer," 73–75.

119. "Vallée des Ténèbres" occurs in Joseph Halévy's translation of the phrase, of which he writes: "c'est-à-dire le Šeôl" (Halévy, *Recherches Bibliques: Notes pour l'interprétation des psaumes, les chants nuptiaux des cantiques, les livres d'Osée, d'Amos, de Michée, etc.*, 3: 52). And while this phrase was rendered in de Sacy's translation, "au milieu de l'ombre de la mort [in the midst of the shadow of death]" (Ps. 23.4), the biblical topos of a valley of shadows was surely known to Baudelaire from Edgar Allan Poe's "Eldorado," where a traveler in search of the land of gold is told to go "Down the Valley of the Shadow" (Poe, *Poetry and Tales*, 101).

120. I have quoted this passage according to *La Bible*, trans. Isaac-Louis Le Maistre de Sacy, 3: 13. There, the verse reads in full: "Vous avez oint ma tête avec une huile *de parfums*. Que mon calice, qui a la force d'enivrer, est admirable!"

121. In his erudite commentary on the Psalms, Halévy retraces this tradition of translations of the verse that is known to today to read: "my cup overflows." Explaining the way the word for abundance came to be understood as drunkenness, he recurs to the Greek translation of the Hebrew Bible, writing of the Septuaginta: "Les Septante, induits en erreur par l'araméen [aleph wav r] 's'enivrer,' ont traduit [ha yod wav daleth] par μεθύκον," and he goes on to note that the Vulgate "a conservé le participe *inebrians*" (Halévy, *Recherches Bibliques*, 53).

122. Of course, the motif of intoxication cannot be reduced to these resonances, either, as Joshua Wilner shows in his perceptive reading of the intersections between Baudelaire's prose poem, "Enivrez-vous," and the second canto of Lord Byron's *Don Juan*. He offers an elegant argument that suggests that getting drunk, for Baudelaire, figures as an antidote to time—as "the mirror image of the 'dictatorship of time' that Baudelaire evokes at the end of 'La Chambre double' " (Wilner, *Feeding on Infinity: Readings in the Romantic Rhetoric of Internalization*, 87–88). Furthermore, insofar as the marking of time was associated with the time of labor in Baudelaire's context in general, Wilner proceeds to point out the historical and political dimension of Baudelaire's imperative, arguing for the "strong evidence that 'Enivrez-vous' is a distant (and mocking) echo of the political slogan 'Enrichissez-vous' [. . .], which figured prominently in the electoral debates in the 1840s over extending suffrage to the millions of disfranchised French citizens who did not pay the two hundred francs in property taxes that was a condition of suffrage under the constitutional monarchy of Louis-Philippe" (Wilner, *Feeding on Infinity*, 93).

123. The downward turn of the voyagers' quest for the "Inconnu" also may recall the opening poem of Théophile Gautier's *España*-cycle, whose speaker proposes to journey to the underworld in similar terms, or "to make, upon my turn to the unknown land, / this voyage from which no one has returned." The French lines read: "de faire à mon tour au pays inconnu / Ce voyage dont nul n'est encore revenu," and as in "Le Voyage," Gautier speaks there, too, of an "amer

savoir," when he writes in the concluding strophe: "Le voyage est un maître aux préceptes amers" (Gautier, *Poésies complètes*, 2: 254). Yet what Gautier elaborates as the bitterness of voyaging is not the repetitive variant on original sin that features in the Baudelairean voyagers' debriefing, but rather one which proceeds from the way the voyage "vous montre l'oubli dans les coeurs les plus chers, / Et vous prouve,— ô misère et tristesse suprême! — / Qu'ingrat à votre tour, vous oubliez vous-même!" (Gautier, *Poésies complètes*, 2: 254).

124. My translation. The French text reads: "cette génération rongie par des ennuis sans remède, repoussée par d'injuste déclassements, atirée vers l'inconnu par les désirs des imaginations déréglées" (Maxime du Camp, *Mémoires d'un suicidé*, 21–22). This generation, in turn, is compared both in du Camp's preface and in Jean-Marc's first-person narrative to Chateaubriand's René (*Mémoires*, 17, 22, 36, 114, 218), the protagonist of the novella *René* and the novel *Les Natchez*, who searches "solely an unknown good for which the instinct pursues me [*seulement un bien inconnu, dont l'instinct me poursuit*]" (François-René de Chateaubriand, *René*, in *Oeuvres romanesques et voyages*, 1: 128, my translation). But whereas Chateaubriand and du Camp maintain the semblance of first-person protagonists suffering from vague passions, Baudelaire draws different consequences from Chateaubriand's description of their cause in his *Génie du christianisme*: "The more people advance in civilization, the more this state of *undulation / vagueness* of the passions augments; for a very sad thing arrives: the great number of examples one has before one's eyes, the multitude of books that treat man and his sentiments, render him skilled without experience. One is disillusioned without having enjoyed; yet there remain desires, and one no longer has illusions" (Chateaubriand, *Génie du christianisme, ou beautés de la religion chrétienne*, in *Essai sur les révolutions; Génie du christianisme*, 714–15), my translation. But if a sense disillusionment may be attributed to the sea of ink and proliferation of dead letters that haunt all processes of life—as is the case in Baudelaire's poem—the phenomenon of exposure to other voices can neither be a matter of personal knowledge, nor can it be historically limited as the modern phenomenon that Chateaubriand makes it out to be. It would have to exceed and dissolve the subject whose experience is crossed by these very letters in singular ways, rendering every articulation of experience singularly plural and plural in its singularity. The notion of a disillusioned individual itself, meanwhile, could only emerge as an effect of the fundamentally impersonal and transpersonal function of the language that Chateaubriand articulates, and that the proliferation of Renés in his own century demonstrates further. Furthermore, the structure of experience that is traced in *Génie du christianisme* and *René* would have been at least as old as the very Scriptures to which Chateaubriand seeks to oppose the dissemination of modern literature, as the wisdom of the Ecclesist testifies in his remarks on the proliferation of seductive and misleading books. On this aspect of Ecclesiastes, see Mendicino, "Newswriting, Historiography," 91–94. There, the following lines of the Ecclesiast are discussed: "The sayings of the wise are like goads, and like nails

firmly fixed are the collected sayings that are given by one shepherd. Of anything beyond these, my child, beware. Of making many books there is no end, and much study is a weariness of the flesh" (Ecc. 12.11–12). Thus, when the transient plural voices of Baudelaire's voyagers do away with the insular individuals who populate Chateaubriand's *René* and the literature of his epigones, the poem draws the furthest consequences of the transpersonal and impersonal languages of the afterlife that Chateaubriand promotes at least as much as he expressly seeks to damn them.

125. Benjamin, *The Arcades Project*, 11; "Das letzte Gedicht der 'Fleurs du mal': Le Voyage. 'O Mort, vieux capitaine, il est temps! levons l'ancre!' Die letzte Reise des Flaneurs: der Tod. Ihr Ziel: das Neue. 'Au fond de l'Inconnu pour trouver du Nouveau!' Das Neue ist eine vom Gebrauchswert der Ware unabhängige Qualität. Es ist der Ursprung des Scheins, der den Bildern unveräußerlich ist, die das kollektive Unbewußte hervorbringt. Es ist die Quintessenz des falschen Bewußtseins, dessen nimmermüde Agentin die Mode ist. Dieser Schein des Neuen reflektiert sich, wie ein Spiegel im andern, im Schein des immer wieder Gleichen" (*Gesammelte Schriften*, 5: 55).

126. With respect to this last point, it is significant that Baudelaire abandoned his initial plan to call the poem "Le Voyageur." See Baudelaire to Maxime du Camp, 23 February 1859, *Correspondance*, 1: 554–55.

127. Baudelaire, *My Heart Laid Bare*, 172; *OC* 1: 666.

128. Nor is the unknown ever found, though it may perhaps be invented in the sense that Arthur Rimbaud would propose, when he wrote, "The inventions of the unknown invoke novelties [*Les inventions d'inconnu réclament des formes nouvelles*]," which Ross Chambers has read as a testimony to the effects of "language's own cracks, gaps, and holes," which may be exposed "in order to *suggest* something that ordinary language is thought to get in the way of our glimpsing" (Chambers, "Inventing Unknownness: The Poetry of Disenchanted Enchantment [Leopardi, Baudelaire, Rimbaud, Justice]," 15, 17).

129. The movement of "Le Voyage" therefore resembles the one that Michael Levine elaborates in his reading of Baudelaire, via Walter Benjamin, Sigmund Freud, and Jacques Derrida, when he describes the scene of Baudelaire's writing as one in which one "hand [. . .] erases as the other writes," before citing Derrida's remarks on Freud's mystic writing pad: "Traces thus produce the space of their inscription only by acceding to the period of their erasure. From the beginning, in the 'present' [*maintenant*] of their first impression, they are constituted by the double force of repetition and erasure, legibility and illegibility" (Levine, *Writing through Repression*, 104). Yet in "Le Voyage," even the intervention of hands, so crucial to the poem that Levine analyzes—Baudelaire's "Le Soleil"—may no longer hold, as the multiple subjects of inscription in "Le Voyage" coincide and blur any precise recognition of who, exactly, will have had a hand in the text. The difference is already suggested by the way in which this poem, with its shifting, first-person plural subjects, abandons the first-person singular pronoun that marks the majority of the poems in *Les Fleurs du mal*.

130. This phrase is a translation of the passage from Plato's *Phaedrus*, where Socrates speaks against those who would share their thoughts on the good and the beautiful "in black water [. . .] through a pen [ἐν ὕδατι μέλανι διὰ [. . .] καλάμου]" (Plato, *Phaedrus* 276d), writing: "De manière que celui qui s'imagine pouvoir établir par l'écriture une seule doctrine claire et durable, EST UN GRAND SOT. S'il possedait réellement les véritables germes de la vérité, il se garderait bien de croire qu'avec *un peu de liqueur noire* et une plume il pourra les faire germer dans l'univers, les défendre contre l'inclémence des saisons et leur communiquer l'efficacité nécessaire" (*Essai sur le principe générateur des constitutions politiques et des autres institutions humaines*, 30).

131. In her text-immanent reading of the poem, Kathryn Oliver Mills also stresses the importance of writing throughout, from the "estampes [*engravings*]" mentioned in the very first line, to the double meanings of words such as "lame" and "rayon," which also refer to etching and cutting (20–21), but because she does not emphasize the connections of these important observations to the additional traces of other texts that are inscribed in Baudelaire's lines, she concludes: "Thus, the images of writing in this poem are controlled and fixed. And since these forms of representation also describe the poem's voyage, the voyagers' journey is by extension controlled and fixed" (Mills, *Formal Revolution*, 21).

Chapter 3

1. As word of voyaging went around, travel literature came to display certain recognizable tendencies such as a commitment "to accomplish[ing] a course whose stages are already fixed by the itineraries of previous voyagers," and "to 'fabricat[ing]' alterity, that is, to respond[ing] to the expectations of a readership avid for displacement, surprise, and novelty" (Sarga Moussa, "Usages de la fiction dans le récit de voyage: l'épisode de la mer Morte chez Lamartine," 52, my translation). For further discussions of other ways in which nineteenth-century voyages traverse written topoi, see Christine Montalbetti, *Le Voyage, le monde et la bibliothèque*. However, even those voyage narratives that appear to retrace well-known itineraries often issue, as Thangam Ravindranathan has recently shown through explorations of twentieth-century literature, into the fundamentally unsettling experience of that which "resists the desire of adequation and refuses to enter any grid of preexisting readings" (Ravindranathan, *Là où je ne suis pas: Récits de dévoyage*, 25, my translation). The trajectory of the final poem from *Les Fleurs du mal* moves in precisely this direction toward the unknown and unknowable dimensions that open through each passage.

2. Alphonse Lamartine, "Sur le chemin de fer de Paris à Avignon," in *Oeuvres oratoires et écrits politiques. Troisième série: 1847–1851*, 6: 143, 159. Translations of

all quotations from Lamartine's oeuvre are mine.

3. In his discourse "Sur l'enseignement" from 24 March 1837, he asserts: "Étudiez l'histoire de tous les peuples, vous retrouverez l'apogée de leur littérature à ce point précis de leur existence" (Lamartine, "Sur l'enseignement," in *La politique de Lamartine*, 125).

4. For a helpful presentation of his contemporary reputation among fellow statesmen and political opponents, see George Armstrong Kelly, "Alphonse de Lamartine: The Poet in Politics;" for a more recent elaboration of the political dimensions of Lamartine's poetry, see Roger Pearson, *Unacknowledged Lawgivers: The Poet as Lawgiver in Post-Revolutionary France: Chateaubriand—Staël—Lamartine—Hugo—Vigny*, 351–70. Furthermore, Lamartine's voyages, as traced in his literary meditations in the *Voyage en Orient*, also served his political advancement. As Moussa has pointed out, Lamartine's record of encounters with prominent figures of the East in his *Voyage en Orient* supported the legitimation of his claims on the Orient in the Chamber. See Sarga Moussa, "Un voyage dans l'Itinéraire: Lamartine contradicteur de Chateaubriand," 93–94.

5. Alphonse Lamartine, "Sur le chemin de fer de Paris à Avignon," 137.

6. Lamartine, "Sur le chemin de fer," 139.

7. Lamartine, "Sur le chemin de fer," 145.

8. Lamartine, "Sur le chemin de fer," 148.

9. Lamartine, "Sur le chemin de fer," 148.

10. Baudelaire, *My Heart Laid Bare*, 173; *OC* 1: 667.

11. "[L]a pensée générale, la pensée politique, la pensée sociale domine et oppresse chaque pensée individuelle. Nous voulons la déposer en vain; elle est autour de nous, en nous, partout; l'air qui nous respirons nous l'apporte, l'écho du monde entier nous la renvoie. En vain nous nous réfugions dans le silence des vallées, dans les sentiers les plus perdus de nos forêts [. . .] nous contemplons d'un regard envieux ce ciel paisible et étoilé qui nous attire et l'ordre harmonieux et durable de l'armée céleste; le souvenir de ce monde mortel qui tremble sous nos pieds, les soucis du présent, la prévision de l'avenir, nous atteignent jusqu'à ces hauteurs mêmes" (Lamartine, "Sur la politique rationelle," *La politique de Lamartine*, 1: 21–22).

12. Lamartine, "Sur le chemin de fer," 148–49.

13. These turns in Lamartine's speech also mark a novel shift in Lamartine's political trajectory, deviating radically from his earlier denouncements of modern institutions of finance in 1838, when he had proclaimed before the Chamber of Deputies under Louis Philippe: "Do we not see the entire country oppressed in its agriculture or in its commerce by the collective interests of a small number of manufacturers of iron, possessors of factories, manufacturers privileged by the incentives that were once granted to them, by the rights that are protective for them alone, and ruinous for all the rest?" In French, the passage reads: "Ne voyons-nous pas le pays tout entier opprimé dans son agriculture ou dans son commerce par ces

intérêts collectifs d'un petit nombre de fabricants de fer, de possesseurs d'usines, de fabricants privilégiés par des primes une fois accordées, par des droits protecteurs d'eux seuls, ruineux pour tout le reste?" (Lamartine, *Sur le projet de loi relatif aux chemins de fer prononcé à la Chambre des Députés* 10 May 1838, 18). In this speech, his characterization of companies grows increasingly worse as he goes on to assert that "leur histoire n'est que celle de nos désastres, de nos ruines, de nos catastrophes industrielles et coloniales; rien de grand ne s'est fait, de grand, de monumental en France, et je dirai dans le monde, que par l'État" (Lamartine, *Sur le projet de loi*, 21–22).

14. Lamartine, "Sur le chemin de fer," 153.

15. He writes at one point, situating the threat of the socialists and communists even beyond the borders of the French Republic: "Messieurs, on a dit qu'il y a des hommes dans notre pays qui ont fait les uns le serment d'Annibal contre la société, les autres le serment de Coriolan contre une République qui froisse leurs habitudes ou leurs souvenirs!" (Lamartine, "Sur le chemin de fer," 157).

16. Lamartine, "Sur le chemin de fer," 154.

17. Lamartine, "Sur le chemin de fer," 154.

18. Lamartine, "Sur le chemin de fer," 157.

19. Lamartine, "Sur le chemin de fer," 155.

20. Lamartine, "Sur le chemin de fer," 155.

21. Baudelaire, *OC* 2: 1044.

22. Baudelaire writes: "Séparons une fois pour toutes le Gouvernement provisoire et ses actes, de la révolution du 24 février et de ses conséquences immédiates. Le crédit public ruiné, toute autorité détruite, toutes les passions surexcitées, toutes les misères aggravées, les ambitions, les cupidités bouillonnantes de ses amis servies et non rassasiées, la justice mise au service de la politique, l'arbitraire effaçant le droit commun, l'imprévoyance régnant, l'inconséquence gouvernante, le dépôt du pouvoir érigé en dictature, tels ont été les actes du Gouvernement provisoire; la confiance, l'union, la fraternité, proclamées sur les barricades, tels ont été les faits de la Révolution" (*OC* 2: 1045).

23. Patrick Hutton, "Legends of a Revolutionary: Nostalgia in the Imagined Lives of Auguste Blanqui," 41.

24. Hutton, "Legends of a Revolutionary," 51.

25. Friedrich Engels, "Programme of the Blanquist Commune Refugees," in MECW 24: 13.

26. Rosa Luxemburg, "Blanquism and Social Democracy," in *Socialism or Barbarism: The Selected Writings of Rosa Luxemburg*, 127.

27. Daniel Bensaïd and Michael Löwy, "Auguste Blanqui, Heretical Communist," 26.

28. Benjamin, *The Arcades Project* [D5, 6], 112.

29. Jacques Rancière, for example, claims that repetition, as understood by Blanqui, renders every second a chance to alter decisively the course of events for

eternity. "With Nietzsche, as with Blanqui," he argues, "the scientific argument counts for less than what he is trying to stage: the redoubling at the very heart of repetition. Repetition does not entail resignation. On the contrary, it splits in two, and this split obliges us, every time, to replay one repetition against another" (Rancière, "The Radical Gap: A Preface to Auguste Blanqui, *Eternity by the Stars*," 24). Peter Hallward pursues the possibilities of bifurcations for revolutionary thought still further, underscoring the way in which Blanqui's hypothesis does not imply determinism or fatalism: "These irreversible and irreducible choices condition the whole of human existence, regardless of scale. However perfectly the world we have shaped thus far may have been (and will be) copied in other worlds in other spaces and at other times, still the path or 'chapter of bifurcations' opens again with every new decision" (Hallward, "Blanqui's Bifurcations," 42). Benjamin too writes: "One should not necessarily conclude from this [*The Eternity by the Stars*] that [Blanqui] was untrue to his political credo. The activity of a professional revolutionary such as Blanqui does not presuppose any faith in progress; it presupposes only the determination to do away with present injustice" (*The Arcades Project* [J61a, 3], 339).

30. Miguel Abensour and Valentin Pelosse, "Libérer l'enfermé," in *Instructions pour une prise d'armes; L'Éternité par les astres*, 420. All translations of quotations from this essay are mine.

31. Abensour and Pelosse, "Libérer l'enfermé," 424.

32. Abensour and Pelosse, "Libérer l'enfermé," 402–03. Rancière's more recent readings of Blanqui also indicate that his most radical practice lies in his linguistic performances, such as his scandalous pronunciation of his profession as "proletariat" before the Court of Assizes in 1832. When Blanqui declares his profession to be "proletariat," he explicates his decision, stating, "It is the profession of thirty thousand Frenchmen who live off their labor and who are deprived of political rights" (quoted in Jacques Ranicière, *Dis-Agreement: Politics and Philosophy*, 37). For Blanqui's dialogue with the court and full defense speech, see *Oeuvres complètes I: Des origines à la Révolution de 1848*, edited by Dominique le Nuz, 183–206. References to this edition of Blanqui's early writings will be distinguished from the earlier edition of Münster (which also bears the title *Oeuvres complètes*) by referring to the full title of le Nuz's volume. Significantly, the French word for "profession" in the scene that Rancière describes is the homonym of the word for "state": "Votre état?" is the question posed by the public prosecutor, to which Blanqui replies, "Prolétaire," (*Oeuvres complètes I: Des origines à la Révolution de 1848*, 186). On this scene, Rancière observes: "Blanqui's [. . .] replies summarize the entire conflict between politics and the police: everything turns on the double acceptance of a single word, *profession*. [. . .] It is clear that proletarian does not designate any occupation whatever [. . .] [b]ut, within revolutionary politics, Blanqui gives the same word a different meaning: a profession is a profession of faith, a declaration of membership of a collective." He continues to emphasize that this collective comprises "the class of the uncounted that only exists in the very declaration in which they are counted as

those of no account. The name *proletarian* defines neither a set of properties (manual labor, industrial labor, destitution, etc.) that would be shared equally by a multitude of individuals nor a collective body, embodying a principle [. . .]. It is part of a process of subjectification identical to the process of expounding a wrong [. . .]. What is subjectified is neither work nor destitution, but the simple counting of the uncounted, the difference between an inegalitarian distribution of social bodies and the equality of speaking beings" (Rancière, *Dis-Agreement*, 37–38). Building upon the work of Rancière, Philippe Le Goff has also turned to Blanqui's and Gustav Tridon's newswritings as revolutionary interventions designed "to expose the plight of the unseen and unheard." Citing Hutton's assertion of Blanqui's "concern for 'aesthetic effect as the leaven of revolutionary agitation' " and Dommanget's emphasis upon Blanqui's stylistic "clarté, concision et, en même temps, grâce et mouvement,' " Le Goff writes: "Writing had to serve the ideal: newspapers, like essays and pamphlets, were conceived as major political interventions, as weapons in the struggle against oppression, as vehicles for the idea of communism" (Le Goff, " 'La faim justifie les moyens': Auguste Blanqui, 'Structural' Violence and the Socialist Press," 17–18). Later, Le Goff reaffirms several of the points that have been emphasized throughout this chapter, but on the basis of different selections from the published corpus of Blanqui and Tridon: "For a doctrine defined by the primacy of human agency and the subject, by the rejection of 'la fatalité du progrès' and the 'mauvaise plaisanterie' of political, social or economic laws, it is the suffering *here* and *now* that justifies if not requires our full, uncompromising engagement and devotion *here* and *now*. Imagining 'the end' is not the concern. For the Blanquists emancipatory politics is not about drawing up a vision of a future society or believing in the inexorable forward march of history as the means to arrive there. Only recognising and tackling existing injustice through a dedicated and determined mobilisation—in which 'la deception ou l'insuccès n'apporte ni repentir ni découragement'—and uniting under the moral, creative power of an idea will the conditions for emancipation emerge" (Le Goff, " 'La faim justifie les moyens,' " 21).

33. His imprisonment followed his invasion of the National Assembly with a group of protesters in order to plea for the cause of Polish refugees fleeing oppression under the Russian tsar, as well as for the cause of the unemployed and famished people of France. The Assembly was declared dissolved, at which point the people retreated to the Hôtel de Ville, where a new popular government was briefly declared, until troops arrived, and the workers fled. For a summary of these events and the documentation of Blanqui's disruption of the National Assembly, see Blanqui, *Oeuvres complètes*, 204–13.

34. See Lamartine, "Sur le chemin de fer," 154.

35. Blanqui, *Oeuvres complètes*, 211–12. All translations from this text are mine.

36. Louis-Auguste Blanqui, *Critique sociale*, 2: 100. All translations of quotations from Blanqui's oeuvre are, unless otherwise noted, mine.

37. Lamartine, *Harmonies poétiques et religieuses*, 1: 8.

38. Lamartine, *Souvenirs, impressions, pensées et paysages pendant un voyage en Orient (1832–1833), ou notes d'un voyageur*, 2: 216.

39. Shortly thereafter, Blanqui also emphasizes the theological resonance of Lamartine's account of finance by posing the question as to how "the local divinity, marveling over these novel accents," might have received its latest guest. See Blanqui, *Critique sociale*, 2: 100.

40. Blanqui, *Critique sociale*, 2: 101.

41. Blanqui, *Critique sociale*, 2: 101.

42. Blanqui, *Critique sociale*, 2: 101.

43. "M. de Rothschild pompe aussi, il pompe énormément. Lorsqu'il n'est pas satisfait des révolutionnaires, il retient toutes les vapeurs pompées et ne lâche pas une goutte d'eau, moyen infaillible de rôtir les perturbateurs, et de les calciner jusqu'à l'état de momie" (Blanqui, *Critique sociale*, 2: 102). With this remark, Blanqui also alludes to the ways in which the provisional government of the Second Republic had already accepted provisions from major sources of finance. James Rothschild had lent money, for example, to Louis Bonaparte in 1848 around the time of his presidential election, as Betrand Gille has documented in his history of this financial dynasty. See Betrand Gille, *Histoire de la maison Rothschild*, 1: 53. In *The Eighteenth Brumaire*, Marx too emphasizes the intimate connection between finance and the regimes of both the Second Republic and the Second Empire, underscoring how the major financier Achille Fould figured prominently in the ministry of Louis Bonaparte; see MECW 11: 159, 163.

44. Blanqui's allusion to the *ancien régime* is also solicited by the anachronisms in Lamartine's presentation of credit as a transcendent function that spans from the Middle Ages to the present. See Lamartine, "Sur le chemin de fer," 148.

45. Baudelaire, *My Heart Laid Bare*, 171–72, translation modified; *OC* 1: 665–66.

46. "Baudelaire as the poet of *Spleen of Paris*: 'One of the central motifs of this poetry is, in effect, boredom in the fog, ennui and indiscriminate haze (fog of the cities). In a word, it is spleen.' François Porche, *La Vie douloureuse de Charles Baudelaire* (Paris, 1926), p. 184" (Walter Benjamin, *The Arcades Project*, [D1, 4], 102).

47. Quoted in Benjamin, *The Arcades Project* [a10a, 1], 716, translation modified. Cf. Walter Benjamin, *Gesammelte Schriften*, 5: 872–73. In his recent book, *Atmospherics of the City*, Ross Chambers likewise attends to the natural and technological "foggy atmosphere" that characterizes "humanity's long fall into the nightmare of history," as it is registered in the poetry of Baudelaire. See especially Chambers, *Atmospherics of the City: Baudelaire and the Poetics of Noise*, 17–18.

48. Lamartine, "Sur le chemin de fer," 138.

49. Marx, *The Eighteenth Brumaire*, in MECW 11: 106–07.

50. Blanqui, *Critique sociale*, 2: 103.

51. Michel Chevalier, *Lettres sur l'Amérique du nord*, 1: 37, my translation. The immediate context of this passage is Manchester; the later chapter on railways

in the United States concludes, however, with a reproach to the French for not having invested in the construction of railway networks, which have proven to be so productive and inspiring for the people of America according to Chevalier: "En France, nous sommes certainement le peuple le plus audacieux dans l'ordre des idées et des théories; nous nous sommes montrés hardis à faire trembler en fait d'expérimentation politique; mais nous sommes depuis vingt ans le plus timide des peuples en fait de réalisations matérielles" (Chevalier, *Lettres*, 135, my translation).

52. At first, the Assembly concluded that "the most important lines are to be executed and possessed by the State," before a shift in majority opinion took place, which prevented the enterprise. The representatives of the center-left, writes J. Lobet, "feared in their defiance that the [state] might abuse the means of influence that this vast enterprise would give it, and refused to confide the execution of the network to it. The part played by financial influences was no less considerable, and this consideration that the State could ruin certain stock operations did not appear to be unfamiliar when it came to the vote of the chamber" (J. Lobet, *Des chemins de fer en France*, 602, my translation).

53. Blanqui, *Critique sociale*, 2: 103–04.
54. Blanqui, *Critique sociale*, 2: 104.
55. Blanqui, *Critique sociale*, 2: 104.
56. Blanqui, *Critique sociale*, 2: 104.
57. Blanqui, *Critique sociale*, 2: 112.
58. In this same text, they later write of French utopian models: "In its positive aims, however, this form of Socialism aspires either to restoring the old means of production and of exchange, and with them the old property relations, and the old society, or to cramping the modern means of production and of exchange, within the framework of the old property relations that have been, and were bound to be, exploded by those means. In either case, it is both reactionary and Utopian" (MECW 6: 509–10).
59. Blanqui, *Critique sociale*, 2: 112.
60. Blanqui, *Critique sociale*, 2: 114.
61. The full passage reads: "L'organisme social ne peut être l'ouvrage ni d'un seul, ni de quelques-uns, ni de la bonne foi, ni du dévouement, ni même du génie. Il ne saurait être une improvisation. Il est l'oeuvre de tous, par le temps, les tâtonnements, l'expérience progressive, par un courant inconnu, spontané" (Blanqui, *Critique sociale*, 2: 115).
62. "Une révolution détermine dans le corps social un travail instantané de réorganisation semblable aux combinaisons tumultueuses des éléments d'un corps dissous qui tendent à se recomposer en une forme nouvelle. Ce travail ne peut commencer tant qu'un soufflé de vie anime encore la vieille agrégation. Ainsi les idées reconstitutives de la société ne prendront jamais corps aussi longtemps qu'un cataclysme, frappant de mort la vieille société décrépite, n'aura pas mis en liberté les éléments captifs dont la fermentation spontanée et rapide doit organiser le monde

nouveau. Toutes les puissances de la pensée, toutes les tensions de l'intelligence ne sauraient anticiper ce phénomène créateur qui n'éclate qu'à un moment donné. [. . .] Jusqu'à l'instant de la mort et de la renaissance, les doctrines, bases de la société future, restent à l'état de vagues aspirations, d'aperçus lointains et vaporeux" (Blanqui, *Oevures complètes*, 307–08).

63. Werner Hamacher, "Affirmative, Strike," 1139.

64. Blanqui, *Critique sociale*, 2: 115–16.

65. Lamartine, "Sur le chemin de fer," 155.

66. Blanqui, *Critique sociale*, 2: 115. Bensaïd and Löwy give this point due emphasis in their study of Blanqui's communism, writing: "Convinced that future generations must be allowed the freedom to choose their own path, he assigns the Revolution only the role of clearing the terrain, thus opening up 'the routes, or rather the multiple paths, that lead to the new order' " (Bensaïd and Löwy, "Auguste Blanqui, Heretical Communist," 30).

67. Friedrich Engels, MECW 24: 13.

68. Blanqui, *Critique sociale*, 2: 114.

69. The full passage reads: "L'organisme social ne peut être l'ouvrage ni d'un seul, ni de quelques-uns, ni de la bonne foi, ni du dévouement, ni même du génie. Il ne saurait être une improvisation. Il est l'oeuvre de tous, par le temps, les tâtonnements, l'expérience progressive, par un courant inconnu, spontané" (Blanqui, *Critique sociale*, 2: 115).

70. Blanqui, *Critique sociale*, 2: 58.

71. Blanqui, *Critique sociale*, 2: 58.

72. Blanqui, *Critique sociale*, 2: 58. For the text from 1850, see *Critique sociale*, 2: 115.

73. Blanqui, *Critique sociale*, 2: 58.

74. Blanqui also calls the skeptic in this passage "un aveugle volontaire" (Blanqui, *Critique sociale*, 2: 58).

75. Lamartine, *La politique de Lamartine: Choix de discours et écrits politiques*, 2: 357–58, my translation. The phrase in French reads as follows: "comme principe divin, comme loi de Dieu, et non pas comme loi humaine, comme fibre constitutive de la nature de l'homme." This speech was delivered before the National Assembly on 6 September 1848.

76. These remarks had appeared in his article, "Notre drapeau, c'est l'Égalité," from the issue of *Le Libérateur* from 2 February 1834, where the phrase in French reads, "l'égoïsme et les viles passions qui en découlent, divise les hommes, pour les isoler [. . .] n'enfante que la concurrence, la guerre, et a pour dernière conséquence logique, la destruction" (Blanqui, *Oeuvres complètes I: Des origines à la Révolution de 1848*, 262). He goes on to speak of equality as "justice" on this page, but this principle no longer defines the notion as it appears in the more radical, because less formulaic text from 1870, "Political Economy without Morals." What does persist from this early text through to his latest writings, however, is Blanqui's emphasis on

the impropriety of fixed definitions of the person, which extend, for example, to his gestures of appealing to the "voice of public opinion" as the "sole legitimate verdict" during his defense speech on 9 March 1849. There, moreover, he also identifies himself as "one of those voyagers" who "called themselves yesterday revolutionaries, and today, socialists," and whose sole goal is to draw the people "from the limbo of ignorance and misery to introduce well-being and fraternity to the brilliant light of day" (Blanqui, *Oeuvres complètes*, 243, 258, 254–55). Nor does his identification with the proletariat coincide with his biographical or social history—again, it does not accord with what might be called individual "identity"—as he remarks in his letter to Maillard from 1852, while imprisoned in Belle-Ile. There, he writes, "according to my family, my education, I am a bourgeois and so are you; perhaps [. . .] there are many bourgeois in the proletarian camp" (Blanqui, *Oeuvres complètes*, 356).

77. For arguments in favor of the latter interpretation, see Patrick Hutton, *The Cult of the Revolutionary Tradition: The Blanquists in French Politics, 1863–1893*, 58. Hutton especially emphasizes how Blanqui and his followers attempted to cultivate a sense of civic responsibility by honoring the legacy of the Revolution and performing pilgrimages to the graves of its proponents. See, for example, Hutton's account of the honors that the Blanquists paid to Alphonse Baudin, a doctor who was killed "resisting the coup d'etat of Louis Napoleon": "As one among a number of republican groups promoting the cult of Baudin, the Blanquists, beginning in 1867, made pilgrimages to his grave at the Montmartre cemetery on the anniversary of his death in the hope that remembrance of his role in the last days of the Second Republic might hasten the coming revolutionary days in which the Third would be born" (*The Cult of the Revolutionary Tradition*, 55).

78. Blanqui, *Critique sociale*, 2: 58. For the text from 1850, see *Critique sociale*, 2: 115.

79. Rancière, *Dis-Agreement*, 40.

80. Blanqui, *Oeuvres complètes*, 257.

81. There, he had said, "Il y a des penseurs qui rêvent une société plus fraternelle, et cherchent à découvrir une terre promise dans les brumes mouvantes de l'horizon. Mais l'insensé qui voudrait s'élancer d'un bond vers le point inconnu se précipiterait dans le vide," before quoting the motto of these thinkers: "Marchons! voici la route! elle traverse des contrées ignorées; nous suivrons, en frayant la voie, les ondulations du sol, l'oeil toujours fixé sur l'étoile qui nous guide" (*Oeuvres complètes*, 257). Soon thereafter, he continues: "Je suis un de ces voyageurs. Ils s'appelaient hier des révolutionnaires, aujourd'hui des socialistes. Devant leur marche infatigable, la distance s'efface, l'horizon soulève peu à peu son voile et découpe la silhouette de la terre promise. Nous avançons" (*Oeuvres complètes*, 258).

82. Marx, *The Eighteenth Brumaire*, in MECW 11: 106–07.

83. "La parole elle-même est le lieu et l'occasion d'une expérience de l'excès de l'être" (Abensour and Pelosse, "Libérer l'enfermé," 405).

84. Blanqui, *Critique sociale*, 1: 1–2. The convolute of fragments, which include many of the pieces that have been cited in this chapter, are dated from a range of years, from the late 1840s to the 1870s. Cf. *Critique sociale*, 2: 67, 225, 366.

85. Blanqui, *Critique sociale*, 1: 53.

86. Blanqui, *Critique sociale*, 1: 63–64.

87. Honoré de Balzac, "L'illustre Gaudissart," 584, my translation. It is also highly likely that Blanqui is alluding to Balzac's "La Fille aux yeux d'or," which similarly equates the arm, fingers, and tongue of a disabled worker—along with his feet, back, and hands—with the economic resources that allow him to make a living: "L'ouvrier, le prolétaire, l'homme qui remue ses pieds, ses mains, sa langue, son dos, son seul bras, ces cinq doigts pour vivre; eh! bien, celui-là qui, le premier, devrait économiser le principe de sa vie, il outrepasse ses forces, attelle sa femme à quelque machine, use son enfant et le cloue à un rouage" (Balzac, "La Fille aux yeux d'or," 1041). Within the sphere of capital, then, the organs and members of the living body become reconfigured as tools to gain a livelihood, which are extended by members of the family, and ultimately, mechanized appendages. The likelihood that Blanqui refers to this passage in "Capital and Labor" is all the greater, since Blanqui goes on to call the voice of political economy "le Dieu panthéiste, ce capital-Protée" (Blanqui, *Critique sociale*, 1: 64), recalling Balzac's subsequent words on the more successful man of business: "N'est-ce pas le mouvement fait homme, l'espace incarné, le Protée de la civilisation?" (Balzac, *La Fille aux yeux d'or*, 1044).

88. Balzac, "L'illustre Gaudissart," 584.

89. The concept of "embodied capital" has been most thoroughly explored and elaborated by Pierre Bourdieu, who considers it primarily to consist in the habits, dispositions, and cultural literacy that are acquired by an individual, and that prove to be advantageous to his advancement. In *Distinction: A Social Critique of the Judgement of Taste*, for example, Bourdieu writes of "docility towards the [educational] institution itself" as an example of "embodied capital" (*Distinction*, 81).

90. Blanqui, *Critique sociale*, 1: 63.

91. Blanqui, *Critique sociale*, 1: 64.

92. Blanqui, *Critique sociale*, 1: 72.

93. Blanqui, *Critique sociale*, 1: 73. Although the identification of capital with theft was not entirely new—Pierre-Joseph Proudhon had famously defined property as theft in *What Is Property?* from 1840—the immanent critique of capital that Blanqui offers through citations of political economy and popular parlance differs from the theoretical work of his contemporary. See Pierre-Joseph Proudhon, *What Is Property?* 13.

94. Blanqui, *Critique sociale*, 1: 74.

95. Blanqui, *Oevures complètes*, 1: 307–08.

96. Blanqui, *Critique sociale*, 1: 53.

97. Blanqui, *Critique sociale*, 1: 74–75.

98. Blanqui, *Critique sociale*, 1: 75.

99. For a historical account of these events, see Jill Harsin, *Barricades: The War of the Streets in Revolutionary Paris, 1830–1848*. For a specific account of Blanqui's involvement in the various revolutionary movements of nineteenth-century Paris, see Gustave Geffroy's biography, *L'Enfermé*, as well as Maurice Dommanget's *Auguste Blanqui à Belle-Ile, 1850–1857* and *Blanqui et l'opposition à la fin du Second Empire*.

100. Blanqui, *Oeuvres complètes*, 331.

101. Benjamin, *The Arcades Project* [J24, 2], 271.

102. Bejamin, *The Arcades Project*, [J24, 2], 271.

103. Blanqui, *Critique sociale*, 1: 54.

104. Blanqui, *Critique sociale*, 2: 114.

105. Again, the emphasis upon "decomposition" and "recomposition" is borrowed from Rancière, *Dis-Agreement*, 40.

106. Blanqui, *Eternity by the Stars*, 114; *Éternité par les astres*, 297.

107. Blanqui, *Eternity by the Stars*, 123; *Éternité par les astres*, 309–10.

108. Blanqui, *Eternity by the Stars*, 98; *Éternité par les astres*, 278.

109. Blanqui, *Eternity by the Stars*, 125–26; *Éternité par les astres*, 313.

110. Blanqui, *Eternity by the Stars*, 125; *Éternité par les astres*, 312.

111. Eduardo Cadava draws connections between Benjamin's concerns over the modes of mechanical reproducibility that make up the modern structure of experience and Blanqui's photographic theory of the cosmos. He states explicitly: "The linguistic physiognomy of Blanqui's theory of the eternal return is in fact a photographic one," supporting his arguments with reference to Blanqui's language, which "focuses on the questions of repetition, reproduction, images, negatives, originals, copies, transitions, death, and mourning" (Cadava, "Sternphotographie: Benjamin, Blanqui, and the Mimesis of the Stars," 19). The political consequences of such a structure reside not in a program, but in the way that the cosmos, viewed through this aperture, is "the name of what globalizes, of the processes whereby whatever we call the world is reproduced, infinitely and heterogeneously," which means too "that we can never globalize the meaning of the world," but would be involved at all times in the work "of transforming it" (Cadava, "Sternphotographie," 26).

112. Benjamin, *The Arcades Project* [D5, 6], 112.

113. Benjamin, *The Arcades Project* [D5a, 2], 111. As an anonymous reviewer in *La Critique philosophique, politique, scientifique, littéraire* from 9 May 1872 had noted, these are also the premises that were put forth by the Ecclesiast and by "Stoic pantheism, which admits the eternity of the world," and "infers from this a regular and perpetual alternation of creations and destructions" (in Blanqui, *Instructions pour une prise d'armes; L'Éternité par les astres*, 370, my translation).

114. Benjamin, *The Arcades Project*, [D5a, 2], 111.

115. Cadava, "Sternphotographie," 20.

116. Blanqui, *Eternity by the Stars*, 137; *Éternité par les astres*, 328–29.

117. Blanqui, *Oevures complètes*, 307–08.
118. Blanqui, *Eternity by the Stars*, 127, translation modified; *Éternité par les astres*, 314–15; cf. *Eternity by the Stars*, 69; *Éternité par les astres*, 236.
119. Blanqui, *Eternity by the Stars*, 127, translation modified; *Éternité par les astres*, 315.
120. This reduction is implicit, moreover, from the very first page of *Eternity by the Stars*, where Blanqui modifies Blaise Pascal's thought, "The universe is a circle, whose center is everywhere and its circumference nowhere [*nulle part*]" to read: "The universe is a sphere, whose center is everywhere and its surface nowhere [*nulle part*]" (Blanqui, *Eternity by the Stars*, 66; *Éternité par les astres*, 315). It is almost as if he were suggesting that, without limitations—without limes and lines of demarcation—the second dimension of surface is eliminated, and with it, the third dimension of depth.
121. Blanqui, *Eternity by the Stars*, 139.
122. Blanqui, *Éternité par les astres*, 330.
123. Edgar Allan Poe, *Eureka*, in *Poetry and Tales*, 1272.
124. Edgar Allan Poe, *Eureka*, translated by Charles Baudelaire, 33.
125. Blanqui, *Eternity by the Stars*, 129; *Éternité par les astres*, 318.
126. "Quand vient la Saint-Sylvestre, il ne se trouve pas plus avancé qu'au Premier de l'an et sa seule perspective est de recommencer" (Frédéric Bastiat, *Oeuvres complètes*, 5: 29–30, my translation).
127. "Mais si le second, le rentier, consomme dans l'année sa rente de l'année, il a, l'année d'après, et les années suivantes, et pendant l'éternité entière, une rente toujours égale, intarissable, *perpétuelle*. Le capital est donc rémunéré non pas une fois ou deux fois, mais un nombre indéfini de fois!" (Bastiat, *Oeuvres complètes*, 5: 30, my translation).
128. Blanqui, *Critique sociale*, 1: 130–31.
129. Blanqui observes: "Pas l'ombre d'une preuve en faveur de la rente. Pas un mot qui réfute l'accusation d'iniquité [. . .]. Rien que de burlesques doléances sur la méchante querelle faite à l'usure, comme si on insultait de gaieté de coeur une sainte dans sa châsse" (*Critique sociale*, 1: 124).
130. "Les tonneaux se rempliront, sans qu'il s'en mêle" (Blanqui, *Critique sociale*, 1: 37). Later, he explicitly refers to the "supplice des Danaïdes" as the *comparandum* for the repetitive tasks of modern labor that serve in the futile production of luxury goods, even as many members of the proletariat were lacking necessities (*Critique sociale*, 1: 97).
131. Blanqui, *Eternity by the Stars*, 129; *Éternité par les astres*, 318–19.
132. Benjamin, *The Arcades Project*, 25, 26. It should also be noted here that Blanqui's general expressions of suspicion toward positivism in his manuscripts have been well recognized on the parts of his readers, such as Hallward, who refers to Blanqui's "polemic against Comte and Comtean positivism" and resistance to "any

deterministic account that might justify, on either religious or pseudo-scientific grounds, 'the doctrine of the fatality of social suffering' " (Hallward, "Blanqui's Bifurcations," 37). Even the scientific theories that Blanqui borrows from Pierre-Simon Laplace are not left untouched by the ways in which he presents them in *Eternity by the Stars,* where he opposes, as Abensour and Pelosse have written, his " 'warm' vision of renovating conflagrations" to Laplace's " 'cool' representation of the universe-clockwork" (Abensour and Pelosse, "Libérer l'enfermé," 424). For a partial reproduction of Blanqui's dossier of notes from 1869, "Contre le positivisme," see Abensour and Pelosse, *Instructions pour une prise d'armes; L'Éternité par les astres,* 197–225. Interestingly, in the first of the notes, Blanqui criticizes the potential oppression that print technologies may serve, should they be used for the spread of fixed dogmas, instead of democratically multiplying the "communication of thought" ("Contre le positivisme," 197). Blanqui argues that "the maintenance of [a] so-called absolute truth and the eternal immobilization of thought" would be "to attempt murder upon humanity in its entirety" ("Contre le positivisme," 197). While the role of the printing press in the dissemination of religion is the capital example that he cites for such fatal dogmatism, Blanqui goes on to criticize the valorization of historical facts as a dogma of another sort: "because things have followed this course, it seems that they could not have followed another. The *fait accompli* has an irresistible power. [. . .] Spirit (finds itself) overwhelmed by it and does not dare to revolt (stiffen). The ground is lacking for it. It could not support itself except upon the void (the nothing)" ("Contre le positivisme," 205). Against this possible impossibility for change, he asserts that the "gears of human matters are not fatal like those of the universe. They are modifiable at every minute" ("Contre le positivisme," 206). Here, it is implied that the assumption of an ineluctable course of events would itself be a quasi-religious myth, whose form is the tautology, and whose validation could only come from the values of those who promote it.

133. Blanqui, *Eternity by the Stars,* 143; *Éternité par les astres,* 336.

134. Perpetual exchange is one of the principles to which Blanqui frequently appeals in *Capital and Labor* as well, envisaging, for example, a scenario in which all individuals labor from youth onward, in which case, "il ne restera plus d'ouvriers, il n'y aura plus que des patrons. Ou plutôt ouvriers et patrons auront également disparu, et on ne verra que des citoyens s'occupant, chacun à part pour son compte" (*Critique sociale,* 1: 120). The question is whether this affirmation of exchange would accord with the more radical economy that Blanqui offers in *Eternity by the Stars,* where the processes of alteration that he traces allow nothing to stand as equivalent, commensurable, or exchangeable with itself or with another.

135. Blanqui, *Eternity by the Stars,* 104; *Éternité par les astres,* 285.

136. Benjamin, *The Arcades Project,* [D5a, 2], 111.

137. Blanqui, *Eternity by the Stars,* 148–49; *Éternité par les astres,* 343. My emphasis.

138. For a survey of the organic and cosmological tropes that organize much of the rhetoric of nineteenth-century French socialism, as well as an extensive bibliography, see Volny Fages, "Ordonner le monde changer la société: Les systèmes cosmologiques des socialistes du premier XIXᵉ siècle," 123–34. I disagree, however, with the way in which Fages takes Blanqui's universal hypothesis as a straightforward argument apart from the contexts of his other writings and those details of the text that speak against the very scientific principles that he evokes. Nothing could be less certain than the notion that, as Fages puts it, "[l]'univers de Blanqui est cyclique" (Fages, "Ordonner le monde," 132).

139. Blanqui, *Eternity by the Stars*, 143; *Éternité par les astres*, 335.

140. Blanqui, *Critique sociale*, 2: 115.

141. My underlining. Blanqui, *Eternity by the Stars*, 72; cf. *Éternité par les astres*, 243: "Sur notre globe jusqu'à nouvel ordre, la nature a pour éléments uniques à sa disposition les 64 *corps simples*, dont les noms viennent ci-après. Nous disons 'jusqu'à nouvel ordre,' parce que le nombre de ces corps n'était que 53 il y a peu d'années."

142. My underlining. Blanqui, *Eternity by the Stars*, 72; cf. *Éternité par les astres*, 243: "On les dénomme *corps simples*, parce qu'on les a trouvés jusqu'à présent irréductibles."

143. Blanqui, *Oeuvres complètes*, 257–58.

144. Blanqui, *Eternity by the Stars*, 90; *Éternité par les astres*, 266.

145. Blanqui, *Eternity by the Stars*, 90; *Éternité par les astres*, 266. According to the narrator of the *Thousand and One Nights*, "the prophet Solomon, the son of David," sent "Asif ibn-Abarkhiya" to take a rebellious demon "by force" and bid him to "be led in defeat and humiliation before the prophet Solomon" (*The Arabian Nights*, 34). Upon the demon's refusal to submit to him, Solomon confined him in a brass jar "and sealed it with a lead seal on which he imprinted God's Almighty name" (*The Arabian Nights*, 34). Discovered by a fisherman nearly two thousand years later, the demon threatens his latest liberator with death, before being tricked to return to the bottle. But the threat of this figure to all authority persists—otherwise the fisherman would not choose to "build a house right here, and sit here and stop any fisherman who comes to fish and warn him that there is a demon" (*The Arabian Nights*, 35).

146. "Les sympathies des masses, retrempées par un système de terreur, se réveillent plus vives; c'est un ressort rendu plus énergique par la compression et qui ne demande qu'à se défendre" (*Oeuvres complètes I: Des origines à la Révolution de 1848*, 313).

147. "Eh bien! ne nous effrayons pas, nous, hommes d'État; nous qui avons l'habitude d'envisager d'un regard un peu plus perçant et plus ferme la portée des doctrines qui traversent comme des comètes l'horizon de l'humanité, et qui vont se perdre dans les régions inaccessibles de l'utopie" (Lamartine, "Sur le chemin de fer," 154).

Chapter 4

1. Walter Benjamin, *The Arcades Project*, [D8, 8], 116.
2. For the historical background of this text, see Anneliese Griese and Gerd Pawelzig, "Natur und Naturwissenschaft im philosophischen Denken von Friedrich Engels," 9–37.
3. Friedrich Engels, *Dialectic of Nature*, in MECW 25: 321–22, 324.
4. Baudelaire, *OC* 1: 665.
5. Blanqui, *Critique sociale*, 2: 114.
6. Louis Althusser, *For Marx*, 164–65.
7. Althusser, *Pour Marx*, 165.
8. Cf. Althusser, *For Marx*, 65. This topological rhetoric, like Althusser's famous description of an "epistemological break" in Karl Marx's thinking, resonates with the language of his contemporary Gaston Bachelard, who speaks of the "topologie du champ épistémologique" in order to elaborate the relations between the practices of experimental and theoretical science in his study from 1949, *Le rationalisme appliqué*. In *Le rationalisme appliqué*, Bachelard grounds his use of spatial metaphors in his description of the scene of scientific instruction. Even in those cases where the object of study cannot be reduced to a two-dimensional plane—as when, for example, the matter in question is the dynamics of force—its illustration nonetheless takes place pedagogically "sur une représentation plane, sur une représentation à deux dimensions," leading him to the conclusion: "Un axe *spatial* est alors le représentant de commerce de tout espace" (Bachelard, *Le rationalisme appliqué*, 62). For the notion of an epistemological break, which Bachelard introduces to describe what he calls the fourth era of the sciences, where technical instruments and measures no longer have a "signification *directe* dans la vie commune," see Bachelard, *Le rationalisme appliqué*, 102–05. Althusser also develops Bachelard's notion of a "problem" as the structure that mediates both the subject and object of cognition, which Bachelard describes as follows: "Il nous faut d'abord poser l'objet comme un sujet de problème et le sujet du cogito comme une conscience de problème. L'être pensant pense ainsi à la limite de son savoir après avoir fait le dénombrement de ses connaissances propres à résoudre le problème proposé. Ce dénombrement, conscience d'un ordre dynamique d'idées, est donc polarisé par le problème à résoudre. Dans le rationalisme enseigné, le dénombrement est codifié; il est resserré sur une ligne bien définie, bien appuyé sur ses bases. Mais dans le rationalisme questionnant, les bases elles-mêmes sont à l'épreuve, elles sont mises en question par la question. Le Problème est le sommet actif de la recherche. Fondation, cohérence, dialectique et problème, voilà tous les éléments du dénombrement rationnel, tous les moments de cette mobilisation de l'intelligence" (*Le rationalisme appliqué*, 55–57). Bachelard's notion of a problem lends itself to Althusser's thinking because it is defined according to a social dynamic of collective production through instruction and scientific exchange. To be sure, Althusser explicitly states that he borrows the notion of a "problematic" from

Jacques Martin in his introduction to *For Marx*, but he acknowledges his debt to Bachelard explicitly at several points in this same work (*For Marx*, 32, 168). More recent scholars have emphasized the affinity between Althusser's usage of the notion of the problem and Bachelard's elaboration of it, on which see Sereni. For a careful description of the implications of Althusser's appropriation of Bachelard's concept of an "epistemological break," see Balibar, *Écrits pour Althusser*, 9–57.

9. Jacques Derrida, *Théorie et pratique: Cours de l'ENS-Ulm 1975–1976*, 18. All translations from this recently published seminar are mine.

10. Derrida, *Théorie et pratique*, 18–19.

11. Althusser, *For Marx*, 170; cf. *Pour Marx*, 170.

12. Althusser, *For Marx*, 177; cf. *Pour Marx*, 181.

13. Althusser *For Marx*, 172; cf. *Pour Marx*, 173.

14. Althusser, *For Marx*, 174; cf. *Pour Marx*, 176.

15. Derrida, *Théorie et pratique*, 18.

16. See Jacob and Wilhelm Grimm, *Deutsches Wörterbuch*, 5: 2194–222.

17. Althusser, *For Marx*, 174; cf. *Pour Marx*, 176.

18. Derrida, *Théorie et pratique*, 104.

19. Jacques Derrida, *Specters of Marx: The State of Debt, the Work of Mourning and the New International*, 113.

20. Étienne Balibar, *The Philosophy of Marx*, 4. He continues: "An irreversible event has occurred, one which is not comparable with the emergence of a new philosophical point of view, because it not only obliges us to change our ideas or methods, but to transform the practice of philosophy" (*Philosophy of Marx*, 4).

21. Althusser, *For Marx*, 33; cf. *Pour Marx*, 25.

22. Ovid, *Metamorphoses*, book 1, lines 381–83, in *Metamorphoses Volume 1: Books 1–8*, translation modified. The complication arises because Deucalion's wife Pyrrha perceives the oracular injunction to be sacrilege toward the remains of her mother, Pandora—who had been sent by Zeus as a bane to man before, and whose ire over the desecration of her remains is perhaps all the more to be feared. At the same time, however, disobeying Themis would amount to transgression in the name of a goddess and in the name of justice, θέμις. Caught between divine justice and chthonic piety, just as Antigone and Orestes were in the Theban trilogy of Sophocles and in the *Oresteia* of Aeschylus, the sole remaining human pair on earth confronts a paradoxical dilemma that places at risk all that is left of life after the flood. The solution to the alternatives that appear to be available, however, will not be sublation. For a time, they delay a fatal decision regarding their lot by repeating the words of the oracle: "In the meantime," it is told, "they repeat the obscure words of their given lot in their dark retreat [*Interea repetunt caecis obscura latebris verba datae sortis*]" (Ovid, *Metamorphoses*, book 1, lines 388–89, my translation). Then, for no explicable reason, the repetition of these lines breaks off—not unlike those moments in the history of philosophy that "[den] Fortgang der graden Linie abbrechen"—when Deucalion offers a reinterpretation of the injunction, in good

faith that the oracle must be just, and that their initial interpretation of the words according to their common senses must therefore be in error: "either our skill of mind is false, or pious are the oracles and never persuade the nefarious. The great (female) parent is the earth, it is stones in the body of the earth that I reckon are said to be bones; we are adjured to throw them behind our backs [*aut fallax [. . .] est sollertia nobis, / aut pia sunt nullumque nefas oracula suadent. / Magna parens terra est, lapides in corpore terrae / ossa reor dici; iacere hos post terga iubemur*]" (Ovid, *Metamorphoses*, book 1, lines 391–94, my translation). Taking up the bones of a different mother in order to obey the oracle—and therefore doing nothing of the sort—Deucalion and Pyrrha perform the gesture of throwing stones behind their back, which eventually soften and take the shape of men. Moving from the blind cave to blind faith thanks to a most dubious hermeneutics, Deucalion and Pyrrha thus turn from their cave to the world without understanding or enlightenment. "Nicht mehr begreifend," they emerge as the ironic counterpart to the spectators who rise from Plato's cave in the central myth of the *Republic* and act behind their own backs to save the world.

23. Hans Blumenberg, *Work on Myth*, 588; cf. *Arbeit am Mythos*, 637.

24. G. W. F. Hegel, *Die Phänomenologie des Geistes*, 370. All translations of passages from this text are mine.

25. Hegel, *Phänomenologie*, 348.

26. Hegel, *Phänomenologie*, 316.

27. Hegel, *Phänomenologie*, 348–49.

28. Hegel, *Phänomenologie*, 353.

29. Hegel, *Phänomenologie*, 352.

30. Hegel, *Phänomenologie*, 355, 354.

31. Hegel, *Phänomenologie*, 371.

32. Hegel, *Phänomenologie*, 370.

33. Hegel, *Phänomenologie*, 366.

34. Hegel, *Phänomenologie*, 370.

35. Here, I cite the passage as it appears Marx's *Economic-Philosophical Manuscripts from 1844* (MECW 3: 323, MEGA 1.3: 146).

36. Hegel, *Phänomenologie*, 371.

37. See Hegel, *Phänomenologie*, 472.

38. Hegel, "Die Verfassung Deutschlands," in *Hegels Schriften zur Politik und Rechtsphilosophie*, 47, my translation.

39. Ferdinand Christian Baur, *Das Christliche des Platonismus, oder Sokrates und Christus*, 26. All translations from this work are mine.

40. Baur, *Das Christliche des Platonismus*, 26, 27–28.

41. A sustained analysis of Marx's discussions of irony can be found in John Evan Seery, *Political Returns: Irony in Politics and Theory, from Plato to the Antinuclear Movement*. However, Seery does not address Marx's remarks in the context of Baur's work, and therefore does not attend to the rupture in the course of Marx's discussion

of irony that is traced in this chapter. His reading also differs from mine, in that he suggests that Marx's evocation of the ironies of Heraclitus, Thales, and Fichte merely affirms that "[i]rony has an 'objective content' in its ability to abstract from existing reality and empirical conditions," rather than noticing the irony *of* abstraction in Marx's writing, and the way in which irony would therefore persist through both abstract and 'concrete' linguistic presentations (Seery, *Political Returns*, 245). For this same reason, I cannot follow him in his assertion that Marx "is saying that we need 'ironists,' or those who are able to break with totalizing views of reality, and then can act on their own, like the self-initiating motion of Epicurus' swerving atom" (Seery, *Political Returns*, 250), because the operations of irony in language, as Marx addresses them, would exceed individual choice and necessity alike, and already affect any "totalizing views" that could come to expression.

42. Friedrich Schlegel, "On Incomprehensibility," in *Friedrich Schlegel's Lucinde and the Fragments*, 265. See Friedrich Schlegel, "Über die Unverständlichkeit," in *Charakteristiken und Kritiken I. Kritische Friedrich Schlegel-Ausgabe*, 368. Here, the English translation of Peter Firchow has been modified for accuracy. Where I have translated the passages myself, I refer to Firchow's English edition for ease of reference by prefacing the reference with the abbreviation "cf."

43. Schlegel, "Über die Unverständlichkeit," 368; cf. "On Incomprehensibility," 265.

44. Schlegel, "Über die Unverständlichkeit," 369; cf. "On Incomprehensibility," 267. My emphases.

45. Schlegel, "Über die Unverständlichkeit," 369; cf. "On Incomprehensibility," 267.

46. Werner Hamacher, *Premises: Essays on Philosophy and Literature from Kant to Celan*, 249.

47. According to Marx's description, myth would therefore coincide with the structure that the concept assumes, as soon as it would grasp empirical data of any kind. For if the absolute is not to be purely negative, it must grasp something that it is not, one way or another. If it is not to bury all "in the one dark night in which [. . .] all cows are black," Marx writes, it cannot but give way to a "positive interpretation," which means turning "limited positive reality" into a colorful myth that illustrates the ideal (MECW 1: 497, MEGA 4.1: 105–06). And although Marx here associates this optics solely with "myth and allegory," his formulation more generally suggests that any attempt to shed light on the world through concepts and ideals would likewise be mythic, and that any philosophical interpretation of the world would be illusory to the same extent that it is elucidating, because it ascribes significance to empirical data, and therefore submits its objects to a philosophically inflected interpretation. In a certain respect, the non-opposition between mythos and conceptual logos that emerges here also resonates with Blumenberg's major thesis, namely, that "the classical 'disinformation' that is contained in the formula 'from mythos to logos' and that still lies innocently dormant in Plato's indecision

between myth and logos is complete where the philosopher recognizes in myth only the identity of the objects for which he believes he has found the definitive mode of treatment. The mischief of that obvious historical formula lies in the fact that it does not permit one to recognize in myth itself one of the modes of accomplishment of logos. That the course of things proceeded 'from mythos to logos' is a dangerous misconstruction because we think that we assure ourselves by it that somewhere in the distant past the irreversible 'spring forward' [*Fort*sprung] took place that determined that something had been put far behind us and that from then on only 'steps forward' [*Fort*schritte 'progresses'] had to be executed" (*Work on Myth*, 27; cf. *Arbeit am Mythos*, 34). He then turns to a comparison between the mythographer Hesiod and the philosopher Thales, posing the question: "But was the spring really between the 'myth' that had said that the earth rests on the ocean or rises out of it and the 'logos' that had translated this into the so much paler universal formula that everything comes out of water and accordingly is composed of it?" (*Work on Myth*, 27; cf. *Arbeit am Mythos*, 34). Marx, however, suggests that because Thales develops his theory as a philosophical universal that opposes empirical reality, it becomes a mythic reflection of reality, rendering the opposition of "mythos" and "logos" subject to ironies that thoroughly undermine any such "Gegensatz."

48. Paul de Man, *Aesthetic Ideology*, 165.

49. Kevin Newmark, *Irony on Occasion: From Schlegel and Kierkegaard to Derrida and de Man*, 16. Numerous insightful commentaries on Schlegel's essay similarly highlight the ineluctable irony and incomprehensibility of language, and as a result, the resistence of irony to definition, as a trope or as any other circumscribable mode of expression. Without pretending to approximate an exhaustive list, I refer to Peter Szondi, "Friedrich Schlegel und die romantische Ironie: Mit einer Beilage über Tiecks Komödie;" Georgia Albert, "Understanding Irony: Three Essais on Friedrich Schlegel;" and J. Hillis Miller, *Others*. What these readers do not tend to emphasize as strongly, however, is the way in which the paradox that Schlegel bespeaks not only entails the logical consequence "of constitutive and irreducible self-contradiction, of the simultaneous co-presence of mutually elusive elements," as Albert writes ("Understanding Irony," 828), for irony also operates with and besides every utterance, opening it to alterity beyond the more restrictive definition of contrariety. This opening, as Schlegel's critical question indicates, forms the condition of possibility for all varieties of understanding (including non-understanding).

50. See Margaret Rose, *Reading the Young Marx and Engels*, 120.

51. All quotations from the writings of Epicurus are provided according to Bailey's dual-language edition, though his translations have been occasionally modified. For an excellent reading of this passage that elaborates the grammatical ambiguities within the Greek quotation, which imply that the utterances themselves, rather than the speakers, may be the ones who are "choosing by reasoning" in the process of altering language, see Wilson Shearin, *The Language of Atoms: Performativity and Politics in Lucretius'* De rerum natura, 38–49.

52. Marx speaks similarly of commodity fetishism in the opening chapter of *Capital*, when he writes of his discovery: "The recent scientific discovery, that the products of labour, so far as they are values, are but material expressions of the human labour spent in their production, marks, indeed, an epoch in the history of the development of the human race, but, by no means, dissipates the mist through which the social character of labour appears to us to be an objective character of the products themselves" (MECW 35: 85, MEGA 2.10: 73).

53. Jan Mieszkowski, *Labors of Imagination: Aesthetics and Political Economy from Kant to Althusser*, 142.

54. Such gestures occur when, for example, they say that the "division of labour and private property are, after all, identical expressions: in the one the same thing is affirmed with reference to activity as is affirmed in the other with reference to the product of the activity" (MECW 5: 46, MEGA 1.5: 22).

55. Georg Lukács would later describe this feature of Marx's writing as the most promising aspect of Marxist philosophy in *History and Class Consciousness*. "It was left to Marx" writes Lukács, "to make the concrete discovery of 'truth as the subject' and hence to establish the unity of theory and practice. This he achieved by focusing the known totality upon the reality of the historical process and by confining it to this. By this means he determined both the knowable totality and the totality to be known" (*History and Class Consciousness: Studies in Marxist Dialectics*, 39). Consistent with his premises, Lukács also describes the historical conditions for this simultaneity of theory and praxis when he addresses the emergence of the proletariat: "It was necessary for the proletariat to be born for social reality to become fully conscious. The reason for this is that the discovery of the class-outlook of the proletariat provided a vantage point from which to survey the whole of society. With the emergence of historical materialism there arose the theory of the 'conditions for the liberation of the proletariat' and the doctrine of reality understood as the total process of social evolution. This was only possible because for the proletariat the total knowledge of its class-situation was a vital necessity, a matter of life and death; because its class situation becomes comprehensible only if the whole of society can be understood; and because this understanding is the inescapable precondition of its actions. Thus the unity of theory and practice is only the reverse side of the social and historical position of the proletariat. From its own point of view self-knowledge coincides with knowledge of the whole so that the proletariat is at one and the same time the subject and object of its own knowledge" (*History and Class Consciousness*, 19–20). This is not to say, however, that insight into this unity suffices to bring it about completely; among the symptoms that, according to Lukács, indicate the insufficiency of current critique, which continues to proceed "from the standpoint of capitalism," is what he later calls the "separation of the various theatres of war" (*History and Class Consciousness*, 76).

56. Derrida, *Théorie et pratique*, 71.

57. Althusser, *For Marx*, 33; cf. *Pour Marx*, 25.

58. Althusser, *For Marx*, 82; cf. *Pour Marx*, 80.

59. Louis Althusser, Étienne Balibar, Roger Establet, Pierre Macherey, and Jacques Rancière, *Reading Capital: The Complete Edition*, 344; cf. *Lire* Le Capital, 404.

60. Dominick LaCapra, *Rethinking Intellectual History: Texts, Contexts, Language*, 168–69.

61. In *Capital*, the ventriloquism of impersonal personifications—in a language that no one had spoken before—forms one of the major strategies of presentation, signaling that there is no end to character masks in Marx's latest writings. For example, over the course of Marx's elaboration of the transformation of the working day under capital, a critical moment arises when "[s]uddenly the voice of the labourer, which had been stifled in the storm and stress of the process of production, rises: 'The commodity that I have sold to you differs from the crowd of other commodities, in that its use creates value, and a value greater than its own. That is why you bought it. That which on your side appears a spontaneous expansion of capital, is on mine extra expenditure of labour power. You and I know on the market only one law, that of the exchange of commodities. And the consumption of the commodity belongs not to the seller who parts with it, but to the buyer, who acquires it. To you, therefore, belongs the use of my daily labour power. But by means of the price that you pay for it each day, I must be able to reproduce it daily, and to sell it again. Apart from natural exhaustion through age, &c., I must be able on the morrow to work with the same normal amount of force, health and freshness as today. You preach to me constantly the gospel of 'saving' and 'abstinence.' Good! I will, like a sensible saving owner, husband my sole wealth, labour power, and abstain from all foolish waste of it" (MECW 35: 241–42, MEGA 2.10: 209). Reading the earlier passages devoted to commodity fetishism, Nicole Pepperell also insists upon the theatrical dimensions of Marx's language in "Impure Inheritances: Spectral Materiality in Derrida and Marx," 43–72. In his brief commentary on the same chapter on commodity fetishism, LaCapra poses the question with regard to less overtly dialogic passages: "To what extent is Marx putting forth propositions in his own voice (for example, a labor theory of value) and to what extent does he furnish an ironic deconstruction of the system of classical economics and the capitalistic practice it subtended (including the assumption of a labor theory of value)?" (*Rethinking Intellectual History*, 170). The question already implies that there is no voice of one's "own" to be secured in the writings of Marx or anyone else, insofar as the sheer possibility of citation exposes language *a priori* to citation and alteration, ironization and deconstruction.

62. And as far as ghosts are concerned, Jacques Derrida has pointed out in his careful reading of many of the texts addressed in this chapter that the exorcisms Marx undertakes cannot but leave remnants that return: "This hostility toward ghosts, a terrified hostility that sometimes fends off terror with a burst of laughter, is perhaps what Marx will always have had in common with his adversaries. He too will have tried to conjure (away) the ghosts, and everything that was neither

life nor death, namely, the re-apparition of an apparition that will never be either the appearing or the disappeared, the phenomenon or its contrary. He will have tried to conjure (away) the ghosts like the conspirators [*conjurés*] of old Europe on whom the *Manifesto* declares war. However inexpiable this war remains, and however necessary this revolution, it conspires [*conjure*] with them in order to exorc-analyze the spectrality of the specter. And this is today, as perhaps it will be tomorrow, our problem" (Derrida, *Specters of Marx*, 58).

63. Martin Puchner, *Poetry of the Revolution: Marx, Manifestos, and the Avant-Gardes*, 12. The historical sense of the "manifesto" to which Puchner helpfully contrasts Marx and Engels's text includes its traditional usage as "a communication, authored by those in authority, by the state, the military, or the church, to let their subjects know their sovereign intentions and laws" (*Poetry of the Revolution*, 12). In a less radical way, Kenneth Burke, to whom Puchner also refers, had emphatically called the *Manifesto* a "*constitution*" in his argument that it "ground[s] its statement of political principles in statements about the nature of the universal scene," and is designed to culminate in "a great 'World-Historical' act" that it anticipates, announces, and thereby calls forth (Burke, *A Grammar of Motives*, 202, 207). Similarly, Janet Lyon argues, with reference to the *Declaration of Independence* and the *Communist Manifesto*, that "[t]he manifesto's revolutionary speaking position constructs political certainty [. . .] not just by reinforcing polemical fields, but also by assuming control of the language of history, the conditions of plot" (Lyon, *Manifestoes: Provocations of the Modern*, 60).

64. Derrida, *Théorie et pratique*, 19.

65. For an excellent study of the infinite judgment, see Daniel Heller-Roazen's recent book, *No-One's Ways: An Essay on Infinite Naming*.

66. Derrida, *Specters of Marx*, 10.

67. Puchner, *Poetry of the Revolution*, 52.

68. Puchner, *Poetry of the Revolution*, 56.

69. Puchner, *Poetry of the Revolution*, 56.

70. Schlegel, "On Incomprehensibility," 261–62; "Über die Unverständlichkeit," 365.

71. Hegel, *Phänomenologie*, 370.

72. Puchner, *Poetry of the Revolution*, 31.

73. Hamacher, "Lingua Amissa: The Messianism of Commodity-Language and Derrida's *Specters of Marx*," 175.

74. See the discussion of this logic in other instances of revolutionary rhetoric above, chapter 2.

75. See the notebooks on Epicurean philosophy, where Marx recurs to a passage that precedes the discussion of action and passion in this very text: συντόμως δὲ καὶ νῦν λεκτέον, ὅτι τρόπον μέν τινα ἐκ μὴ ὄντος ἁπλῶς γίνεται, τρόπον δὲ ἄλλον ἐξ ὄντος ἀεί· τὸ γὰρ δυνάμει ὂν ἐντελεχείᾳ δὲ μὴ ὂν ἀνάγκη προϋπάρχειν λεγόμενον ἀμφοτέρως (317b 16–18, MECW 1: 411, MEGA 4.1: 17). Quotations

from Aristotle in Greek and English have been taken from the Loeb editions of his works and cited according to the standard Bekker pagination; however, translations have been occasionally modified. The importance of Aristotle to Marx's thought is a frequent topic in scholarship, but there is little commentary on the categories evoked in the *Communist Manifesto*. Instead, Marx's engagement with Aristotle has been addressed more often with reference to the *Metaphysics*, the *Nicomachean Ethics*, and the *Politics* in debates over Marx's critique of money or the organization of activity and community that would lead to the good life. The arguments also tend to emphasize not the specific linguistic and conceptual modifications of Aristotle's thought that take place in passages from Marx's oeuvre, but rather the more general comparisons that might be drawn between the two thinkers. See, for example, Richard W. Miller, "Marx and Aristotle: A Kind of Consequentialism," and Alan Gilbert, "Marx's Moral Realism: Eudaimonism and Moral Progress." For a nuanced description of Marx's adoption of Aristotelian notions such as "praxis" within a mode of historical thinking that deviates from the Aristotelian ontology that would establish "man's changeless nature," see Margolis, "Praxis and Meaning: Marx's Species Being and Aristotle's Political Animal," 335. This basic distinction was also drawn in Georges Sorel's elaboration of a Bergsonian version of Marxism, which contrasts the ancient metaphysical tendency to seek, amidst changing phenomena, "une science immuable" with a modern metaphysics of innovation within a socially and economically determined context; see Sorel, *D'Aristote à Marx*, 161, 193. With reference to Marx's early writings, David J. Depew argues that Marx adopts those premises from Aristotle's *De anima* that, in contradistinction to Hegel, do not privilege the intellective part of the soul over the "reproductive soul," which is "not just a blind comminution between individual and bits of the world, but aims at the continuation of the species through the continuation of the individual" (Depew, "Aristotle's *De Anima* and Marx's Theory of Man," 149). Georg Lukács also recurs to the distinctions between Aristotle and Marx, noting Aristotle's valuable insights into the "Waren- und Wertprobleme" that Marx draws upon in *Kapital*, as well as the limitations of Aristotle's thinking, due to his historical position within an economy predicated upon slavery. See Lukács, *Prolegomena: Zur Ontologie des gesellschaftlichen Seins*, 226–27.

76. Althusser, *Machiavelli and Us*, 38; cf. *Écrits philosophiques et politiques*, 2: 86.

77. Thus, Althusser goes on to write, "Machiavelli has no sooner alluded to the classical problem of the *typology* of governments than he changes terrain and problem, offering us an example and problem that transport us to a quite different world" (Althusser, *Machiavelli and Us*, 39; cf. *Écrits philosophiques*, 2: 86–87).

78. In her reading of the opening chapters of *Capital*, Pepperell argues from a similar premise that "the various ontological claims put forward overtly [. . .] can instead be read as set pieces designed to portray the conflicting claims of political economic theory" (Pepperell, "Impure Inheritances," 44). However, her reading is also highly inflected by a theatrical vocabulary in ways that differ from the anaylsis

offered here: "The text as a whole," she argues, "can be read as a play in which personifications of contradictory tenets of political economic discourse stride successively onto *Capital*'s economic 'stage'" ("Impure Inheritances," 44).

79. The original Greek text reads: πλὴν εἰ μή που κατὰ συμβεβηκός, οἷον εἰ συμβέβηκε λευκὴν ἢ μέλαιναν εἶναι τὴν γραμμήν· οὐκ ἐξίστησι γὰρ ἄλληλα τῆς φύσεως ὅσα μήτ᾽ ἐναντία μήτ᾽ ἐξ ἐναντίων ἐστίν. ἀλλ᾽ ἐπεὶ οὐ τὸ τυχὸν πέφυκε πάσχειν καὶ ποιεῖν, ἀλλ᾽ ὅσα ἢ ἐναντία ἐστὶν ἢ ἐναντίωσιν ἔχει (323b 27–32).

80. See Johann Wolfgang von Goethe, *Gedichte und Singspiele. Goethes Werke: Berliner Ausgabe*, 1: 90–92.

81. Goethe, *Gedichte*, 1: 91.

82. See Aristotle, *Metaphysics* 1013b 21, 1014a 8.

83. Martin Heidegger, "The Thing," 163.

84. Heidegger, "The Thing," 163, 164.

85. Heidegger, "The Thing," 164, 174.

86. This phrase is borrowed from Mieszkowski, *Labors of Imagination*, 129. There, Mieszkowski unfolds the complicated and ambivalent role that "labor" plays in Marx's writings, since its alienating effects imply that labor, "[c]onsidered as a predicate of a self [. . .] is never simply an activity of self-confirmation or self-realization. It is always a process of self-externalization and self-expropriation, to the point that the act of labor is no longer self-evidently the act of a self that performs it. As a result, one cannot simply appeal to labor as a naturally liberating power [. . .]" (Mieszkowski, *Labors of Imagination*, 132).

87. After discussing the preconditions for a "productive dialogue with Marxism" in his *Letter on 'Humanism,'* which include freeing "oneself from naive notions about materialism," Heidegger insists that "[t]he essence of materialism is concealed in the essence of technology" (Heidegger, *Letter on 'Humanism,'* 259). This assertion is in keeping with Heidegger's earlier description of the tendency in Marx to present the society he envisions as one in which "human 'nature,' that is, the totality of 'natural needs' (food, clothing, reproduction, economic sufficiency), is equably secured" (Heidegger, *Letter on 'Humanism,'* 244). This vision for society, however, does not radically challenge the paradigm of domination that Heidegger already locates in the "public realm itself," which consists of "the metaphysically conditioned establishment and authorization of the openness of beings in the unconditional objectification of everything" (Heidegger, *Letter on 'Humanism,'* 242).

88. For a further discussion of this aspect of Heidegger's thought, see especially his inquiry into "another beginning" in his *Beiträge zur Philosophie*. For an excellent reading of Heidegger's response to Aristotle that exposes many of the ways in which Heidegger does not read "Aristotle as *the* metaphysician *par excellence*," but "offers a persuasive and revolutionary rethinking of Aristotle's work, which he argues is more original and radical than that of his teacher Plato," see Walter Brogan, *Heidegger and Aristotle: The Twofoldness of Being*, 4.

89. Epicurus, *The Extant Remains*, 134.

90. Lucretius, *De rerum natura*, book 1, lines 1021–28.

91. Lucretius frequently refers to "federations" in the formation of bonds among atoms, as when he writes in book 1, lines 584–92: "Denique iam quoniam generatim reddita finis / crescendi rebus constat vitamque tenendi, / et quid quaeque queant per foedera naturai, / quid porro nequeant, [. . .] inmutabilis materiae quoque corpus habere / debent."

92. Lucretius, *De rerum natura*, book 1, lines 459–61.

93. Sextus Empiricus, *Adversus mathematicos*, 10.219. Marx cites this passage in his dissertation; see MECW 1: 96, MEGA 1.1: 75.

94. For an excellent commentary on this phrase, see Derrida's remarks in his essay on atomism, "Mes chances," where he writes: "Dans tous les cas, l'incidence se laisse remarquer dans le système d'une coïncidence, cela même qui tombe, bien ou mal, *avec* autre chose, en même temps ou dans le même lieu qu'autre chose. Tel est aussi en grec le sens de *symptôma*, mot qui signifie d'abord l'affaissement, l'effondrement, puis la coïncidence, l'événement fortuit, la rencontre, ensuite l'événement malchanceux et enfin le symptôme comme signe, par exemple clinique" (Derrida, "Mes chances," 10).

95. The temporal significance of this word form corresponds so closely to the atomistic interpretation of temporality that it remains significant, whether or not its usage was motivated by metrical constraints, as Cyril Bailey suggests in his erudite prolegomenon to his edition and commentary of *De rerum natura*. There, Bailey offers a metrical explanation for Lucretius's usage of *positura*, as well as similarly formed coinages, such as *compositura, dispositura*, and *flexura*, writing: "It has been seen that many of the forms [. . .] were used or even invented by Lucretius as substitutes for abstract substantives, which in the normal form would not scan in a hexameter" (Lucretius, *De rerum natura*, 135).

96. This interpretation of positioning *qua* event thus approximates what Gilles Deleuze writes of the clinamen, interpreting its occurrence "*nec regione loci certa nec tempore certo*" (Lucretius, *De rerum natura*, book 2, lines 292–93) to mean "en un temps plus petit que le minimum de temps continu pensable" (Deleuze, *Logique du sens*, 312).

97. For a most incisive reading of the remarks on "tempus" in Lucretius's poem, see Thomas Schestag's discussion in *para—Titus Lucretius Carus, Johann Peter Hebel, Francis Ponge*, 16–19. See also Michael Levine's excellent readings of the implications of atomistic temporality for the poetry of Paul Celan in *Atomzertrümmerung*.

98. Lucretius, *De rerum natura*, book 2, lines 1013–18. It is along the same lines that fire and firewood, "ignis et lignum," can be said to differ (Lucretius, *De rerum natura*, book 1, lines 912, 914), such that wood may come to blaze, not due to an inherent fiery potential that need only be activated in order to ignite, but due to the slightest rearrangement of the elements of wood itself, which is not a substantial material at all, but a result of atomic compositions that can break down and break into conflagration. This illustration of the conversion of fire to

2. Blanqui, *Eternity by the Stars*, 72; cf. *Éternité par les astres*, 243.
3. Blanqui, *Eternity by the Stars*, 72; cf. *Éternité par les astres*, 243.
4. Hamacher, "Afformative, Strike," 1139.
5. Samuel Beckett, *Murphy*, 3.
6. William Carlos Williams, *The Great American Novel*, in *Imaginations*, 165.

Works Cited

Abensour, Miguel, and Valentin Pelosse. "Libérer l'enfermé." In *Instructions pour une prise d'armes; L'Éternité par les astres*. Edited by Miguel Abensour and Valentin Pelosse, 377–442. 2nd ed. Paris: Sens & Tonka, 2000.

Adorno, Theodor W. *Aesthetic Theory*. Translated by Robert Hullot-Kentor. London: Continuum, 1997.

Albert, Georgia. "Understanding Irony: Three Essais on Friedrich Schlegel." *MLN* 108, no. 5 (1993): 825–48.

Alexandrova, Alena, Ignaas Devisch, Laurens ten Kate, and Aukje van Rooden, eds. *Re-treating Religion: Deconstructing Christianity with Jean-Luc Nancy*. New York: Fordham University Press, 2012.

Althusser, Louis. *For Marx*. Translated by Ben Brewster. New York: Pantheon, 1969.

———. *Écrits philosophiques et politiques*. Vol. 2. Edited by François Matheron. Paris: Stock/IMEC, 1995.

———. *Machiavelli and Us*. Edited by François Matheron. Translated by Gregory Elliott. London: Verso, 1999.

———. *Philosophy of the Encounter: Later Writings, 1978–87*. Edited by François Matheron and Oliver Corpet. Translated by G. M. Goshgarian. London: Verso, 2006.

———. *Pour Marx*. Paris: La Découverte, 2005.

Althusser, Louis, Étienne Balibar, Roger Establet, Pierre Macherey, and Jacques Rancière. *Lire* Le Capital, 3rd ed. Paris: PUF, 1996.

———. *Reading Capital: The Complete Edition*. Translated by Ben Brewster and David Fernbach. London: Verso, 2015.

The Arabian Nights. Edited by Muhsin Mahdi. Translated by Husain Haddawy. New York: Norton, 1990.

Aristotle. *The Categories, On Interpretation, Prior Analytics*. Translated and edited by Harold P. Cooke and Hugh Tredennick. Cambridge, MA: Harvard University Press, 2002.

———. *Metaphysics*. Translated by Hugh Tredennick. 2 vols. Cambridge, MA: Harvard University Press, 1933–35.

---. *On Sophistical Refutations, On Coming-to-Be and Passing Away*. Translated by E. S. Forster. Cambridge, MA: Harvard University Press, 1965.

---. *Physics*. Translated by P. H. Wicksteed and F. M. Cornford. 2 vols. Cambridge, MA: Harvard University Press, 1957, 1960.

---. *Poetics*. In *Aristotle: Poetics, Longinus: On the Sublime, and Demetrius: On Style*. Translated and edited by Stephen Halliwell. Cambridge, MA: Harvard University Press, 1995.

Ataeian, Azadeh. *Vom Standpunkt des Erkennens: Nietzsches Philosophie des Perspektivismus*. Berlin: LIT Verlag, 2013.

Austin, J. L. *Poetic Principles and Practice: Occasional Papers on Baudelaire, Mallarmé, and Valéry*. Cambridge, UK: Cambridge University Press, 1987.

Avni, Abraham. "The Bible and *Les Fleurs du mal*." *PMLA* 88, no. 2 (1973): 299–310.

Azzam, Abed. *Nietzsche Versus Paul*. New York: Columbia University Press, 2015.

Babuts, Nicolae. "Baudelaire's 'Le Voyage': The Dimension of Myth." *Nineteenth-Century French Studies* 25, no. 3/4 (1997): 348–59.

Bach, Heinrich. *Handbuch der Luthersprache. Laut- und Formenlehre in Luthers Wittenberger Drucken bis 1545. Teil 2*. Copenhagen: Gad, 1985.

Bachelard, Gaston. *Le rationalisme appliqué*. 3rd ed. Paris: PUF, 1966.

Badiou, Alain. *Being and Event*. Translated by Oliver Feltham. London: Continuum, 2005.

---. *Nietzsche: L'antiphilosophie I: 1992–1993*. Edited by Véronique Pineau. Paris: Fayard, 2015.

---. "Who is Nietzsche?" Translated by Alberto Toscano. *Pli* 11 (2001): 1–11.

Balfour, Ian. "Reversal, Quotation (Benjamin's History)." *MLN* 106, no. 3 (1991): 622–47.

Balibar, Étienne. *Écrits pour Althusser*. Paris: La Découverte, 1991.

---. *The Philosophy of Marx*. Translated by Chris Turner. London: Verso, 2007.

Balzac, Honoré de. "L'illustre Gaudissart." In *La Comédie humaine*. Edited by Pierre Barbéris, vol. 4, 561–98. Paris: Gallimard, 1976.

---. *La Fille aux yeux d'or*. In *La Comédie humaine*. Edited by Rose Fortassier, vol. 5, 1039–1109. Paris: Gallimard, 1977.

Barash, Jeffrey A. *Martin Heidegger and the Problem of Historical Meaning*. New York: Fordham University Press, 2003.

Barnes, David. "Fascist Aesthetics: Ezra Pound's Cultural Negotiations in 1930s Italy." *Modern Literature* 34, no. 1 (2010): 19–35.

Bastiat, Frédéric. *Oeuvres complètes*. Vol. 5: *Sophismes économiques*. Paris: Guillaumin et Cie, 1854.

Baudelaire, Charles. *Correspondance: 1832–1860*. Vol. 1. Edited by Claude Pichois and Jean Ziegler. Paris: Gallimard, 1973.

---. *The Flowers of Evil*. Translated by James McGowan. Oxford: Oxford University Press, 2008.

———. *My Heart Laid Bare and Other Prose-Writings*. Translated by Norman Cameron. London: Weidenfeld & Nicolson, 1950.

———. *Oeuvres complètes*. Edited by Claude Pichois. 2 vols. Paris: Gallimard, 1976.

———. *Oeuvres posthumes et correspondances inédites*. Edited by Eugène Crépet. Paris: Quantin, 1887.

Baur, Ferdinand Christian. *Das Christliche des Platonismus, oder Sokrates und Christus*. Tübingen: Fues, 1837.

Beckett, Samuel. *Murphy*. London: Faber and Faber, 2009.

Benjamin, Walter. *The Arcades Project*. Translated by Howard Eiland and Kevin McLaughlin. Cambridge, MA: Harvard University Press, 2002.

———. *Gesammelte Schriften*. Edited by Rolf Tiedemann and Hermann Schweppenhäuser. 7 vols. Frankfurt am Main: Suhrkamp Verlag, 1972–89.

———. "On the Concept of History." Translated by Harry Zohn. In *Walter Benjamin: Selected Writings*. Edited by Howard Eiland and Michael W. Jennings, vol. 4, 389–400. Cambridge, MA: Harvard University Press, 2006.

———. "The Storyteller: Observations on the Works of Nikolai Leskov." Translated by Harry Zohn. In *Walter Benjamin: Selected Writings*. Edited by Howard Eiland and Michael W. Jennings, vol. 3, 143–66. Cambridge, MA: Harvard University Press, 2002.

———. *Über den Begriff der Geschichte*. Edited by Gérard Raulet. Frankfurt am Main: Suhrkamp, 2010.

Bennholdt-Thomsen, Anke. *Nietzsches* Also sprach Zarathustra *als literarisches Phänomen*. Frankfurt am Main: Athenäum, 1974.

Bensaïd, Daniel, and Michael Löwy. "Auguste Blanqui, Heretical Communist." Translated by Philippe le Goff. *Radical Philosophy* 185 (2014): 26–35.

La Bible. Translated by Isaac-Louis Lemaistre de Sacy. Vol. 3. Paris: Guiraudet and Jouaust, 1837.

Blanchot, Maurice. "Literature and the Right to Death." Translated by Lydia Davis. In *The Work of Fire*, 300–44. Stanford, CA: Stanford University Press, 1995.

———. "Littérature et le droit de la mort." In *La part du feu*, 291–331. Paris: Gallimard, 1949.

Blanqui, Louis-Auguste. *Critique sociale*. 2 vols. Paris: Germer, 1885.

———. *Eternity by the Stars: An Astronomical Hypothesis*. Translated by Frank Chouraqui. New York: Contra Mundum Press, 2013.

———. *Instructions pour une prise d'armes; L'Éternité par les astres*. Edited by Miguel Abensour and Valentin Pelosse. 2nd ed. Paris: Sens & Tonka, 2000.

———. *Oeuvres complètes*. Edited by Arno Münster. Vol. 1. Paris: Galilée, 1977.

———. *Oeuvres complètes I: Des origines à la Révolution de 1848*. Edited by Dominique le Nuz. Nancy: Presses Universitaires de Nancy, 1993.

Bloch, Ernst. *The Principle of Hope*. Translated by Neville Plaice, Stephen Plaice, and Paul Knight. Vol. 1. Cambridge, MA: MIT Press, 1986.

Blumenberg, Hans. *Arbeit am Mythos*. Frankfurt am Main: Suhrkamp, 1996.
———. *The Legitimacy of the Modern Age*. Translated by Robert M. Wallace. Cambridge, MA: MIT Press, 1983.
———. *Die Legitimität der Neuzeit*. Frankfurt am Main: Suhrkamp, 1966.
———. *Work on Myth*. Trans. Robert M. Wallace. Cambridge, MA: MIT Press, 1985.
Bourdieu, Pierre. *Distinction: A Social Critique of the Judgement of Taste*. Translated by Richard Nice. Cambridge, MA: Harvard University Press, 1984.
Brogan, Walter. *Heidegger and Aristotle: The Twofoldness of Being*. Ithaca, NY: State University of New York Press, 2005.
Brombert, Victor. "The Rhetoric of Contemplation: Hugo's 'La pente de la rêverie.'" In *Nineteenth-Century French Poetry: Introductions to Close Reading*. Edited by Christopher Prendergast, 48–61. Cambridge, UK: Cambridge University Press, 1990.
Brunel, Pierre. *Baudelaire antique et moderne*. Paris: Presses de l'Université Paris-Sorbonne, 2007.
Bürger, Peter. *Theory of the Avant-Garde*. Translated by Michael Shaw. Minneapolis: University of Minnesota Press, 1984.
Burke, Kenneth. *A Grammar of Motives*. New York: Prentice Hall, 1945.
Burt, E. S., Elissa Marder, and Kevin Newmark, eds. *Time for Baudelaire (Poetry, Theory, History)*. Yale French Studies 125/126 (2014).
Burton, Richard. *Baudelaire and the Second Republic: Writing and Revolution*. Oxford: Clarendon, 1991.
———. *Baudelaire in 1859: A Study in the Sources of Poetic Creativity*. Cambridge, UK: Cambridge University Press, 1988.
Cadava, Eduardo. "Sternphotographie: Benjamin, Blanqui, and the Mimesis of the Stars." *Qui Parle* 9, no. 1 (1995): 1–32.
Chateaubriand, François-René de. *Essai sur les révolutions; Génie du christianisme*. Edited by Maurice Regard. Paris: Gallimard, 1978.
———. *Oeuvres romanesques et voyages*. Vol. 1. Edited by Maurice Regard. Paris: Gallimard, 1969.
Chambers, Ross. *Atmospherics of the City: Baudelaire and the Poetics of Noise*. New York: Fordham University Press, 2015.
———. "Inventing Unknownness: The Poetry of Disenchanted Enchantment (Leopardi, Baudelaire, Rimbaud, Justice)." *French Forum* 33, no. 1/2 (2008): 15–36.
Chevalier, Michel. *Lettres sur l'Amérique du nord*. Vol. 1. Brussels: Hauman, Cattoir et Ce, 1837.
Chrostowska, S. D. "Angelus Novus, Angst of History." *diacritics* 40, no. 1 (2012): 42–68.
Creuzer, Friedrich. *Symbolik und Mythologie der alten Völker*. Vol. 1. 2nd ed. Leipzig and Darmstadt: Heyer and Leske, 1819.
Culler, Jonathan. "Intertextuality and Interpretation: Baudelaire's 'Correspondances.'" In *Nineteenth-Century French Poetry: Introductions to Close Reading*. Edited by

Christopher Prendergast, 118–37. Cambridge, UK: Cambridge University Press, 1990.

Dastur, Françoise. "Who Is Nietzsche's Zarathustra? A Note on the Iranian-Persian Background." Translated by David Farrell Krell. *Comparative and Continental Philosophy* 1, no. 1 (2009): 39–54.

Deleuze, Gilles. *Difference and Repetition*. Translated by Paul Patton. London: Continuum, 2004.

———. *Logique du sens*. Paris: Minuit, 1969.

———. *Nietzsche and Philosophy*. Translated by Hugh Tomlinson. London: Continuum, 2002.

de Man, Paul. *Aesthetic Ideology*. Edited by Andrzej Warminski. Minneapolis: University of Minnesota Press, 1996.

———. *Allegories of Reading: Figural Language in Rousseau, Nietzsche, Rilke, and Proust*. New Haven, CT: Yale University Press, 1979.

———. *Blindness and Insight: Essays in the Rhetoric of Contemporary Criticism*. Minneapolis: University of Minnesota Press, 1983.

Depew, David J. "Aristotle's *De Anima* and Marx's Theory of Man." *Graduate Faculty Philosophy Journal* 8, no. 1/2 (1981): 133–87.

Derrida, Jacques. "Mes chances: Au rendez-vous de quelques stéréophonies épicuriennes." *Tijdschrift voor Filosofie* 45, no. 1 (1983): 3–40.

———. "Psyche: Invention of the Other." Translated by Catherine Porter. In *Psyche: Inventions of the Other, Volume 1*. Edited by Peggy Kamuf and Elizabeth Rottenberg, 1–47. Stanford, CA: Stanford University Press, 2007.

———. *Specters of Marx: The State of the Debt, the Work of Mourning, and the New International*. Translated by Peggy Kamuf. New York: Routledge, 1994.

———. *Spectres de Marx: L'État de la dette, le travail du deuil et la nouvelle Internationale*. Paris: Galilée, 1993.

———. *Spurs / Éperons: Nietzsche's Styles*. Translated by Barbara Harlow. Chicago: University of Chicago Press, 1978.

———. *Théorie et pratique: Cours de l'ENS-Ulm 1975–1976*. Edited by Alexander García Düttmann. Paris: Galilée, 2017.

Descartes, René. *Meditations on First Philosophy: With Selections from the Objections and Replies*. Translated by John Cottingham. 2nd ed. Cambridge, UK: Cambridge University Press, 2017.

———. *Oeuvres philosophiques: Tome II (1638–1642)*. Edited by Ferdinand Alquié. Paris: Garnier, 1967.

Diogenes Laertes. *Lives of Eminent Philosophers: Books 6–10*. Translated by R. D. Hicks. Cambridge, MA: Harvard University Press, 1931.

D'Iorio, Paulo. "The Eternal Return: Genesis and Interpretation." *Lexicon Philosophicum* 2 (2014): 41–96.

Dommanget, Maurice. *Auguste Blanqui à Belle-Ile, 1850–1857*. Paris: Librairie du Travail, 1935.

———. *Blanqui et l'opposition à la fin du Second Empire*. Paris: Armand Colin, 1960.
Du Camp, Maxime. *Mémoires d'un suicidé*. Paris: Flammarion, 1890.
Enderwitz, Susanne. "Shahrazâd is One of Us: Practical Narrative, Theoretical Discussion, and Feminist Discourse." *Marvels & Tales* 18, no. 2 (2004): 187–200.
Epicurus. *The Extant Remains*. Edited and translated by Cyril Bailey. Oxford: Clarendon Press, 1926.
Fages, Volny. "Ordonner le monde changer la société: Les systèmes cosmologiques des socialistes du premier XIXe siècle." *Romantisme* 159, no. 1 (2013): 123–34.
Fox, Michael V. *A Time to Tear Down and a Time to Build Up: A Rereading of Ecclesiastes*. Eugene: Wopf & Stock, 2010.
Frey, Hans-Jost. *Studies in Poetic Discourse: Mallarmé, Baudelaire, Rimbaud, Hölderlin*. Translated by William Whobrey. Stanford, CA: Stanford University Press, 1996.
Gauchet, Marcel. *The Disenchantment of the World: A Political History of Religion*. Translated by Oscar Burge. Princeton, NJ: Princeton University Press, 1997.
Gautier, Théophile. *Poésies complètes*. Edited by René Jasinski. 3 vols. Paris: Firmin-Didot, 1932.
Geffroy, Gustave. *L'Enfermé*. 2 vols. Paris: Crès, 1927.
Gelikman, Oleg. "The Crisis of the Messianic Claim: Scholem, Benjamin, Baudelaire." In *Messianic Thought Outside Theology*. Edited by Anna Glazova and Paul North, 171–94. New York: Fordham University Press, 2014.
Gilbert, Alan. "Marx's Moral Realism: Eudaimonism and Moral Progress." In *Marx and Aristotle: Nineteenth-Century German Social Theory and Classical Antiquity*. Edited by George E. McCarthy, 303–28. Savage: Rowman & Littlefield, 1992.
Gille, Betrand. *Histoire de la maison Rothschild*. Vol. 1. Geneva: Droz, 1965.
Goethe, Johann Wolfgang von. *Gedichte und Singspiele. Goethes Werke: Berliner Ausgabe*. Vol. 1. Edited by Regine Otto. Berlin: Aufbau, 1976.
Gooding-Williams, Robert. *Zarathustra's Dionysian Modernism*. Stanford, CA: Stanford University Press, 2001.
Griese, Anneliese, and Gerd Pawelzig. "Natur und Naturwissenschaft im philosophischen Denken von Friedrich Engels." *Marx-Engels Jahrbuch* 8 (1985): 9–37.
Grimm, Jacob, and Wilhelm Grimm. *Deutsches Wörterbuch*. 33 vols. Munich: Deutscher Taschenbuch Verlag, 1984.
Groys, Boris. *On the New*. Translated by G. M. Goshgarian. London: Verso, 2014.
Halévy, Joseph. *Recherches Bibliques: Notes pour l'interprétation des psaumes, les chants nuptiaux des cantiques, les livres d'Osée, d'Amos, de Michée, etc.* Vol. 3. Paris: Leroux, 1905.
Hallward, Peter. "Blanqui's Bifurcations." *Radical Philosophy* 185 (2014): 36–44.
Hamacher, Werner. "Afformative, Strike." Translated by Dana Hollander. *Cardozo Law Review* 13, no. 4 (1991): 1133–157.
———. "History, Teary: Some Remarks on *La Jeune Parque*." Translated by Michael Shae. *Yale French Studies* 74 (1988): 67–94.
———. "Lingua Amissa: The Messianism of Commodity-Language and Derrida's *Specters of Marx*." Translated by Kelly Barry. In *Ghostly Demarcations: A Sym-*

posium on Jacques Derrida's Specters of Marx. Edited by Michael Sprinker, 168–212. London: Verso, 1999.

———. *95 Theses on Philology.* Translated by Catherine Diehl. In *Minima Philologica*, 3–105. New York: Fordham University Press, 2015.

———. *Pleroma—Reading in Hegel.* Translated by Nicholas Walker and Simon Jarvis. Stanford, CA: Stanford University Press, 1998.

———. *Premises: Essays on Philosophy and Literature from Kant to Celan.* Translated by Peter Fenves. Cambridge, MA: Harvard University Press, 1996.

———. "What Remains to Be Said: On Twelve and More Ways of Looking at Philology." Translated by Kristina Mendicino. In *Give the Word: Responses to Werner Hamacher's 95 Theses on Philology*. Edited by Gerhard Richter and Ann Smock, 217–354. Lincoln: University of Nebraska Press, 2019.

Harsin, Jill. *Barricades: The War of the Streets in Revolutionary Paris, 1830–1848.* New York: Palgrave, 2002.

Hartmann, Eduard von. *Philosophie des Unbewussten.* Vol. 1. Leipzig: Kröner, 1923.

A Hebrew and English Lexicon of the Old Testament. William Gesenius and Edward Robinson. Oxford: Clarendon Press, 1951.

Hegel, G. W. F. *Die Phänomenologie des Geistes.* Edited by Johannes Hoffmeister. Hamburg: Meiner, 1952.

———. "Die Verfassung Deutschlands." In *Hegels Schriften zur Politik und Rechtsphilosophie.* Edited by Georg Lasson, 3–136. Leipzig: Meiner, 1913.

Heidegger, Martin. *Basic Questions of Philosophy: Selected 'Problems' of 'Logic.'* Translated by Richard Rojcewicz and André Schuwer. Bloomington and Indianapolis: Indiana University Press, 1994.

———. *Beiträge zur Philosophie (Vom Ereignis).* Edited by Friedrich-Wilhelm von Herrmann. 3rd ed. Frankfurt am Main: Klostermann, 2003.

———. *Contributions to Philosophy (From Enowning).* Translated by Parvis Emad and Kenneth Maly. Bloomington and Indianapolis: Indiana University Press, 1999.

———. *Grundfragen der Philosophie: Ausgewählte 'Probleme' der 'Logik.'* Edited by Friedrich-Wilhelm von Herrmann. Frankfurt am Main: Klostermann, 1984.

———. "Letter on 'Humanism.'" Translated by Frank A. Capuzzi. In *Pathmarks.* Edited by William McNeill, 239–76. Cambridge, UK: Cambridge University Press, 1998.

———. *Nietzsche.* Vol. 1. Pfullingen: Neske, 1961.

———. *Poetry, Language, Thought.* Translated by Albert Hofstadter. New York: Harper Collins, 2001.

———. *Was heißt Denken?* Edited by Paola-Ludivika Coriando. Frankfurt am Main: Klostermann, 2002.

———. *Wegmarken.* Edited by Friedrich-Wilhelm von Herrmann. Frankfurt am Main: Klostermann, 2004.

———. "Who is Nietzsche's Zarathustra?" Translated by Bernd Magnus. *The Review of Metaphysics* 20, no. 3 (1967): 411–31.

Heller-Roazen, Daniel. *No-One's Ways: An Essay on Infinite Naming*. New York: Zone Books, 2017.
Heine, Heinrich. *Concerning the History of Religion and Philosophy in Germany.* Translated by Helen Mustard. In *The Romantic School and Other Essays*. Edited by Jost Hermand and Robert C. Holub, 128–244. New York: Continuum, 2002.
Hesiod. *Works and Days*. In *Theogony, Works and Days, Testimonia*. Translated by Glenn W. Most. Cambridge, MA: Harvard University Press, 2006.
Hirt, André. *Baudelaire: Le monde va finir*. Paris: Kimé, 2010.
Holland, Eugene W. *Baudelaire and Schizoanalysis: The Sociopoetics of Modernism*. Cambridge, UK: Cambridge University Press, 2006.
Holmes, Brooke. "Deleuze, Lucretius, and the Simulacrum of Naturalism." In *Dynamic Reading: Studies in the Reception of Epicureanism*. Edited by Brooke Holmes and W. H. Shearin, 316–42. New York: Oxford University Press, 2012.
Hugo, Victor. *Oeuvres poétiques*. Vol. 1. Edited by Pierre Albouy. Paris: Gallimard, 1964.
———. *Selected Poems of Victor Hugo: A Bilingual Edition*. Translated by E. H. and A. M. Blackmore. Chicago and London: University of Chicago Press, 2004.
Hutton, Patrick. "Legends of a Revolutionary: Nostalgia in the Imagined Lives of Auguste Blanqui." *Historical Reflections / Réflexions Historiques* 39, no. 3 (2013): 41–54.
———. *The Cult of the Revolutionary Tradition: The Blanquists in French Politics, 1864–1893*. Berkeley: University of California Press, 1981.
Jauss, Hans Robert. *Literaturgeschichte als Provokation*. Frankfurt am Main: Suhrkamp, 1970.
———. "Tradition, Innovation, and Aesthetic Experience." *Journal of Aesthetics and Art Criticism* 46, no. 3 (1988): 375–88.
———. "Ursprung und Bedeutung der Fortschrittsidee in der Querelle des Anciens et des Modernes." In *Die Philosophie und die Frage nach dem Fortschritt*. Edited by Helmut Kuhn and Franz Wiedmann, 51–72. Munich: Pustet, 1964.
Kelly, George Armstrong. "Alphonse de Lamartine: The Poet in Politics." *Daedelus* 116, no. 2 (1987): 157–80.
Kenner, Hugh. *The Poetry of Ezra Pound*. Lincoln: University of Nebraska Press, 1985.
Kittler, Friedrich. *Aufschreibesysteme 1800 · 1900*. Munich: Fink, 1985.
Klenker, J. F. *Zend-Avesta, Zoroasters lebendiges Wort: Erster Theil*. Riga: Hartknoch, 1776.
Klossowski, Pierre. *Nietzsche and the Vicious Circle*. Translated by Daniel W. Smith. Chicago: University of Chicago Press, 1997.
Krell, David Farrell. *Infectious Nietzsche*. Bloomington: Indiana University Press, 1996.
Krüger, Thomas. "Dekonstruktion und Rekonstruktion prophetischer Eschatologie im Qohelet-Buch." In *"Jedes Ding hat seine Zeit . . .": Studien zur israelitischen*

und altorientalischen Weisheit: Diethelm Michel zum 65. Geburtstag. Edited by Anja A. Diesel, Reinhard G. Lehmann, Eckart Otto, and Andreas Wagner, 107–29. Berlin: Walter de Gruyter, 1996.

LaCapra, Dominick. *Rethinking Intellectual History: Texts, Contexts, Language*. Ithaca, NY: Cornell University Press, 1983.

Lamartine, Alphonse. *Harmonies poétiques et religieuses*. Vol. 1. Paris: C. Gosselin, 1830.

———. *La politique de Lamartine*. Vol. 1. Paris: Hachette, 1854.

———. *Oeuvres oratoires et écrits politiques. Troisième série: 1847–1851*. Vol. 6. Paris: Lacroix, Verboeckhoven et Cie, 1865.

———. *La politique de Lamartine: Choix de discours et écrits politiques*. Vol. 2. Paris: Hachette & Cie—Furne, Jouvet & Cie, 1878.

———. *Souvenirs, impressions, pensées et paysages pendant un voyage en Orient (1832–1833), ou notes d'un voyageur*. Vol. 2. Paris: C. Gosselin, 1835.

———. *Sur le projet de loi relatif aux chemins de fer prononcé à la Chambre des Députés* 10 May 1838. Paris: Duverger, 1838.

Leakey, F. W. *Baudelaire and Nature*. Manchester, UK: University of Manchester Press, 1969.

Le Goff, Philippe. "'La faim justifie les moyens': Auguste Blanqui, 'Structural' Violence and the Socialist Press." Paper delivered at Stanford University. 1–2 November 2013. 1–23.

Le Rider, Jacques. "Nietzsche et Baudelaire." *Littérature* 86 (1992): 85–101.

Levine, Michael. *Atomzertrümmerung: Zu einem Gedicht von Paul Celan*. Vienna: Turia + Kant, 2018.

———. *Writing through Repression*. Baltimore, MD: Johns Hopkins University Press, 1994.

Ljungquist, Kent. "Poe's Nubian Geographer." *American Literature* 48, no. 1 (1976): 73–75.

Lobet, J. *Des chemins de fer en France*. Paris: Parent-Desbarres, 1845.

Löwith, Karl. *Meaning in History*. Chicago: University of Chicago Press, 1949.

———. *Nietzsche's Philosophy of the Eternal Recurrence of the Same*. Trans. J. Harvey Lomax. Berkeley: University of California Press, 1997.

Lucretius. *De rerum natura: Libri Sex*. Edited and translated by Cyril Bailey. Vol. 1. Oxford: Clarendon Press, 1966.

Lüdemann, Hermann. *Die Anthropologie des Apostels Paulus*. Kiel: Toeche, 1872.

Lukács, Georg. *Geschichte und Klassenbewußtsein. Frühschriften II*. Neuweid and Berlin: Luchterhand, 1968.

———. *History and Class Consciousness: Studies in Marxist Dialectics*. Translated by Rodney Livingstone. Cambridge, MA: MIT Press, 1971.

———. "Nietzsche als Vorläufer der faschistischen Ästhetik." In *Probleme der Ästhetik*, 307–39. Neuweid: Luchterhand, 1969.

———. *Prolegomena: Zur Ontologie des gesellschaftlichen Seins*. Edited by Frank Benseler. Darmstadt: Luchterhand, 1984.

Luxemburg, Rosa. "Blanquism and Social Democracy." Translated by Peter Manson. In *Socialism or Barbarism: The Selected Writings of Rosa Luxemburg*. Edited by Paul Le Blanc and Helen C. Scott, 126–33. London: Pluto, 2010.

Lyon, Janet. *Manifestoes: Provocations of the Modern*. Ithaca, NY: Cornell University Press, 1999.

Lyotard, Jean-François. *L'inhumain: Causeries sur le temps*. Paris: Galilée, 1988.

———. *The Inhuman: Reflections on Time*. Translated by Geoffrey Bennington and Rachel Bowlby. Cambridge, UK: Polity, 1991.

Magnus, Bernd. *Nietzsche's Existential Imperative*. Bloomington: Indiana University Press, 1978.

de Mailla, Joseph-Anne-Marie de Moyriac, *Histoire générale de la Chine, ou annales de cet Empire, traduites du Tong-Kien-Kang-Mou*. Edited by. J.-B. Grosier et al. Vol. 1. Paris: Clousier, 1777.

Maistre, Joseph de. *St. Petersburg Dialogues: Or, Conversations on the Temporal Government of Providence*. Translated by Richard A. Lebrun. Montreal: McGill-Queen's University Press, 1993.

———. *Essai sur le principe générateur des constitutions politiques et des autres institutions humaines*. Paris: Société Typographique, 1814.

Marder, Elissa. *Dead Time: Temporal Disorders in the Wake of Modernity (Baudelaire and Flaubert)*. Stanford, CA: Stanford University Press, 2001.

Margolis, Joseph. "Praxis and Meaning: Marx's Species Being and Aristotle's Political Animal." In *Marx and Aristotle: Nineteenth-Century German Social Theory and Classical Antiquity*. Edited by George E. McCarthy, 329–55. Savage: Rowman & Littlefield, 1992.

Martinon, Jean-Paul. *On Futurity: Malabou, Nancy, Derrida*. Basingstoke and New York: Palgrave Macmillan, 2007.

Marx, Karl, and Friedrich Engels. *Collected Works (MECW)*. Translated by Richard Dixon et al., 50 vols. New York: International Publishers, 1975–2004.

———. *Gesamtausgabe (MEGA)*. Edited by Günter Heyden, Anatoli Jegorow et al., 79 vols. Berlin: Dietz and Akademie Verlag, 1972–.

Meltzer, Françoise. *Seeing Double: Baudelaire's Modernity*. Chicago: University of Chicago Press, 2011.

Mendicino, Kristina. "Newswriting, Historiography, and the Controversion of the Present (After Heine)." *diacritics* 44, no. 3 (2016): 80–112.

Michaud, Stéphane. "Nietzsche et Baudelaire." In *Le Surnaturalisme français: De Baudelaire au Surréalisme*, 133–61. Neuchâtel: Bacconière, 1979.

Mieszkowski, Jan. *Labors of Imagination: Aesthetics and Political Economy from Kant to Althusser*. New York: Fordham University Press, 2006.

———. "What's in a Slogan?" *Mediations: Journal of the Marxist Literary Group* 29, no. 2 (2016): 149–60.

Miller, J. Hillis. *Others*. Princeton, NJ: Princeton University Press, 2001.
Miller, Louis. "Foucault, Nietzsche, Enlightenment: Some Historical Considerations." *Historical Reflections / Réflexions Historiques* 25, no. 2 (1999): 341–64.
Miller, Richard W. "Marx and Aristotle: A Kind of Consequentialism." In *Marx and Aristotle: Nineteenth-Century German Social Theory and Classical Antiquity*. Edited by George E. McCarthy, 275–302. Savage: Rowman & Littlefield, 1992.
Mills, Kathryn Oliver. *Formal Revolution in the Work of Baudelaire and Flaubert*. Newark: University of Delaware Press, 2012.
Montalbetti, Christine. *Le Voyage, le monde et la bibliothèque*. Paris: PUF, 1997.
Moog-Grünewald, Maria. "Ennui—Curiosité—Nouveau." In *Sprachgewinn: Festschrift für Günter Bader*. Edited by Heinrich Assel and Hans Askani, 126–39. Münster: LIT, 2008.
Moussa, Sarga. "Un voyage dans l'Itinéraire: Lamartine contradicteur de Chateaubriand." *Bulletin de la Société Chateaubriand* 50 (2007): 93–102.
———. "Usages de la fiction dans le récit de voyage: l'épisode de la mer Morte chez Lamartine." In *Roman et récit du voyage*. Edited by Marie-Christine Gomez-Géraud and Philippe Antoine, 47–54. Paris: Presses de l'Université de Paris-Sorbonne, 2001.
Mundt, Theodor. *Die Geschichte der Gesellschaft in ihren neueren Entwickelungen und Problemen*. Berlin: M. Simion, 1844.
Nancy, Jean-Luc. *Dis-Enclosure: The Deconstruction of Christianity*. Translated by Bettina Bergo, Gabriel Malenfant, and Michael B. Smith. New York: Fordham University Press, 2008.
Newmark, Kevin. *Irony on Occasion: From Schlegel and Kierkegaard to Derrida and de Man*. New York: Fordham University Press, 2012.
———. "Off the Charts: Walter Benjamin's Depiction of Baudelaire." In *Baudelaire and the Poetics of Modernity*. Edited by Patricia A. Ward, 72–84. Nashville, TN: Vanderbilt University Press, 2001.
The New Oxford Annotated Bible. Edited by Michael D. Coogan et al. Oxford: Oxford University Press, 2010.
Nietzsche, Friedrich. *Beyond Good and Evil*. Edited by Rolf-Peter Horstmann and Judith Norman. Translated by Judith Norman. Cambridge, UK: Cambridge University Press, 2002.
———. *The Gay Science*. Translated by Walter Kaufmann. New York: Vintage Books, 1974.
———. *Human, All Too Human: A Book for Free Spirits*. Translated by R. J. Hollingdale. Cambridge, UK: Cambridge University Press, 1996.
———. *Kritische Studienausgabe*. Edited by Giorgio Colli and Mazzino Montinari. 2nd ed. 15 vols. Berlin: de Gruyter, 1999.
———. *Nachgelassene Aufzeichnungen Herbst 1858–Herbst 1862*. Edited by Giorgio Colli, Mazzino Montinari et al. Berlin: de Gruyter, 2000.

---. *On the Genealogy of Morals and Ecce Homo*. Translated by Walter Kaufmann. New York: Random House, 1967.

---. *Sämtliche Briefe: Kritische Studienausgabe*. Edited by Giorgio Colli and Mazzino Montinari. 6 vols. Berlin: de Gruyter, 2003.

---. *Selected Letters of Friedrich Nietzsche*. Translated by Christopher Middleton. Chicago: University of Chicago Press, 1969.

---. *Thus Spoke Zarathustra*. Translated by Walter Kaufmann. New York: Random House, 1995.

North, Michael. *Novelty: A History of the New*. Chicago: University of Chicago Press, 2013.

Oehler, Dolf. *Le Spleen contre l'oubli, juin 1848: Baudelaire, Flaubert, Heine, Herzen*. Translated by Guy Petitdemange. Paris: Payot, 1996.

---. *Pariser Bilder I: 1830–1848: Antibourgeoise Ästhetik bei Baudelaire, Daumier und Heine*. Frankfurt am Main: Suhrkamp, 1979.

Ovid. *Metamorphoses Volume 1: Books 1–8*. Translated by Frank Justus Miller. 3rd ed. Cambridge, MA: Harvard University Press, 1977.

Pautrat, Bernard. "Nietzsche Medused." In *Looking After Nietzsche*. Edited by Laurence A. Rickels, 159–73. Albany, NY: State University of New York Press, 1990.

Pearson, Roger. *Unacknowledged Lawgivers: The Poet as Lawgiver in Post-Revolutionary France: Chateaubriand—Staël—Lamartine—Hugo—Vigny*. Oxford: Oxford University Press, 2016.

Pepperell, Nicole. "Impure Inheritances: Spectral Materiality in Derrida and Marx." In *Messianic Thought Outside Theology*. Edited by Anna Glazova and Paul North, 43–72. New York: Fordham University Press, 2014.

Pestalozzi, Karl. "Nietzsches Baudelaire-Rezeption." *Nietzsche-Studien* 7, no. 1 (1978): 158–88.

Poe, Edgar Allan. *Poetry and Tales*. Edited by Patrick F. Quinn. New York: Literary Classics of the United States, 1984.

---. *Eureka*. Translated by Charles Baudelaire. Paris: Lévy, 1864.

Pound, Ezra. *The Cantos*. New York: New Directions, 1950.

---. *Confucius: The Unwobbling Pivot, The Great Digest, The Analects*. New York: New Directions, 1969.

Proudhon, Pierre-Joseph. *What Is Property?* Edited and translated by Donald R. Kelley and Bonnie G. Smith. Cambridge, UK: Cambridge University Press, 1993.

Puchner, Martin. *Poetry of the Revolution: Marx, Manifestos, and the Avant-Gardes*. Princeton, NJ: Princeton University Press, 2005.

de Quincey, Thomas. *Confessions of an English Opium Eater, and Other Writings*. Edited by Barry Milligan. London: Penguin, 2003.

Rancière, Jacques. *Dis-Agreement: Politics and Philosophy*. Translated by Julie Rose. Minneapolis: University of Minnesota Press, 1999.

---. "The Radical Gap: A Preface to Auguste Blanqui, *Eternity by the Stars*." Translated by Olivia Lucca Fraser. *Radical Philosophy* 185 (2014): 19–25.

Rasula, Jed. "Make It New." *Modernism/modernity* 174 (2010): 713–33.
Ravindranathan, Thangam. *Là où je ne suis pas: Récits de dévoyage*. Paris: Presses Universitaires de Vincennes, 2012.
Richter, Gerhard. *Afterness: Figures of Following in Modern Thought and Aesthetics*. New York: Columbia University Press, 2011.
Roberts, Leslie J. "Etienne Cabet and his *Voyage en Icarie*, 1840." *Utopian Studies* 2, no. 1/2 (1991): 77–94.
Robespierre, Maximilien. "Dernier discours." In *Oeuvres de Maximilien Robespierre*. Vol. 3. Edited by Albert Laponneraye, 689–736. Paris: Éditeur, 1840.
Rosen, Stanley. *The Mask of Enlightenment: Nietzsche's* Zarathustra. Cambridge, UK: Cambridge University Press, 1995.
Rosenberg, Harold. *The Tradition of the New*. 2nd ed. Cambridge, MA: Da Capo Press, 1994.
Rosenthal, Alan S. "Baudelaire's 'Mysterious Enemy.'" *Nineteenth-Century French Studies* 4, no. 3 (1976): 286–94.
Russ, Charles V. J. "Nominalization in Martin Luther's Word Formation." *Journal of Germanic Linguistics* 16, no. 3 (2004): 245–68.
Saint-Simon, Henri, and Prosper Enfantin. *Œuvres de Saint-Simon & d'Enfantin*. Edited by Jean-Barthélemy Arlès-Dufour et al. 47 vols. Paris: Leroux, 1877.
Salaquarda, Jörg. "Friedrich Nietzsche und die Bibel unter besonderer Berücksichtigung von *Also sprach Zarathustra*." *Nietzscheforschung* 7 (2000): 323–33.
Sanyal, Debrati. "Reading Baudelaire in the Age of Terror." *Time for Baudelaire: Poetry, Theory, History. Yale French Studies* 124, no. 2 (2014): 102–18.
Schestag, Thomas. *para—Titus Lucretius Carus, Johann Peter Hebel, Francis Ponge*. Munich: Klaus Boer Verlag, 1991.
Schlegel, Friedrich. "On Incomprehensibility." Translated by Peter Firchow. In *Friedrich Schlegel's* Lucinde *and the Fragments*, 258–71. Minneapolis: University of Minnesota Press, 1971.
———. "Über die Unverständlichkeit." In *Charakteristiken und Kritiken I. Kritische Friedrich Schlegel-Ausgabe*. Edited by Hans Eichner, 363–72. Munich and Paderborn: Schöning, 1967.
Schoors, Anton. *Ecclesiastes: Historical Commentary on the Old Testament*. Leuven: Peters, 2013.
Seery, John Evan. *Political Returns: Irony in Politics and Theory, from Plato to the Antinuclear Movement*. Boulder, CO: Westview Press, 1990.
Sereni, Paul. "Marx, Althusser et 'l'homme communautaire': le problème de la coupure." *Penser la transformation: Pour Althusser* (2013). http://www.penser-la-transformation.org/colloque/2013-05-27%20sereni.htm. Accessed 19 January 2018.
Serres, Michel. *La naissance de la physique dans le texte de Lucrèce: Fleuves et turbulences*. Paris: Minuit, 1977.

Sextus Empiricus. *Adversus mathematicos*. In *Sexti Empirici opera*. Vols. 2–3. Edited by J. Mau and H. Mutschmann. Leipzig: Teubner 1914, 1961.
Shapiro, Gary. "Nietzsche on Geophilosophy and Geoaesthetics." In *A Companion to Nietzsche*. Edited by Keith Ansell Pearson, 477–94. Oxford: Blackwell, 2006.
———. *Nietzschean Narratives*. Bloomington: Indiana University Press, 1989.
Shearin, Wilson H. *The Language of Atoms: Performativity and Politics in Lucretius' De rerum natura*. Oxford: Oxford University Press, 2014.
Sloterdijk, Peter. *You Must Change Your Life*. Translated by Wieland Hoban. Cambridge, UK: Polity, 2013.
Snyder, Jane McIntosh. *Puns and Poetry in Lucretius' De rerum natura*. Amsterdam: B. B. Grüner, 1980.
Sorel, Georges. *D'Aristote à Marx*. Paris: Rivière, 1935.
Szondi, Peter. "Friedrich Schlegel und die romantische Ironie: Mit einer Beilage über Tiecks Komödie." *Euphorian* 48 (1954): 397–411.
Taubes, Jacob. *Occidental Eschatology*. Translated by David Ratmoko. Stanford, CA: Stanford University Press, 2009.
Terrell, Carroll F. *A Companion to the Cantos of Ezra Pound*. Berkeley: University of California Press, 1993.
Wasser, Audrey. *The Work of Difference: Modernism, Romanticism, and the Production of Literary Form*. New York: Fordham University Press, 2016.
Weidner, Daniel. "'Und ihr—ihr machtet schon ein Leier-Lied daraus': Nietzsche als Prophet." *arcadia* 47, no. 2 (2012): 361–84.
Westfall, Joseph. "Zarathustra's Germanity: Luther, Goethe, Nietzsche." *The Journal of Nietzsche Studies* 27 (2004): 42–63.
Williams, William Carlos. *Imaginations*. Edited by Webster Scott. New York: New Directions, 1970.
Wilner, Joshua. *Feeding on Infinity: Readings in the Romantic Rhetoric of Internalization*. Baltimore, MD: Johns Hopkins University Press, 2000.
Wohlfarth, Irving. "Die Willkür der Zeichen: Zu einem sprachphilosophischen Grundmotiv Walter Benjamins." *Anthropology & Materialism*, Special Issue: *Discontinuous Infinities* (2017): 1–32.

Index

address, 8–16, 115–16, 118–19, 131–32, 136, 154, 170n41, 185n42
Adorno, Theodor, xviii, xix, xxiii, 161n37
Althusser, Louis, 112–16, 130–31, 138–39, 152, 210–11n8, 218n77, 221n101
anachrony, 16–19, 41–42, 48–50, 70, 142, 170n41, 201n44
Aristotle, 118–19, 122, 138, 143, 217–18n75, 219n88; *Categories*, 139; *De generatione et corruptione*, 138–40; *Metaphysics*, 140, 148, 178n89; *Physics*, 148; *Poetics*, 179n2
atomism, 102, 112, 119, 128–29, 143–49, 158n19, 184n37, 213n41, 214n51, 220–22nn91–103
avant-garde, 157–58n16, 162n41

Bacon, Francis, ix
Badiou, Alain, 17–18, 21, 163n6, 174nn52–54
Bakunin, Mikhail, 177n85
Balfour, Ian, xxiii–xxiv
Balibar, Étienne, 116, 210–11n8, 211n20
Balzac, Honoré de, 98–99, 101, 205n87
Bastiat, Frédéric, 104–05, 207n126–27

Baudelaire, Charles, xix, xxii–xxiv, 37–78, 79, 81, 83, 85, 87, 92, 101, 104, 111, 142, 153–54, 182n21, 183–84n32, 184–85n42, 185–86nn45–46, 186–87n55, 201n46; "À une passante," 48; *Fusées*, 37, 41, 182n21; and Victor Hugo, 73–75; and journalism, 42, 45–46, 60, 61–64; "La Chevelure," 48; "L'Horloge," 68; "Le Balcon," 191n106; "Le Léthé," 61; "Le Monde va finir," 37–50; "Le Voyage," 49–78, and Joseph de Maistre 60–61, 78, 196n130; and Nietzsche, *see* "Nietzsche"; *The Painter of Modern Life*, 72, 191n108; and Edgar Allan Poe, 76, 103–04, 192–93n118; and Thomas de Quincey, 69–72, 190n103; *Salon of 1846*, 185n43
Baur, Ferdinand Christian, 122–24
Beckett, Samuel, 155
Benjamin, Walter, xix–xxiv, 3, 37, 44, 49, 76–77, 84, 87–88, 101, 102, 105, 106, 111, 206n111; *The Arcades Project*, xix–xxiii, 3, 37, 44, 76–77, 87–88, 101, 102, 105, 106, 111, 161–62n41; *Central Park*, 49; *On the Concept of History*, xxiii–xxiv; "The Storyteller," xx, 161–62n41

Bible, the, xiii, xvi–xvii, xxii, 3, 15, 18–24, 44–47, 72–73, 76, 90–91, 159n24, 184nn36–37, 184n41, 193n121, 194–95n124, 206n113; Ecclesiastes, xiii, xvi, xvii, xxii, 3, 44–47, 72–73, 90–91, 159n24, 184nn36–37, 186n41, 194–95n124, 206n113; Isaiah, xvii–xviii, 46, 184n41; Psalms, 76, 193n121; Revelation, xvii, 44
Blanchot, Maurice, 153, 155
Blanqui, Louis-Auguste, xix–xxiv, 42, 45, 63, 64, 77, 83–109, 111–14, 142, 153, 183n27, 198–99n29, 199–200n32, 200n33, 203–04n76, 204n77, 205n93, 206n111, 207n120, 207–08n132, 208n134, 209n138; "Capital and Labor," 96–101; "Discourse of Lamartine," 88–91; *Eternity by the Stars*, xx–xxi, 84, 88, 101–09, 153, 154, 206n111, 207n120; "Lamartine and Rothschild," 86–88, 201nn43–44; "On the Revolution," 91–92; "Political Economy without Morals," 93–95; and positivism, 207–08n132; "The Sects and the Revolution" 91, 95–96, 107
Bloch, Ernst, ix–x, xii
Blumenberg, Hans, 17–18, 118–19, 160n33, 213–14n47
Bürger, Peter, 157–58n16

Cabet, Étienne, 64, 188n79
Cadava, Eduardo, 102, 206n111
capitalism, ix–x, xix, xxii–xxiii, 49, 63, 66, 76–77, 79–109, 114, 131–44, 147–52, 161n37, 171–72n42, 205n87, 205n89, 205n93, 215n55, 216–17nn61–62, 221n101
Chateaubriand, René, 79, 194–95n124

Chevalier, Michel, 88–90, 92, 201–02n51
citation, xix, 6–8, 18–19, 24, 31, 37–46, 48, 69–78, 86–89, 97–99, 101, 118, 136–37, 192n114, 205n93, 216n61
clinamen, 148–49, 220n96, 221n101, 222nn102–03
colonialism, 49, 138, 198n13
commodity, xix–xx, 76, 136, 150, 158n17, 161n37, 215n52, 216n61
cosmology, xxi–xxii, 2, 84, 88, 101–09, 111–14, 144, 148, 158n20, 162n48, 206n111, 209n138
credit, 80–83, 85–88, 104–06, 198n22
Creuzer, Friedrich, 12–13, 169n36, 169–70n39, 170n41

Darstellung, 130–31, 152, 165–66n16
décadence, 35–37, 41, 44, 49, 59, 64, 77, 169n33, 179–80n7
deconstruction, x–xi, xxi, xxiii, 83, 92, 216n61
Deleuze, Gilles, 5–6, 163–64n10, 222n103
de Man, Paul, xv–xvi, 5, 16–17, 126, 189n95, 192n117
Democritus, 148–49, 220–21n98
de Quincey, Thomas, 69, 71, 190n103
Derrida, Jacques, x–xi, xxi, xxiii, 113–16, 130, 134, 166n16, 195n129, 216–17n62, 220n94; *Psyche: Inventions of the Other*, xi–xi, xxi, xxiii; *Specters of Marx*, 116, 134, 216–17n62; *Théorie et pratique*, 113–15, 130, 134
Descartes, René, 47–48
Deucalion, 117–19, 211–12n22
dialectic, 21–22, 112–13, 119–22, 125
dialectical materialism, 114, 131, 137
Diogenes Laertes, 28

Index

Du Camp, Maxime, xxii, 50, 76, 79, 194–95n124, 195n126

Ecclesiastes, *see* "Bible"
Engels, Friedrich, 63, 77, 84, 91, 92, 111–15, 121, 127–52, 153
Epicurus, 118–19, 128–29, 138, 144–48, 213n41, 214n51, 221n100
epistemological break, 116–17, 131, 210–11n8
equivalence, xx–xxi, 97–99, 120, 135–36, 150, 208n134
eternal recurrence, xix–xxii, xxv, 2–8, 10–11, 44–45, 84, 101–05, 106, 109, 111–12, 144, 163–64n10, 164n11, 165–66n16, 174n54, 184n37, 206n111

French Revolution, the, 17–21, 39–40, 42–43, 45, 63, 65, 173–74n51, 174n52

Gautier, Théophile, 193–94n123
Gelikman, Oleg, 38–39, 41, 179n6, 181n18, 182n21, 185n43
goal, *see* "teleology"
Goethe, Johann Wolfgang von, 24, 32, 141, 149, 176n73
Groddeck, Wolfram, 4–5, 30
Groys, Boris, xii, 158n17

Hamacher, Werner, xi–xiii, 8, 10–11, 67, 92, 136, 125, 152, 154; *95 Theses on Philology*, 67; "Affirmative, Strike," 92, 154; "History, Teary: Some Remarks on *La Jeune Parque*," xi–xiii; "Lingua Amissa," 136, 152; *Pleroma—Reading in Hegel*, 10–11; *Premises*, 8, 125; "What Remains to Be Said," xii
Hartmann, Eduard von, 14, 171–72n42

Hegel, G. W. F., 12, 19–20, 112, 117–23, 127, 129, 135, 160–61n35, 218n75, 222n105; "On the Constitution of Germany," 121; *Phenomenology of Spirit*, 119–21, 129; *Philosophy of Right*, 19–20; *Science of Logic*, 118
Heidegger, Martin, xix, 143, 160–61n35, 163–64n10, 165–66n16, 168n30, 174n54, 219nn87–88
Heine, Heinrich, 20–21, 175nn61–62, 178n94
Hesiod, 43–45
Hugo, Victor, 73–76, 191n112, 192n114

irony, 122–27, 131, 212–13n41, 214n49

Jauss, Hans Robert, xii, 75, 158n16, 186n55, 192n117
journalism, *see* "news"
justice, 38, 63, 91, 93–100, 198–99n29, 199–200n32, 203–04n76, 211–12n22

Kittler, Friedrich, 25
Klee, Paul, xxiii–xxiv
Klossowski, Pierre, 6, 163–64n10, 166n21, 174n54

LaCapra, Dominick, 131, 216n61
Lamartine, Alphonse, 79–92, 94, 101, 106–07, 109, 196n1, 197n4, 197–98n13, 198n15, 201n39, 201n44; *Harmonies poétiques et religieuses*, 85–86; "Sur la politique rationelle," 81–82; "Sur le chemin de fer de Paris à Avignon," 79–92, 106–07, 109; *Voyage en Orient*, 79, 85–86

language xi–xiii, xvi–xviii, xxiii–xxiv, 3–7, 15, 18, 21, 23–25, 32–33, 41–42, 48, 50, 66–67, 74, 77–78, 83, 85, 96, 99, 101, 103, 106, 109, 113–15, 119–32, 134–36, 141–42, 144, 146–47, 149–51, 153–55, 158nn19–20, 159n29, 166n21, 170–71n41, 172–73n45, 192n117, 194–95n124, 195n128, 206n111, 212–13n41, 214n51, 216n61, 221nn100–01, 222n105

Laplace, Pierre-Simon, 104, 106, 108, 111–12, 207–08n132

Leroux, Pierre, 43–44

Löwith, Karl, xviii, 64, 160n33, 172–73n45

Lucretius, 144–48, 220n91, 220–21nn95–98, 222n103

Lukács, Georg, 27, 165n15, 215n55, 218n75

Luther, Martin, 18–25, 27, 30, 32, 178n93

Luxemburg, Rosa, 84

Lyotard, Jean-François, 48, 63, 161–62n41

Machiavelli, Nicolo, 138–39, 218n77

Mailla, Joseph-Anne-Marie de Moyriac de, xiv–xv, 159n24

Maistre, Joseph de, 60–61, 78, 185–86n46

Marder, Elissa, 48–49, 61, 68

Marx, Karl, xiv, 19–21, 63–64, 77, 84, 88, 91, 96, 112–19, 121–44, 146–54, 162n48, 165n15, 201n43, 212–13n41, 213–14n47, 215n52, 216n61; and Aristotle, 137–43, 217–18n75; and atomism, 221n101, *see* "notebooks on Epicurean philosophy"; *Capital*, 131, 215n52, 216n61; *Communist Manifesto*, 91, 131–44, 146–52; *The Eighteenth Brumaire of Louis Bonaparte*, 88, 96, 201n43, 222n105; *The German Ideology*, 116, 121, 127–31; notebooks on Epicurean philosophy, 116–19, 121–27, 143–44, 213–14n47

measure, xxi, 24–25, 28–29, 94, 96, 118, 125, 142–43, 145, 210–11n8; *see* "equivalence"

memory, xiv–xv, xviii, 3, 49, 65, 68, 71–73, 146, 191n108

Mieszkowski, Jan, 129–30, 219n86, 222n105

modernism, ix, xii, xviii–xix, xxii, 49, 61, 157–58n16, 159n24, 159n29, 159–60n31, 160n32, 163n7, 168–69n33, 179–80n7, 186–87n55

modernity, xv–xvi, xix–xx, xxiii, 2–4, 8, 12–16, 20–21, 38, 41–44, 48–50, 68–69, 72–73, 76–77, 81, 87, 90, 137–38, 143, 149, 157–58n16, 158n17, 160n33, 161–62n41, 162n48, 170–71nn41–42, 177n85, 185n43, 189n97, 190n105, 191n108, 191n110, 192n117, 194–95n124, 197–98n13, 206n111, 207n130

money, xiv, xx, 42–44, 82, 87, 120, 135–36, 150–52, 201n43, 218n75

Mundt, Theodor, 21–23, 175n66

nature, *see* "atomism," "cosmology"

Newmark, Kevin, 72, 126, 191n108, 214n49

news, xx, xxii–xxiv, 1–4, 24, 42, 59–60, 160–61n35, 161–62n41, 187n63, 199–200n32; *see* "Baudelaire and journalism"

Nietzsche, Friedrich, xx–xxii, xxv, 1–33, 35–42, 44–46, 48, 59–61, 65, 67, 70, 72–73, 77, 84, 154, 163nn6–7, 165n15, 168n30, 168–69n33, 169n36, 169–72nn39–42, 172–73n45, 173n50, 174n54,

176n76, 177n85; and Baudelaire 37–42, 46, 48, 179–80n7, 181–82n19, 182–83n22; *Beyond Good and Evil*, 7; *The Birth of Tragedy*, 1; *Ecce Homo*, 3–4, 20, 173n50; *Human, All Too Human*, 28–29; *The Gay Science*, 1, 22–23, 27; *On the Use and Abuse of History for Life*, 2; *Thus Spoke Zarathustra*, xxv, 1–33, 35–37, 40–41, 59–60, 163nn6–7, 165–66n16, 167n26, 168n30, 168–69n33, 169n36, 169–72nn39–42, 172–73n45, 177n85; *Untimely Meditations*, 14; *see* "eternal recurrence"

Ovid, 118–19, 127, 211–12n22

Paris Commune, the, xxiii, 1, 22, 33, 83, 111
Pautrat, Bernard, 2
philology, xii–xiii, 6, 28, 67
plutocracy, 43–44
Poe, Edgar Allan, 76, 103–04, 186n46, 192–93nn118–19
Pound, Ezra, xiii–xviii, xx, xxii, xxiv, 159n24, 159nn28–29, 159–60n31
practice, 105–06, 112–21, 125, 127–30, 152, 199–200n32, 210–11n8, 215n55
primogeniture, 42–43, 77
proletariat, xxiii, 19–20, 84, 90, 96, 97–98, 136, 146, 151, 184–85n42, 199–200n32, 203–04n76, 205n87, 215n55, 222n105
Prometheus, 118–19
property, 39–40, 77, 94, 98, 102–03, 136–37, 144, 149, 193n122, 202n58, 205n93, 215n54
prophecy, xvii–xviii, xxii, 4, 12–16, 20, 24, 37–38, 46, 169–70n39, 170–71n41, 172–73n45, 209n145

prosopopoeia, 136
Protagoras, 28
Proudhon, Pierre-Joseph, 205n93
Puchner, Martin, 135, 217n63

raison d'État, 82–83
Rancière, Jacques, 84, 95, 102, 198–99n28, 199–200n32
reason, 44, 47–48, 144–45, 185–86nn45–46, 221n101
Reformation, the, 19–25, 28, 175n66
revolution, xix, xxi, xxiii–xxiv, 2, 17–21, 39–40, 42–43, 45–46, 50, 61–65, 77–78, 83–85, 88, 91–93, 95–96, 100–01, 103, 106–07, 109, 112–16, 127, 131–32, 137, 139–40, 142–43, 151–52, 154–55, 161n35, 163n6, 173–74n51, 174n52, 174n54, 174nn58–59, 184–85n42, 198–99n29, 199–200n32, 203n66, 204n77, 206n99, 216–17n62, 217n63, 221n101, 222n105
Revolution of 1848, the, xix, 45–46, 50, 61–64, 65, 77–78, 80, 83, 85, 184–85n42
Robespierre, Maximilien, 63
Rosenberg, Harold, xii, 157n16, 186n55
Rothschild, James de, 81, 85–87, 106, 201n43
Rousseau, Jean-Jacques, 93, 158n20, 163n6

Schlegel, Friedrich, 122–27, 132, 135, 214n49
secularization, xviii, 101, 160n33
Shakespeare, William, 120, 134
skepticism, 93–94, 203n74
Socrates, 122–24, 196n130

Taubes, Jacob, xviii, 160n33
teleology, 26–32, 35–37, 49, 59, 134–35, 154, 178n89

temporality, x, 3, 17–20, 36, 38, 41n 44–49, 61–65, 68–73, 77–78, 98, 101–02, 105–08, 119, 121, 134, 136, 138, 144–46, 148, 152, 161n39, 161–62n41, 164n11, 173–74n51, 181n18, 184nn36–37, 189n95, 189n97, 191n110, 193n122, 220nn95–97; *see* "eternal recurrence"
theory, 84, 92–93, 106–07, 112–21, 125, 127–30, 134, 138–39, 143–44, 149, 152, 214n47, 215n55, 216n61, 218–19n78, 221n101

A Thousand and One Nights, 31–32, 86, 109, 154, 209n145
translation, 18–25, 37, 76, 124, 134–36, 150, 193n121

Vigny, Alfred de, 87–88, 101

Wittgenstein, Ludwig, xii, 158n20

Zend-Avesta, 13, 32, 169–70n39
Zoroaster, 4, 12–14, 169–70n39

www.ingramcontent.com/pod-product-compliance
Ingram Content Group UK Ltd.
Pitfield, Milton Keynes, MK11 3LW, UK
UKHW041917140426
5217IPUK00013B/187